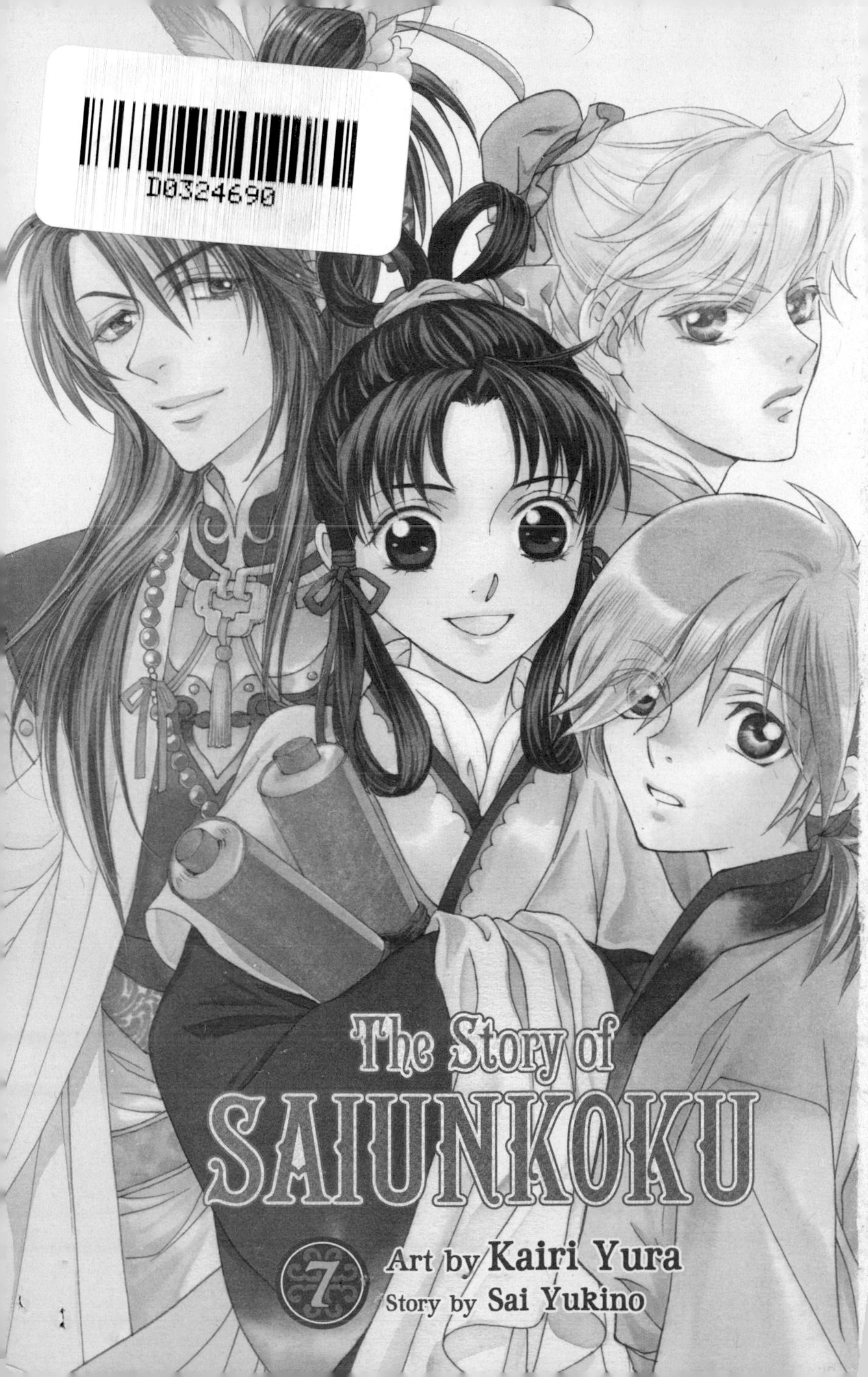
The Story of
SAIUNKOKU
7
Art by Kairi Yura
Story by Sai Yukino

Volume 7
Contents

Story Thus Far

After passing the Imperial Civil Exam with high marks, Shurei Hong becomes the country of Saiunkoku's first female civil servant (currently in training). Yet, almost in exchange for her new position, Shurei finds that the townspeople she grew up with have grown distant, and even her "big sister" Kocho is pulling away. At court she faces prejudice from the officials and escalating bullying from her trainer, Official Ro. Even so, Shurei perseveres determinedly through her trials with the encouragement and support of her fellow inductee civil servants, Eigetsu and Hakumei. However...

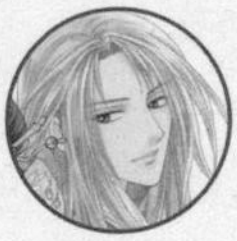

Ryuki Shi
The young emperor of Saiunkoku. He has been pining ceaselessly for Shurei since her departure from the Inner Court.

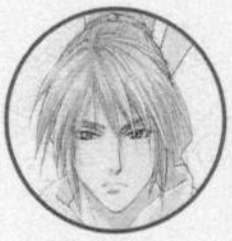

Koyu Ri
A civil servant renowned throughout the court as a genius, currently stuck in a frivolous position (perhaps?) serving Ryuki. He has a hopelessly bad sense of direction.

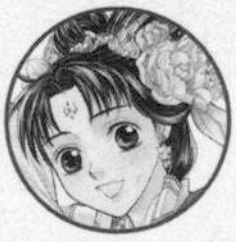

Shurei Hong
A young noblewoman of the prestigious but impoverished Hong Clan. Having passed the Imperial Civil Exam, she is now the country's first female civil servant.

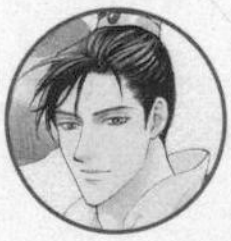

Shuei Ran
A military officer. He is a general of the Yulin Guard, a squad of soldiers charged with protecting the emperor. He is inseparable from Koyu (much to his friend's ire).

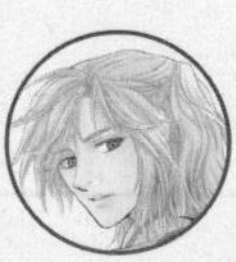

Seiran Shi
After being taken in by Shurei's father, Shoka, Seiran has served the Hong household as its faithful retainer ever since. He is actually Ryuki's older brother.

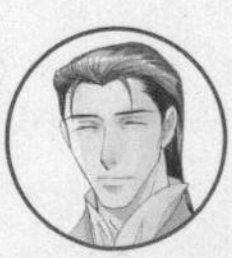

Shoka Hong
The eldest son of the Hong clan and Shurei's father. He holds a leisurely post as the Imperial Archivist, but there is a darker side to this ex-assassin as well.

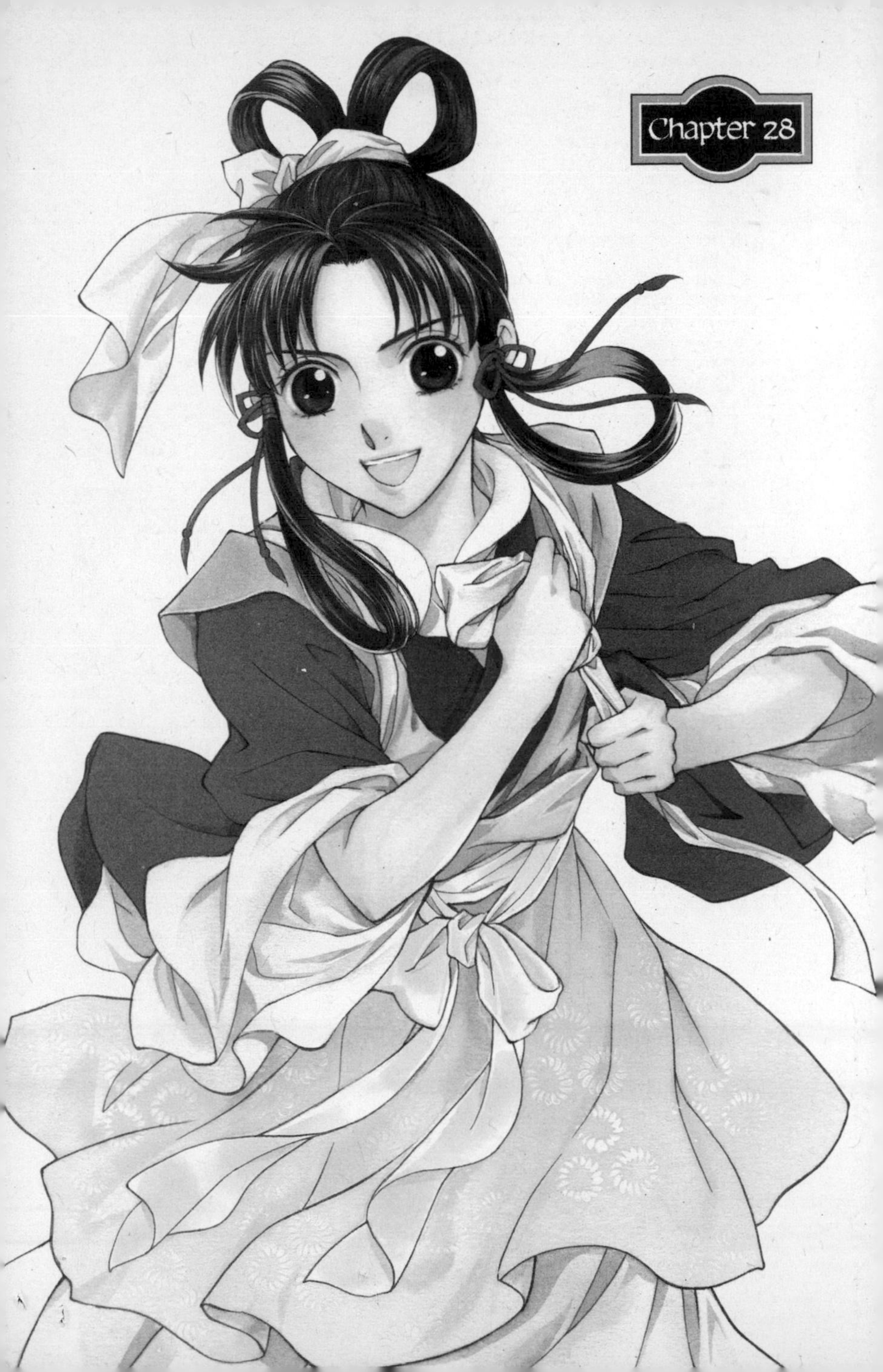
Chapter 28

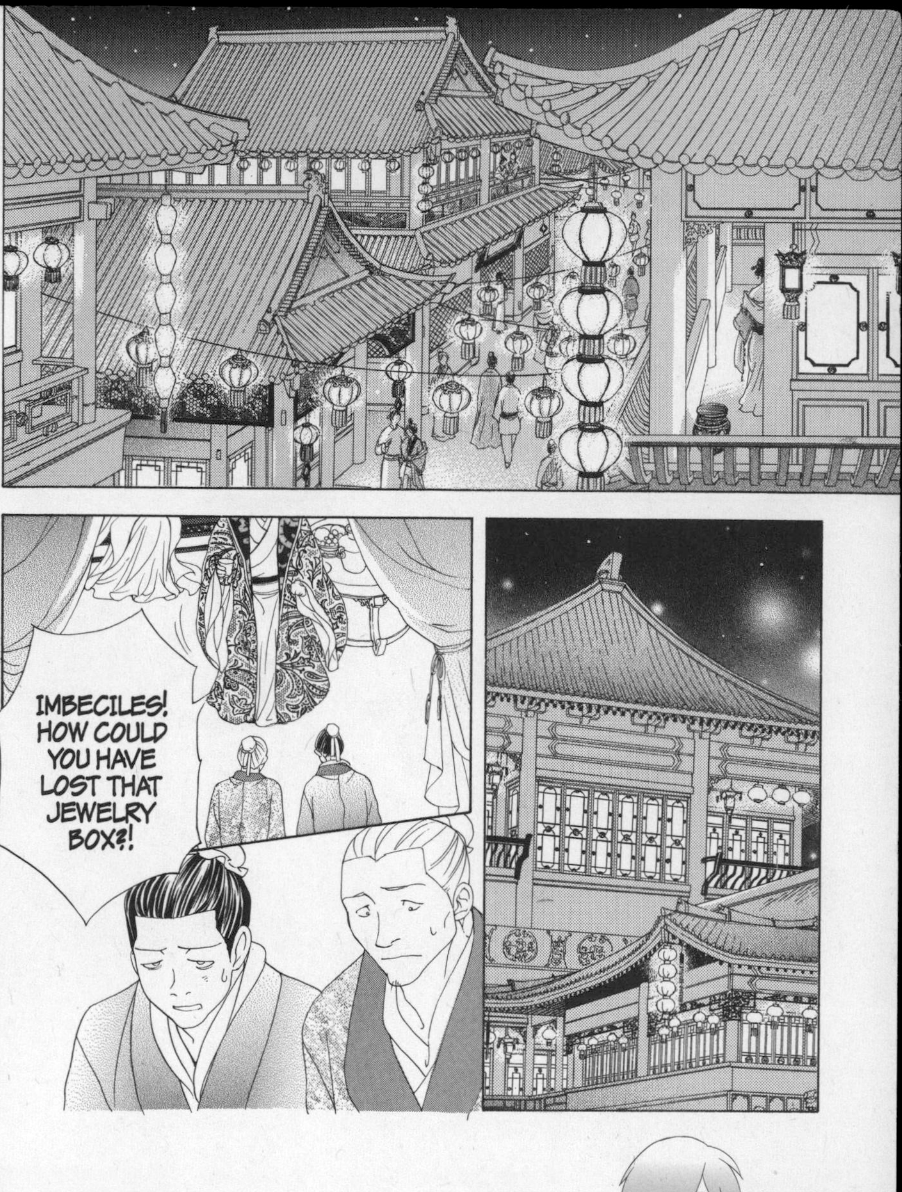
IMBECILES! HOW COULD YOU HAVE LOST THAT JEWELRY BOX?!
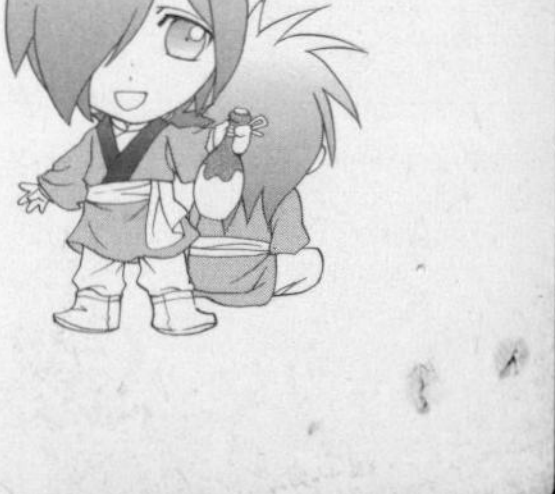

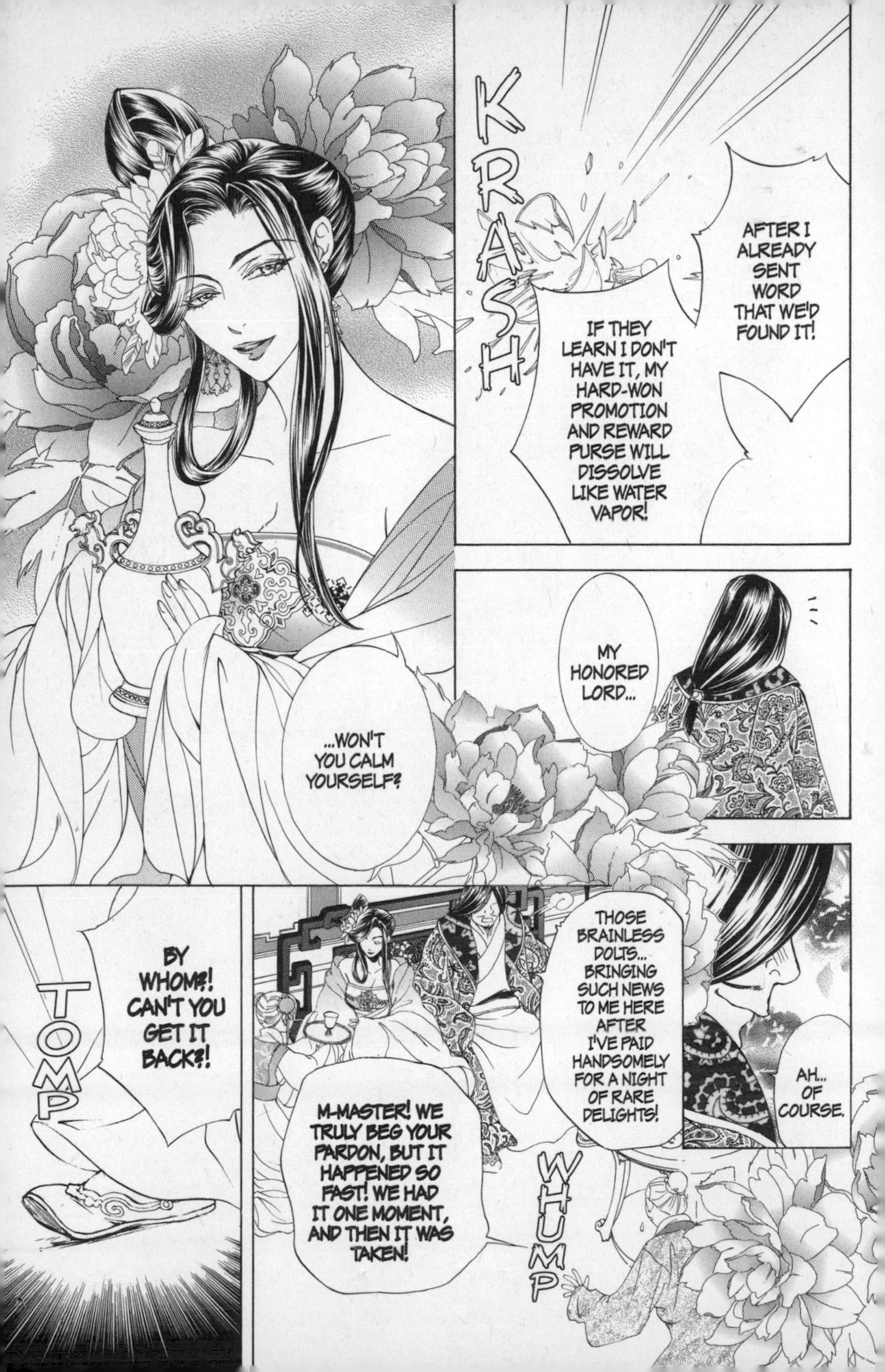
AFTER I ALREADY SENT WORD THAT WE'D FOUND IT!
KRASH
IF THEY LEARN I DON'T HAVE IT, MY HARD-WON PROMOTION AND REWARD PURSE WILL DISSOLVE LIKE WATER VAPOR!
MY HONORED LORD...
...WON'T YOU CALM YOURSELF?
THOSE BRAINLESS DOLTS... BRINGING SUCH NEWS TO ME HERE AFTER I'VE PAID HANDSOMELY FOR A NIGHT OF RARE DELIGHTS!
AH... OF COURSE.
M-MASTER! WE TRULY BEG YOUR PARDON, BUT IT HAPPENED SO FAST! WE HAD IT ONE MOMENT, AND THEN IT WAS TAKEN!
WHUMP
BY WHOM?! CAN'T YOU GET IT BACK?!
TOMP

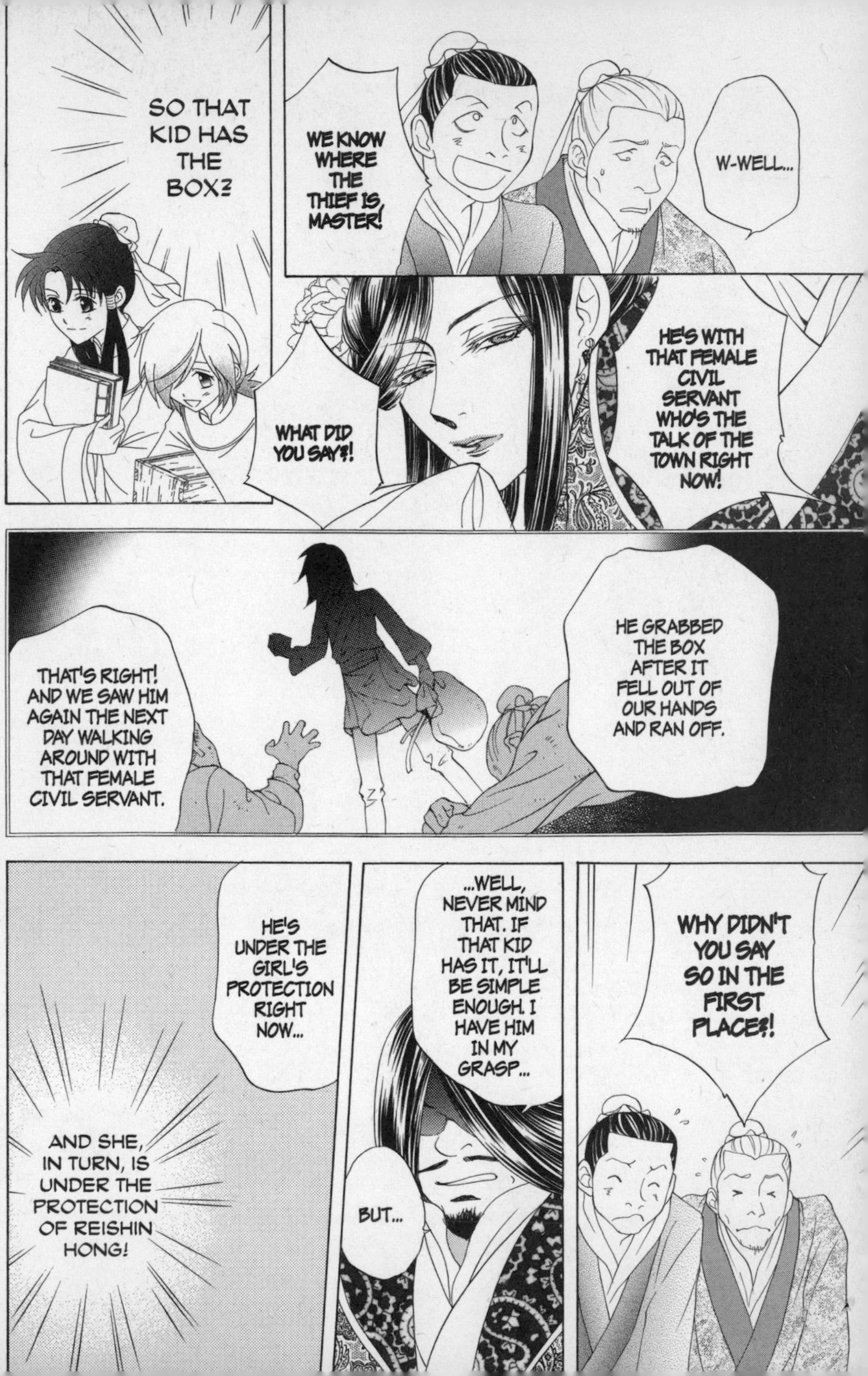
W-WELL...
WE KNOW WHERE THE THIEF IS, MASTER!
HE'S WITH THAT FEMALE CIVIL SERVANT WHO'S THE TALK OF THE TOWN RIGHT NOW!
WHAT DID YOU SAY?!
SO THAT KID HAS THE BOX?
HE GRABBED THE BOX AFTER IT FELL OUT OF OUR HANDS AND RAN OFF.
THAT'S RIGHT! AND WE SAW HIM AGAIN THE NEXT DAY WALKING AROUND WITH THAT FEMALE CIVIL SERVANT.
WHY DIDN'T YOU SAY SO IN THE FIRST PLACE?!
...WELL, NEVER MIND THAT. IF THAT KID HAS IT, IT'LL BE SIMPLE ENOUGH. I HAVE HIM IN MY GRASP...
BUT...
HE'S UNDER THE GIRL'S PROTECTION RIGHT NOW...
AND SHE, IN TURN, IS UNDER THE PROTECTION OF REISHIN HONG!

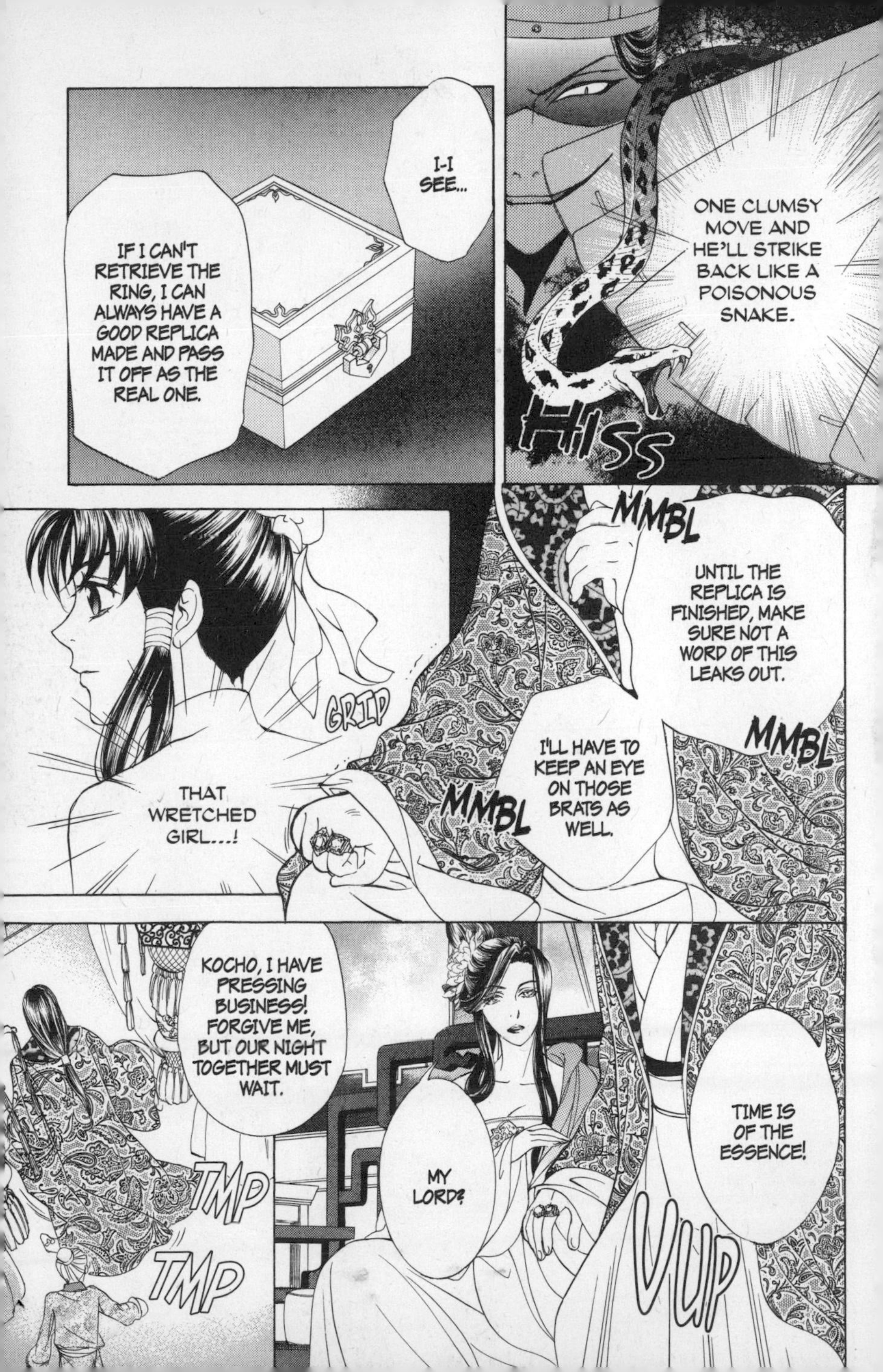
ONE CLUMSY MOVE AND HE'LL STRIKE BACK LIKE A POISONOUS SNAKE.
HISS
I-I SEE...
IF I CAN'T RETRIEVE THE RING, I CAN ALWAYS HAVE A GOOD REPLICA MADE AND PASS IT OFF AS THE REAL ONE.
MMBL
UNTIL THE REPLICA IS FINISHED, MAKE SURE NOT A WORD OF THIS LEAKS OUT.
MMBL
I'LL HAVE TO KEEP AN EYE ON THOSE BRATS AS WELL.
MMBL
GRIP
THAT WRETCHED GIRL...!
KOCHO, I HAVE PRESSING BUSINESS! FORGIVE ME, BUT OUR NIGHT TOGETHER MUST WAIT.
MY LORD?
TIME IS OF THE ESSENCE!
VUP
TMP
TMP

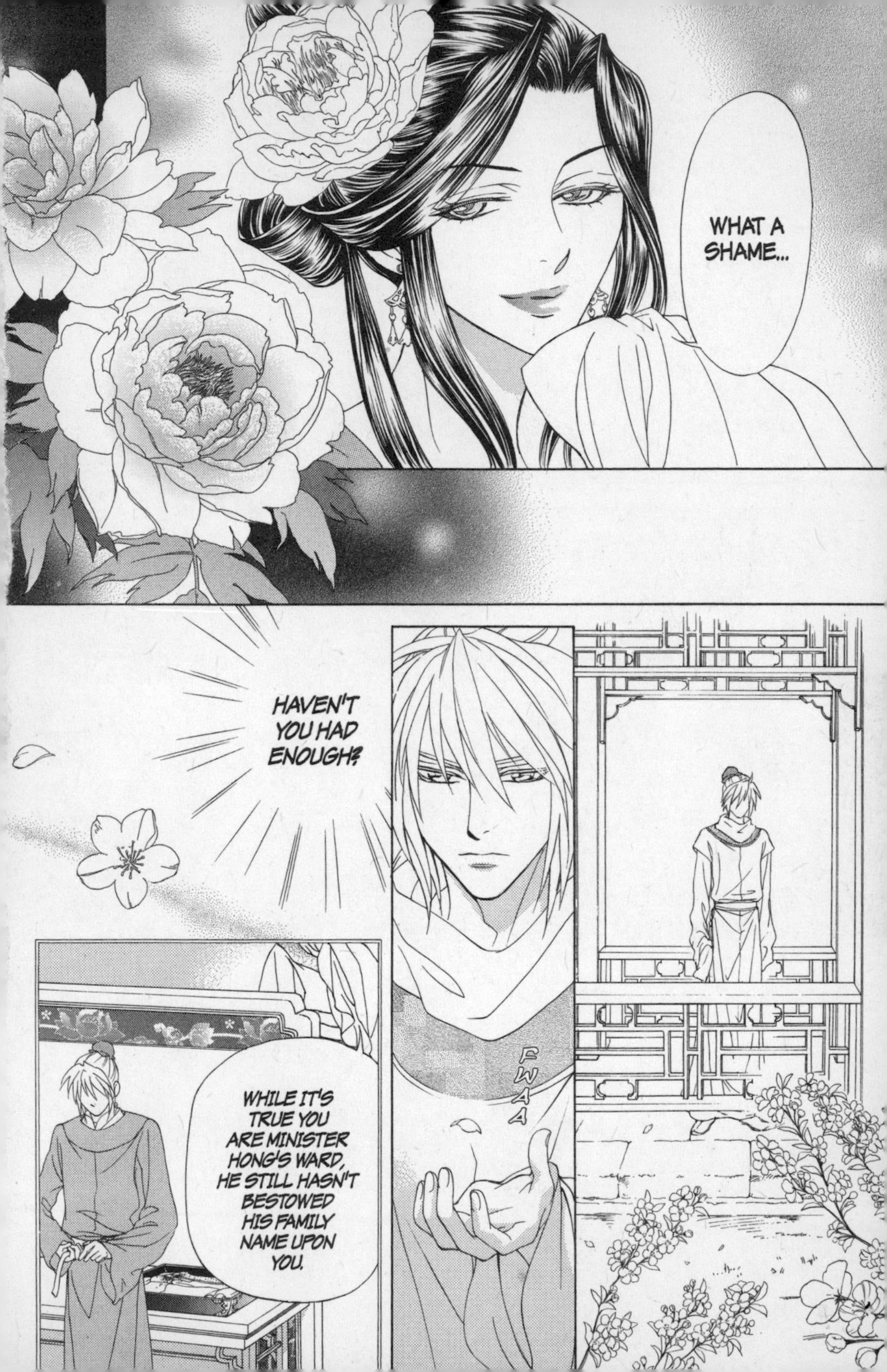
WHAT A SHAME...
FWAA
HAVEN'T YOU HAD ENOUGH?
WHILE IT'S TRUE YOU ARE MINISTER HONG'S WARD, HE STILL HASN'T BESTOWED HIS FAMILY NAME UPON YOU.

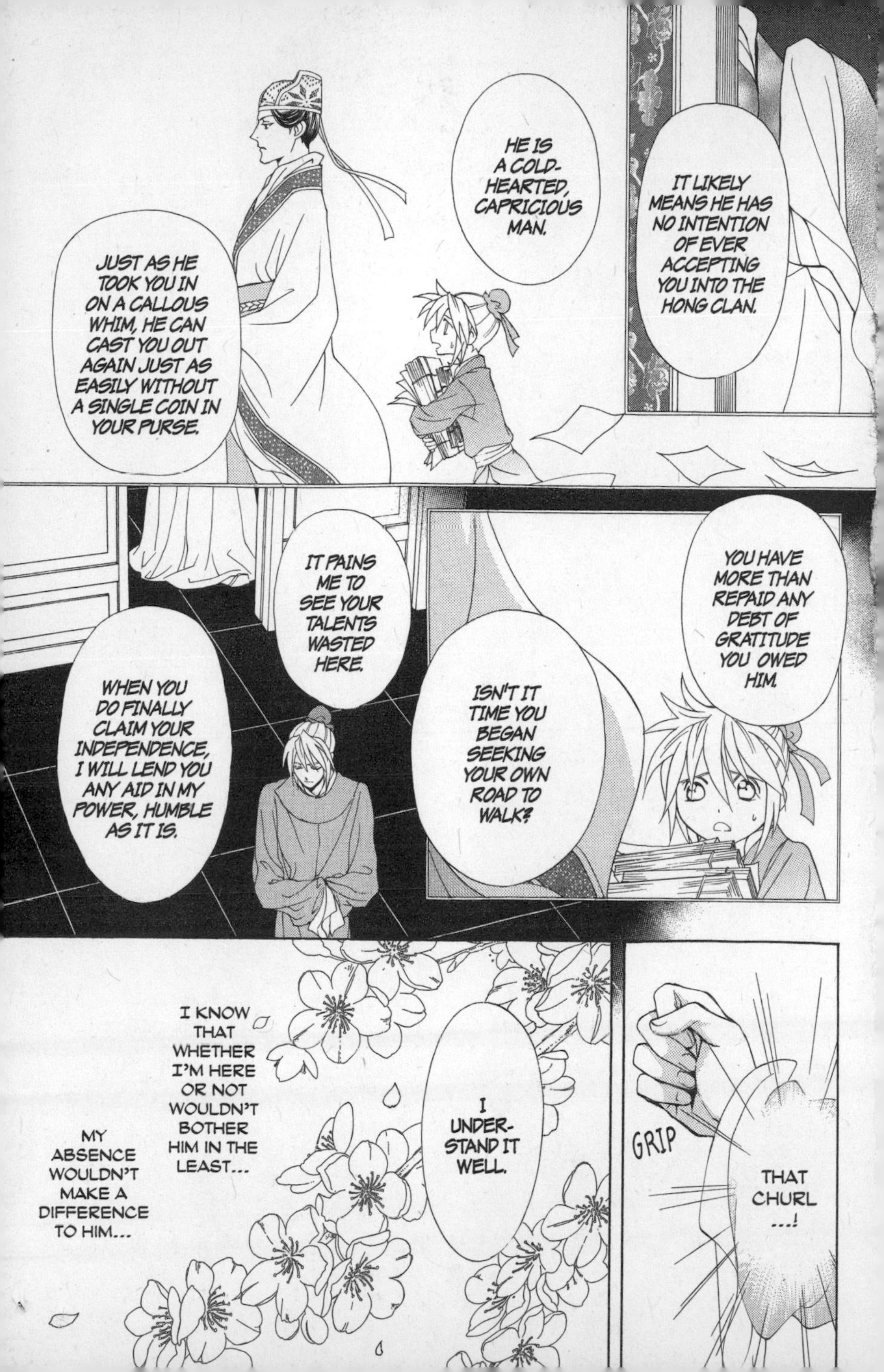
IT LIKELY MEANS HE HAS NO INTENTION OF EVER ACCEPTING YOU INTO THE HONG CLAN.
HE IS A COLD-HEARTED, CAPRICIOUS MAN.
JUST AS HE TOOK YOU IN ON A CALLOUS WHIM, HE CAN CAST YOU OUT AGAIN JUST AS EASILY WITHOUT A SINGLE COIN IN YOUR PURSE.
YOU HAVE MORE THAN REPAID ANY DEBT OF GRATITUDE YOU OWED HIM.
ISN'T IT TIME YOU BEGAN SEEKING YOUR OWN ROAD TO WALK?
IT PAINS ME TO SEE YOUR TALENTS WASTED HERE.
WHEN YOU DO FINALLY CLAIM YOUR INDEPENDENCE, I WILL LEND YOU ANY AID IN MY POWER, HUMBLE AS IT IS.
GRIP
THAT CHURL ...!
I UNDER-STAND IT WELL.
I KNOW THAT WHETHER I'M HERE OR NOT WOULDN'T BOTHER HIM IN THE LEAST...
MY ABSENCE WOULDN'T MAKE A DIFFERENCE TO HIM...

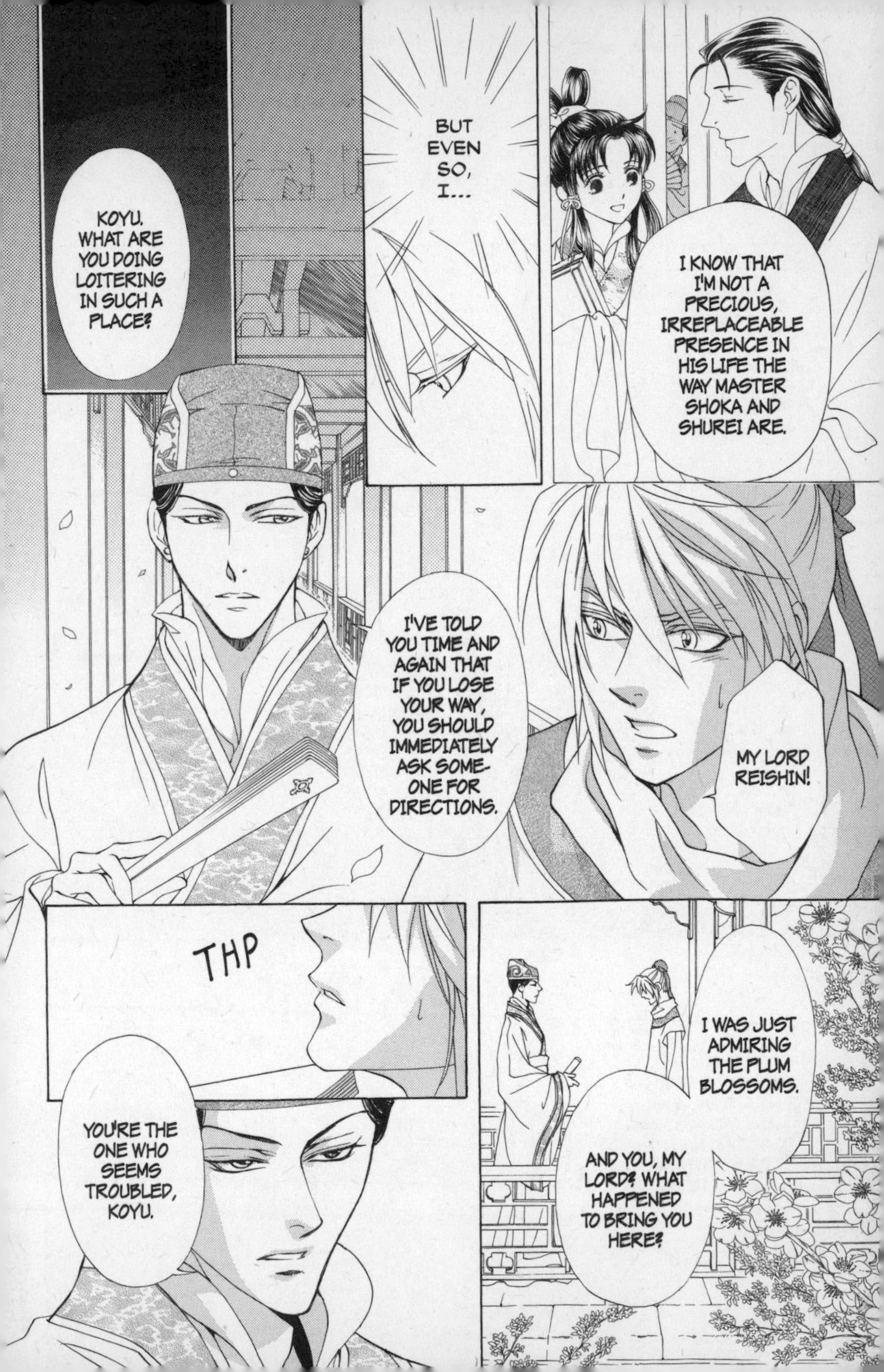
I KNOW THAT I'M NOT A PRECIOUS, IRREPLACEABLE PRESENCE IN HIS LIFE THE WAY MASTER SHOKA AND SHUREI ARE.
BUT EVEN SO, I...
MY LORD REISHIN!
KOYU. WHAT ARE YOU DOING LOITERING IN SUCH A PLACE?
I'VE TOLD YOU TIME AND AGAIN THAT IF YOU LOSE YOUR WAY, YOU SHOULD IMMEDIATELY ASK SOME-ONE FOR DIRECTIONS.
I WAS JUST ADMIRING THE PLUM BLOSSOMS.
AND YOU, MY LORD? WHAT HAPPENED TO BRING YOU HERE?
THP
YOU'RE THE ONE WHO SEEMS TROUBLED, KOYU.

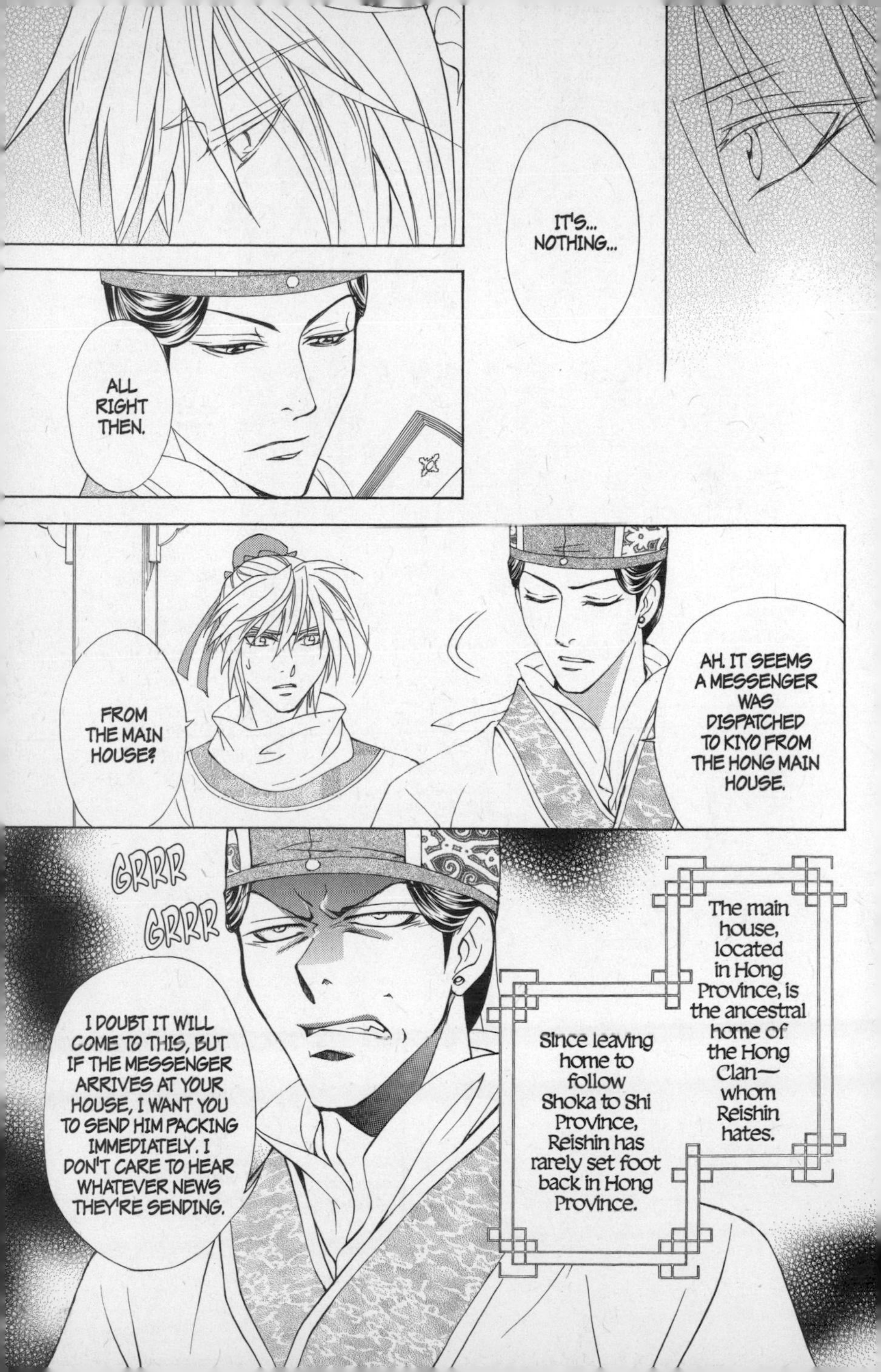
IT'S... NOTHING...
ALL RIGHT THEN.
AH. IT SEEMS A MESSENGER WAS DISPATCHED TO KIYO FROM THE HONG MAIN HOUSE.
FROM THE MAIN HOUSE?
The main house, located in Hong Province, is the ancestral home of the Hong Clan—whom Reishin hates.
Since leaving home to follow Shoka to Shi Province, Reishin has rarely set foot back in Hong Province.
GRRR
GRRR
I DOUBT IT WILL COME TO THIS, BUT IF THE MESSENGER ARRIVES AT YOUR HOUSE, I WANT YOU TO SEND HIM PACKING IMMEDIATELY. I DON'T CARE TO HEAR WHATEVER NEWS THEY'RE SENDING.

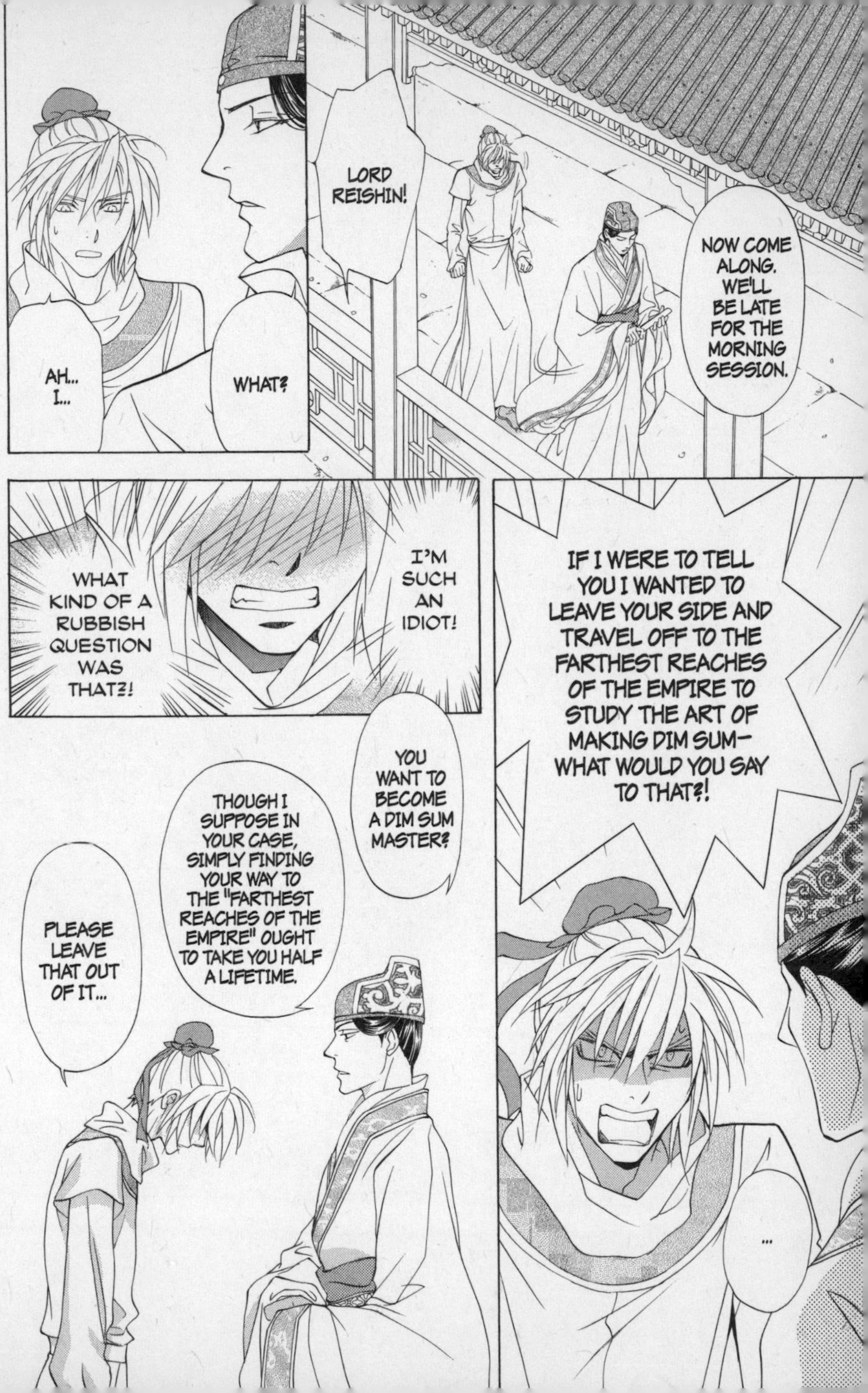
NOW COME ALONG. WE'LL BE LATE FOR THE MORNING SESSION.
LORD REISHIN!
WHAT?
AH... I...
IF I WERE TO TELL YOU I WANTED TO LEAVE YOUR SIDE AND TRAVEL OFF TO THE FARTHEST REACHES OF THE EMPIRE TO STUDY THE ART OF MAKING DIM SUM— WHAT WOULD YOU SAY TO THAT?!
...
I'M SUCH AN IDIOT!
WHAT KIND OF A RUBBISH QUESTION WAS THAT?!
YOU WANT TO BECOME A DIM SUM MASTER?
THOUGH I SUPPOSE IN YOUR CASE, SIMPLY FINDING YOUR WAY TO THE "FARTHEST REACHES OF THE EMPIRE" OUGHT TO TAKE YOU HALF A LIFETIME.
PLEASE LEAVE THAT OUT OF IT...

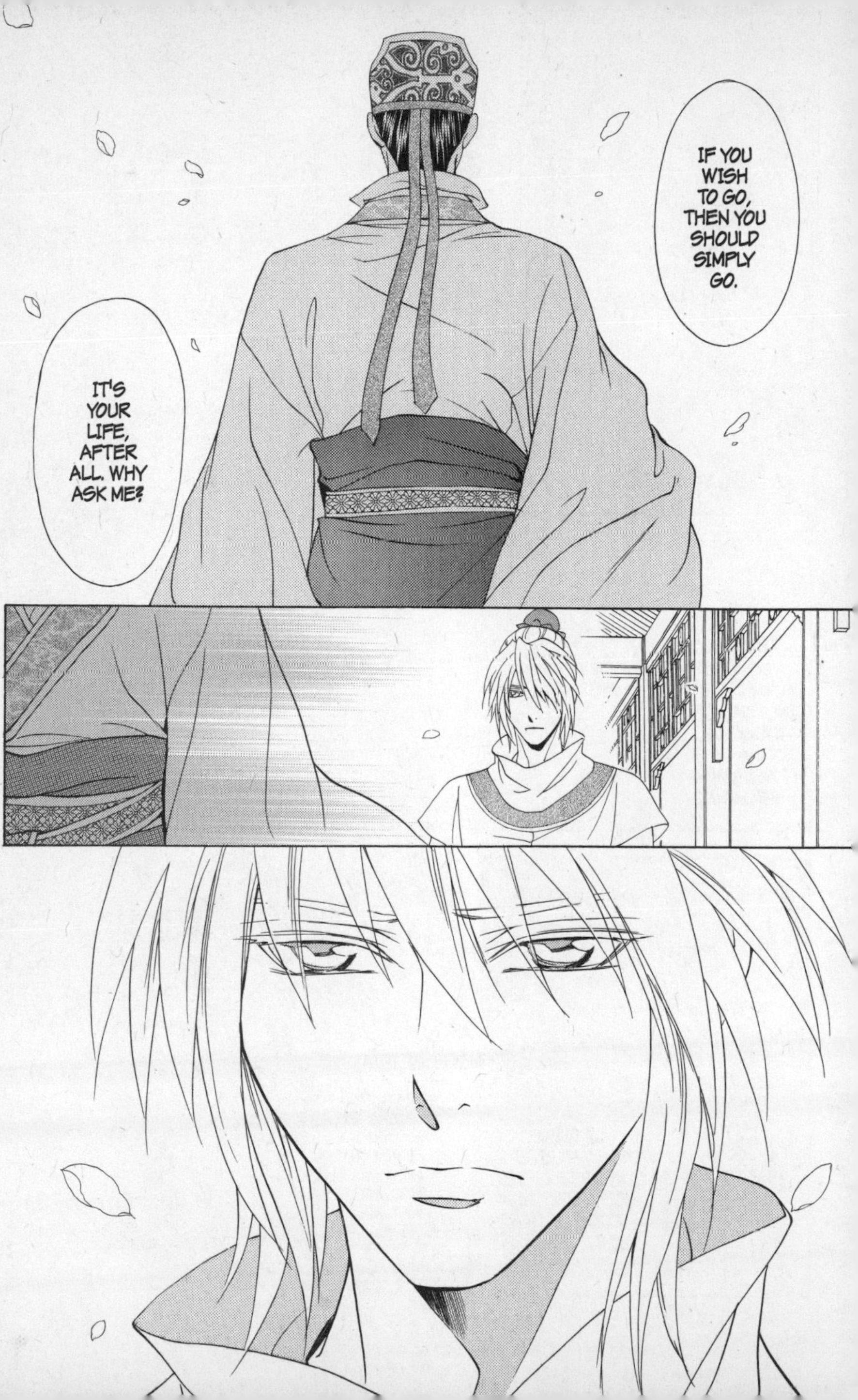
IF YOU WISH TO GO, THEN YOU SHOULD SIMPLY GO.
IT'S YOUR LIFE, AFTER ALL. WHY ASK ME?

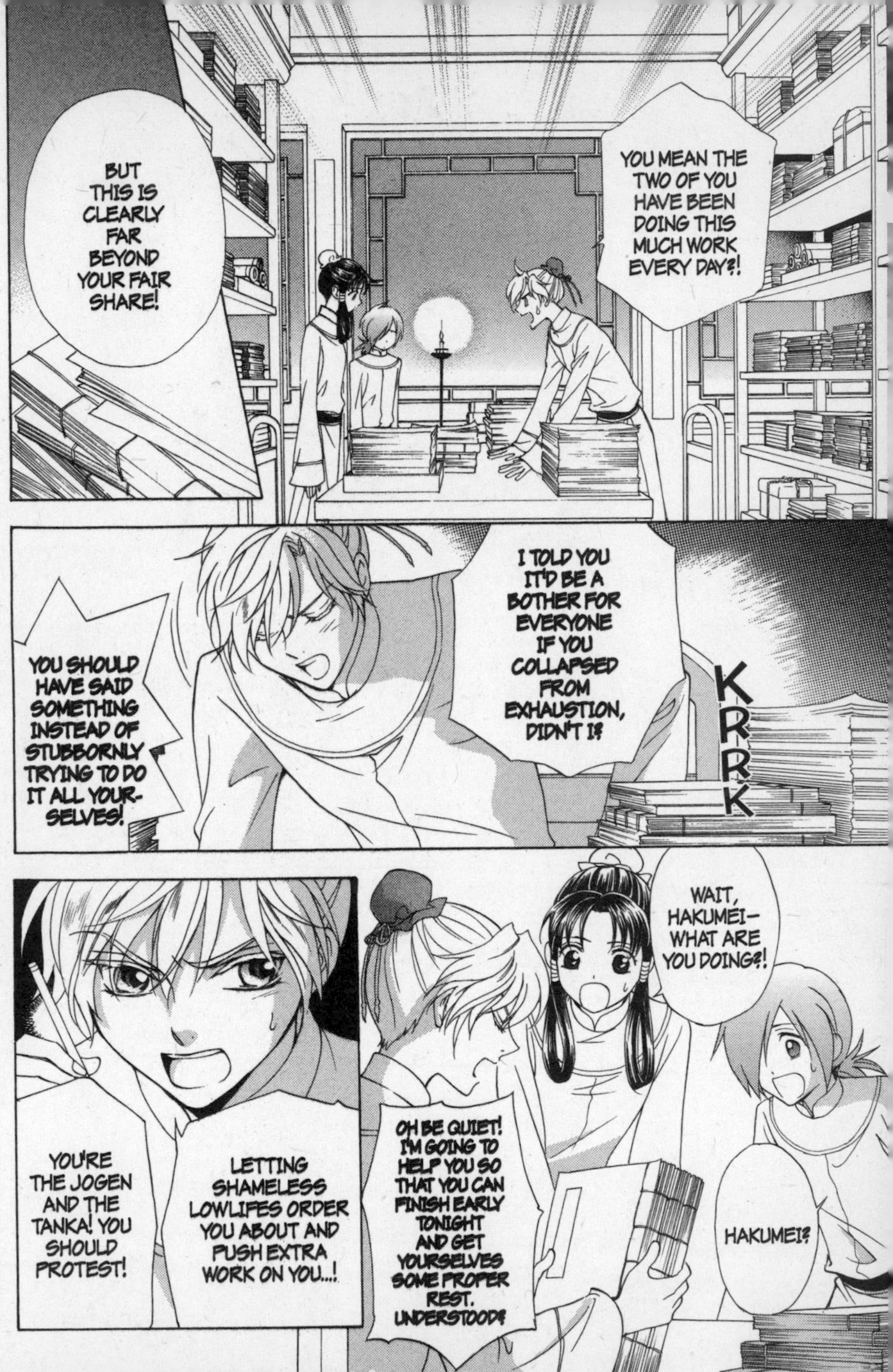
YOU MEAN THE TWO OF YOU HAVE BEEN DOING THIS MUCH WORK EVERY DAY?!
BUT THIS IS CLEARLY FAR BEYOND YOUR FAIR SHARE!
I TOLD YOU IT'D BE A BOTHER FOR EVERYONE IF YOU COLLAPSED FROM EXHAUSTION, DIDN'T I?
KRRK
YOU SHOULD HAVE SAID SOMETHING INSTEAD OF STUBBORNLY TRYING TO DO IT ALL YOUR-SELVES!
WAIT, HAKUMEI— WHAT ARE YOU DOING?!
HAKUMEI?
OH BE QUIET! I'M GOING TO HELP YOU SO THAT YOU CAN FINISH EARLY TONIGHT AND GET YOURSELVES SOME PROPER REST. UNDERSTOOD?
LETTING SHAMELESS LOWLIFES ORDER YOU ABOUT AND PUSH EXTRA WORK ON YOU...!
YOU'RE THE JOGEN AND THE TANKA! YOU SHOULD PROTEST!

*Jogen and Tanka are the first and third top scorers on the Imperial Civil Exam. Second place is called Bogen.

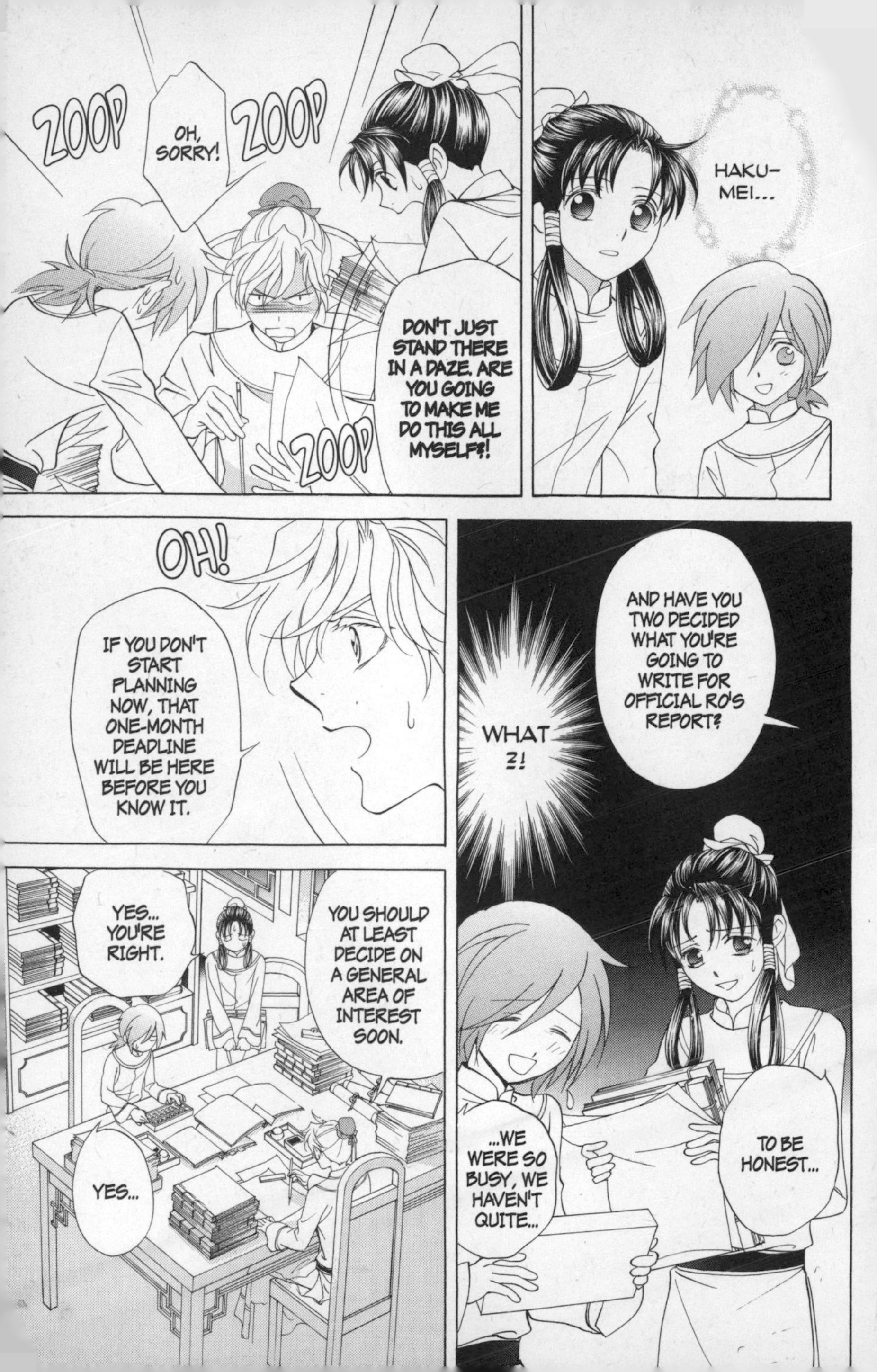
HAKU-MEI...
ZOOP
OH, SORRY!
ZOOP
DON'T JUST STAND THERE IN A DAZE. ARE YOU GOING TO MAKE ME DO THIS ALL MYSELF?!
ZOOP
AND HAVE YOU TWO DECIDED WHAT YOU'RE GOING TO WRITE FOR OFFICIAL RO'S REPORT?
WHAT?!
TO BE HONEST...
...WE WERE SO BUSY, WE HAVEN'T QUITE...
OH!
IF YOU DON'T START PLANNING NOW, THAT ONE-MONTH DEADLINE WILL BE HERE BEFORE YOU KNOW IT.
YOU SHOULD AT LEAST DECIDE ON A GENERAL AREA OF INTEREST SOON.
YES... YOU'RE RIGHT.
YES...

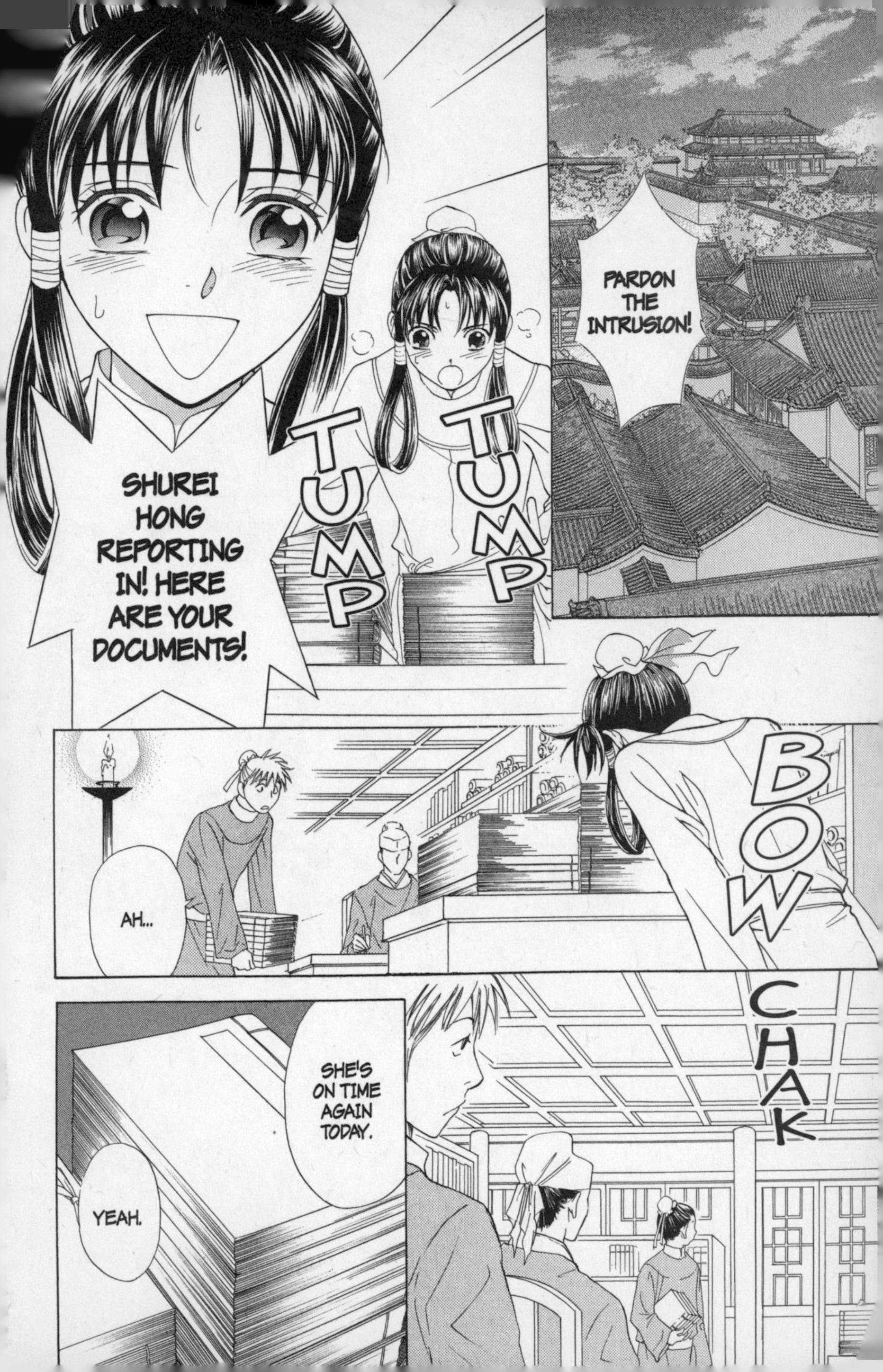
PARDON THE INTRUSION!
TUMP
TUMP
SHUREI HONG REPORTING IN! HERE ARE YOUR DOCUMENTS!
BOW
AH...
CHAK
SHE'S ON TIME AGAIN TODAY.
YEAH.

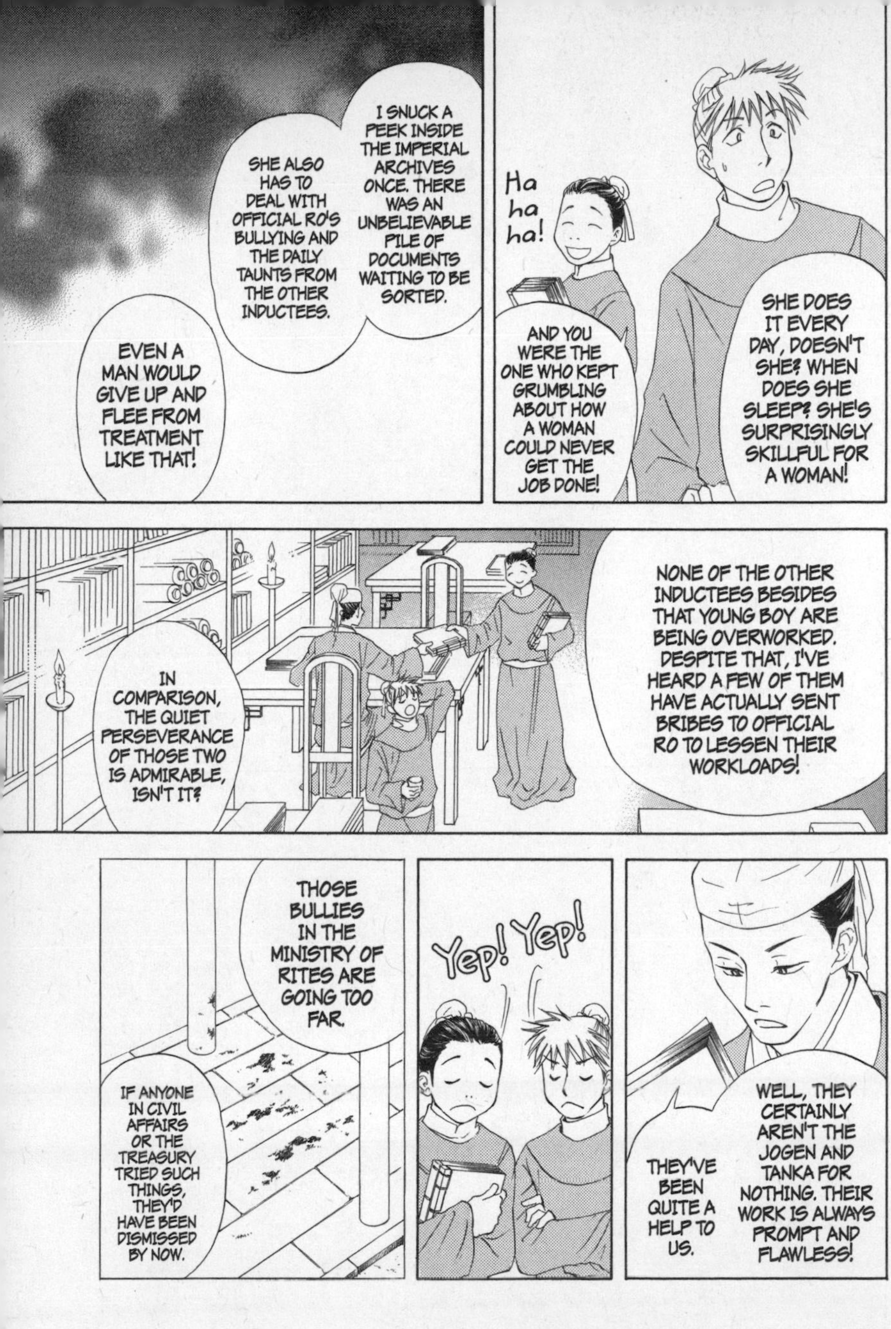
SHE DOES IT EVERY DAY, DOESN'T SHE? WHEN DOES SHE SLEEP? SHE'S SURPRISINGLY SKILLFUL FOR A WOMAN!
Ha ha ha!
AND YOU WERE THE ONE WHO KEPT GRUMBLING ABOUT HOW A WOMAN COULD NEVER GET THE JOB DONE!
I SNUCK A PEEK INSIDE THE IMPERIAL ARCHIVES ONCE. THERE WAS AN UNBELIEVABLE PILE OF DOCUMENTS WAITING TO BE SORTED.
SHE ALSO HAS TO DEAL WITH OFFICIAL RO'S BULLYING AND THE DAILY TAUNTS FROM THE OTHER INDUCTEES.
EVEN A MAN WOULD GIVE UP AND FLEE FROM TREATMENT LIKE THAT!
NONE OF THE OTHER INDUCTEES BESIDES THAT YOUNG BOY ARE BEING OVERWORKED. DESPITE THAT, I'VE HEARD A FEW OF THEM HAVE ACTUALLY SENT BRIBES TO OFFICIAL RO TO LESSEN THEIR WORKLOADS!
IN COMPARISON, THE QUIET PERSEVERANCE OF THOSE TWO IS ADMIRABLE, ISN'T IT?
WELL, THEY CERTAINLY AREN'T THE JOGEN AND TANKA FOR NOTHING. THEIR WORK IS ALWAYS PROMPT AND FLAWLESS!
THEY'VE BEEN QUITE A HELP TO US.
Yep! Yep!
THOSE BULLIES IN THE MINISTRY OF RITES ARE GOING TOO FAR.
IF ANYONE IN CIVIL AFFAIRS OR THE TREASURY TRIED SUCH THINGS, THEY'D HAVE BEEN DISMISSED BY NOW.

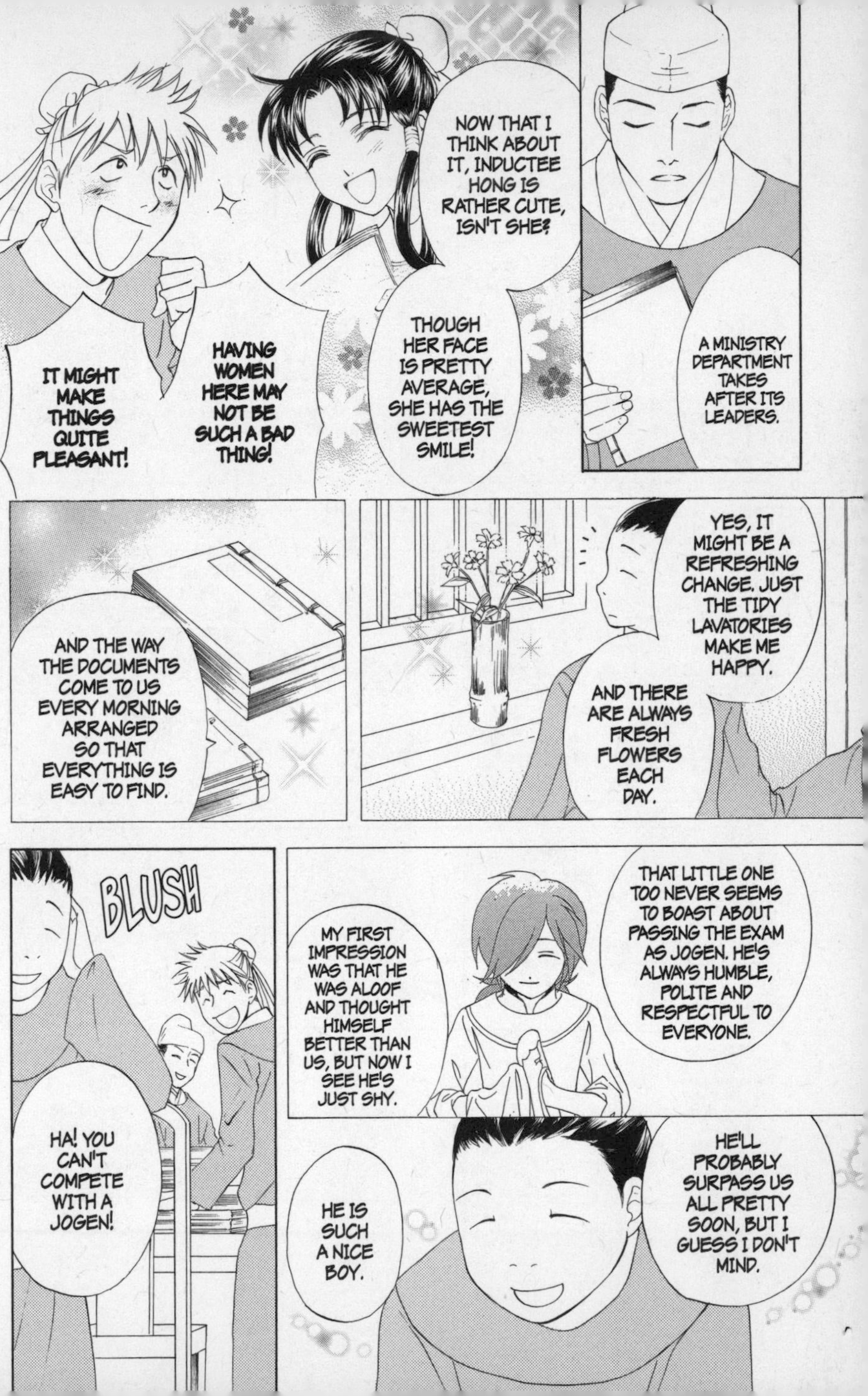
A MINISTRY DEPARTMENT TAKES AFTER ITS LEADERS.
NOW THAT I THINK ABOUT IT, INDUCTEE HONG IS RATHER CUTE, ISN'T SHE?
THOUGH HER FACE IS PRETTY AVERAGE, SHE HAS THE SWEETEST SMILE!
HAVING WOMEN HERE MAY NOT BE SUCH A BAD THING!
IT MIGHT MAKE THINGS QUITE PLEASANT!
YES, IT MIGHT BE A REFRESHING CHANGE. JUST THE TIDY LAVATORIES MAKE ME HAPPY.
AND THERE ARE ALWAYS FRESH FLOWERS EACH DAY.
AND THE WAY THE DOCUMENTS COME TO US EVERY MORNING ARRANGED SO THAT EVERYTHING IS EASY TO FIND.
THAT LITTLE ONE TOO NEVER SEEMS TO BOAST ABOUT PASSING THE EXAM AS JOGEN. HE'S ALWAYS HUMBLE, POLITE AND RESPECTFUL TO EVERYONE.
MY FIRST IMPRESSION WAS THAT HE WAS ALOOF AND THOUGHT HIMSELF BETTER THAN US, BUT NOW I SEE HE'S JUST SHY.
HE'LL PROBABLY SURPASS US ALL PRETTY SOON, BUT I GUESS I DON'T MIND.
HE IS SUCH A NICE BOY.
BLUSH
HA! YOU CAN'T COMPETE WITH A JOGEN!

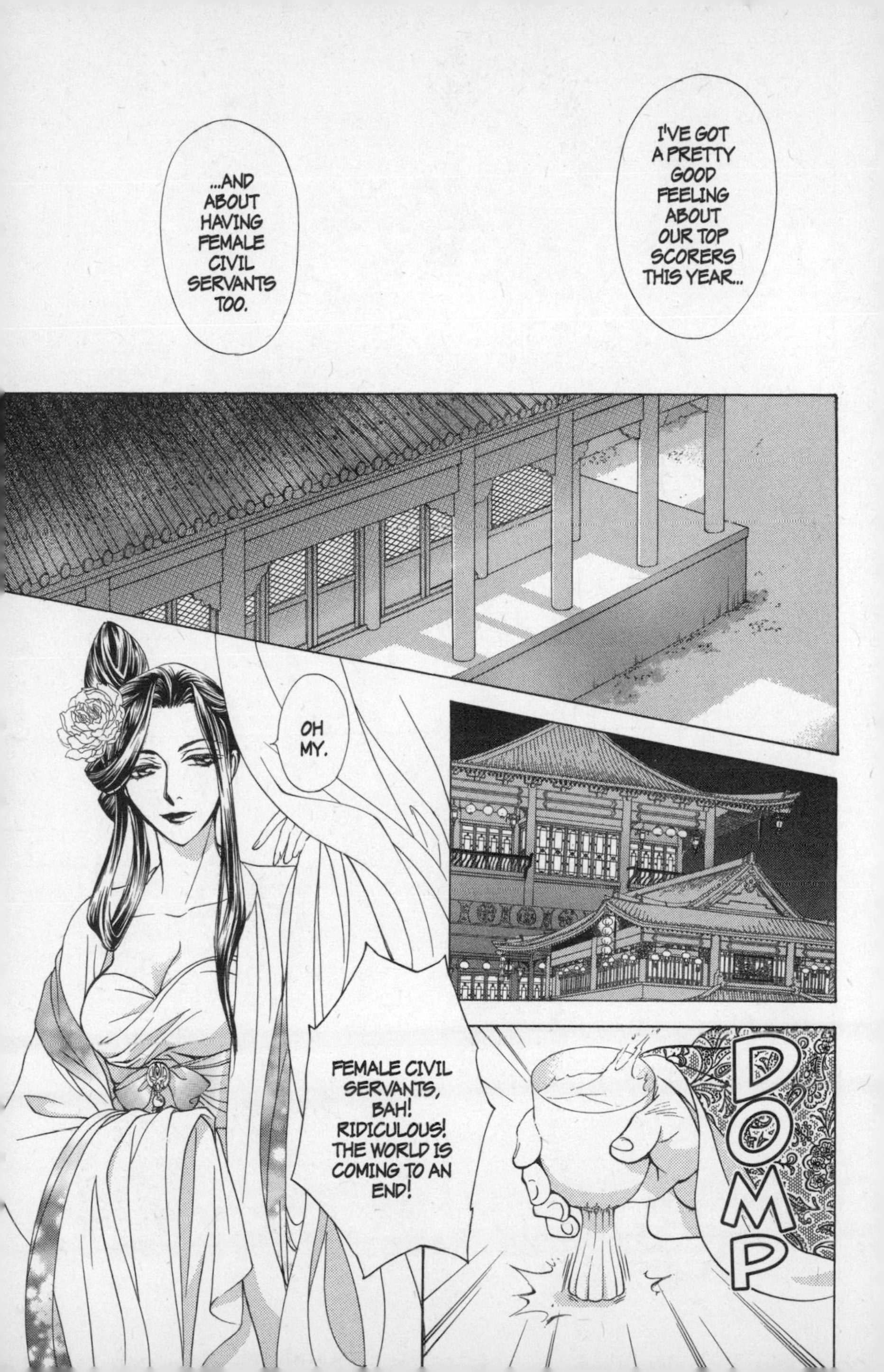
I'VE GOT A PRETTY GOOD FEELING ABOUT OUR TOP SCORERS THIS YEAR...
...AND ABOUT HAVING FEMALE CIVIL SERVANTS TOO.
DOMP
FEMALE CIVIL SERVANTS, BAH! RIDICULOUS! THE WORLD IS COMING TO AN END!
OH MY.

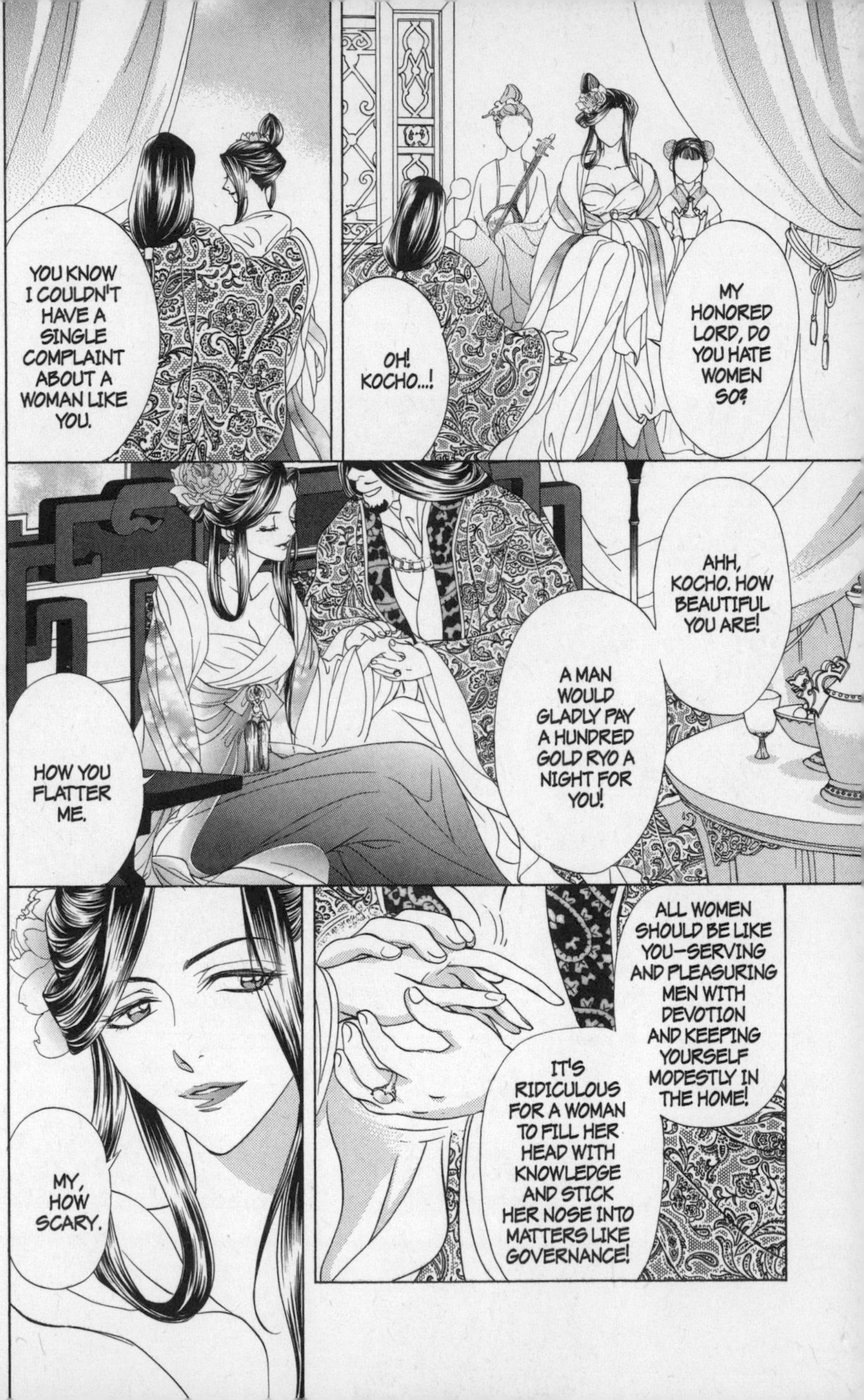
MY HONORED LORD, DO YOU HATE WOMEN SO?
OH! KOCHO...!
YOU KNOW I COULDN'T HAVE A SINGLE COMPLAINT ABOUT A WOMAN LIKE YOU.
AHH, KOCHO. HOW BEAUTIFUL YOU ARE!
A MAN WOULD GLADLY PAY A HUNDRED GOLD RYO A NIGHT FOR YOU!
HOW YOU FLATTER ME.
ALL WOMEN SHOULD BE LIKE YOU—SERVING AND PLEASURING MEN WITH DEVOTION AND KEEPING YOURSELF MODESTLY IN THE HOME!
IT'S RIDICULOUS FOR A WOMAN TO FILL HER HEAD WITH KNOWLEDGE AND STICK HER NOSE INTO MATTERS LIKE GOVERNANCE!
MY, HOW SCARY.

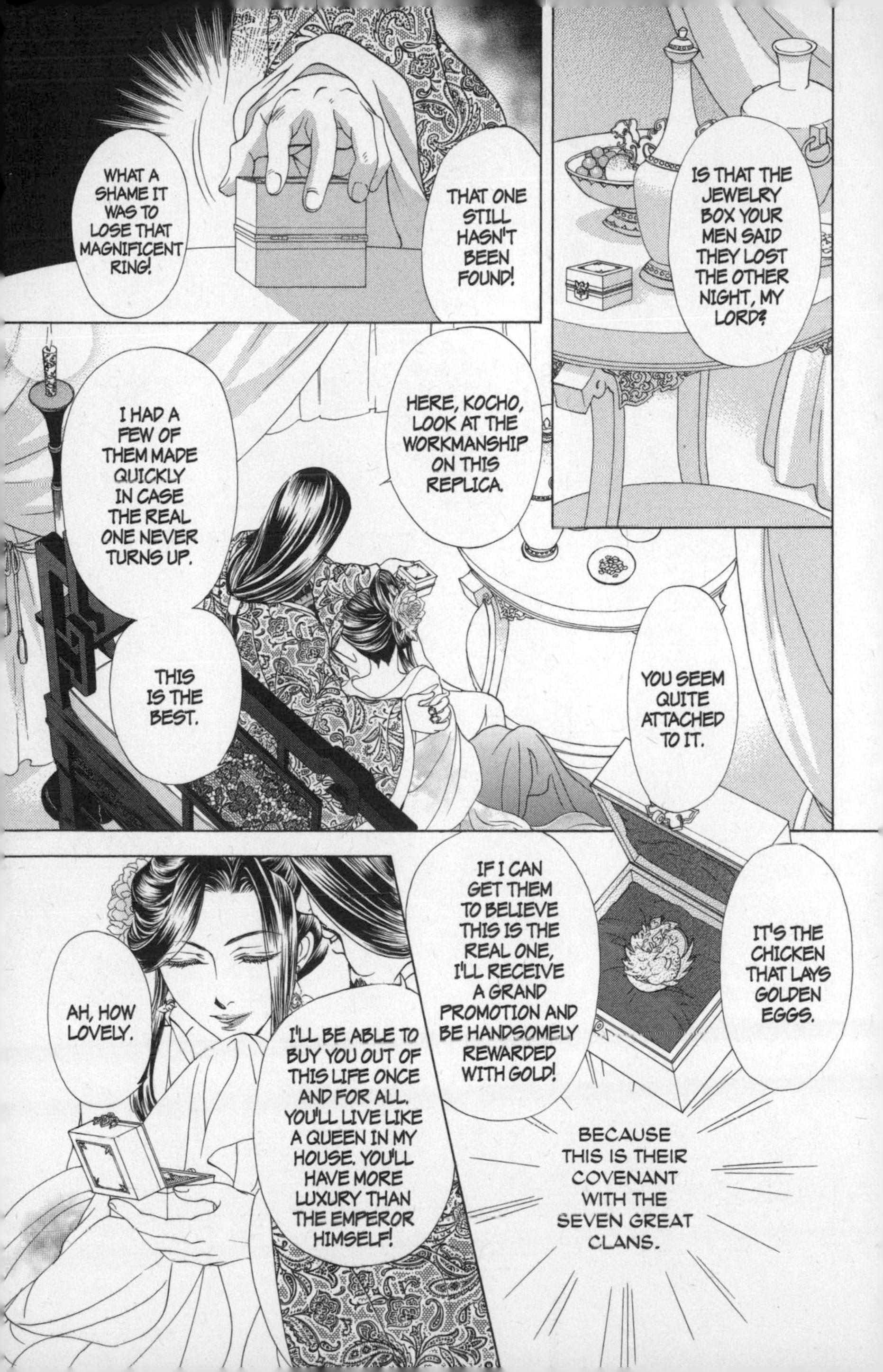
IS THAT THE JEWELRY BOX YOUR MEN SAID THEY LOST THE OTHER NIGHT, MY LORD?
THAT ONE STILL HASN'T BEEN FOUND!
WHAT A SHAME IT WAS TO LOSE THAT MAGNIFICENT RING!
HERE, KOCHO, LOOK AT THE WORKMANSHIP ON THIS REPLICA.
I HAD A FEW OF THEM MADE QUICKLY IN CASE THE REAL ONE NEVER TURNS UP.
THIS IS THE BEST.
YOU SEEM QUITE ATTACHED TO IT.
IT'S THE CHICKEN THAT LAYS GOLDEN EGGS.
IF I CAN GET THEM TO BELIEVE THIS IS THE REAL ONE, I'LL RECEIVE A GRAND PROMOTION AND BE HANDSOMELY REWARDED WITH GOLD!
I'LL BE ABLE TO BUY YOU OUT OF THIS LIFE ONCE AND FOR ALL. YOU'LL LIVE LIKE A QUEEN IN MY HOUSE. YOU'LL HAVE MORE LUXURY THAN THE EMPEROR HIMSELF!
BECAUSE THIS IS THEIR COVENANT WITH THE SEVEN GREAT CLANS.
AH, HOW LOVELY.

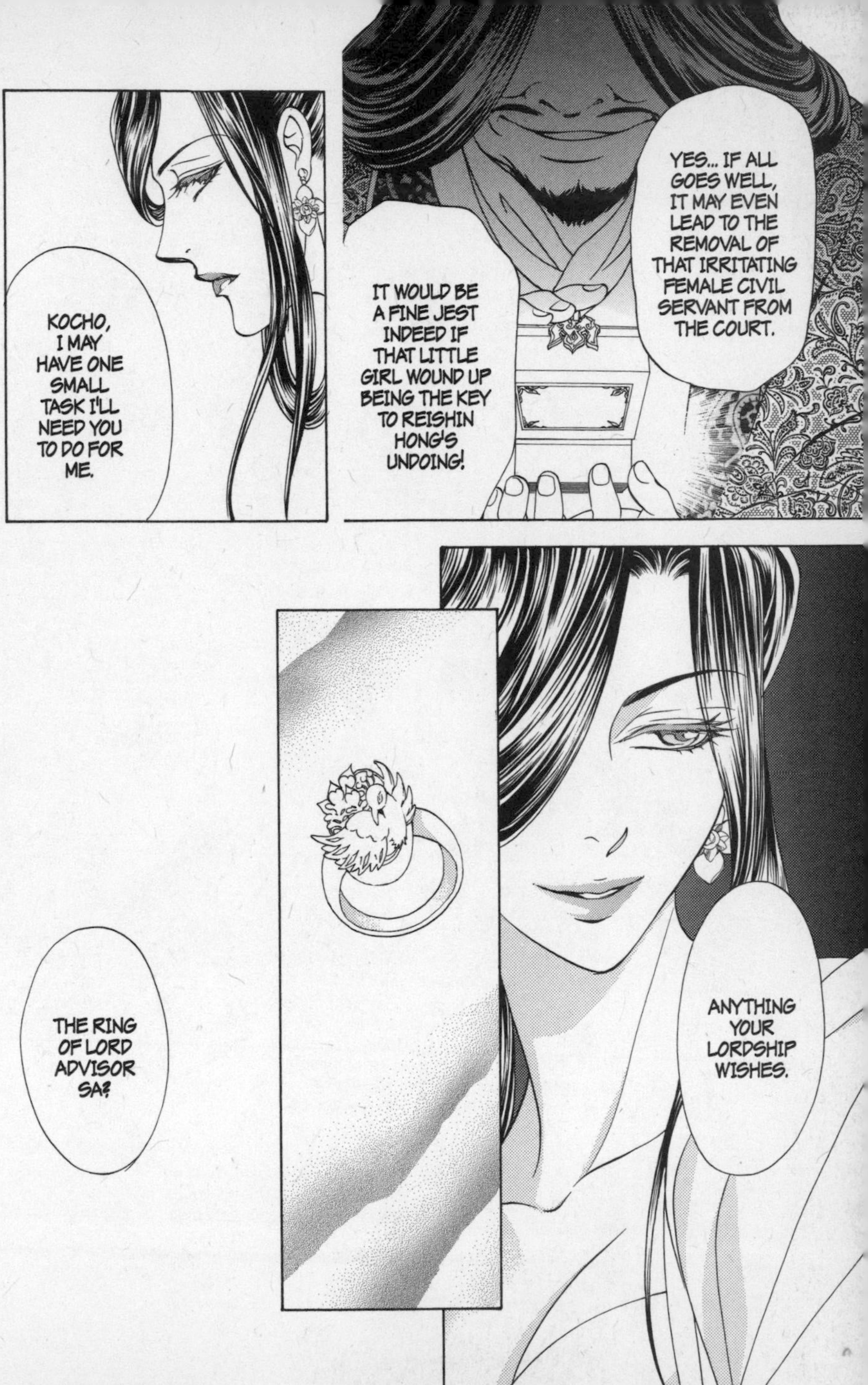
YES... IF ALL GOES WELL, IT MAY EVEN LEAD TO THE REMOVAL OF THAT IRRITATING FEMALE CIVIL SERVANT FROM THE COURT.
IT WOULD BE A FINE JEST INDEED IF THAT LITTLE GIRL WOUND UP BEING THE KEY TO REISHIN HONG'S UNDOING!
KOCHO, I MAY HAVE ONE SMALL TASK I'LL NEED YOU TO DO FOR ME.
ANYTHING YOUR LORDSHIP WISHES.
THE RING OF LORD ADVISOR SA?

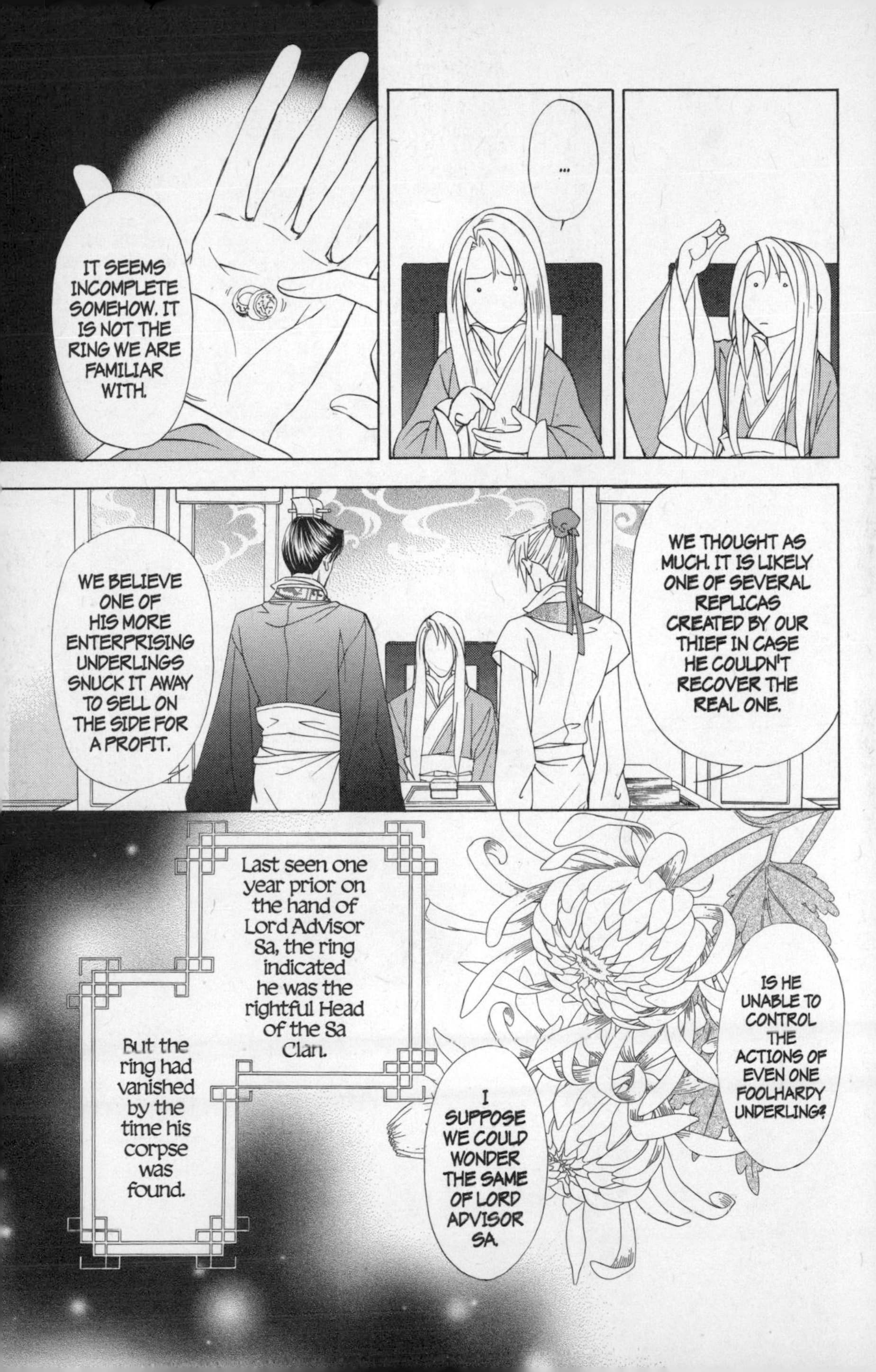
...
IT SEEMS INCOMPLETE SOMEHOW. IT IS NOT THE RING WE ARE FAMILIAR WITH.
WE THOUGHT AS MUCH. IT IS LIKELY ONE OF SEVERAL REPLICAS CREATED BY OUR THIEF IN CASE HE COULDN'T RECOVER THE REAL ONE.
WE BELIEVE ONE OF HIS MORE ENTERPRISING UNDERLINGS SNUCK IT AWAY TO SELL ON THE SIDE FOR A PROFIT.
IS HE UNABLE TO CONTROL THE ACTIONS OF EVEN ONE FOOLHARDY UNDERLING?
I SUPPOSE WE COULD WONDER THE SAME OF LORD ADVISOR SA.
Last seen one year prior on the hand of Lord Advisor Sa, the ring indicated he was the rightful Head of the Sa Clan.
But the ring had vanished by the time his corpse was found.

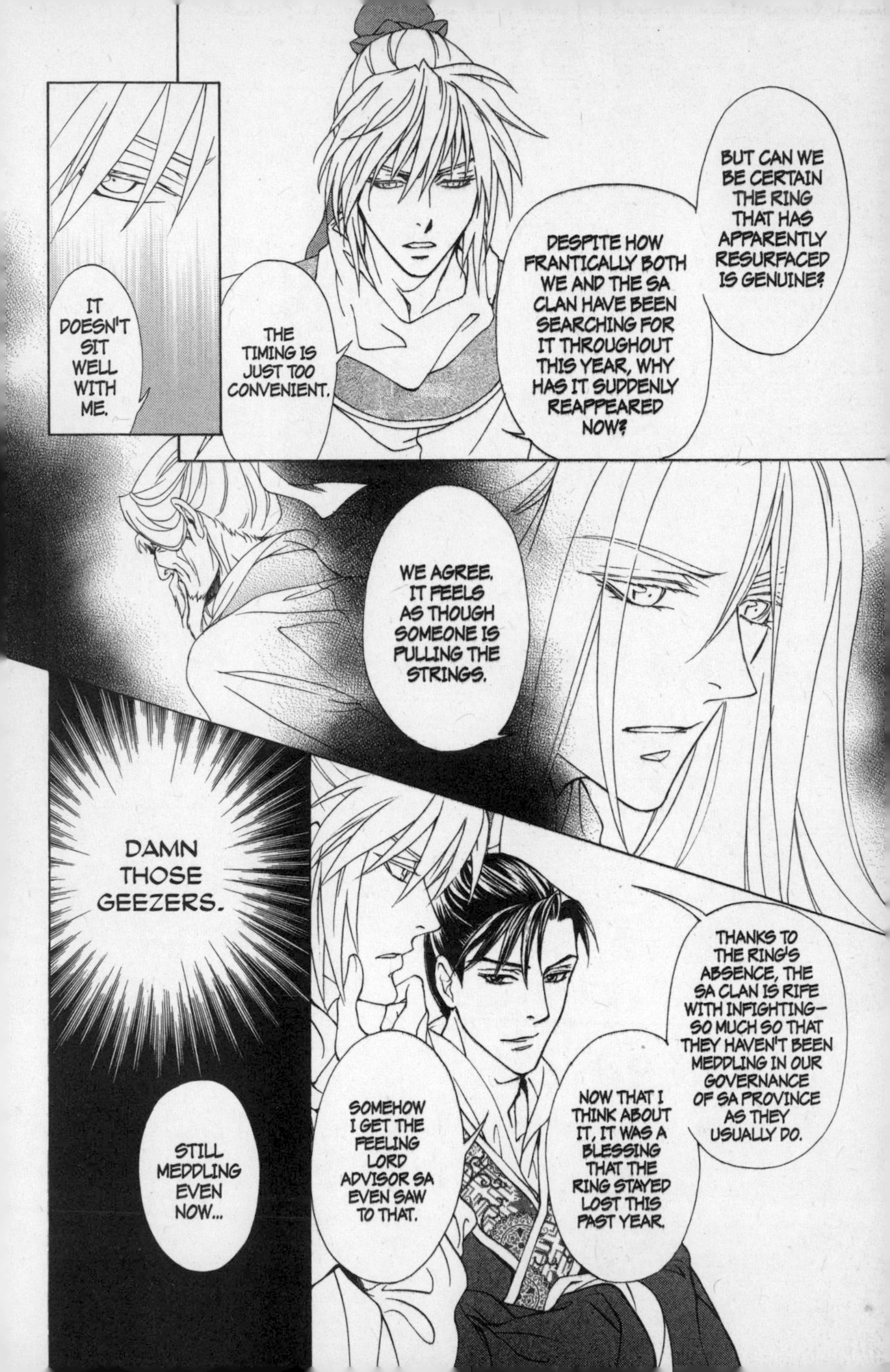
BUT CAN WE BE CERTAIN THE RING THAT HAS APPARENTLY RESURFACED IS GENUINE?
DESPITE HOW FRANTICALLY BOTH WE AND THE SA CLAN HAVE BEEN SEARCHING FOR IT THROUGHOUT THIS YEAR, WHY HAS IT SUDDENLY REAPPEARED NOW?
THE TIMING IS JUST TOO CONVENIENT.
IT DOESN'T SIT WELL WITH ME.
WE AGREE. IT FEELS AS THOUGH SOMEONE IS PULLING THE STRINGS.
THANKS TO THE RING'S ABSENCE, THE SA CLAN IS RIFE WITH INFIGHTING— SO MUCH SO THAT THEY HAVEN'T BEEN MEDDLING IN OUR GOVERNANCE OF SA PROVINCE AS THEY USUALLY DO.
NOW THAT I THINK ABOUT IT, IT WAS A BLESSING THAT THE RING STAYED LOST THIS PAST YEAR.
SOMEHOW I GET THE FEELING LORD ADVISOR SA EVEN SAW TO THAT.
DAMN THOSE GEEZERS.
STILL MEDDLING EVEN NOW...

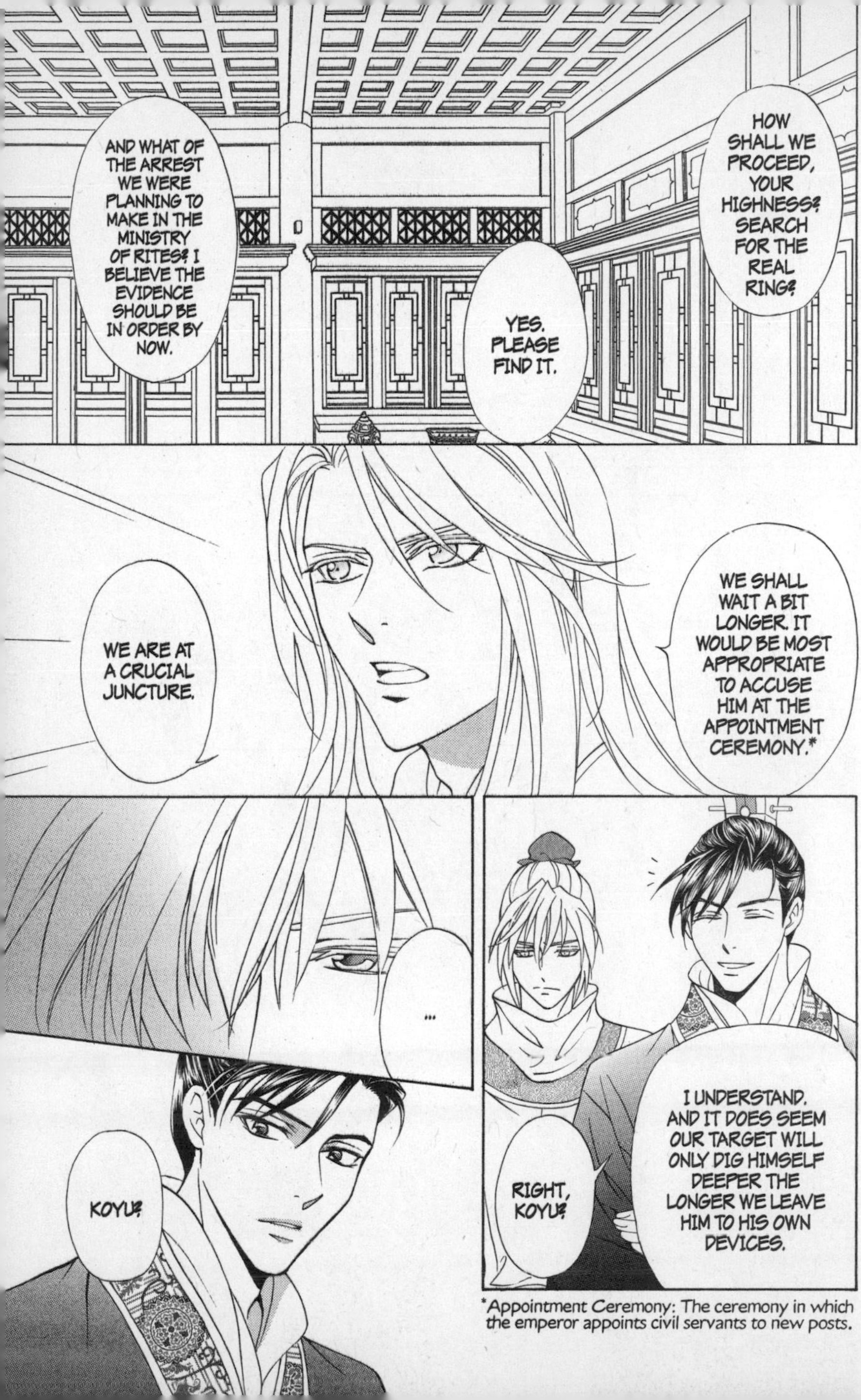
HOW SHALL WE PROCEED, YOUR HIGHNESS? SEARCH FOR THE REAL RING?
YES. PLEASE FIND IT.
AND WHAT OF THE ARREST WE WERE PLANNING TO MAKE IN THE MINISTRY OF RITES? I BELIEVE THE EVIDENCE SHOULD BE IN ORDER BY NOW.
WE SHALL WAIT A BIT LONGER. IT WOULD BE MOST APPROPRIATE TO ACCUSE HIM AT THE APPOINTMENT CEREMONY.*
WE ARE AT A CRUCIAL JUNCTURE.
I UNDERSTAND. AND IT DOES SEEM OUR TARGET WILL ONLY DIG HIMSELF DEEPER THE LONGER WE LEAVE HIM TO HIS OWN DEVICES.
RIGHT, KOYU?
...
KOYU?

*Appointment Ceremony: The ceremony in which the emperor appoints civil servants to new posts.

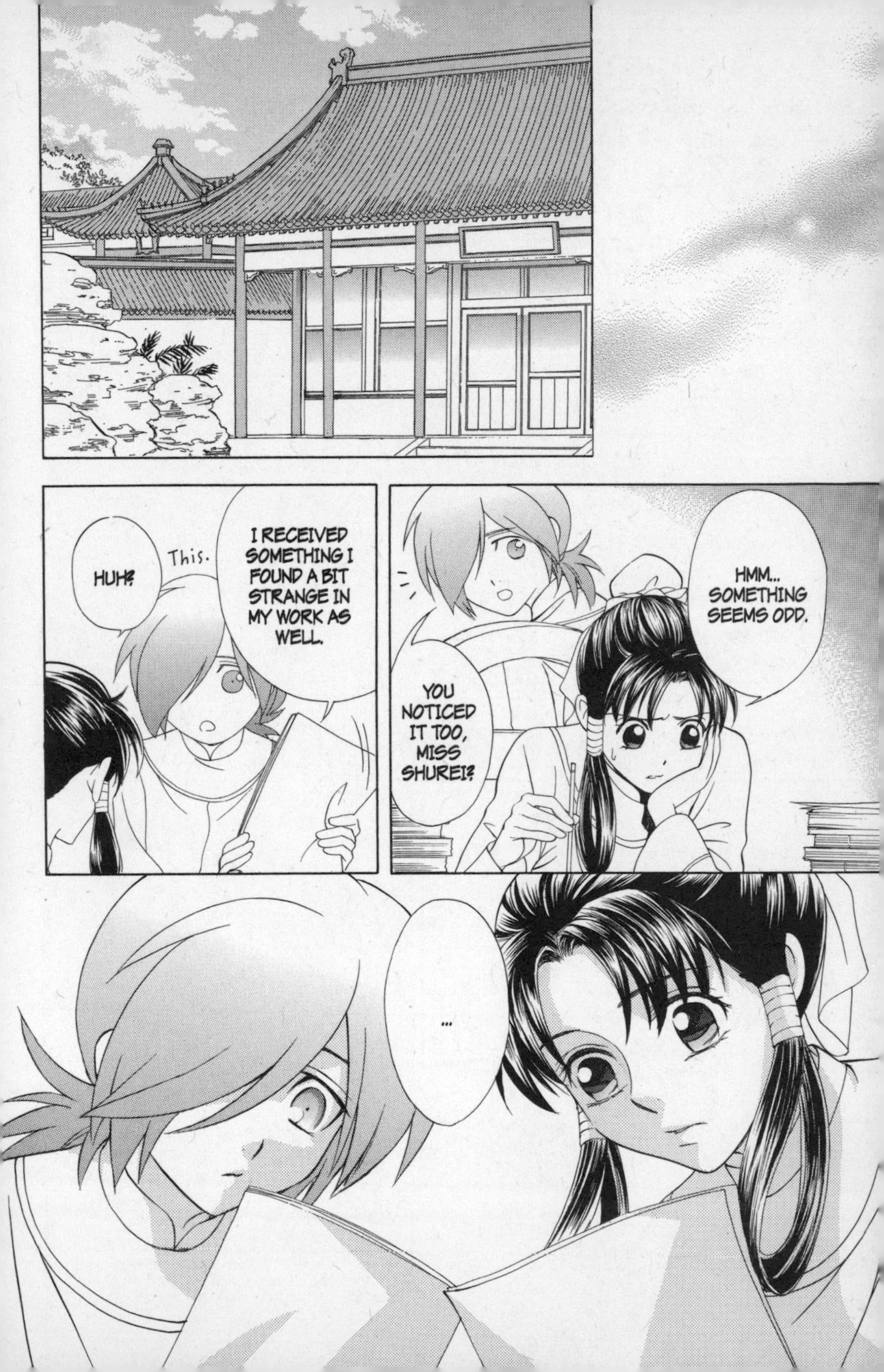

HMM... SOMETHING SEEMS ODD.
YOU NOTICED IT TOO, MISS SHUREI?
I RECEIVED SOMETHING I FOUND A BIT STRANGE IN MY WORK AS WELL.
This.
HUH?
...

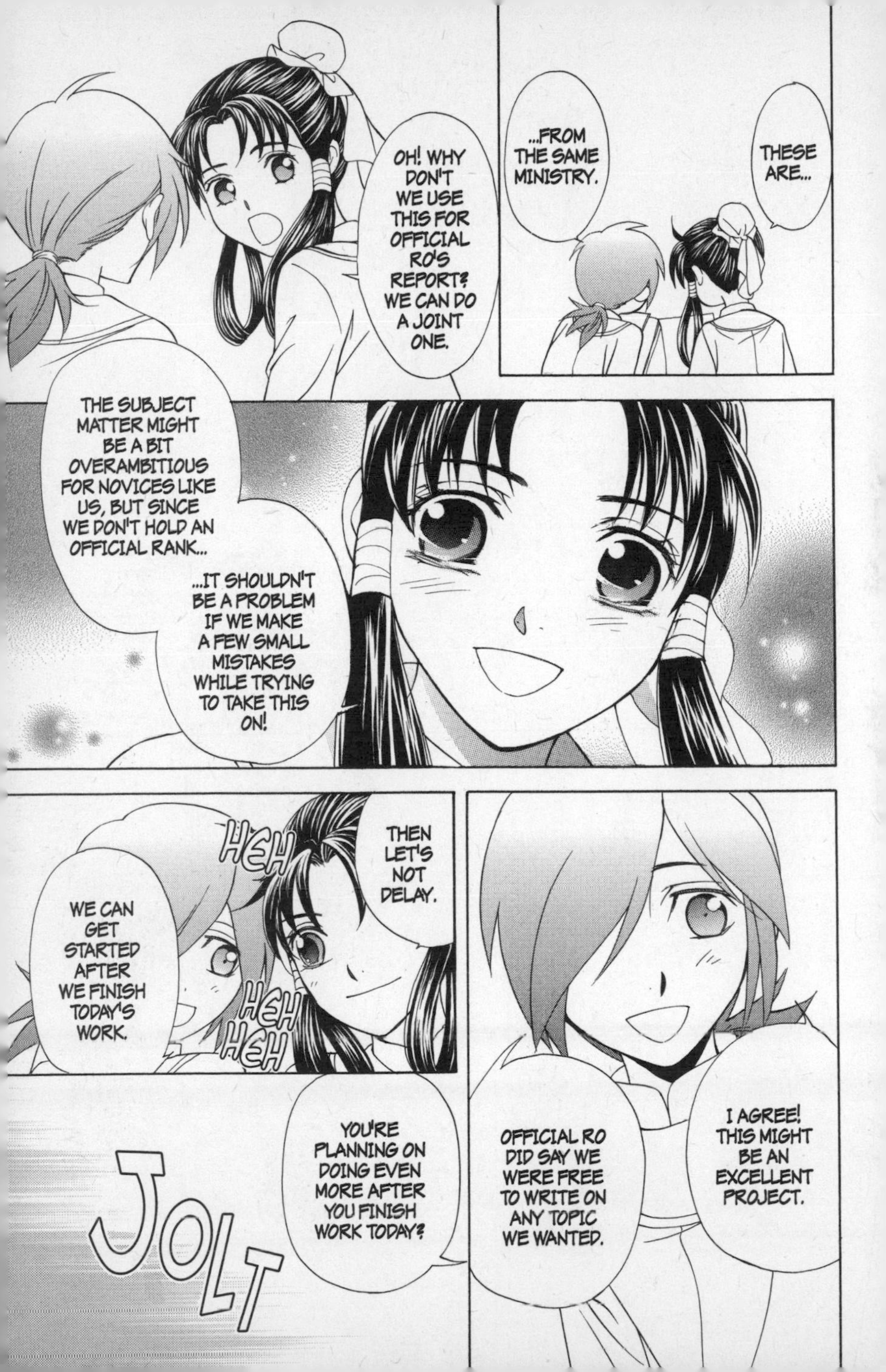
THESE ARE...
...FROM THE SAME MINISTRY.
OH! WHY DON'T WE USE THIS FOR OFFICIAL RO'S REPORT? WE CAN DO A JOINT ONE.
THE SUBJECT MATTER MIGHT BE A BIT OVERAMBITIOUS FOR NOVICES LIKE US, BUT SINCE WE DON'T HOLD AN OFFICIAL RANK...
...IT SHOULDN'T BE A PROBLEM IF WE MAKE A FEW SMALL MISTAKES WHILE TRYING TO TAKE THIS ON!
I AGREE! THIS MIGHT BE AN EXCELLENT PROJECT.
OFFICIAL RO DID SAY WE WERE FREE TO WRITE ON ANY TOPIC WE WANTED.
THEN LET'S NOT DELAY.
HEH
HEH HEH
WE CAN GET STARTED AFTER WE FINISH TODAY'S WORK.
YOU'RE PLANNING ON DOING EVEN MORE AFTER YOU FINISH WORK TODAY?
JOLT

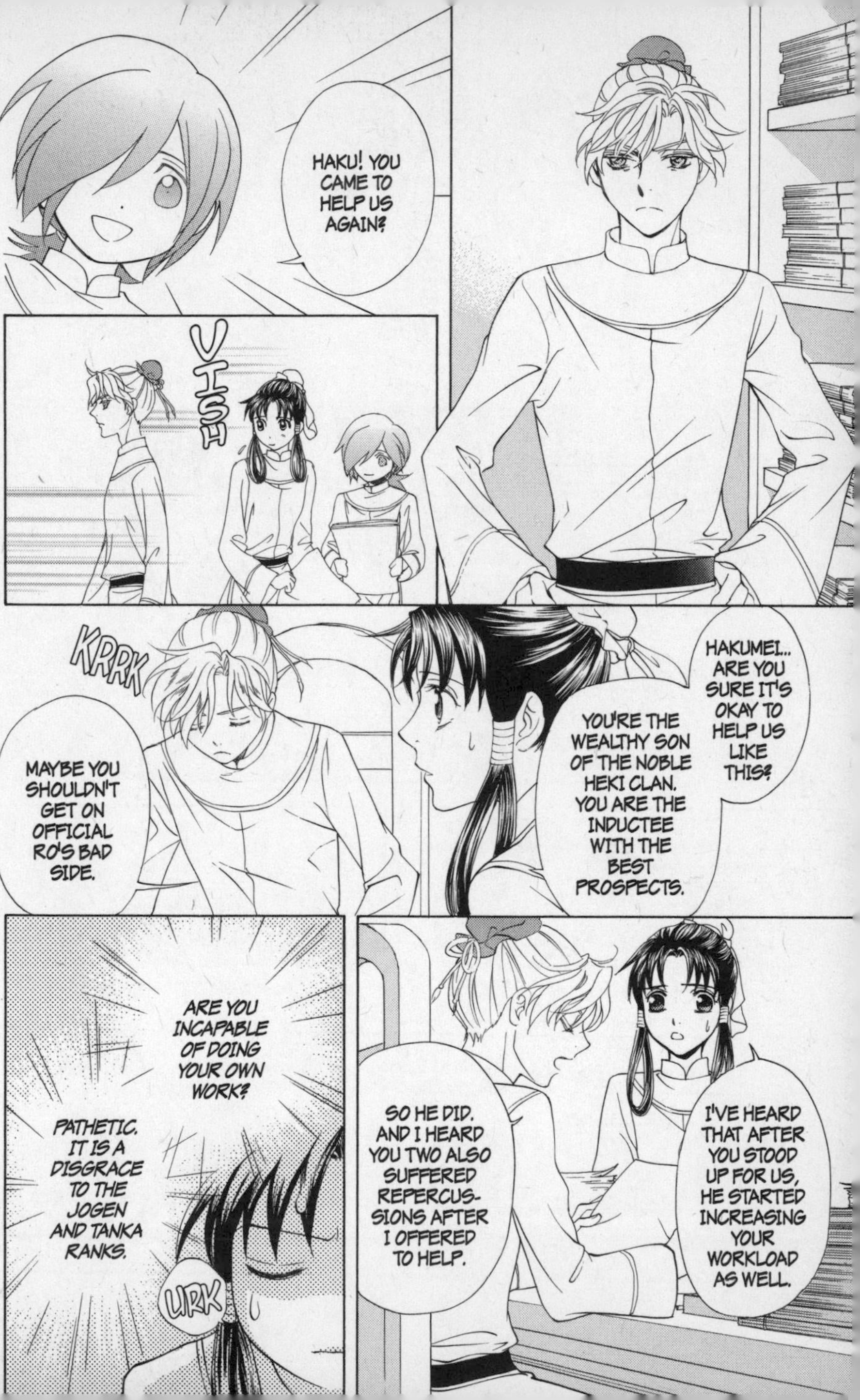
HAKU! YOU CAME TO HELP US AGAIN?
VISH
HAKUMEI... ARE YOU SURE IT'S OKAY TO HELP US LIKE THIS?
YOU'RE THE WEALTHY SON OF THE NOBLE HEKI CLAN. YOU ARE THE INDUCTEE WITH THE BEST PROSPECTS.
KRRK
MAYBE YOU SHOULDN'T GET ON OFFICIAL RO'S BAD SIDE.
I'VE HEARD THAT AFTER YOU STOOD UP FOR US, HE STARTED INCREASING YOUR WORKLOAD AS WELL.
SO HE DID. AND I HEARD YOU TWO ALSO SUFFERED REPERCUSSIONS AFTER I OFFERED TO HELP.
ARE YOU INCAPABLE OF DOING YOUR OWN WORK?
PATHETIC. IT IS A DISGRACE TO THE JOGEN AND TANKA RANKS.
URK

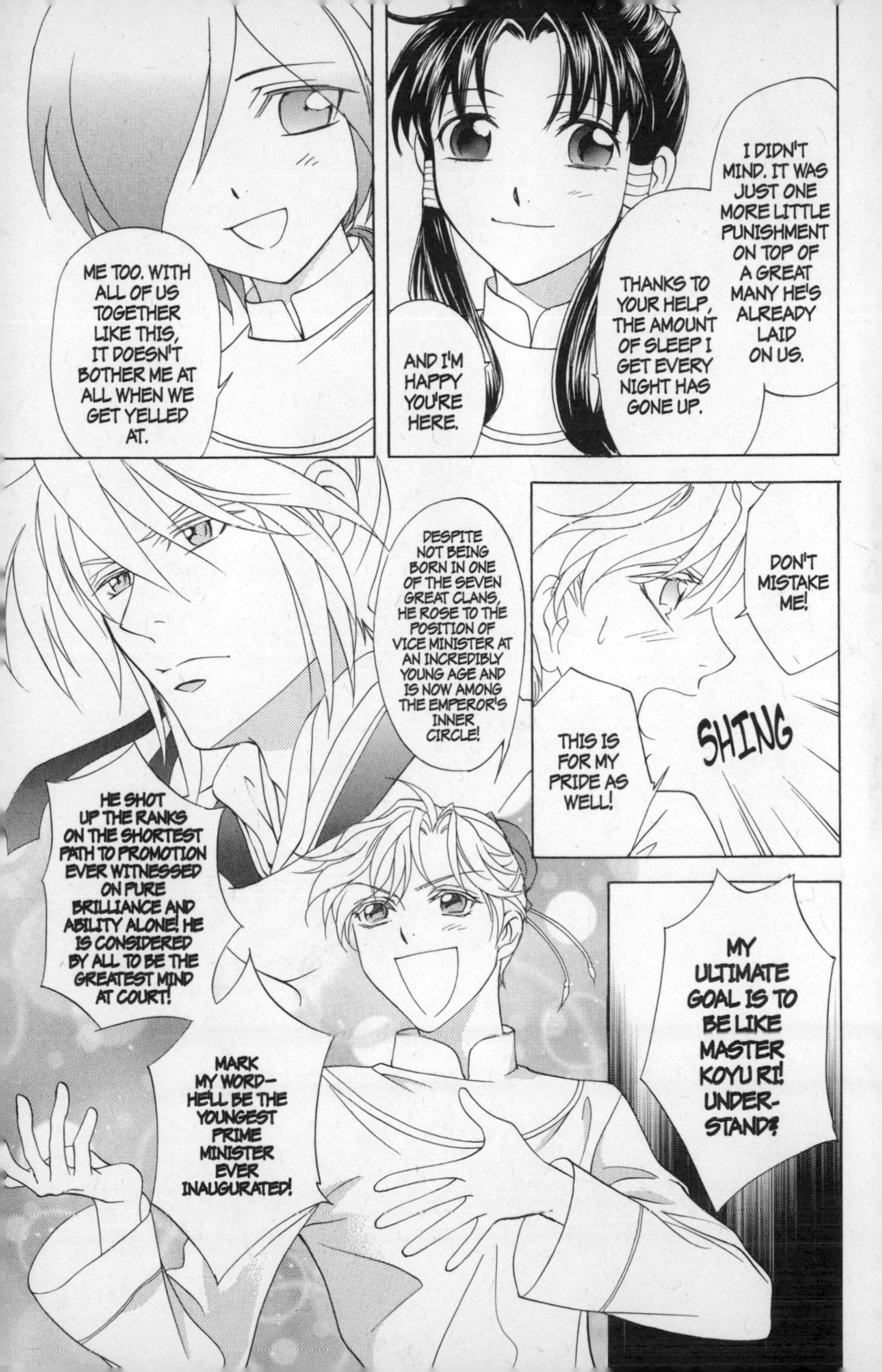
I DIDN'T MIND. IT WAS JUST ONE MORE LITTLE PUNISHMENT ON TOP OF A GREAT MANY HE'S ALREADY LAID ON US.
THANKS TO YOUR HELP, THE AMOUNT OF SLEEP I GET EVERY NIGHT HAS GONE UP.
AND I'M HAPPY YOU'RE HERE.
ME TOO. WITH ALL OF US TOGETHER LIKE THIS, IT DOESN'T BOTHER ME AT ALL WHEN WE GET YELLED AT.
DON'T MISTAKE ME!
SHING
THIS IS FOR MY PRIDE AS WELL!
MY ULTIMATE GOAL IS TO BE LIKE MASTER KOYU RI! UNDER-STAND?
DESPITE NOT BEING BORN IN ONE OF THE SEVEN GREAT CLANS, HE ROSE TO THE POSITION OF VICE MINISTER AT AN INCREDIBLY YOUNG AGE AND IS NOW AMONG THE EMPEROR'S INNER CIRCLE!
HE SHOT UP THE RANKS ON THE SHORTEST PATH TO PROMOTION EVER WITNESSED ON PURE BRILLIANCE AND ABILITY ALONE! HE IS CONSIDERED BY ALL TO BE THE GREATEST MIND AT COURT!
MARK MY WORD—HE'LL BE THE YOUNGEST PRIME MINISTER EVER INAUGURATED!

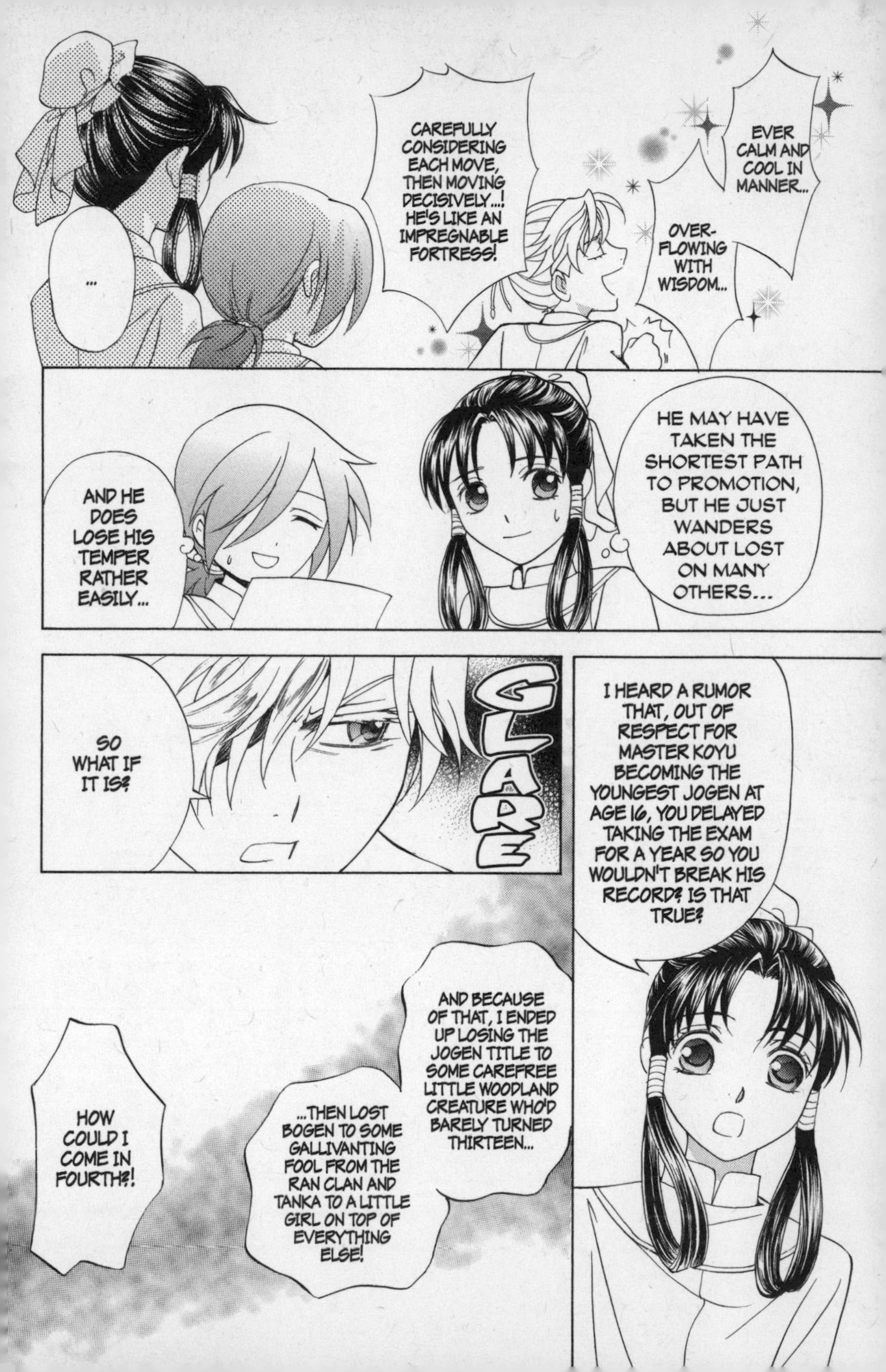
EVER CALM AND COOL IN MANNER...
OVER-FLOWING WITH WISDOM...
CAREFULLY CONSIDERING EACH MOVE, THEN MOVING DECISIVELY...! HE'S LIKE AN IMPREGNABLE FORTRESS!
...
HE MAY HAVE TAKEN THE SHORTEST PATH TO PROMOTION, BUT HE JUST WANDERS ABOUT LOST ON MANY OTHERS...
AND HE DOES LOSE HIS TEMPER RATHER EASILY...
I HEARD A RUMOR THAT, OUT OF RESPECT FOR MASTER KOYU BECOMING THE YOUNGEST JOGEN AT AGE 16, YOU DELAYED TAKING THE EXAM FOR A YEAR SO YOU WOULDN'T BREAK HIS RECORD? IS THAT TRUE?
GLARE
SO WHAT IF IT IS?
AND BECAUSE OF THAT, I ENDED UP LOSING THE JOGEN TITLE TO SOME CAREFREE LITTLE WOODLAND CREATURE WHO'D BARELY TURNED THIRTEEN...
...THEN LOST BOGEN TO SOME GALLIVANTING FOOL FROM THE RAN CLAN AND TANKA TO A LITTLE GIRL ON TOP OF EVERYTHING ELSE!
HOW COULD I COME IN FOURTH?!

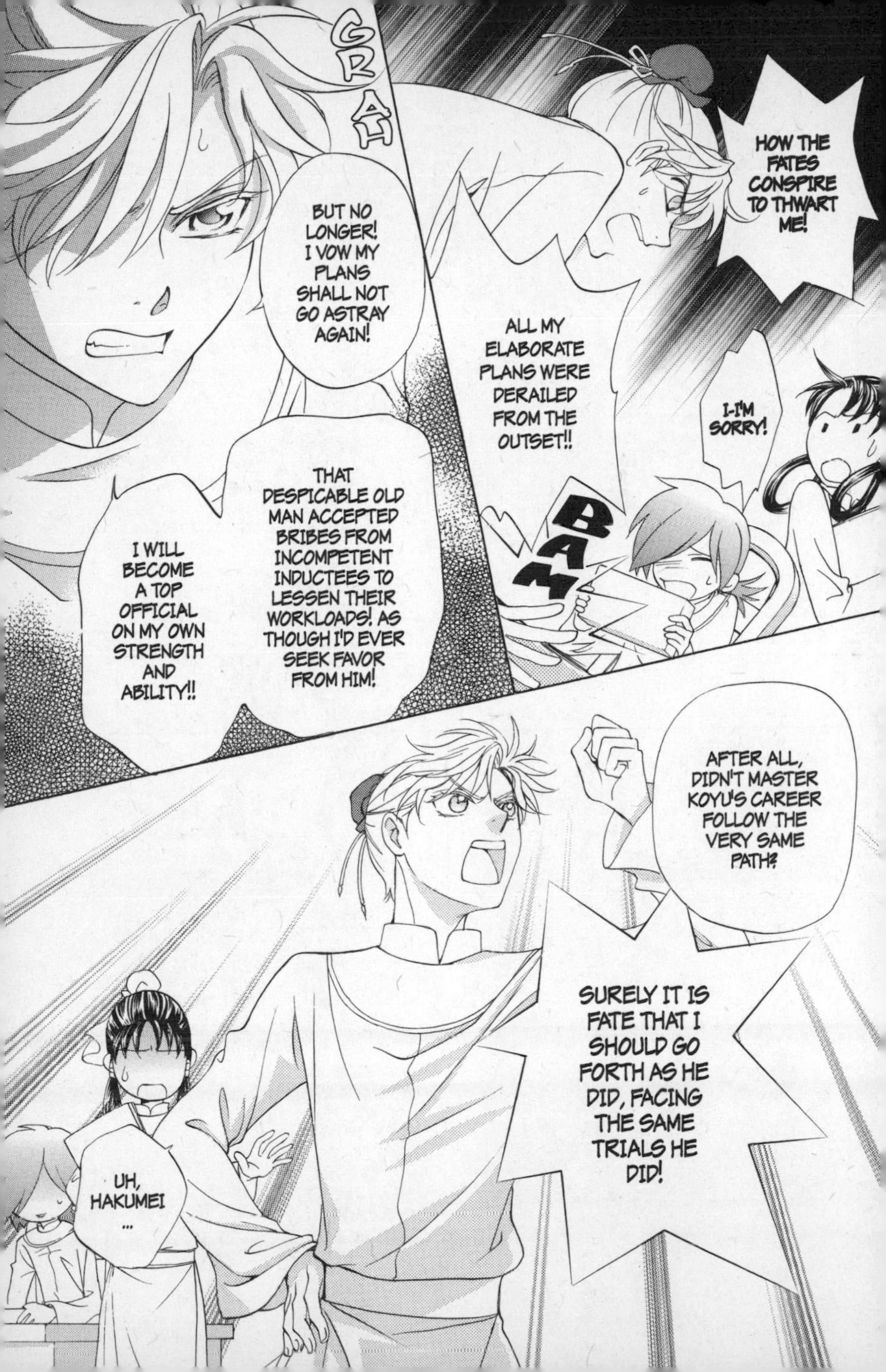
HOW THE FATES CONSPIRE TO THWART ME!
ALL MY ELABORATE PLANS WERE DERAILED FROM THE OUTSET!!
I-I'M SORRY!
BAM
GRAH
BUT NO LONGER! I VOW MY PLANS SHALL NOT GO ASTRAY AGAIN!
THAT DESPICABLE OLD MAN ACCEPTED BRIBES FROM INCOMPETENT INDUCTEES TO LESSEN THEIR WORKLOADS! AS THOUGH I'D EVER SEEK FAVOR FROM HIM!
I WILL BECOME A TOP OFFICIAL ON MY OWN STRENGTH AND ABILITY!!
AFTER ALL, DIDN'T MASTER KOYU'S CAREER FOLLOW THE VERY SAME PATH?
SURELY IT IS FATE THAT I SHOULD GO FORTH AS HE DID, FACING THE SAME TRIALS HE DID!
UH, HAKUMEI ...

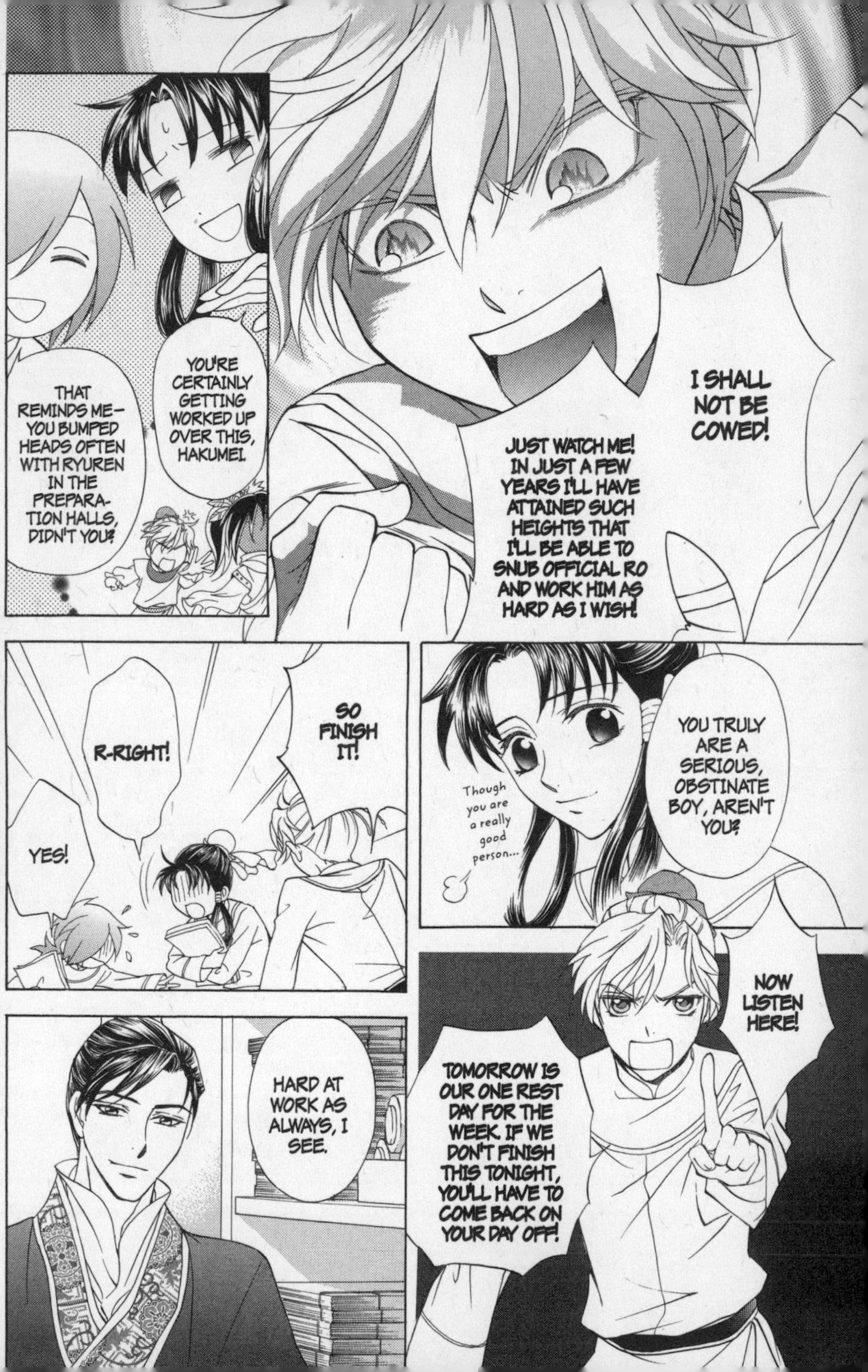
I SHALL NOT BE COWED!
JUST WATCH ME! IN JUST A FEW YEARS I'LL HAVE ATTAINED SUCH HEIGHTS THAT I'LL BE ABLE TO SNUB OFFICIAL RO AND WORK HIM AS HARD AS I WISH!
YOU'RE CERTAINLY GETTING WORKED UP OVER THIS, HAKUMEI.
THAT REMINDS ME— YOU BUMPED HEADS OFTEN WITH RYUREN IN THE PREPARATION HALLS, DIDN'T YOU?
YOU TRULY ARE A SERIOUS, OBSTINATE BOY, AREN'T YOU?
Though you are a really good person...
NOW LISTEN HERE!
TOMORROW IS OUR ONE REST DAY FOR THE WEEK. IF WE DON'T FINISH THIS TONIGHT, YOU'LL HAVE TO COME BACK ON YOUR DAY OFF!
SO FINISH IT!
R-RIGHT!
YES!
HARD AT WORK AS ALWAYS, I SEE.

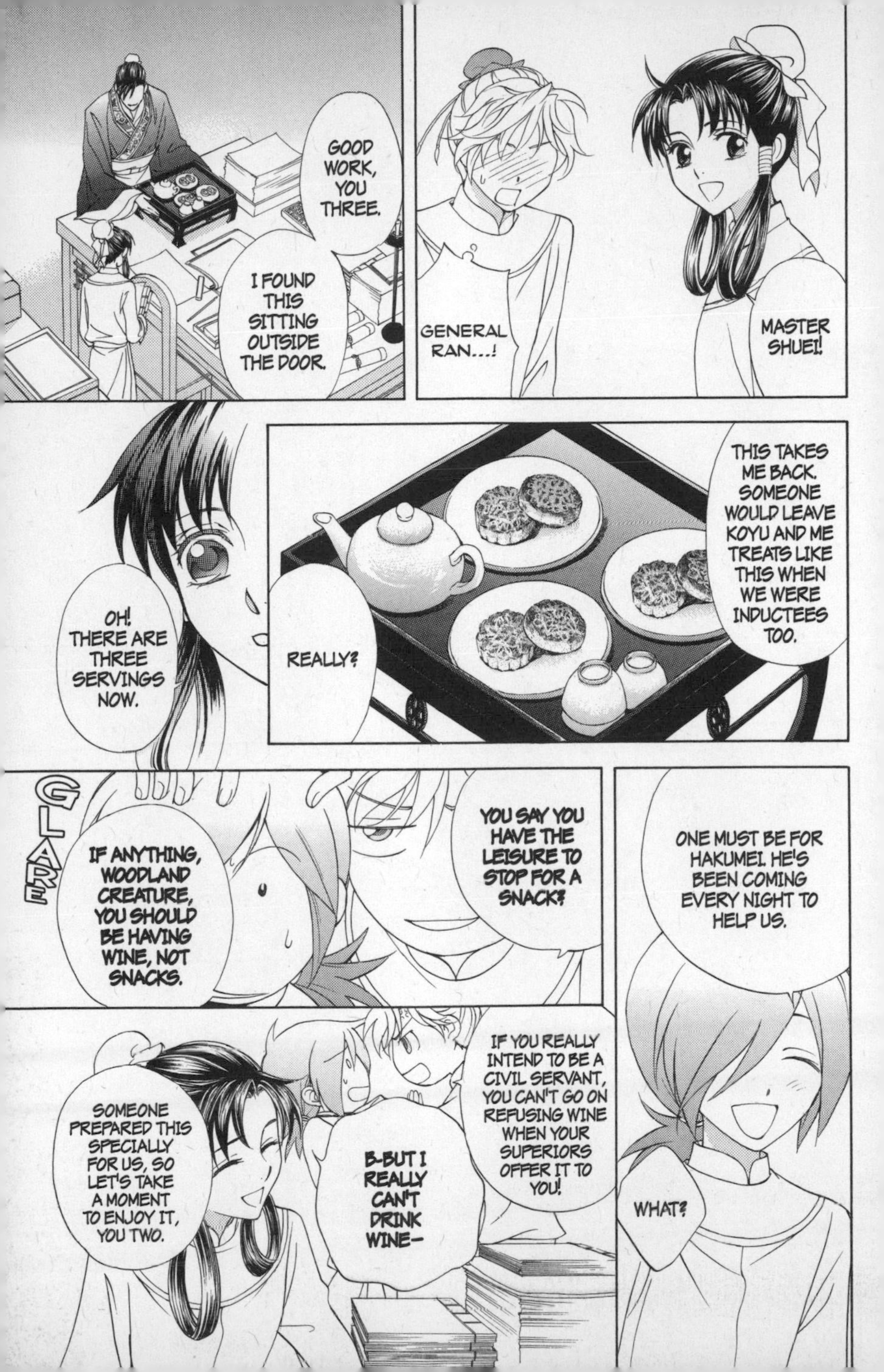
MASTER SHUEI!
GENERAL RAN...!
GOOD WORK, YOU THREE.
I FOUND THIS SITTING OUTSIDE THE DOOR.
THIS TAKES ME BACK. SOMEONE WOULD LEAVE KOYU AND ME TREATS LIKE THIS WHEN WE WERE INDUCTEES TOO.
REALLY?
OH! THERE ARE THREE SERVINGS NOW.
ONE MUST BE FOR HAKUMEI. HE'S BEEN COMING EVERY NIGHT TO HELP US.
WHAT?
YOU SAY YOU HAVE THE LEISURE TO STOP FOR A SNACK?
GLARE
IF ANYTHING, WOODLAND CREATURE, YOU SHOULD BE HAVING WINE, NOT SNACKS.
IF YOU REALLY INTEND TO BE A CIVIL SERVANT, YOU CAN'T GO ON REFUSING WINE WHEN YOUR SUPERIORS OFFER IT TO YOU!
B-BUT I REALLY CAN'T DRINK WINE–
SOMEONE PREPARED THIS SPECIALLY FOR US, SO LET'S TAKE A MOMENT TO ENJOY IT, YOU TWO.

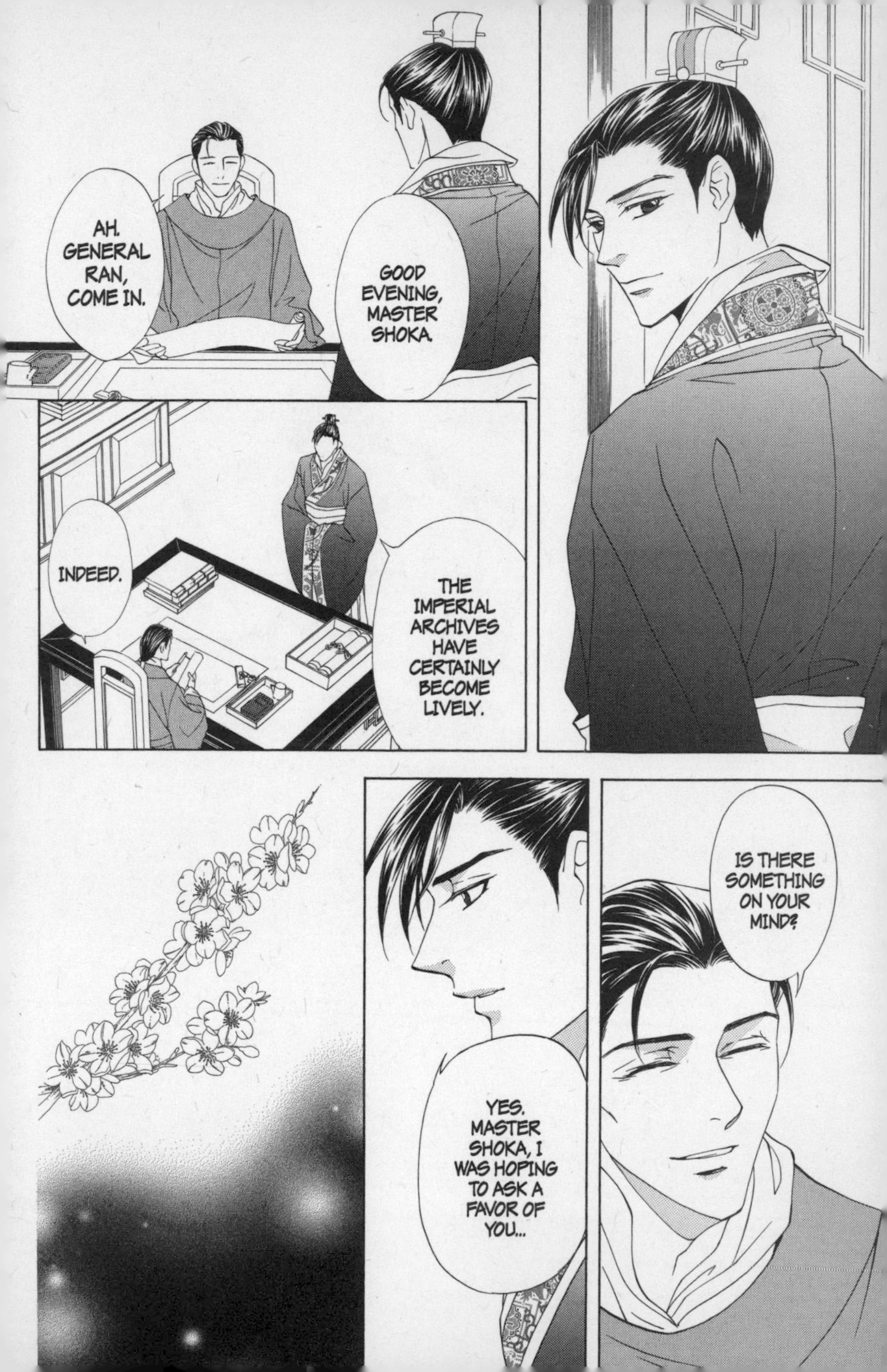
GOOD EVENING, MASTER SHOKA.
AH. GENERAL RAN, COME IN.
THE IMPERIAL ARCHIVES HAVE CERTAINLY BECOME LIVELY.
INDEED.
IS THERE SOMETHING ON YOUR MIND?
YES. MASTER SHOKA, I WAS HOPING TO ASK A FAVOR OF YOU...

The Story of
SAIUNKOKU

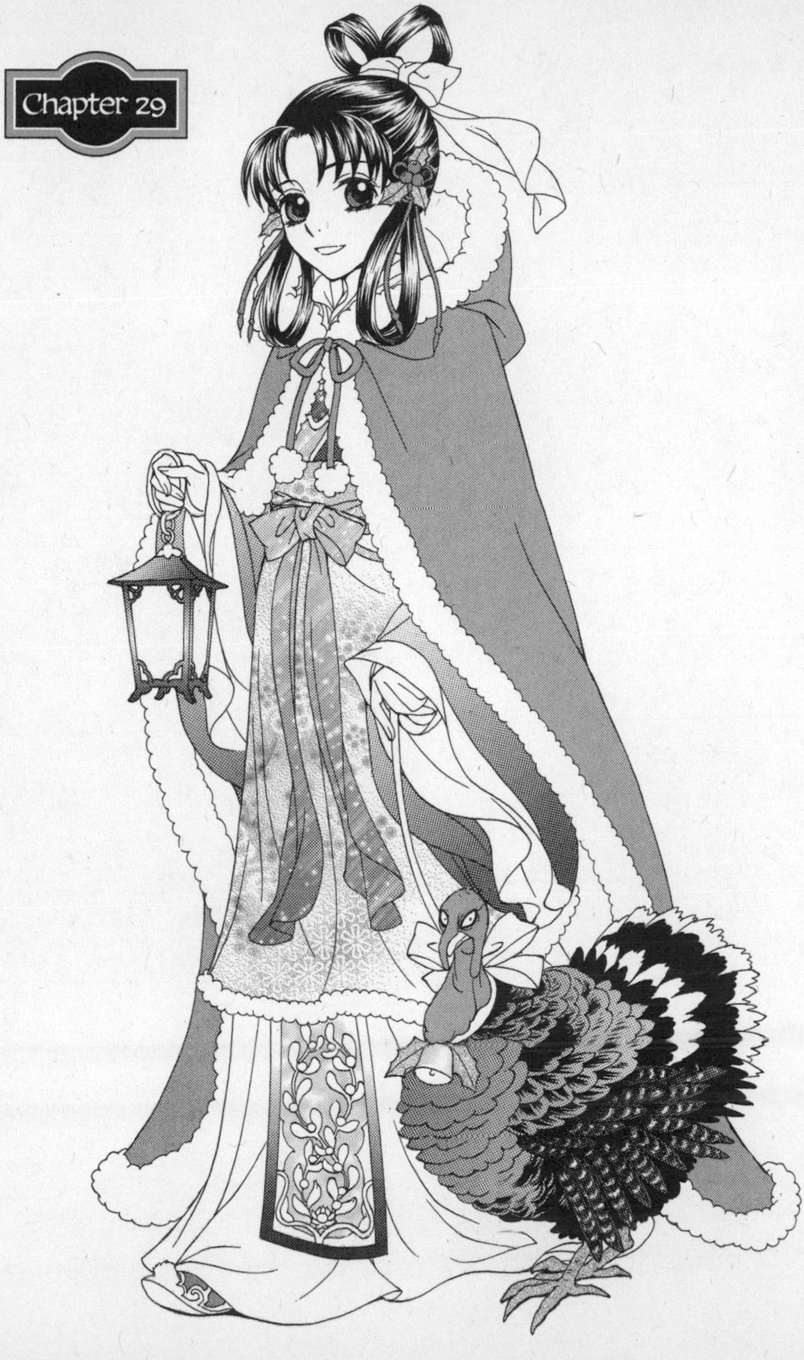
Chapter 29

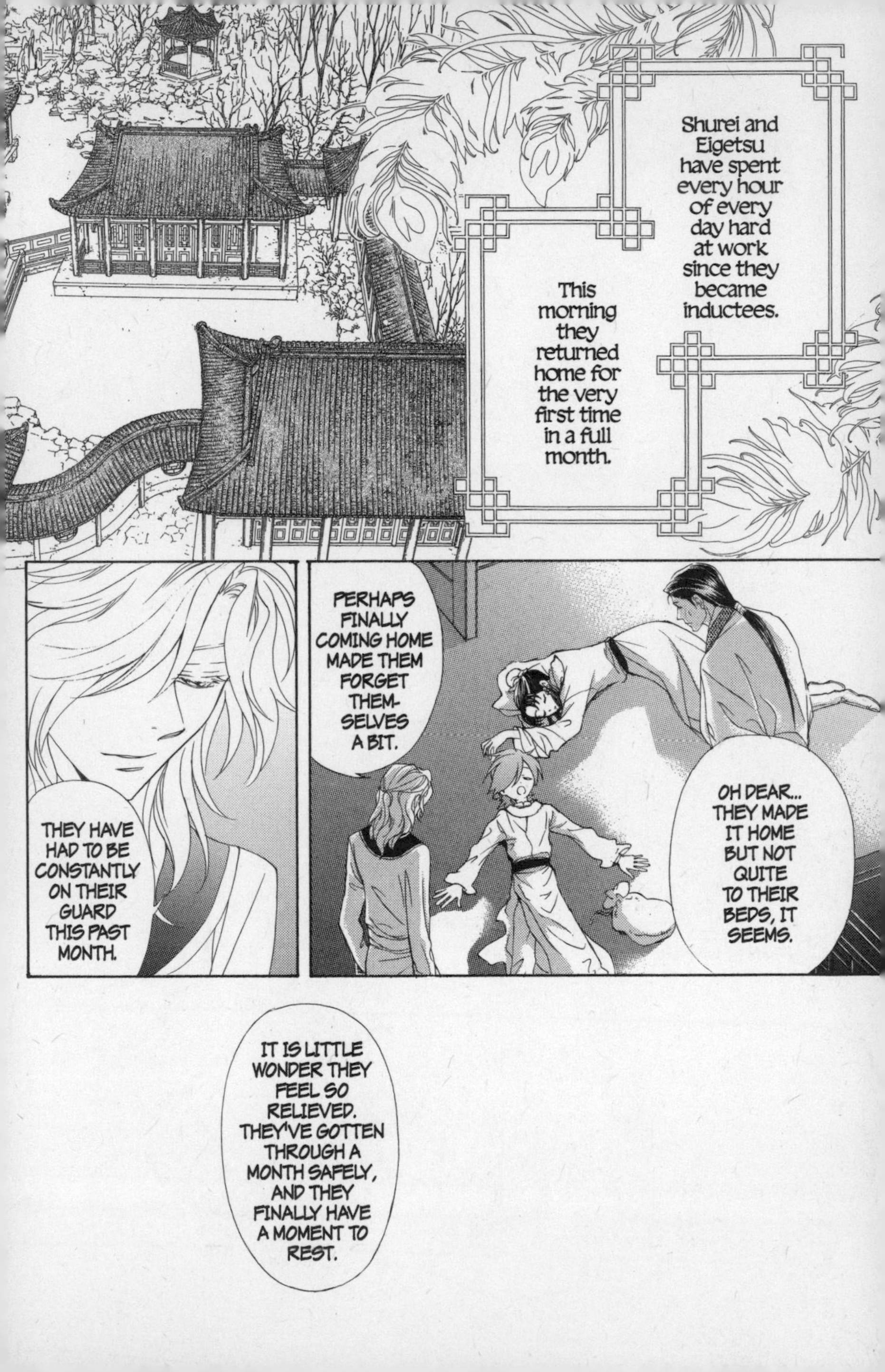
Shurei and Eigetsu have spent every hour of every day hard at work since they became inductees.
This morning they returned home for the very first time in a full month.
OH DEAR... THEY MADE IT HOME BUT NOT QUITE TO THEIR BEDS, IT SEEMS.
PERHAPS FINALLY COMING HOME MADE THEM FORGET THEMSELVES A BIT.
THEY HAVE HAD TO BE CONSTANTLY ON THEIR GUARD THIS PAST MONTH.
IT IS LITTLE WONDER THEY FEEL SO RELIEVED. THEY'VE GOTTEN THROUGH A MONTH SAFELY, AND THEY FINALLY HAVE A MOMENT TO REST.

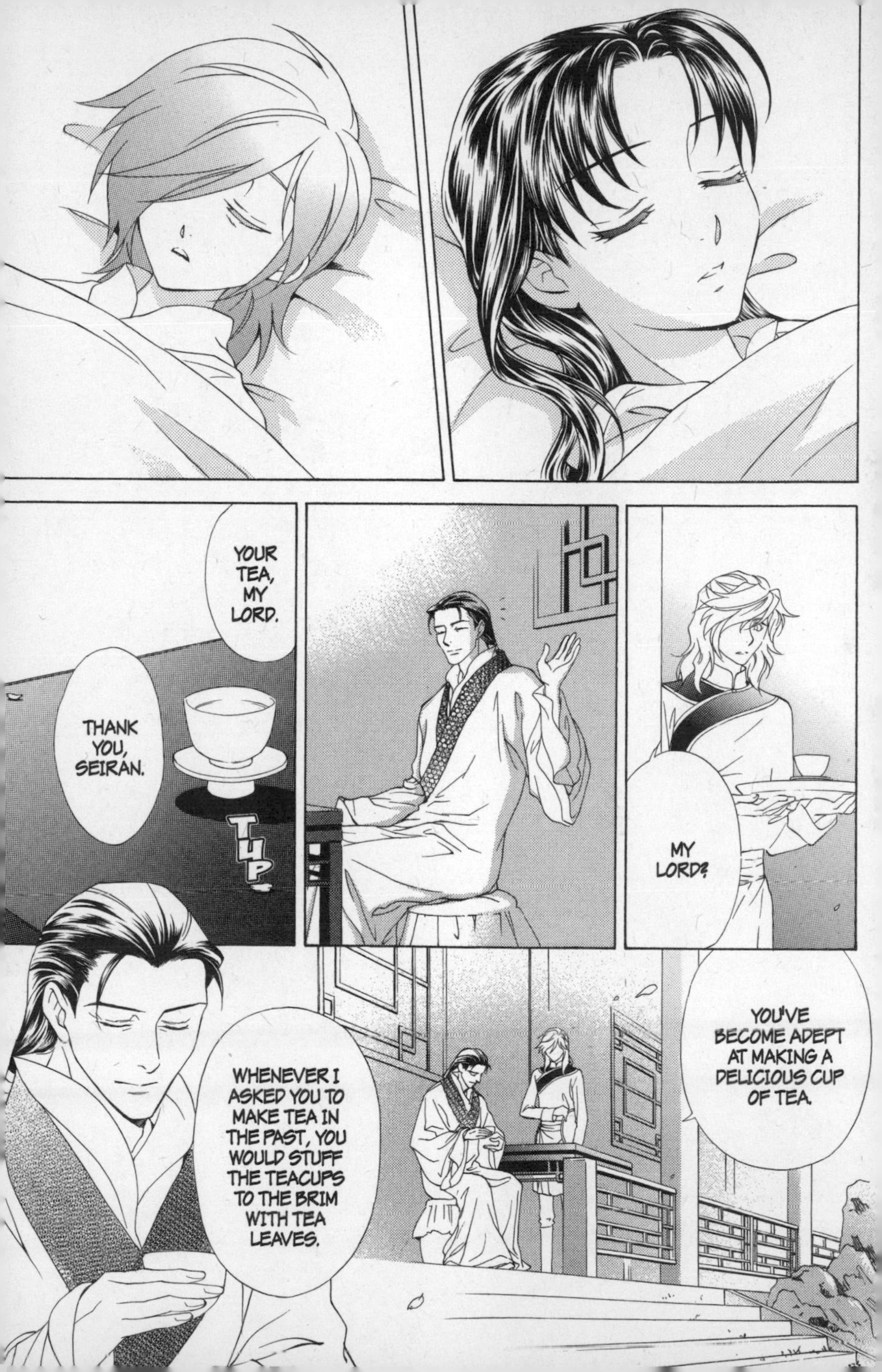
MY LORD?
YOUR TEA, MY LORD.
THANK YOU, SEIRAN.
TUP.
YOU'VE BECOME ADEPT AT MAKING A DELICIOUS CUP OF TEA.
WHENEVER I ASKED YOU TO MAKE TEA IN THE PAST, YOU WOULD STUFF THE TEACUPS TO THE BRIM WITH TEA LEAVES.

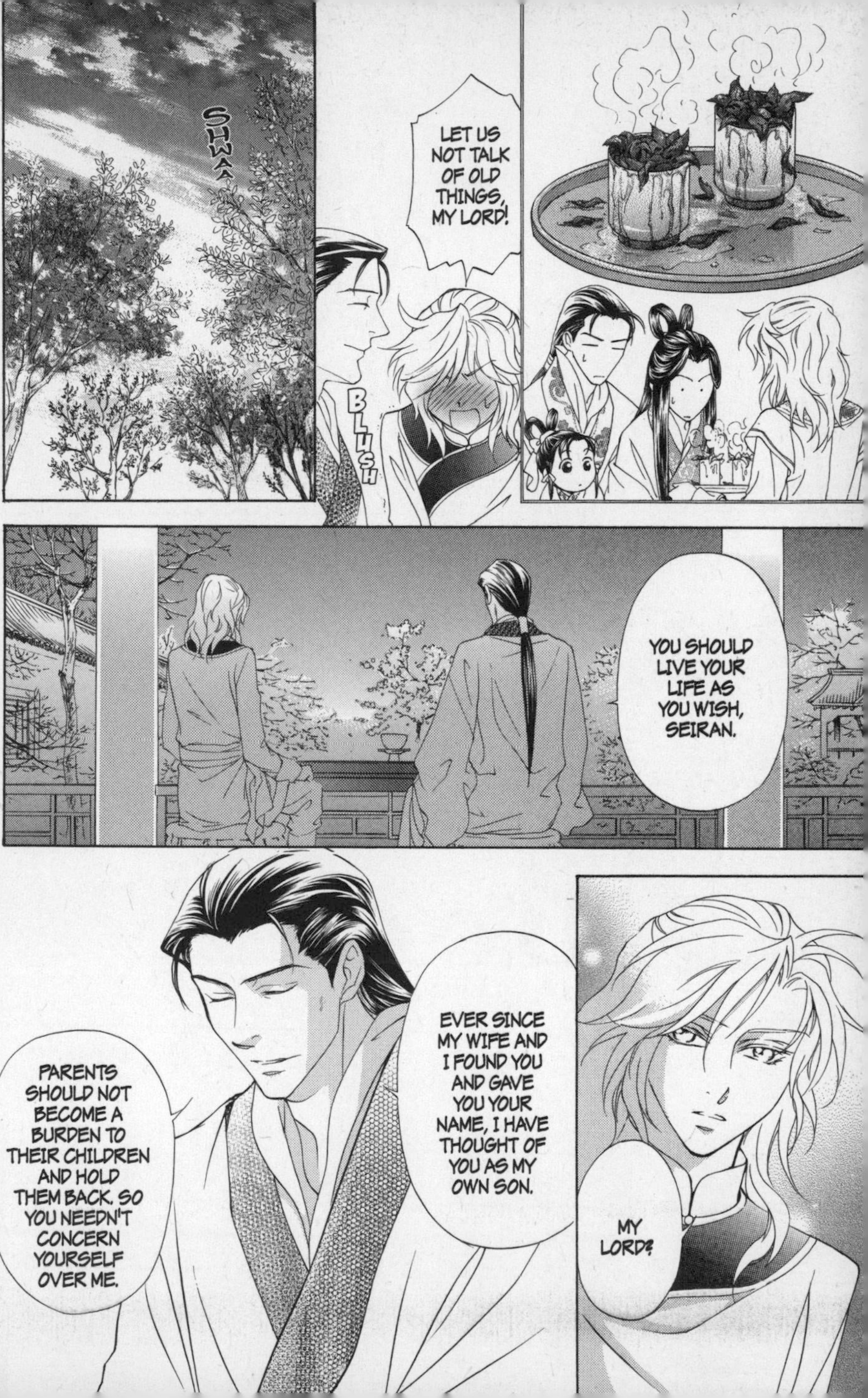
LET US NOT TALK OF OLD THINGS, MY LORD!
BLUSH
SHWAA
YOU SHOULD LIVE YOUR LIFE AS YOU WISH, SEIRAN.
MY LORD?
EVER SINCE MY WIFE AND I FOUND YOU AND GAVE YOU YOUR NAME, I HAVE THOUGHT OF YOU AS MY OWN SON.
PARENTS SHOULD NOT BECOME A BURDEN TO THEIR CHILDREN AND HOLD THEM BACK. SO YOU NEEDN'T CONCERN YOURSELF OVER ME.

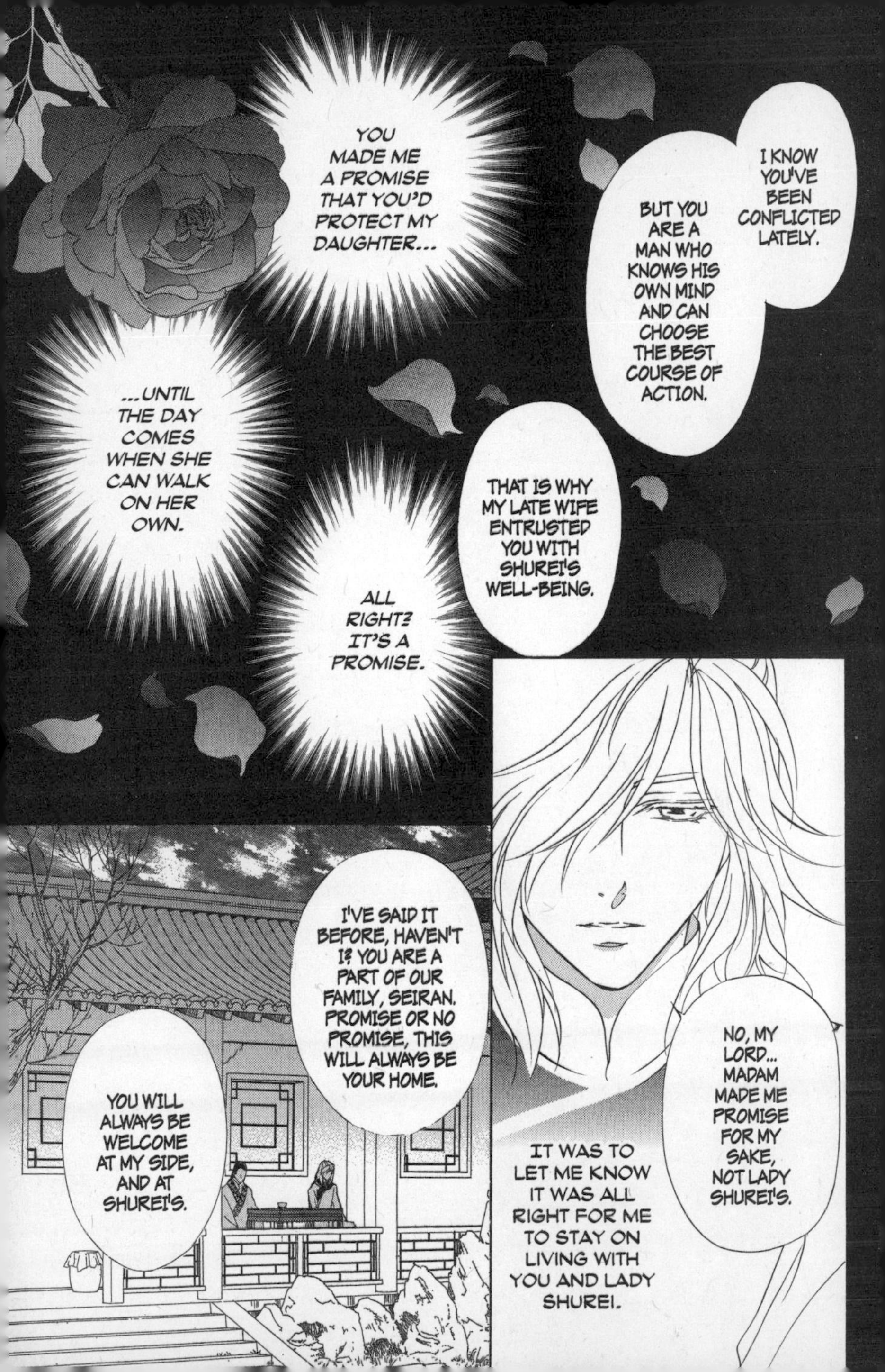
I KNOW YOU'VE BEEN CONFLICTED LATELY.
BUT YOU ARE A MAN WHO KNOWS HIS OWN MIND AND CAN CHOOSE THE BEST COURSE OF ACTION.
THAT IS WHY MY LATE WIFE ENTRUSTED YOU WITH SHUREI'S WELL-BEING.
YOU MADE ME A PROMISE THAT YOU'D PROTECT MY DAUGHTER...
...UNTIL THE DAY COMES WHEN SHE CAN WALK ON HER OWN.
ALL RIGHT? IT'S A PROMISE.
NO, MY LORD... MADAM MADE ME PROMISE FOR MY SAKE, NOT LADY SHUREI'S.
IT WAS TO LET ME KNOW IT WAS ALL RIGHT FOR ME TO STAY ON LIVING WITH YOU AND LADY SHUREI.
I'VE SAID IT BEFORE, HAVEN'T I? YOU ARE A PART OF OUR FAMILY, SEIRAN. PROMISE OR NO PROMISE, THIS WILL ALWAYS BE YOUR HOME.
YOU WILL ALWAYS BE WELCOME AT MY SIDE, AND AT SHUREI'S.

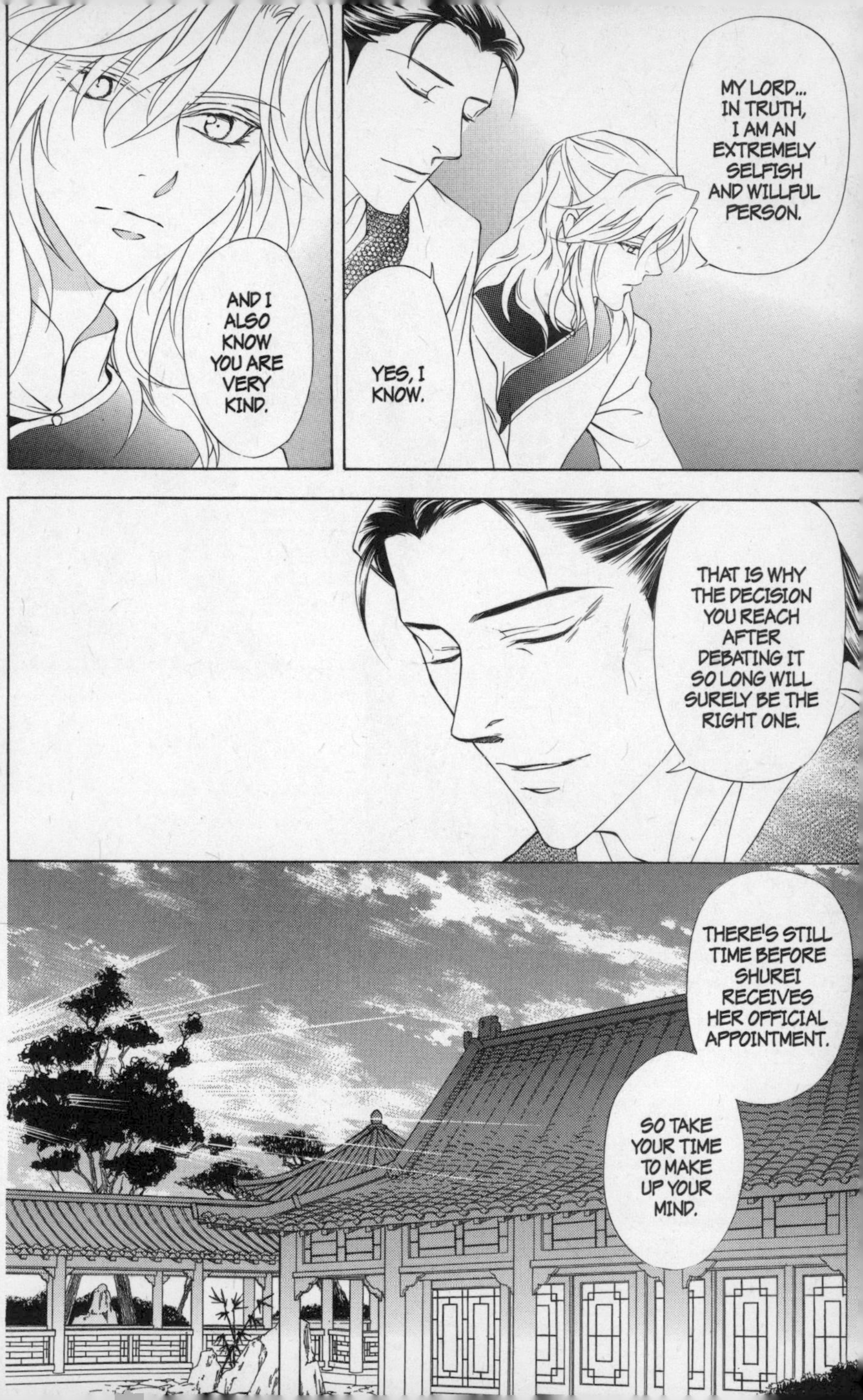
MY LORD... IN TRUTH, I AM AN EXTREMELY SELFISH AND WILLFUL PERSON.
YES, I KNOW.
AND I ALSO KNOW YOU ARE VERY KIND.
THAT IS WHY THE DECISION YOU REACH AFTER DEBATING IT SO LONG WILL SURELY BE THE RIGHT ONE.
THERE'S STILL TIME BEFORE SHUREI RECEIVES HER OFFICIAL APPOINTMENT.
SO TAKE YOUR TIME TO MAKE UP YOUR MIND.

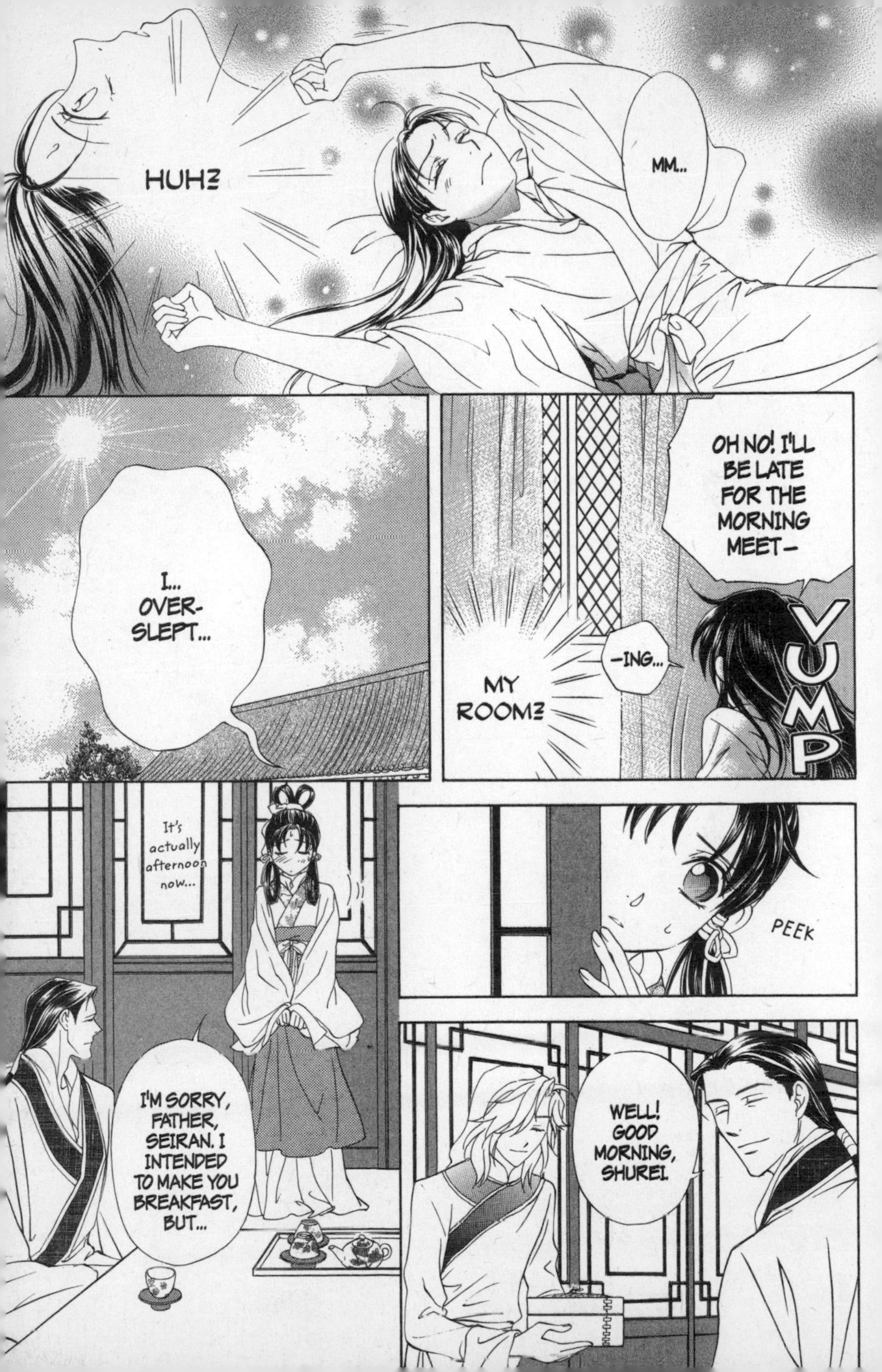
MM...
HUH?
OH NO! I'LL BE LATE FOR THE MORNING MEET-
VUMP
-ING...
MY ROOM?
I... OVER-SLEPT...
PEEK
WELL! GOOD MORNING, SHUREI.
It's actually afternoon now...
I'M SORRY, FATHER, SEIRAN. I INTENDED TO MAKE YOU BREAKFAST, BUT...

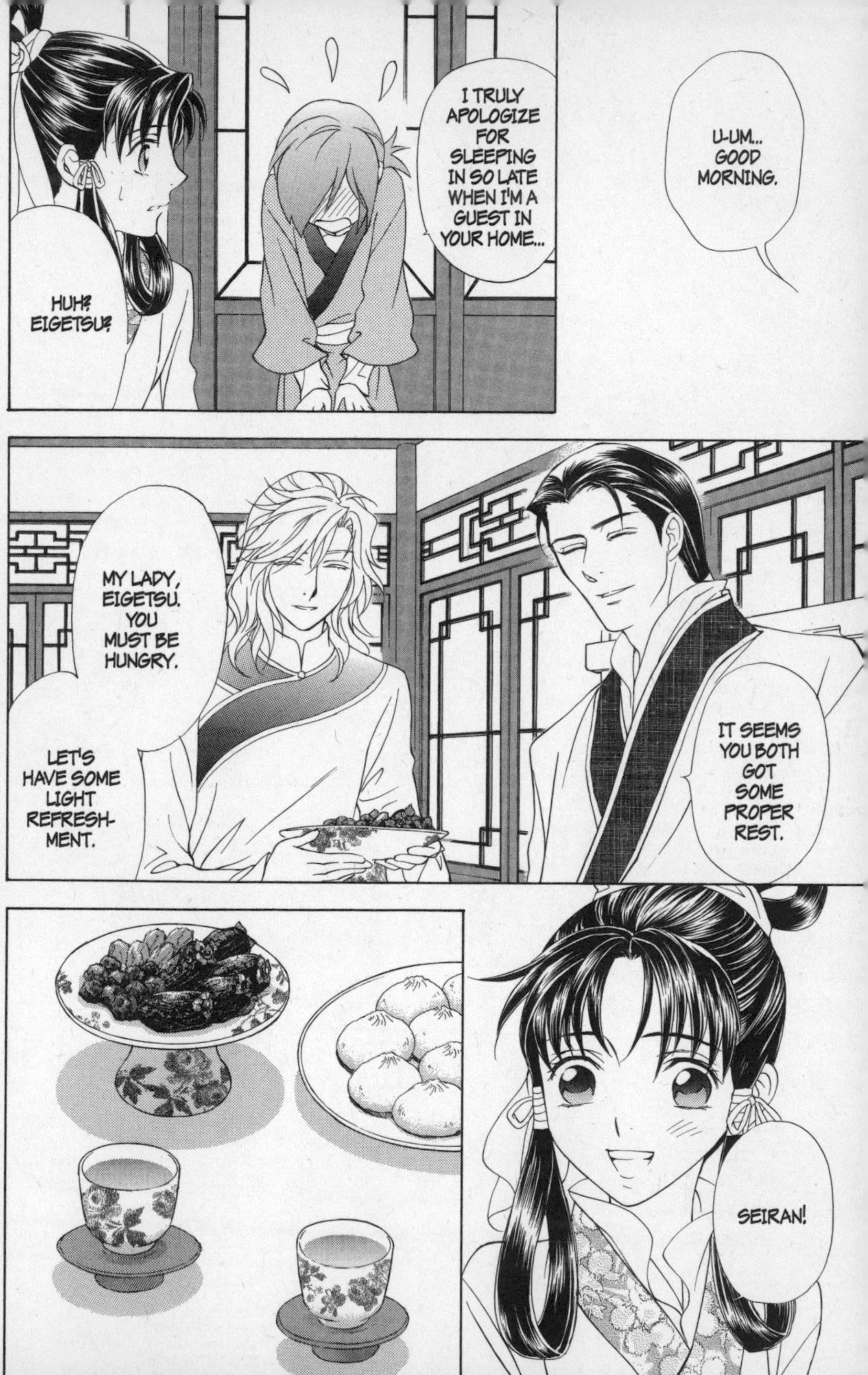
U-UM... GOOD MORNING.
I TRULY APOLOGIZE FOR SLEEPING IN SO LATE WHEN I'M A GUEST IN YOUR HOME...
HUH? EIGETSU?
IT SEEMS YOU BOTH GOT SOME PROPER REST.
MY LADY, EIGETSU. YOU MUST BE HUNGRY.
LET'S HAVE SOME LIGHT REFRESH-MENT.
SEIRAN!

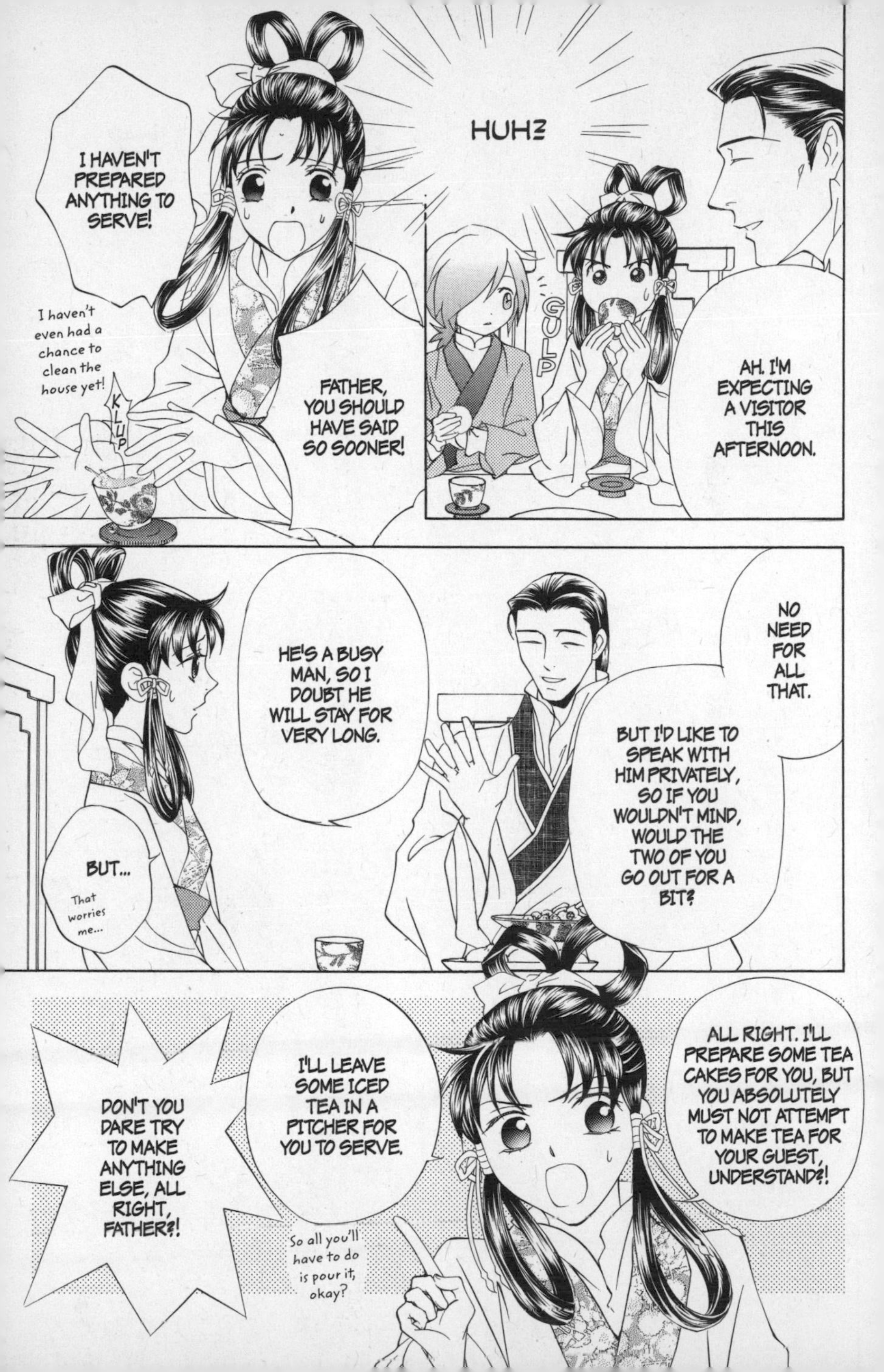
AH. I'M EXPECTING A VISITOR THIS AFTERNOON.
GULP
HUH?
FATHER, YOU SHOULD HAVE SAID SO SOONER!
I HAVEN'T PREPARED ANYTHING TO SERVE!
I haven't even had a chance to clean the house yet!
KLUP
NO NEED FOR ALL THAT.
BUT I'D LIKE TO SPEAK WITH HIM PRIVATELY, SO IF YOU WOULDN'T MIND, WOULD THE TWO OF YOU GO OUT FOR A BIT?
HE'S A BUSY MAN, SO I DOUBT HE WILL STAY FOR VERY LONG.
BUT...
That worries me...
ALL RIGHT. I'LL PREPARE SOME TEA CAKES FOR YOU, BUT YOU ABSOLUTELY MUST NOT ATTEMPT TO MAKE TEA FOR YOUR GUEST, UNDERSTAND?!
I'LL LEAVE SOME ICED TEA IN A PITCHER FOR YOU TO SERVE.
So all you'll have to do is pour it, okay?
DON'T YOU DARE TRY TO MAKE ANYTHING ELSE, ALL RIGHT, FATHER?!

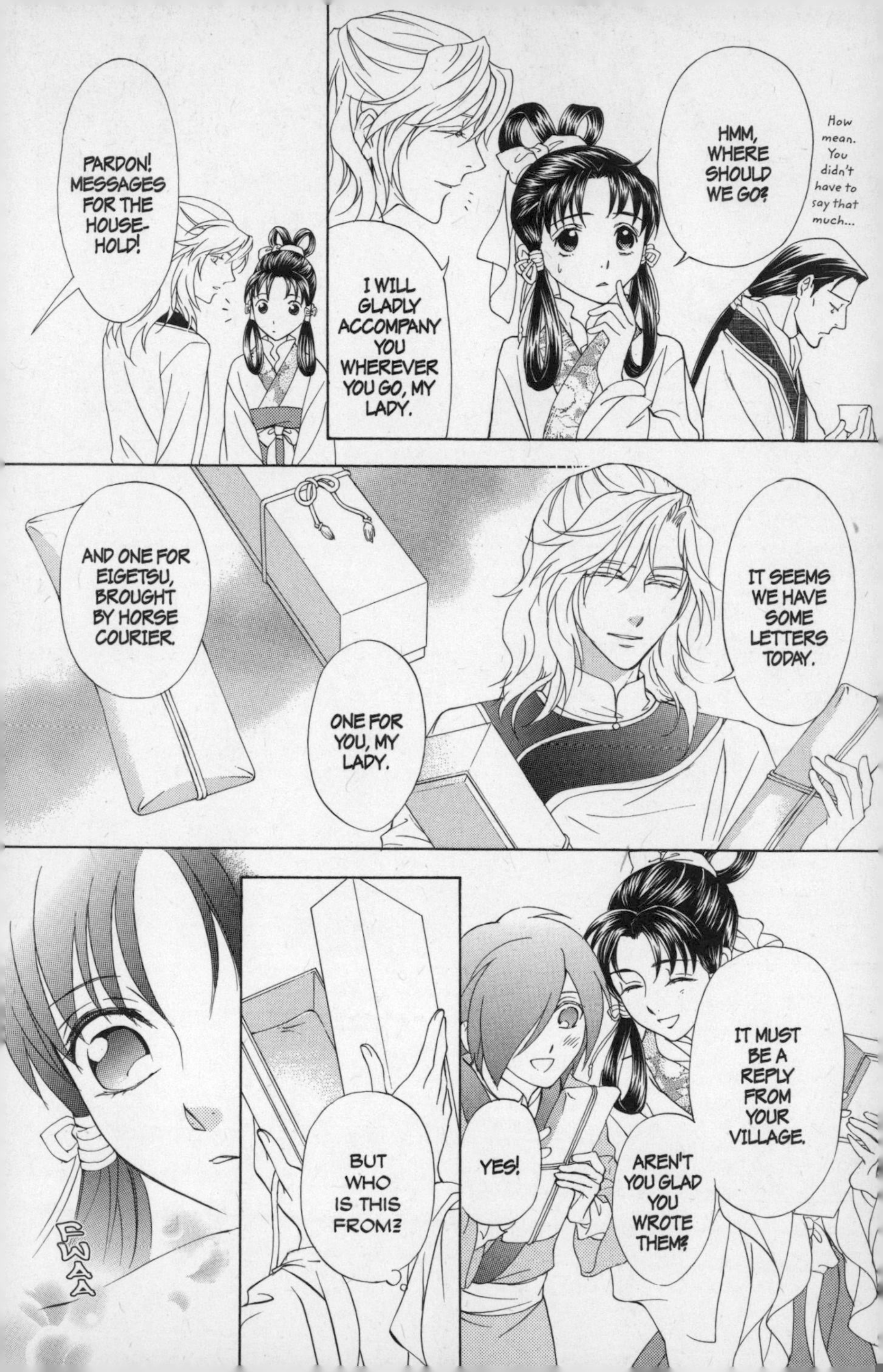
How mean. You didn't have to say that much...
HMM, WHERE SHOULD WE GO?
I WILL GLADLY ACCOMPANY YOU WHEREVER YOU GO, MY LADY.
PARDON! MESSAGES FOR THE HOUSEHOLD!
IT SEEMS WE HAVE SOME LETTERS TODAY.
ONE FOR YOU, MY LADY.
AND ONE FOR EIGETSU, BROUGHT BY HORSE COURIER.
IT MUST BE A REPLY FROM YOUR VILLAGE.
AREN'T YOU GLAD YOU WROTE THEM?
YES!
BUT WHO IS THIS FROM?
FWAA

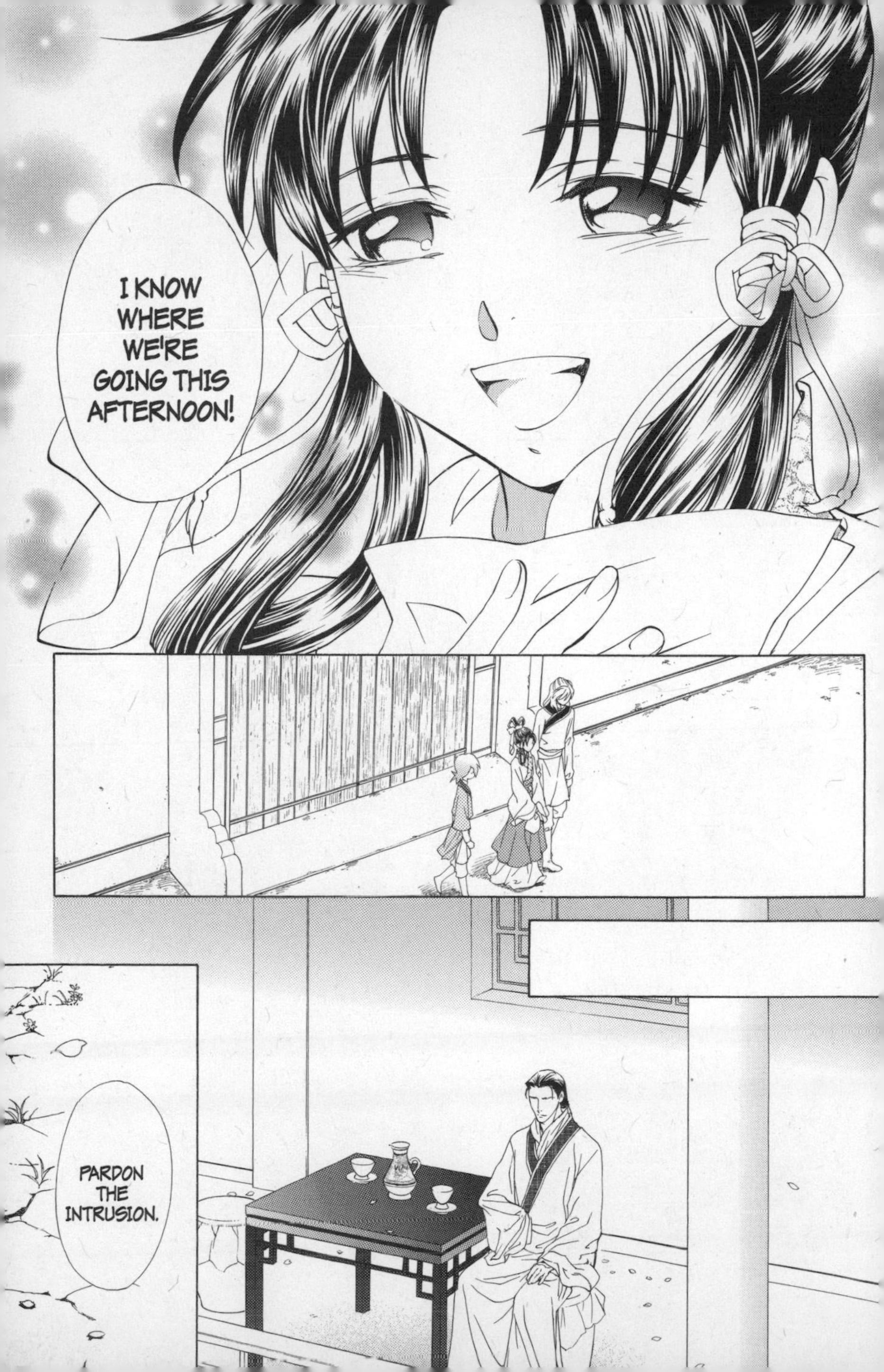
I KNOW WHERE WE'RE GOING THIS AFTERNOON!
PARDON THE INTRUSION.

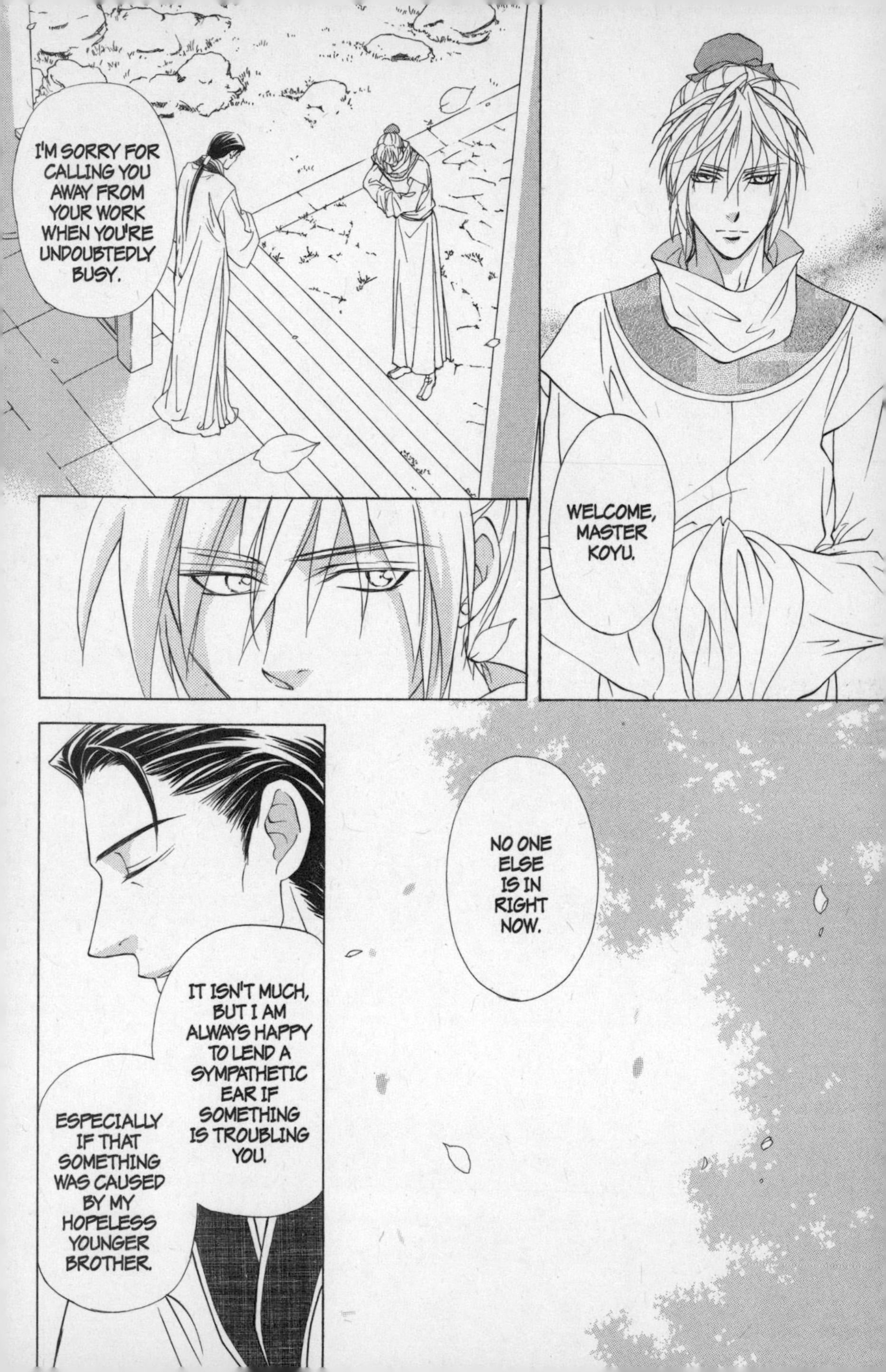
WELCOME, MASTER KOYU.
I'M SORRY FOR CALLING YOU AWAY FROM YOUR WORK WHEN YOU'RE UNDOUBTEDLY BUSY.
NO ONE ELSE IS IN RIGHT NOW.
IT ISN'T MUCH, BUT I AM ALWAYS HAPPY TO LEND A SYMPATHETIC EAR IF SOMETHING IS TROUBLING YOU.
ESPECIALLY IF THAT SOMETHING WAS CAUSED BY MY HOPELESS YOUNGER BROTHER.

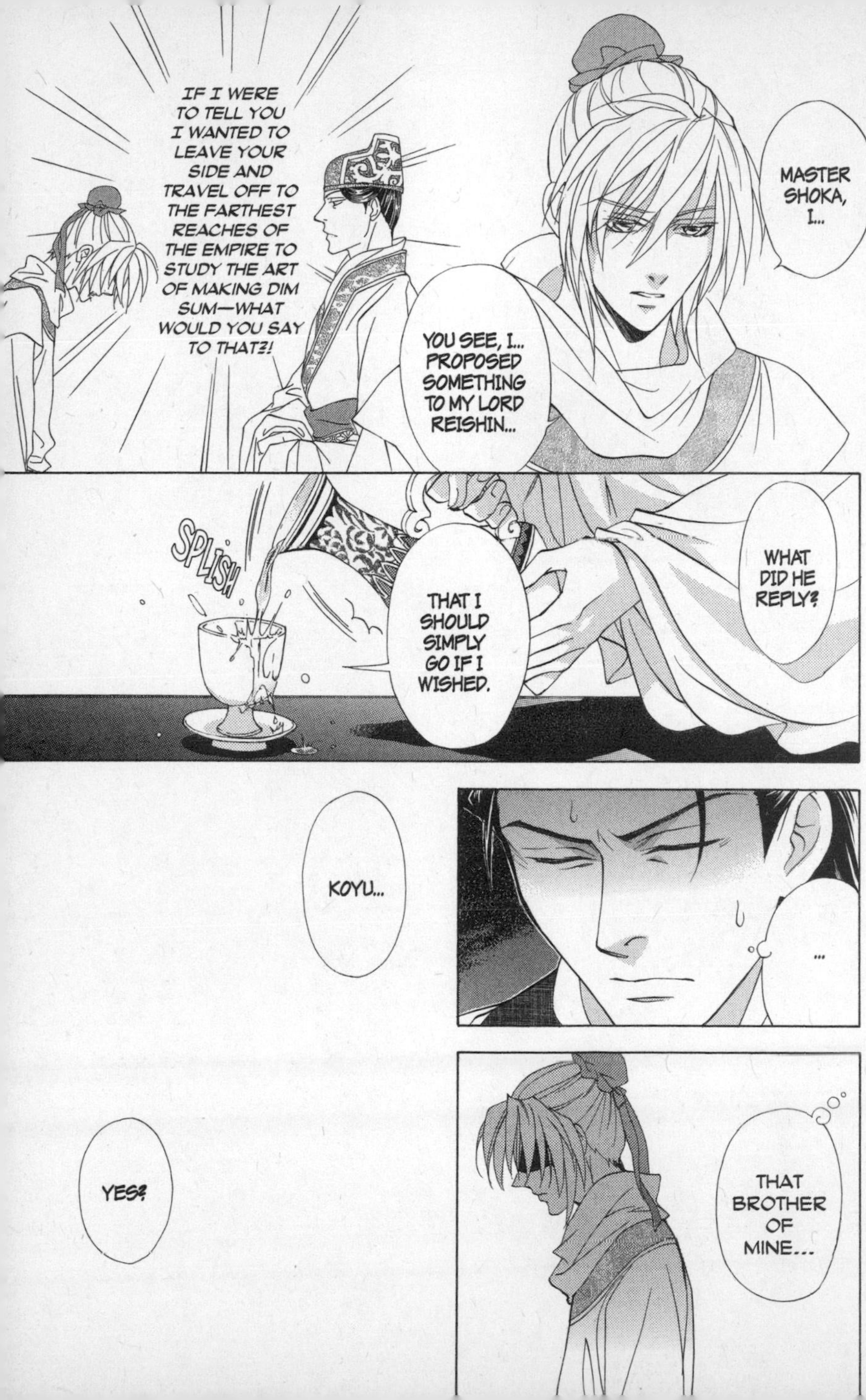
MASTER SHOKA, I...
YOU SEE, I... PROPOSED SOMETHING TO MY LORD REISHIN...
IF I WERE TO TELL YOU I WANTED TO LEAVE YOUR SIDE AND TRAVEL OFF TO THE FARTHEST REACHES OF THE EMPIRE TO STUDY THE ART OF MAKING DIM SUM—WHAT WOULD YOU SAY TO THAT?!
WHAT DID HE REPLY?
THAT I SHOULD SIMPLY GO IF I WISHED.
SPLISH
...
KOYU...
THAT BROTHER OF MINE...
YES?

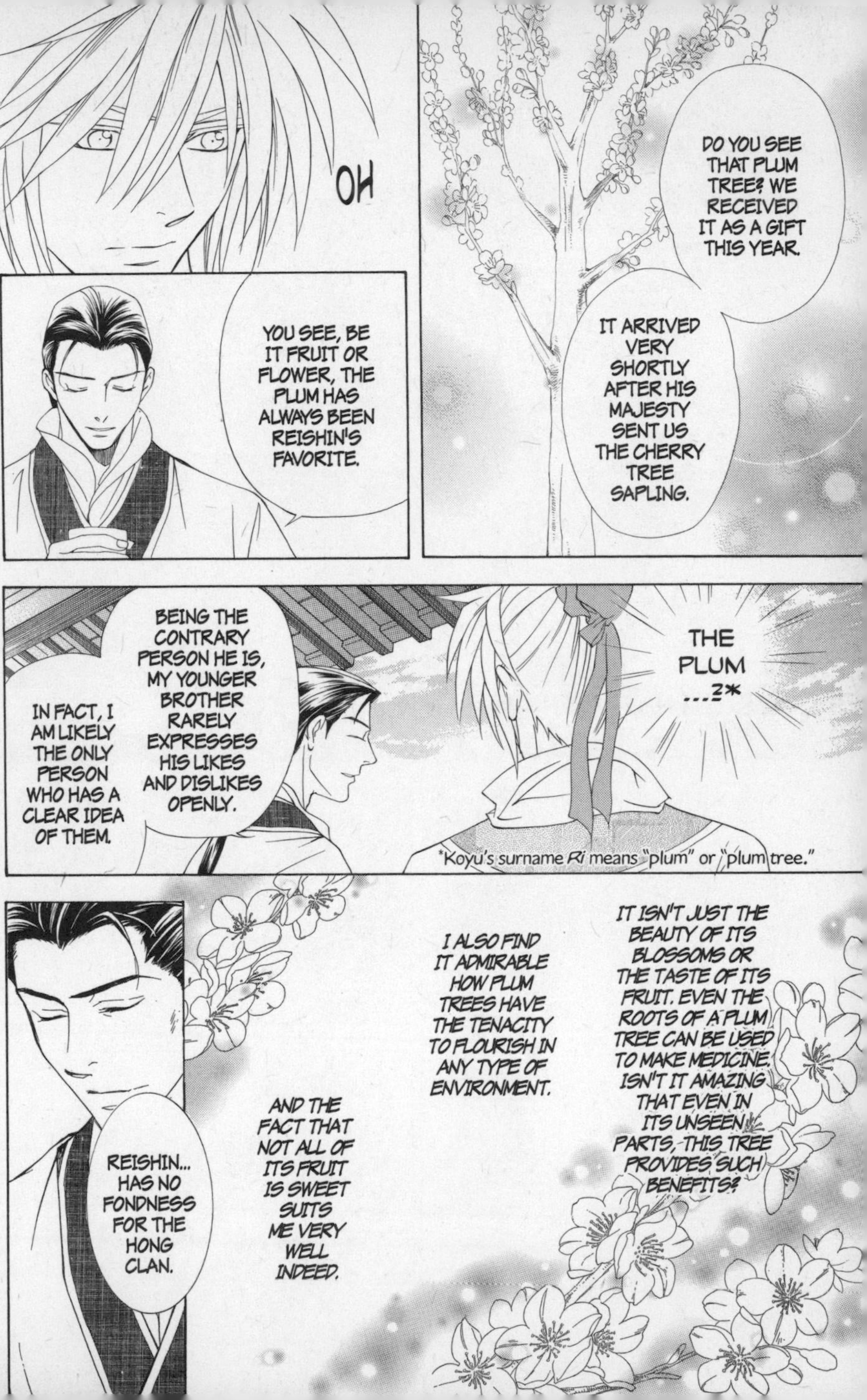
DO YOU SEE THAT PLUM TREE? WE RECEIVED IT AS A GIFT THIS YEAR.
IT ARRIVED VERY SHORTLY AFTER HIS MAJESTY SENT US THE CHERRY TREE SAPLING.
OH
YOU SEE, BE IT FRUIT OR FLOWER, THE PLUM HAS ALWAYS BEEN REISHIN'S FAVORITE.
THE PLUM ...?*
BEING THE CONTRARY PERSON HE IS, MY YOUNGER BROTHER RARELY EXPRESSES HIS LIKES AND DISLIKES OPENLY.
IN FACT, I AM LIKELY THE ONLY PERSON WHO HAS A CLEAR IDEA OF THEM.
*Koyu's surname Ri means "plum" or "plum tree."
IT ISN'T JUST THE BEAUTY OF ITS BLOSSOMS OR THE TASTE OF ITS FRUIT. EVEN THE ROOTS OF A PLUM TREE CAN BE USED TO MAKE MEDICINE. ISN'T IT AMAZING THAT EVEN IN ITS UNSEEN PARTS, THIS TREE PROVIDES SUCH BENEFITS?
I ALSO FIND IT ADMIRABLE HOW PLUM TREES HAVE THE TENACITY TO FLOURISH IN ANY TYPE OF ENVIRONMENT.
AND THE FACT THAT NOT ALL OF ITS FRUIT IS SWEET SUITS ME VERY WELL INDEED.
REISHIN... HAS NO FONDNESS FOR THE HONG CLAN.

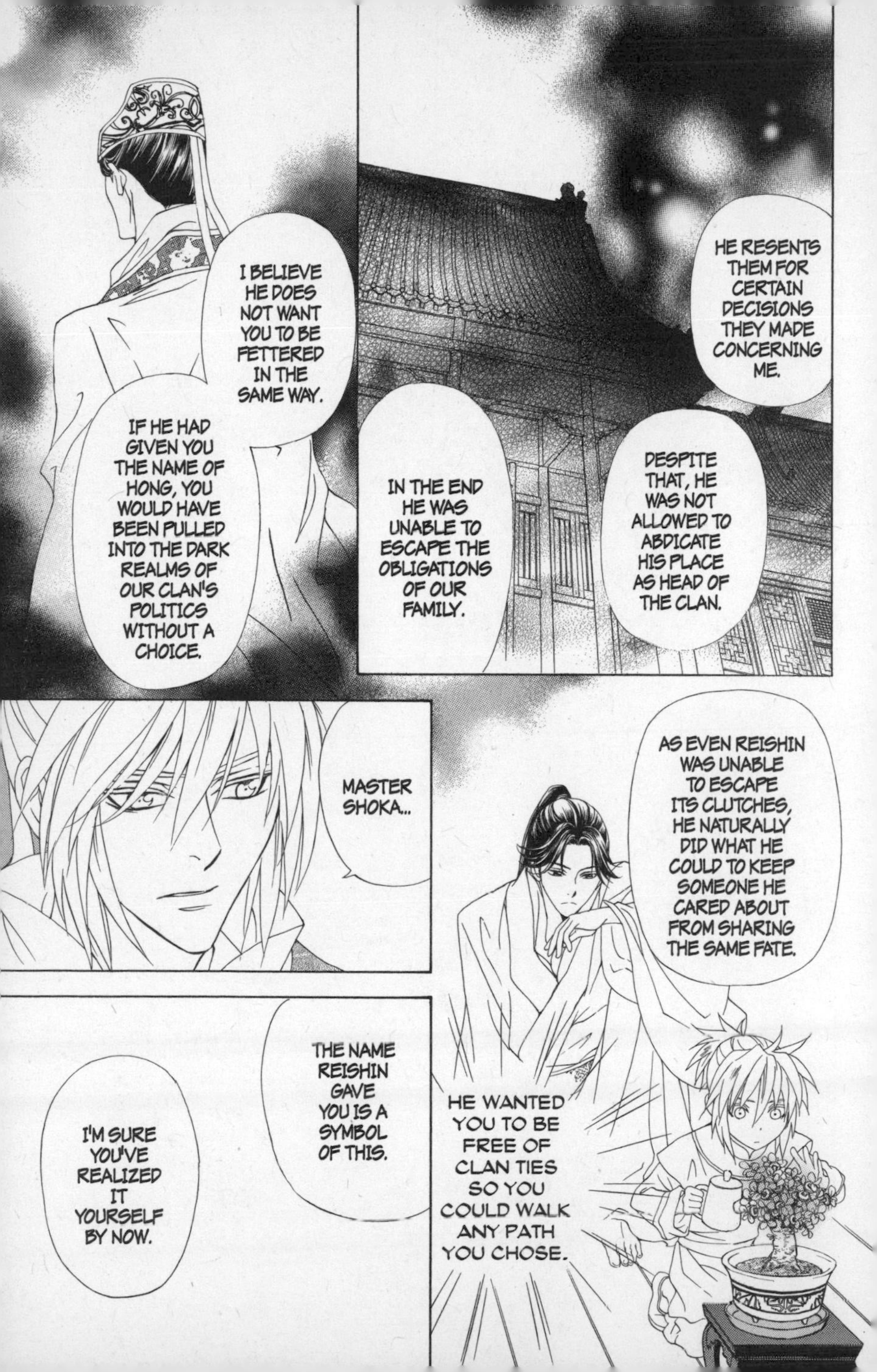
HE RESENTS THEM FOR CERTAIN DECISIONS THEY MADE CONCERNING ME.
DESPITE THAT, HE WAS NOT ALLOWED TO ABDICATE HIS PLACE AS HEAD OF THE CLAN.
IN THE END HE WAS UNABLE TO ESCAPE THE OBLIGATIONS OF OUR FAMILY.
I BELIEVE HE DOES NOT WANT YOU TO BE FETTERED IN THE SAME WAY.
IF HE HAD GIVEN YOU THE NAME OF HONG, YOU WOULD HAVE BEEN PULLED INTO THE DARK REALMS OF OUR CLAN'S POLITICS WITHOUT A CHOICE.
AS EVEN REISHIN WAS UNABLE TO ESCAPE ITS CLUTCHES, HE NATURALLY DID WHAT HE COULD TO KEEP SOMEONE HE CARED ABOUT FROM SHARING THE SAME FATE.
MASTER SHOKA...
HE WANTED YOU TO BE FREE OF CLAN TIES SO YOU COULD WALK ANY PATH YOU CHOSE.
THE NAME REISHIN GAVE YOU IS A SYMBOL OF THIS.
I'M SURE YOU'VE REALIZED IT YOURSELF BY NOW.

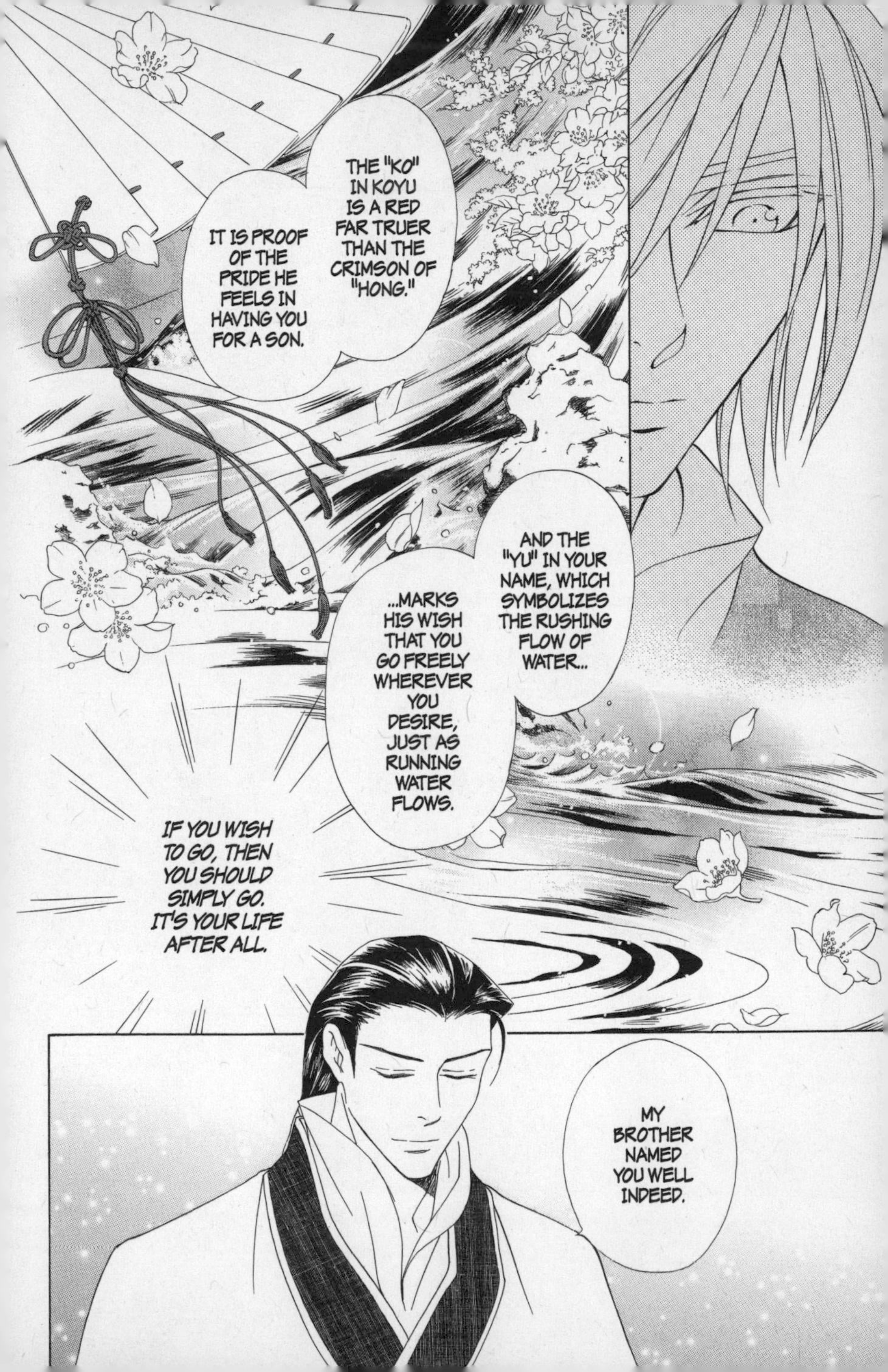
THE "KO" IN KOYU IS A RED FAR TRUER THAN THE CRIMSON OF "HONG."
IT IS PROOF OF THE PRIDE HE FEELS IN HAVING YOU FOR A SON.
AND THE "YU" IN YOUR NAME, WHICH SYMBOLIZES THE RUSHING FLOW OF WATER...
...MARKS HIS WISH THAT YOU GO FREELY WHEREVER YOU DESIRE, JUST AS RUNNING WATER FLOWS.
IF YOU WISH TO GO, THEN YOU SHOULD SIMPLY GO. IT'S YOUR LIFE AFTER ALL.
MY BROTHER NAMED YOU WELL INDEED.

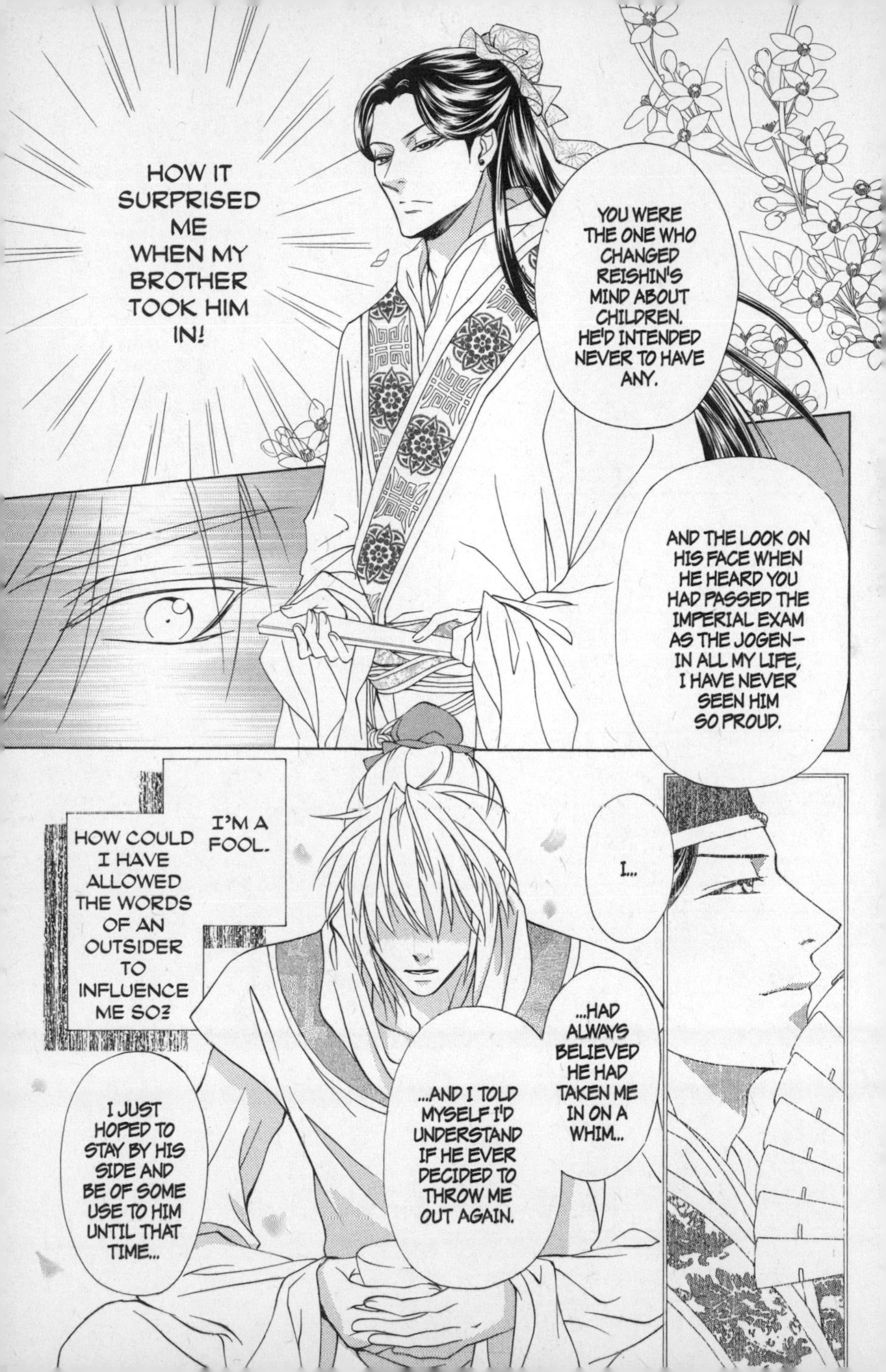
YOU WERE THE ONE WHO CHANGED REISHIN'S MIND ABOUT CHILDREN. HE'D INTENDED NEVER TO HAVE ANY.
HOW IT SURPRISED ME WHEN MY BROTHER TOOK HIM IN!
AND THE LOOK ON HIS FACE WHEN HE HEARD YOU HAD PASSED THE IMPERIAL EXAM AS THE JOGEN—IN ALL MY LIFE, I HAVE NEVER SEEN HIM SO PROUD.
I...
...HAD ALWAYS BELIEVED HE HAD TAKEN ME IN ON A WHIM...
I'M A FOOL.
HOW COULD I HAVE ALLOWED THE WORDS OF AN OUTSIDER TO INFLUENCE ME SO?
...AND I TOLD MYSELF I'D UNDERSTAND IF HE EVER DECIDED TO THROW ME OUT AGAIN.
I JUST HOPED TO STAY BY HIS SIDE AND BE OF SOME USE TO HIM UNTIL THAT TIME...

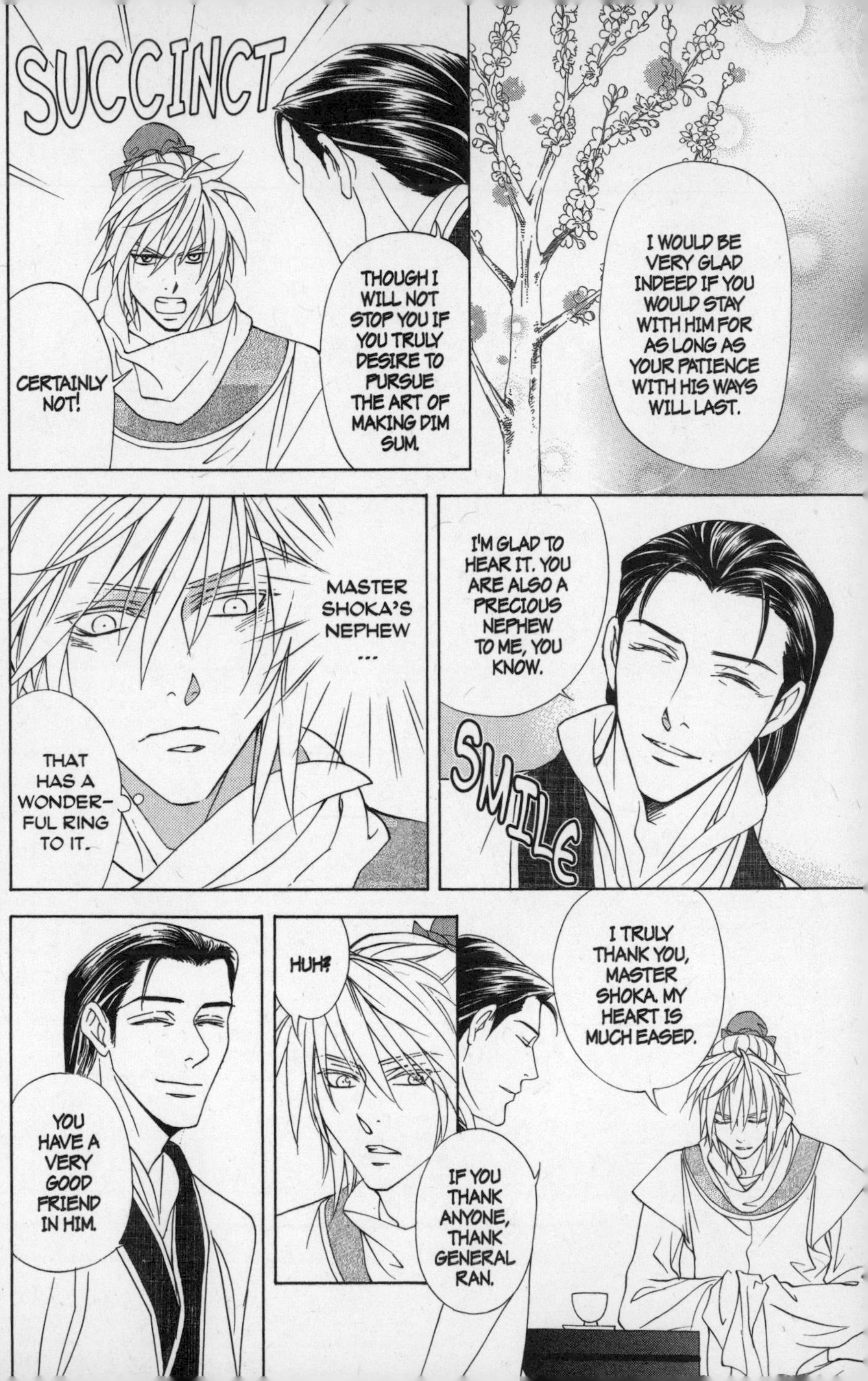
I WOULD BE VERY GLAD INDEED IF YOU WOULD STAY WITH HIM FOR AS LONG AS YOUR PATIENCE WITH HIS WAYS WILL LAST.
SUCCINCT
THOUGH I WILL NOT STOP YOU IF YOU TRULY DESIRE TO PURSUE THE ART OF MAKING DIM SUM.
CERTAINLY NOT!
I'M GLAD TO HEAR IT. YOU ARE ALSO A PRECIOUS NEPHEW TO ME, YOU KNOW.
SMILE
MASTER SHOKA'S NEPHEW...
THAT HAS A WONDERFUL RING TO IT.
I TRULY THANK YOU, MASTER SHOKA. MY HEART IS MUCH EASED.
HUH?
IF YOU THANK ANYONE, THANK GENERAL RAN.
YOU HAVE A VERY GOOD FRIEND IN HIM.

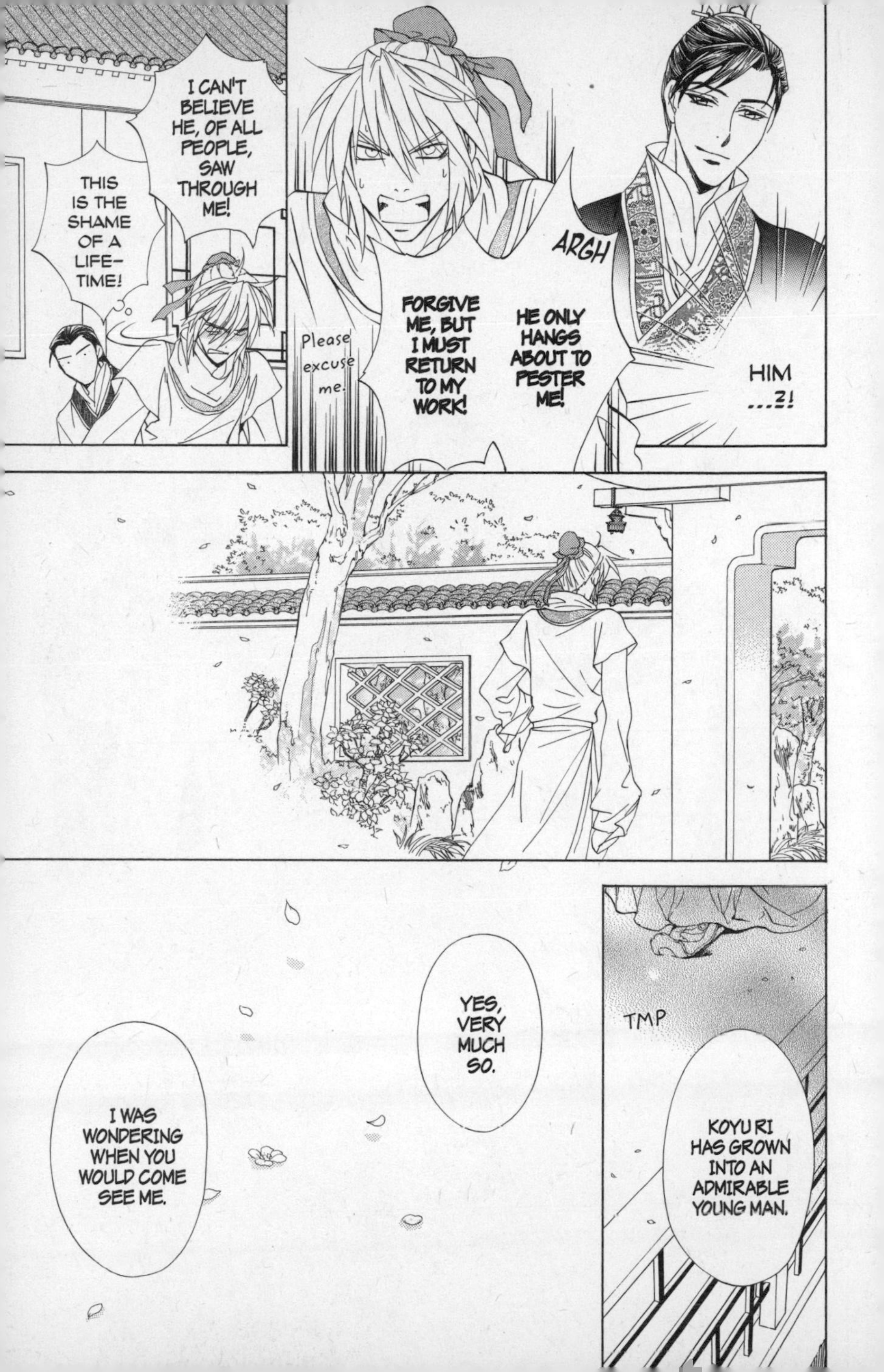

HIM ...?!
ARGH
HE ONLY HANGS ABOUT TO PESTER ME!
FORGIVE ME, BUT I MUST RETURN TO MY WORK!
Please excuse me.
I CAN'T BELIEVE HE, OF ALL PEOPLE, SAW THROUGH ME!
THIS IS THE SHAME OF A LIFE-TIME!
TMP
KOYU RI HAS GROWN INTO AN ADMIRABLE YOUNG MAN.
YES, VERY MUCH SO.
I WAS WONDERING WHEN YOU WOULD COME SEE ME.

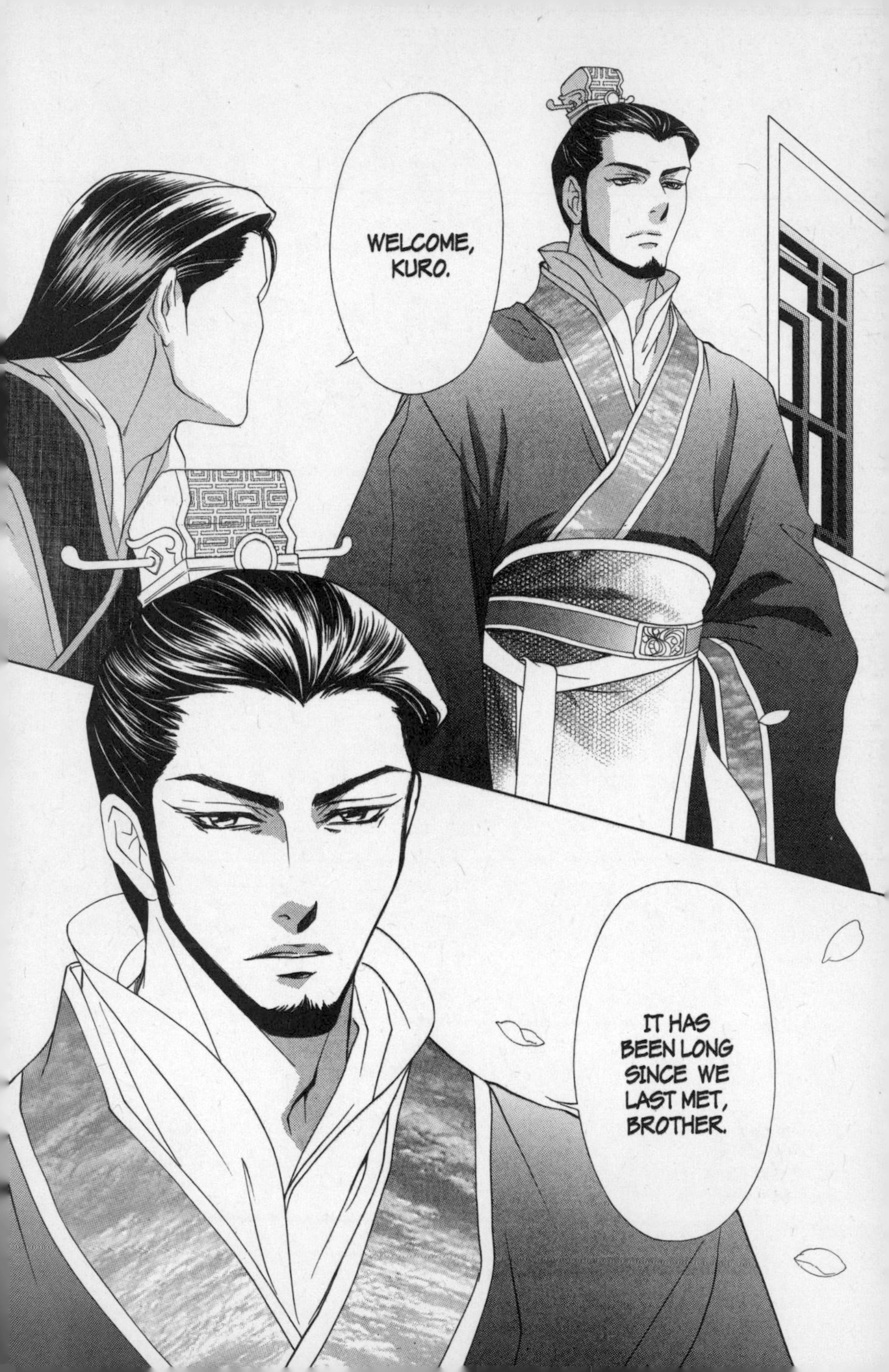
WELCOME, KURO.
IT HAS BEEN LONG SINCE WE LAST MET, BROTHER.

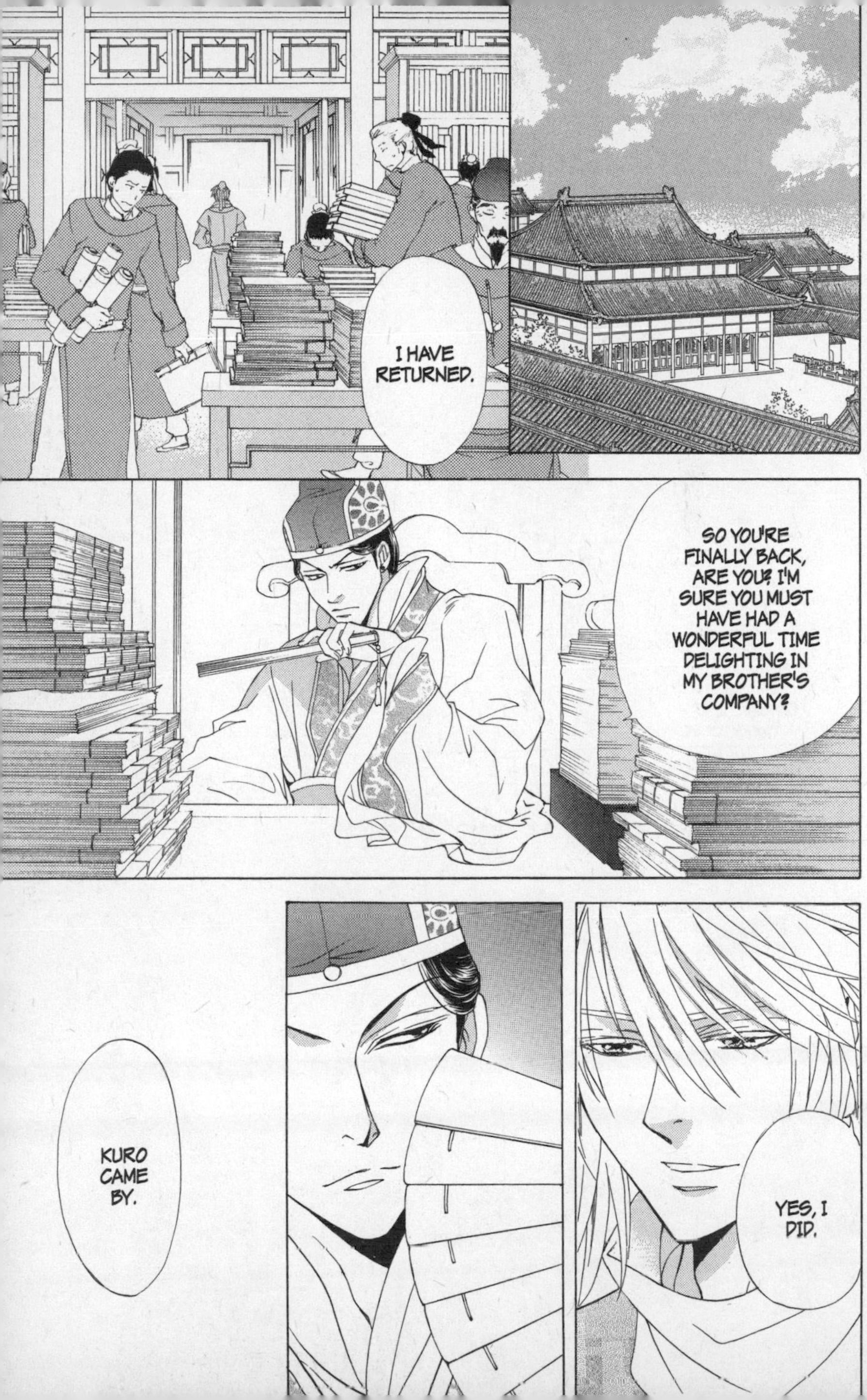
I HAVE RETURNED.
SO YOU'RE FINALLY BACK, ARE YOU? I'M SURE YOU MUST HAVE HAD A WONDERFUL TIME DELIGHTING IN MY BROTHER'S COMPANY?
YES, I DID.
KURO CAME BY.

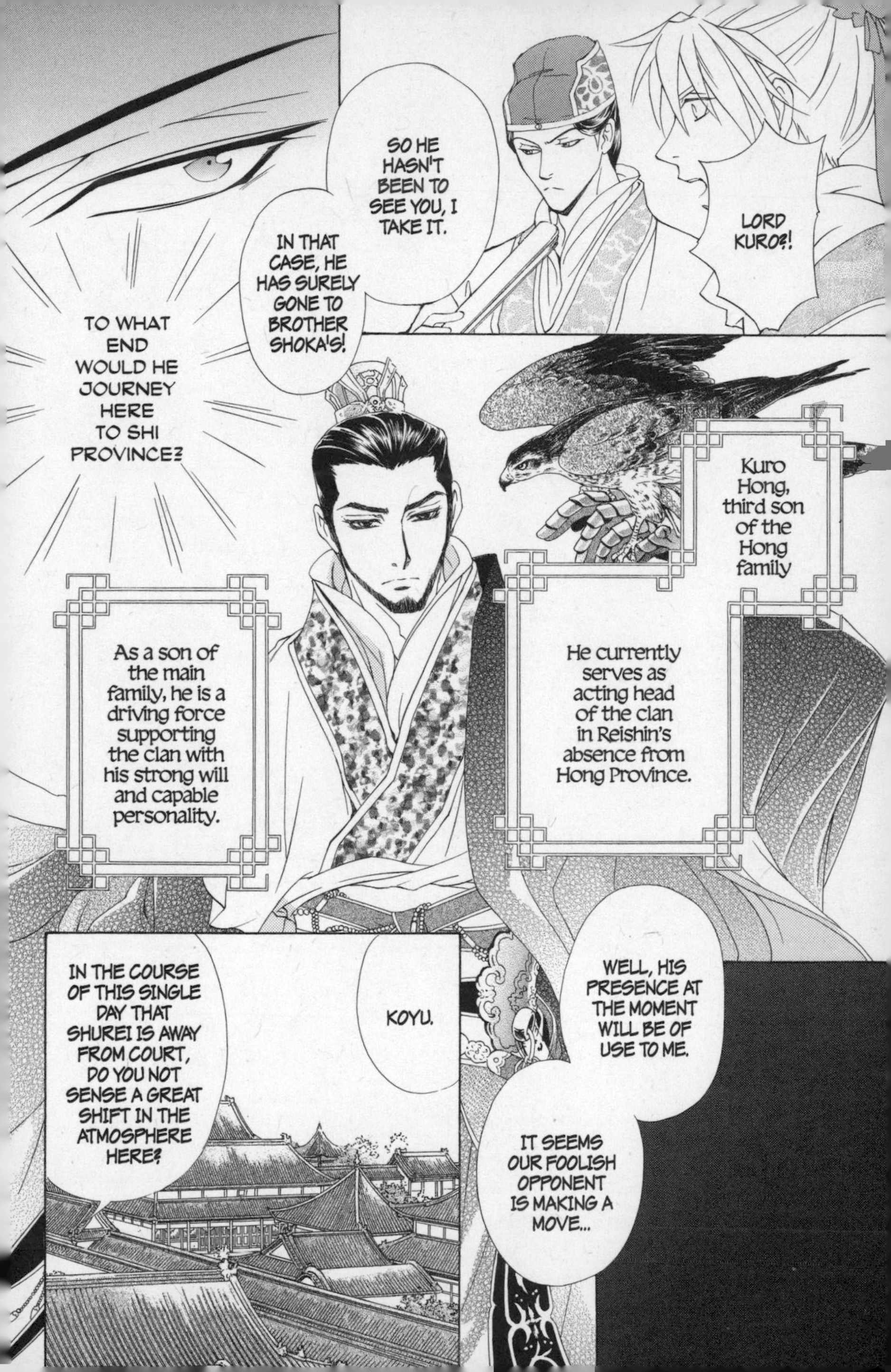
LORD KURO?!
SO HE HASN'T BEEN TO SEE YOU, I TAKE IT.
IN THAT CASE, HE HAS SURELY GONE TO BROTHER SHOKA'S!
TO WHAT END WOULD HE JOURNEY HERE TO SHI PROVINCE?
Kuro Hong, third son of the Hong family
He currently serves as acting head of the clan in Reishin's absence from Hong Province.
As a son of the main family, he is a driving force supporting the clan with his strong will and capable personality.
WELL, HIS PRESENCE AT THE MOMENT WILL BE OF USE TO ME.
IT SEEMS OUR FOOLISH OPPONENT IS MAKING A MOVE...
KOYU.
IN THE COURSE OF THIS SINGLE DAY THAT SHUREI IS AWAY FROM COURT, DO YOU NOT SENSE A GREAT SHIFT IN THE ATMOSPHERE HERE?

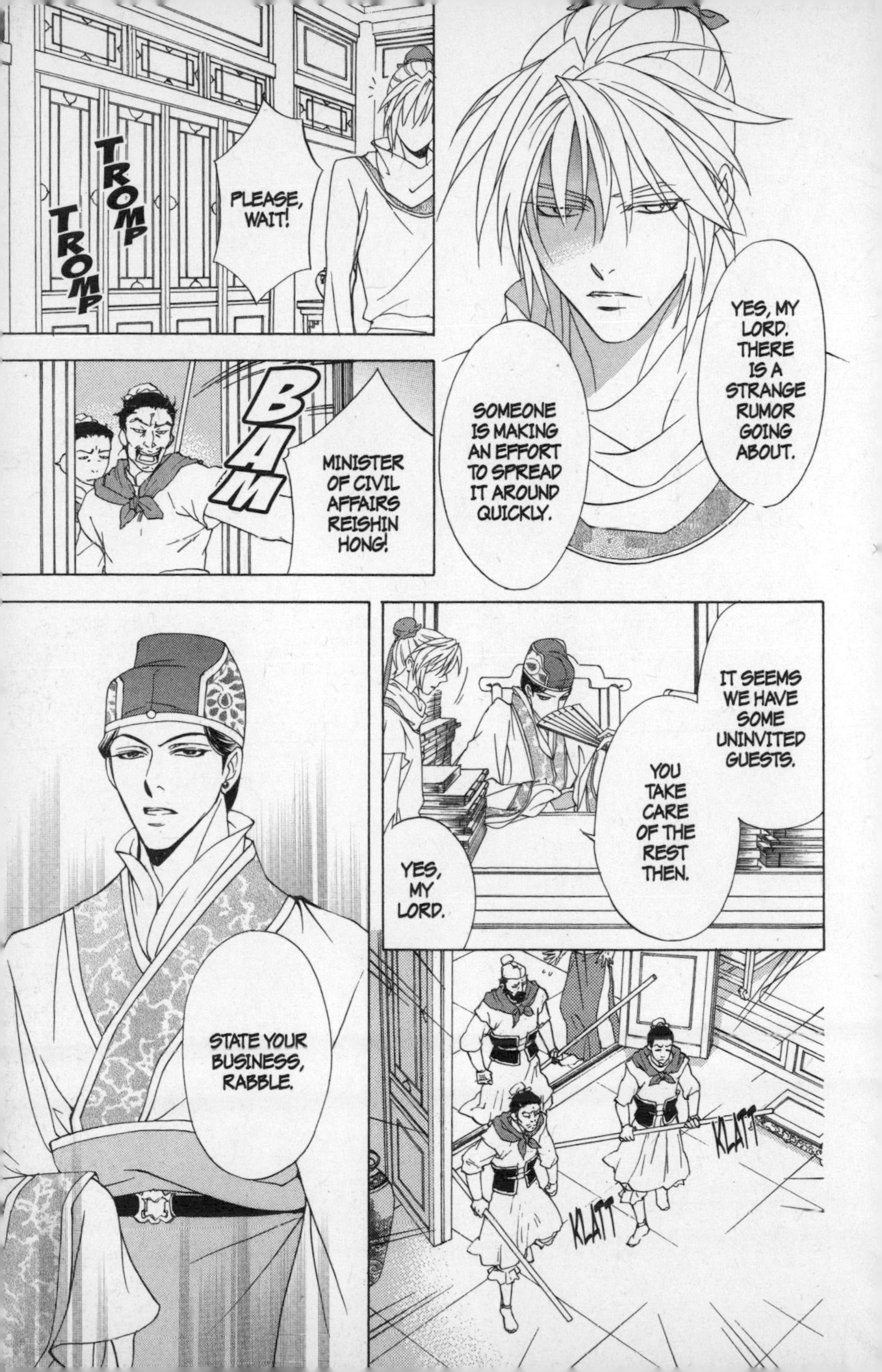
YES, MY LORD. THERE IS A STRANGE RUMOR GOING ABOUT.
SOMEONE IS MAKING AN EFFORT TO SPREAD IT AROUND QUICKLY.
TROMP TROMP
PLEASE, WAIT!
BAM
MINISTER OF CIVIL AFFAIRS REISHIN HONG!
IT SEEMS WE HAVE SOME UNINVITED GUESTS.
YOU TAKE CARE OF THE REST THEN.
YES, MY LORD.
KLATT
KLATT
STATE YOUR BUSINESS, RABBLE.

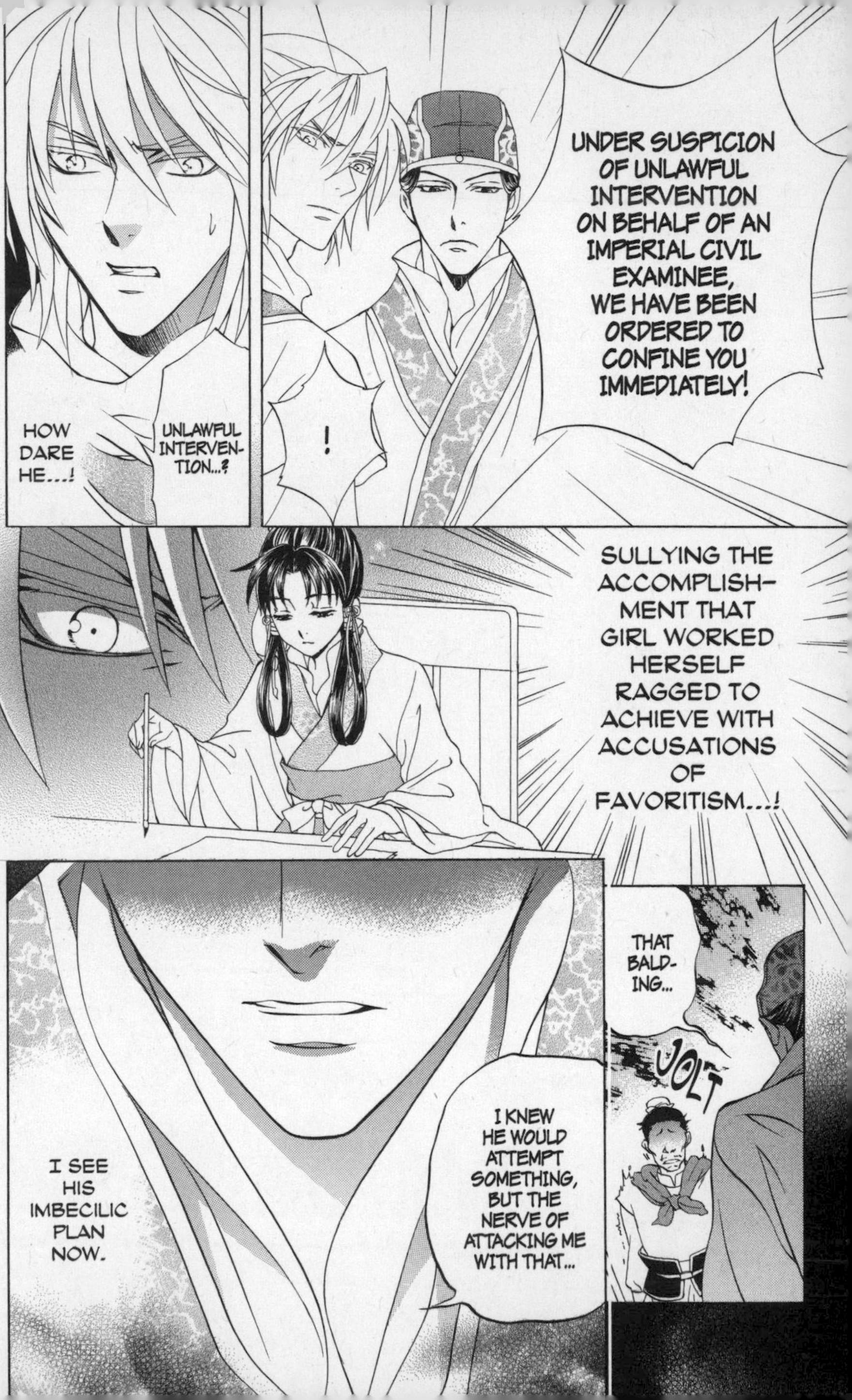
UNDER SUSPICION OF UNLAWFUL INTERVENTION ON BEHALF OF AN IMPERIAL CIVIL EXAMINEE, WE HAVE BEEN ORDERED TO CONFINE YOU IMMEDIATELY!
!
UNLAWFUL INTERVEN-TION...?
HOW DARE HE...!
SULLYING THE ACCOMPLISH-MENT THAT GIRL WORKED HERSELF RAGGED TO ACHIEVE WITH ACCUSATIONS OF FAVORITISM...!
THAT BALD-ING...
JOLT
I KNEW HE WOULD ATTEMPT SOMETHING, BUT THE NERVE OF ATTACKING ME WITH THAT...
I SEE HIS IMBECILIC PLAN NOW.

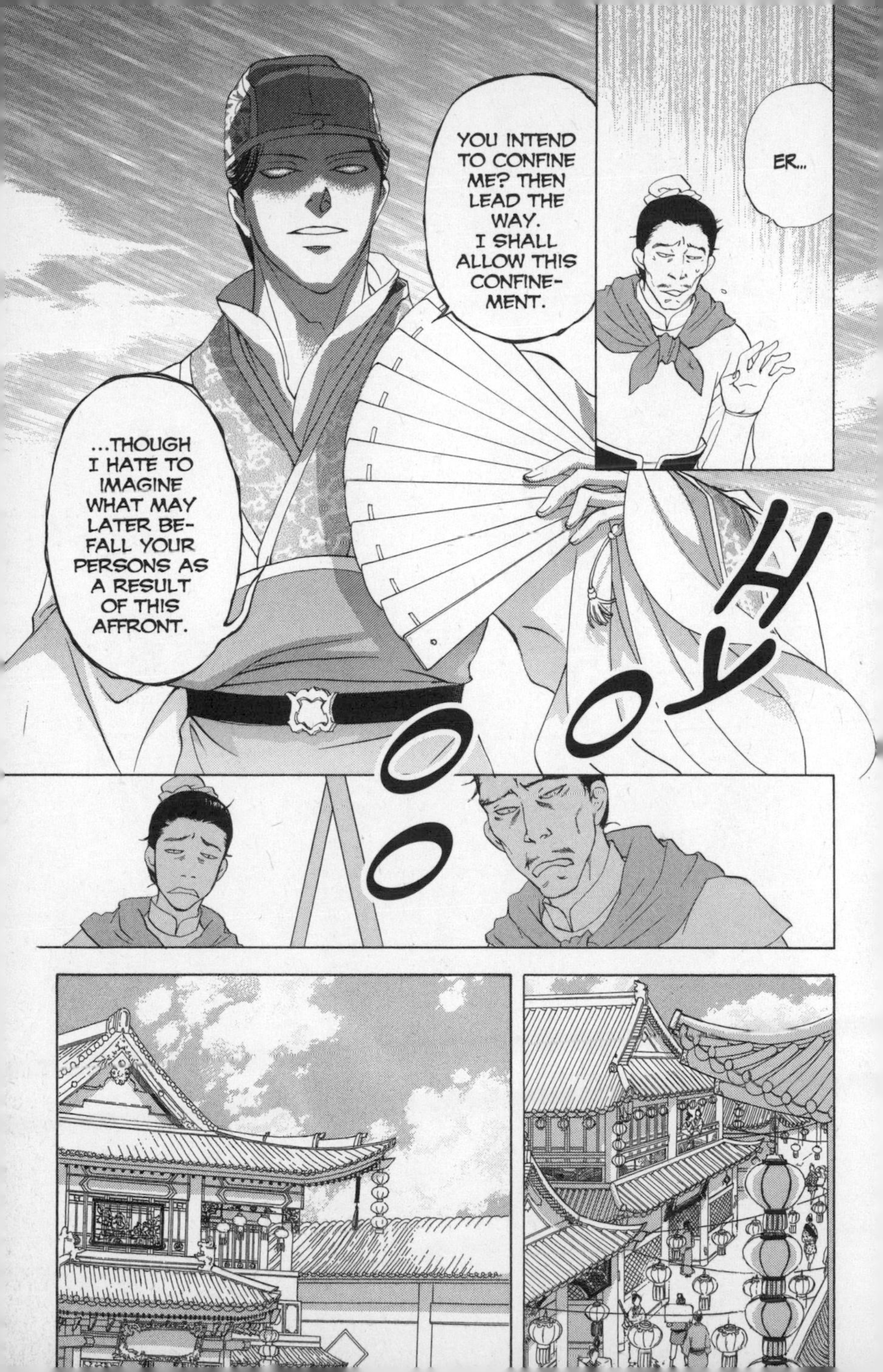
ER...
YOU INTEND TO CONFINE ME? THEN LEAD THE WAY. I SHALL ALLOW THIS CONFINE-MENT.
...THOUGH I HATE TO IMAGINE WHAT MAY LATER BE-FALL YOUR PERSONS AS A RESULT OF THIS AFFRONT.
HYOOOO

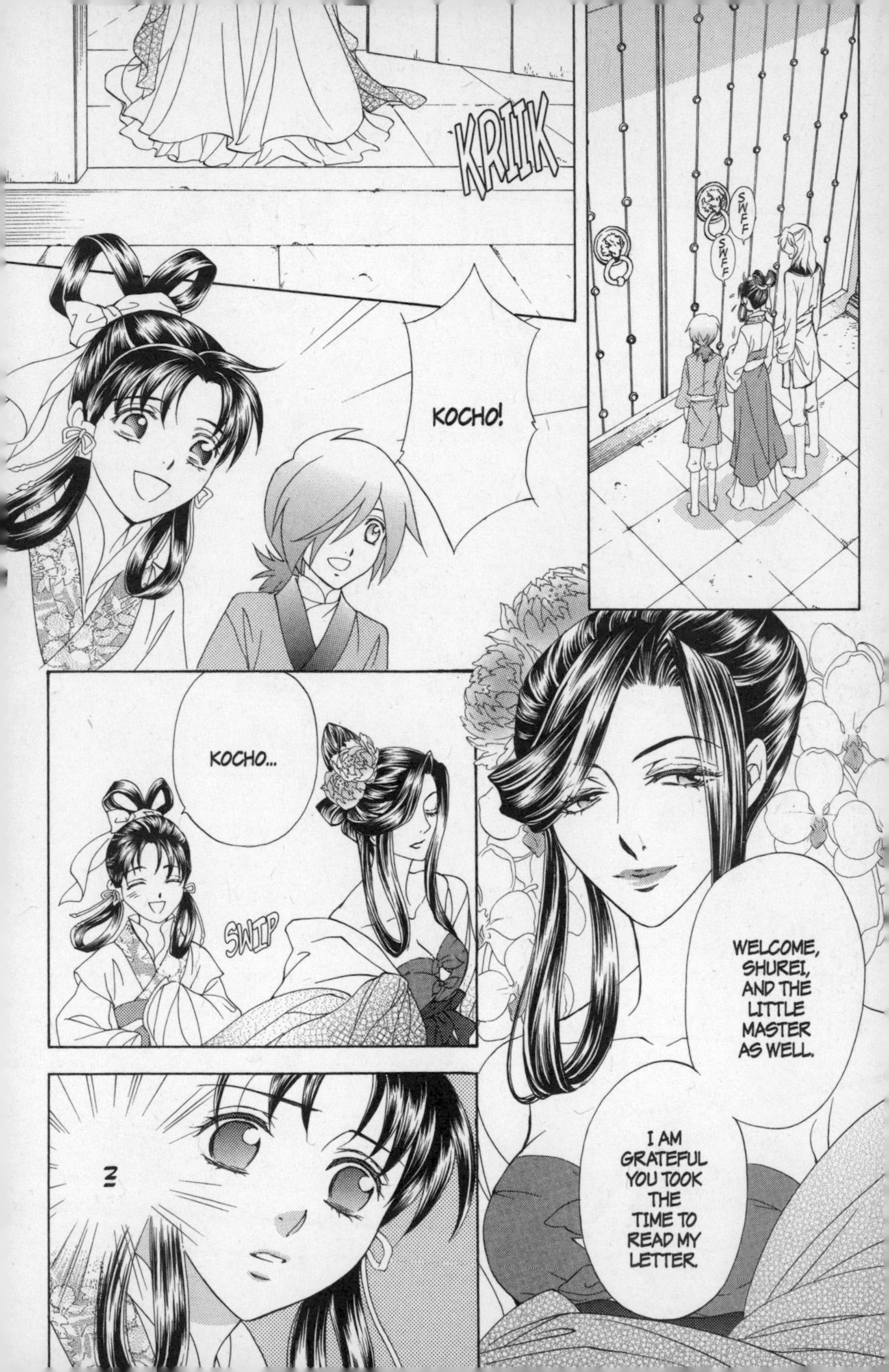
SWFF
SWFF
KRIIK
KOCHO!
WELCOME, SHUREI, AND THE LITTLE MASTER AS WELL.
I AM GRATEFUL YOU TOOK THE TIME TO READ MY LETTER.
KOCHO...
SWIP

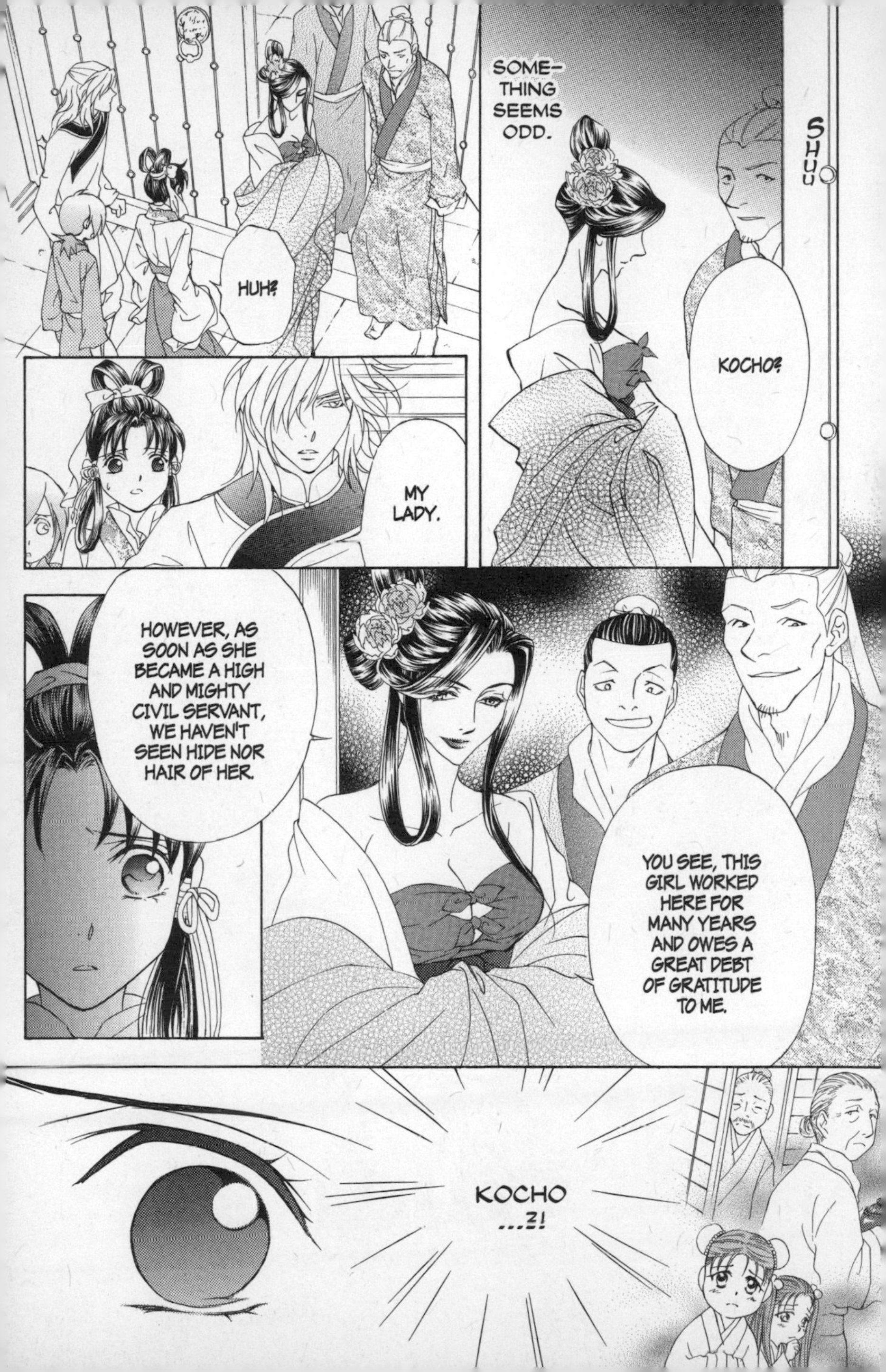
SOME-THING SEEMS ODD.
SHUU
KOCHO?
HUH?
MY LADY.
YOU SEE, THIS GIRL WORKED HERE FOR MANY YEARS AND OWES A GREAT DEBT OF GRATITUDE TO ME.
HOWEVER, AS SOON AS SHE BECAME A HIGH AND MIGHTY CIVIL SERVANT, WE HAVEN'T SEEN HIDE NOR HAIR OF HER.
KOCHO ...?!

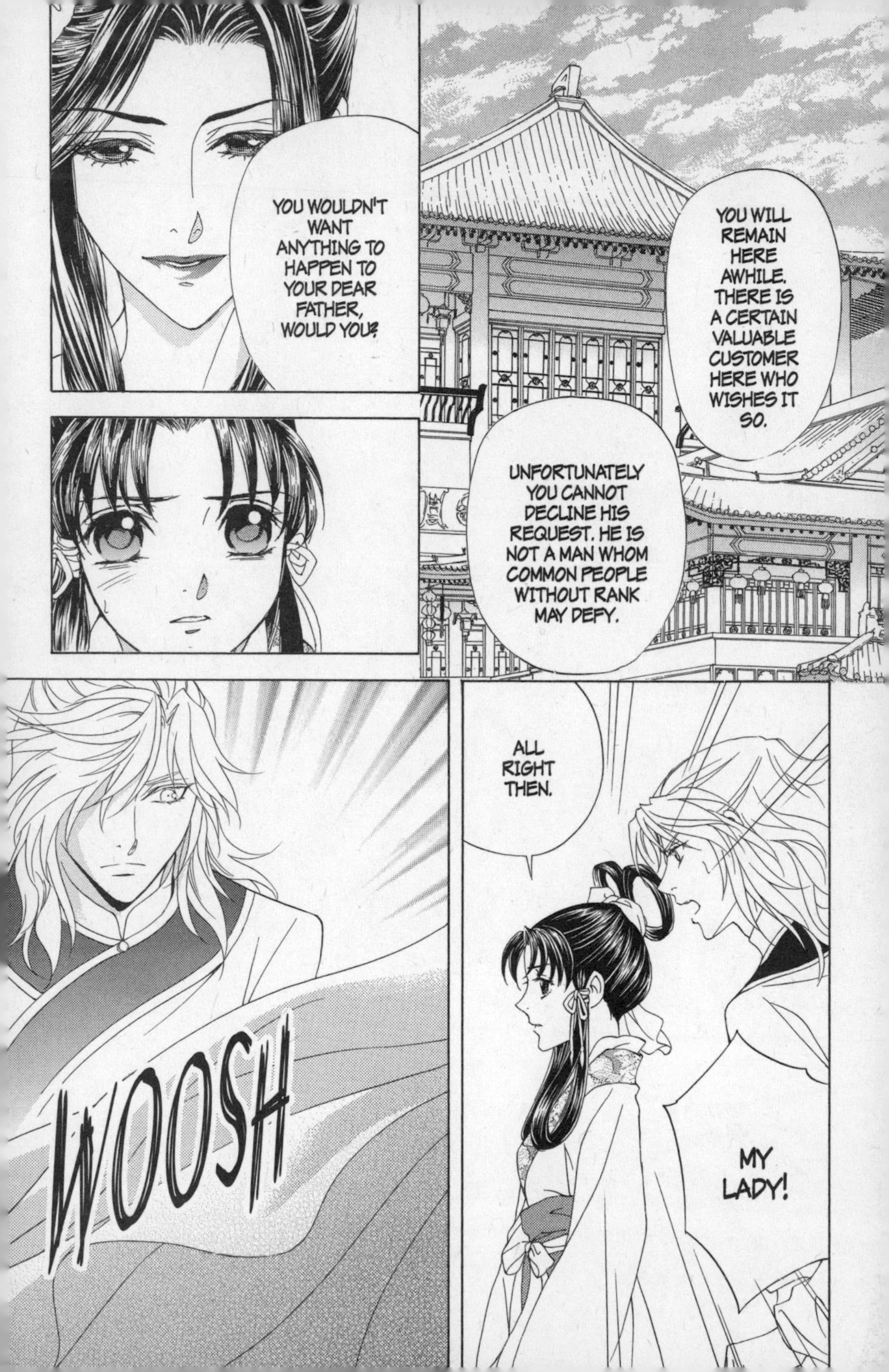

YOU WILL REMAIN HERE AWHILE. THERE IS A CERTAIN VALUABLE CUSTOMER HERE WHO WISHES IT SO.
UNFORTUNATELY YOU CANNOT DECLINE HIS REQUEST. HE IS NOT A MAN WHOM COMMON PEOPLE WITHOUT RANK MAY DEFY.
YOU WOULDN'T WANT ANYTHING TO HAPPEN TO YOUR DEAR FATHER, WOULD YOU?
ALL RIGHT THEN.
MY LADY!
WOOSH

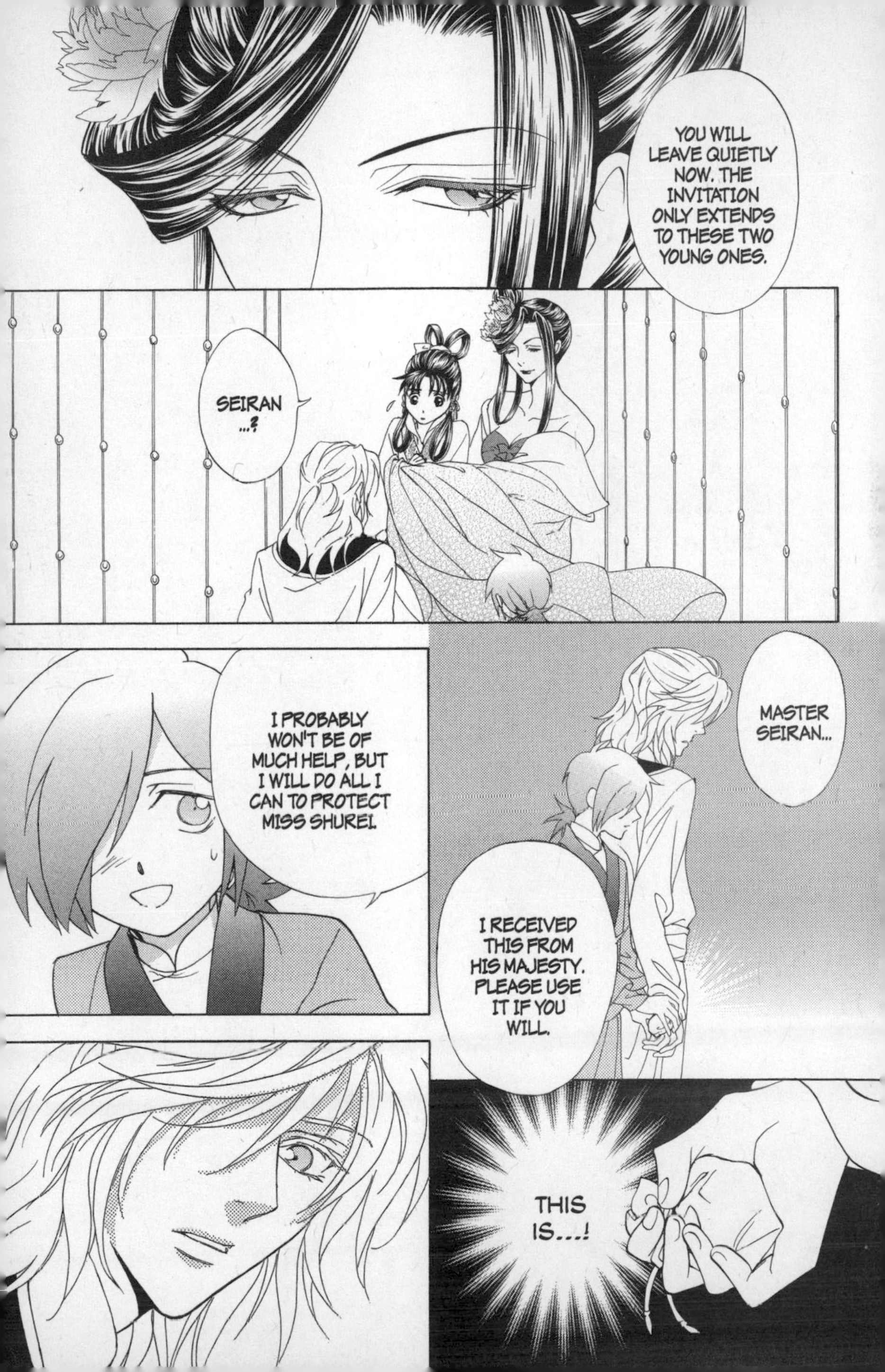
YOU WILL LEAVE QUIETLY NOW. THE INVITATION ONLY EXTENDS TO THESE TWO YOUNG ONES.
SEIRAN ...?
MASTER SEIRAN...
I PROBABLY WON'T BE OF MUCH HELP, BUT I WILL DO ALL I CAN TO PROTECT MISS SHUREI.
I RECEIVED THIS FROM HIS MAJESTY. PLEASE USE IT IF YOU WILL.
THIS IS...!

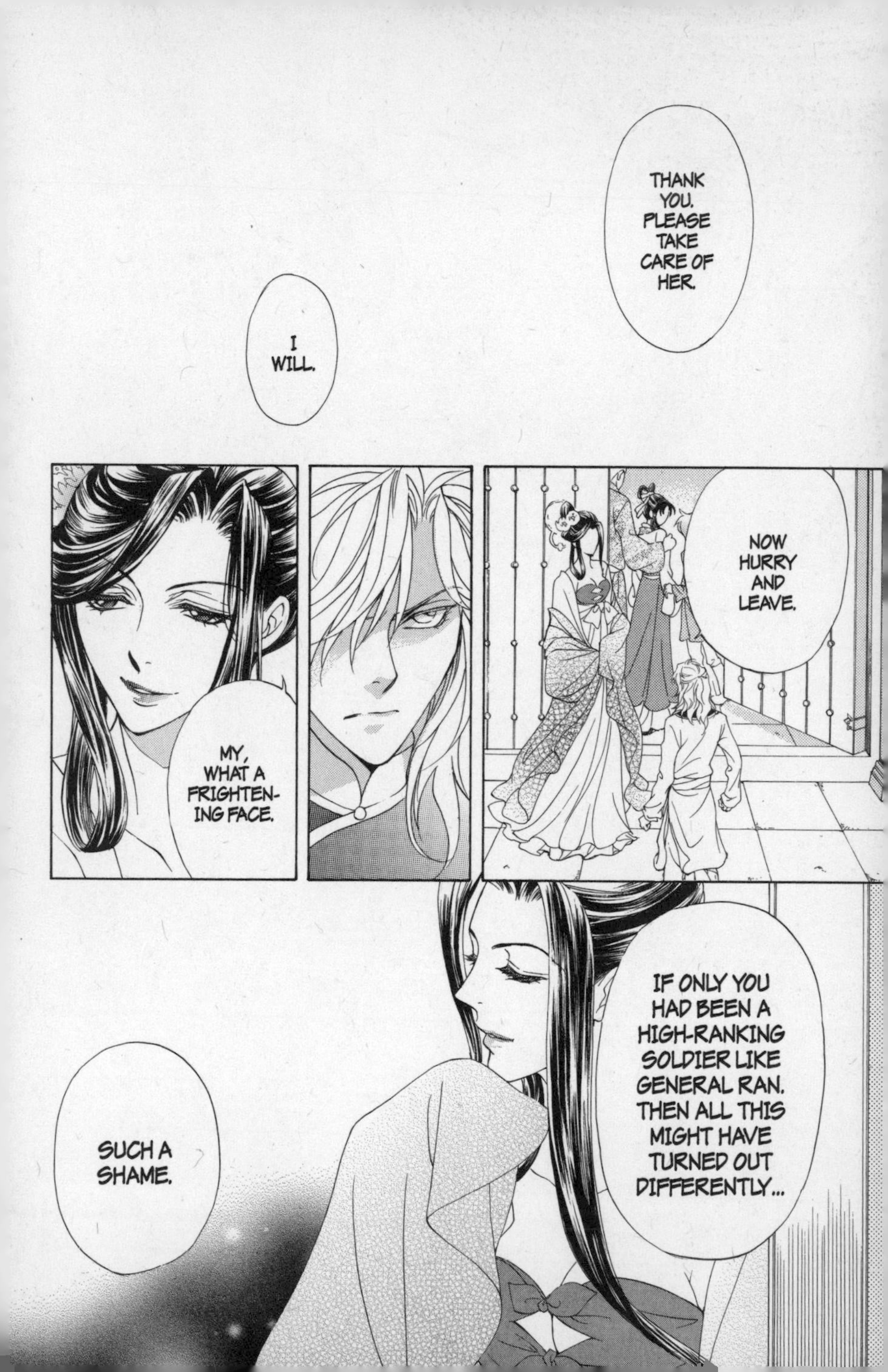
THANK YOU. PLEASE TAKE CARE OF HER.
I WILL.
NOW HURRY AND LEAVE.
MY, WHAT A FRIGHTEN-ING FACE.
IF ONLY YOU HAD BEEN A HIGH-RANKING SOLDIER LIKE GENERAL RAN. THEN ALL THIS MIGHT HAVE TURNED OUT DIFFERENTLY...
SUCH A SHAME.

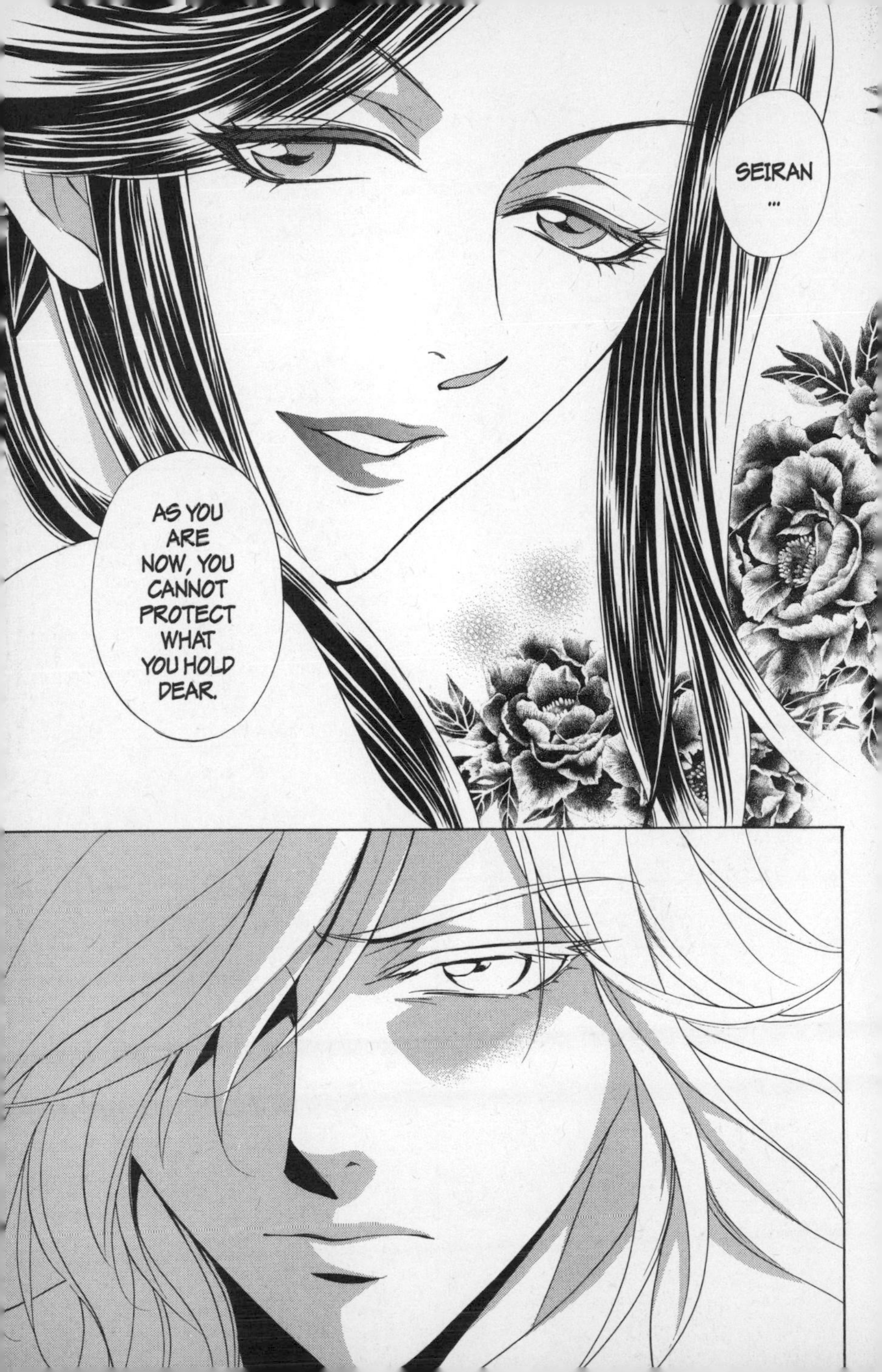
SEIRAN ...
AS YOU ARE NOW, YOU CANNOT PROTECT WHAT YOU HOLD DEAR.

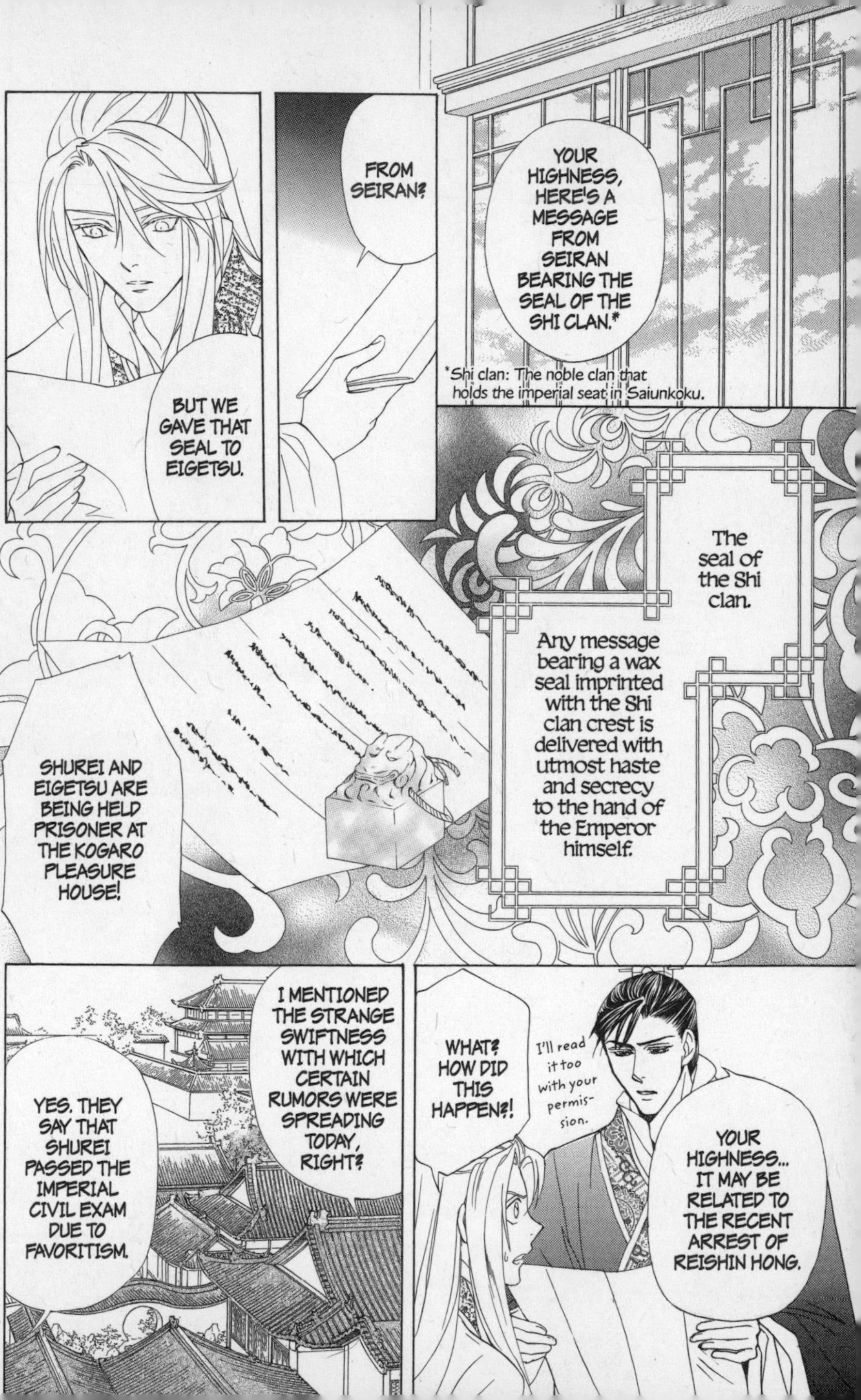
YOUR HIGHNESS, HERE'S A MESSAGE FROM SEIRAN BEARING THE SEAL OF THE SHI CLAN.*
*Shi clan: The noble clan that holds the imperial seat in Saiunkoku.
FROM SEIRAN?
BUT WE GAVE THAT SEAL TO EIGETSU.
The seal of the Shi clan.
Any message bearing a wax seal imprinted with the Shi clan crest is delivered with utmost haste and secrecy to the hand of the Emperor himself.
SHUREI AND EIGETSU ARE BEING HELD PRISONER AT THE KOGARO PLEASURE HOUSE!
WHAT? HOW DID THIS HAPPEN?!
I'll read it too with your permission.
YOUR HIGHNESS... IT MAY BE RELATED TO THE RECENT ARREST OF REISHIN HONG.
I MENTIONED THE STRANGE SWIFTNESS WITH WHICH CERTAIN RUMORS WERE SPREADING TODAY, RIGHT?
YES. THEY SAY THAT SHUREI PASSED THE IMPERIAL CIVIL EXAM DUE TO FAVORITISM.

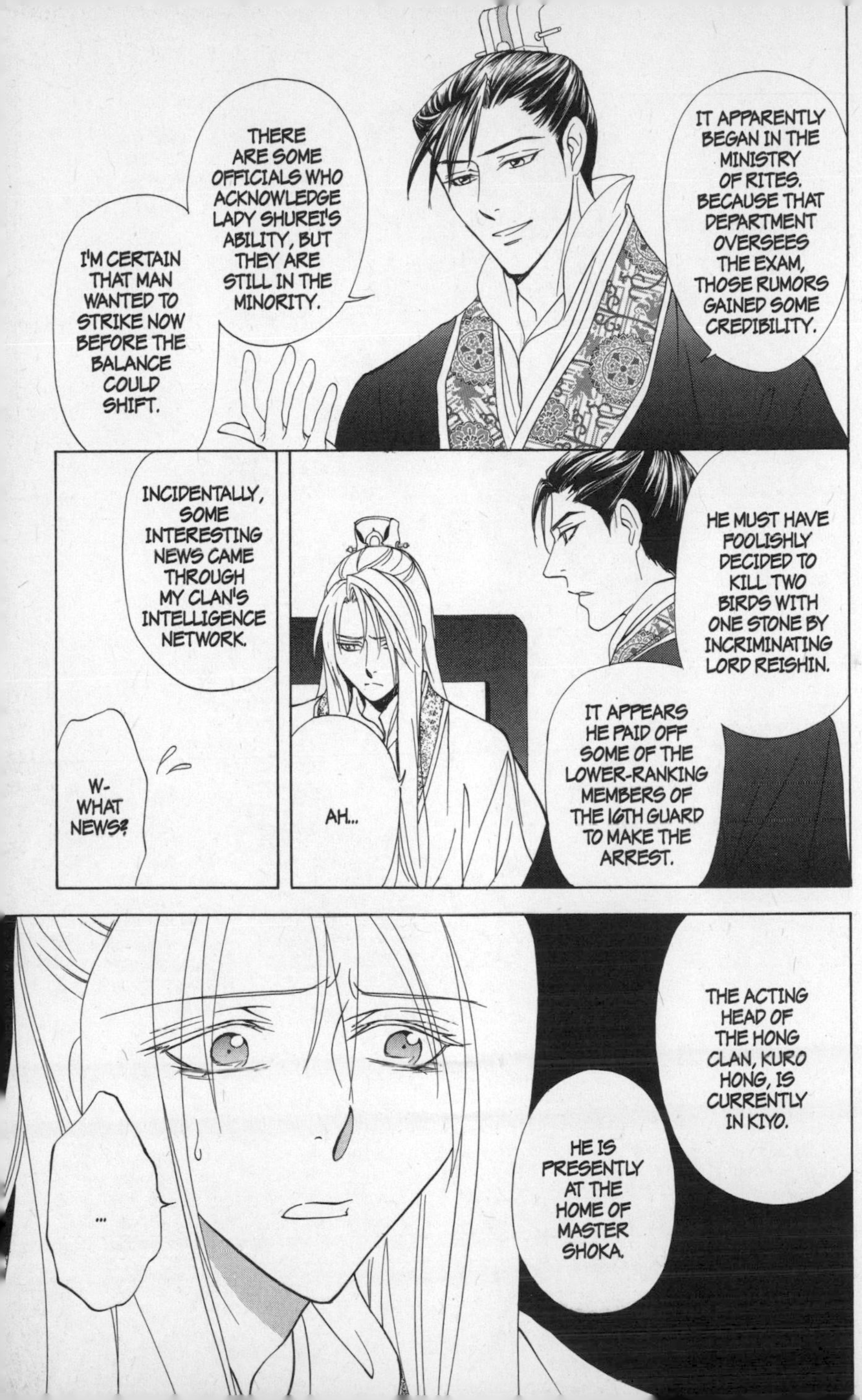
IT APPARENTLY BEGAN IN THE MINISTRY OF RITES. BECAUSE THAT DEPARTMENT OVERSEES THE EXAM, THOSE RUMORS GAINED SOME CREDIBILITY.
THERE ARE SOME OFFICIALS WHO ACKNOWLEDGE LADY SHUREI'S ABILITY, BUT THEY ARE STILL IN THE MINORITY.
I'M CERTAIN THAT MAN WANTED TO STRIKE NOW BEFORE THE BALANCE COULD SHIFT.
HE MUST HAVE FOOLISHLY DECIDED TO KILL TWO BIRDS WITH ONE STONE BY INCRIMINATING LORD REISHIN.
IT APPEARS HE PAID OFF SOME OF THE LOWER-RANKING MEMBERS OF THE 16TH GUARD TO MAKE THE ARREST.
AH...
INCIDENTALLY, SOME INTERESTING NEWS CAME THROUGH MY CLAN'S INTELLIGENCE NETWORK.
W-WHAT NEWS?
THE ACTING HEAD OF THE HONG CLAN, KURO HONG, IS CURRENTLY IN KIYO.
HE IS PRESENTLY AT THE HOME OF MASTER SHOKA.
...

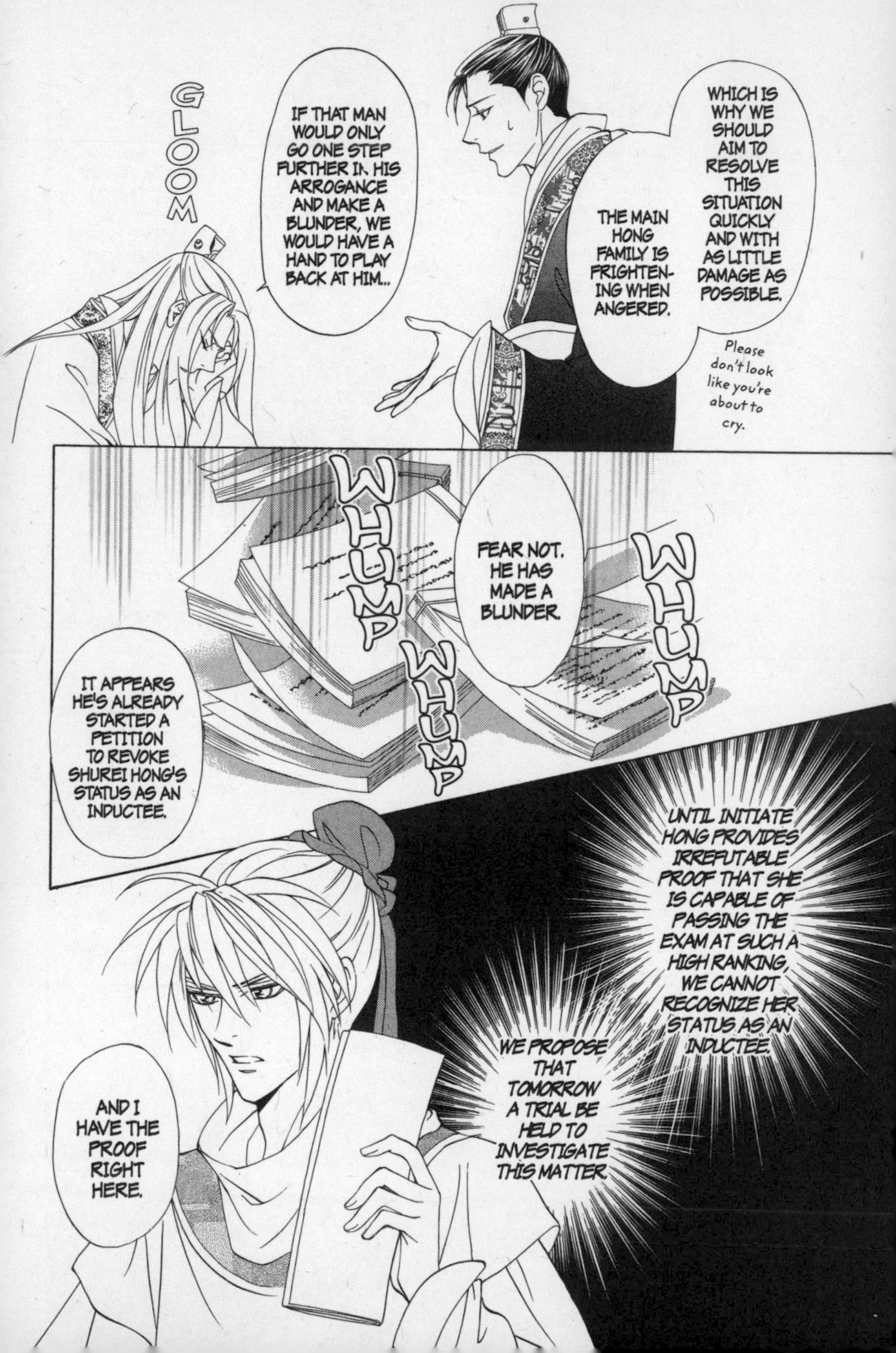

THE MAIN HONG FAMILY IS FRIGHTENING WHEN ANGERED.
WHICH IS WHY WE SHOULD AIM TO RESOLVE THIS SITUATION QUICKLY AND WITH AS LITTLE DAMAGE AS POSSIBLE.
Please don't look like you're about to cry.
IF THAT MAN WOULD ONLY GO ONE STEP FURTHER IN HIS ARROGANCE AND MAKE A BLUNDER, WE WOULD HAVE A HAND TO PLAY BACK AT HIM...
GLOOM
WHUMP
FEAR NOT. HE HAS MADE A BLUNDER.
WHUMP
WHUMP
IT APPEARS HE'S ALREADY STARTED A PETITION TO REVOKE SHUREI HONG'S STATUS AS AN INDUCTEE.
UNTIL INITIATE HONG PROVIDES IRREFUTABLE PROOF THAT SHE IS CAPABLE OF PASSING THE EXAM AT SUCH A HIGH RANKING, WE CANNOT RECOGNIZE HER STATUS AS AN INDUCTEE.
WE PROPOSE THAT TOMORROW A TRIAL BE HELD TO INVESTIGATE THIS MATTER.
AND I HAVE THE PROOF RIGHT HERE.

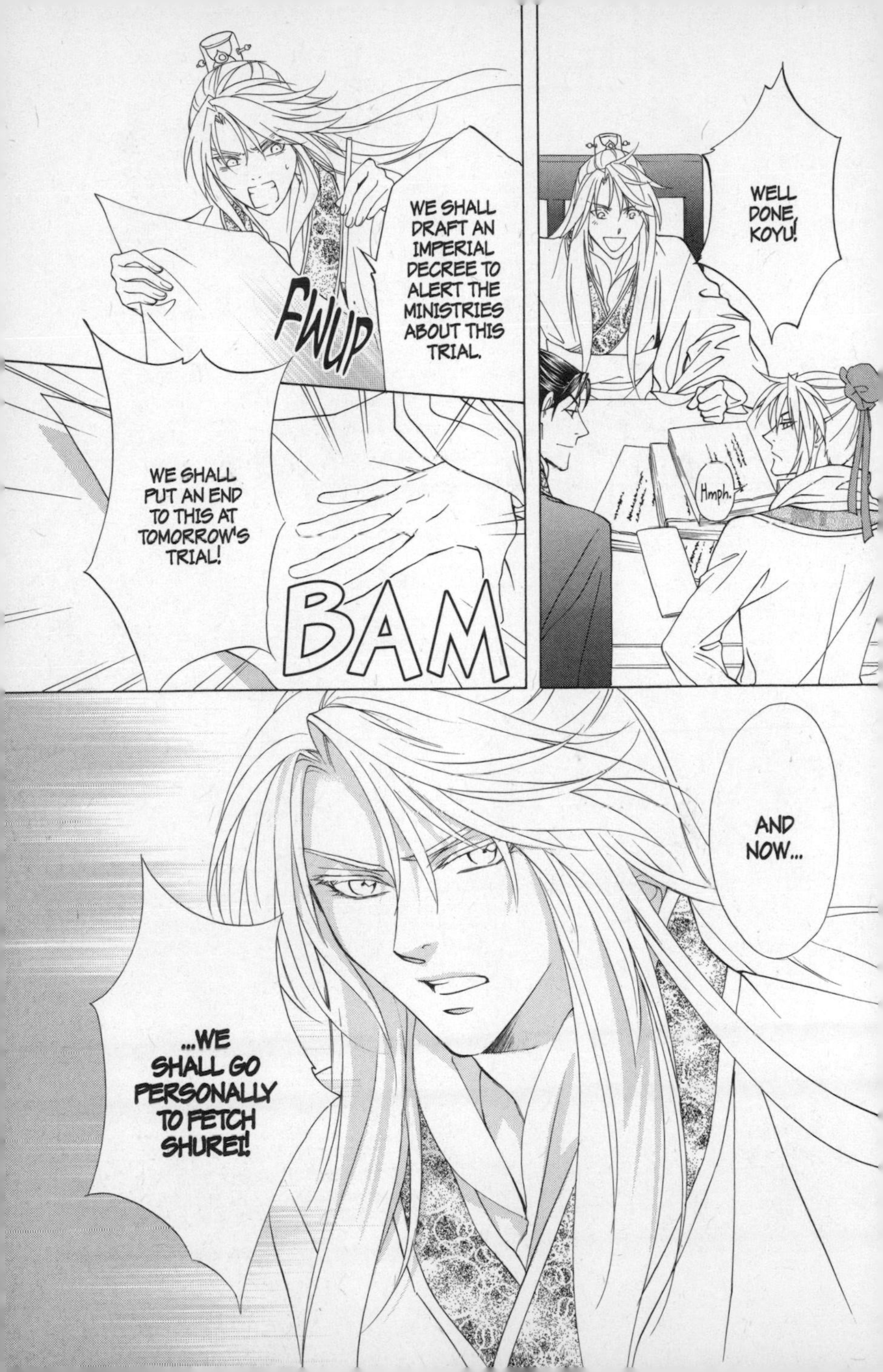
WELL DONE, KOYU!
Hmph.
WE SHALL DRAFT AN IMPERIAL DECREE TO ALERT THE MINISTRIES ABOUT THIS TRIAL.
FWUP
WE SHALL PUT AN END TO THIS AT TOMORROW'S TRIAL!
BAM
AND NOW...
...WE SHALL GO PERSONALLY TO FETCH SHUREI!

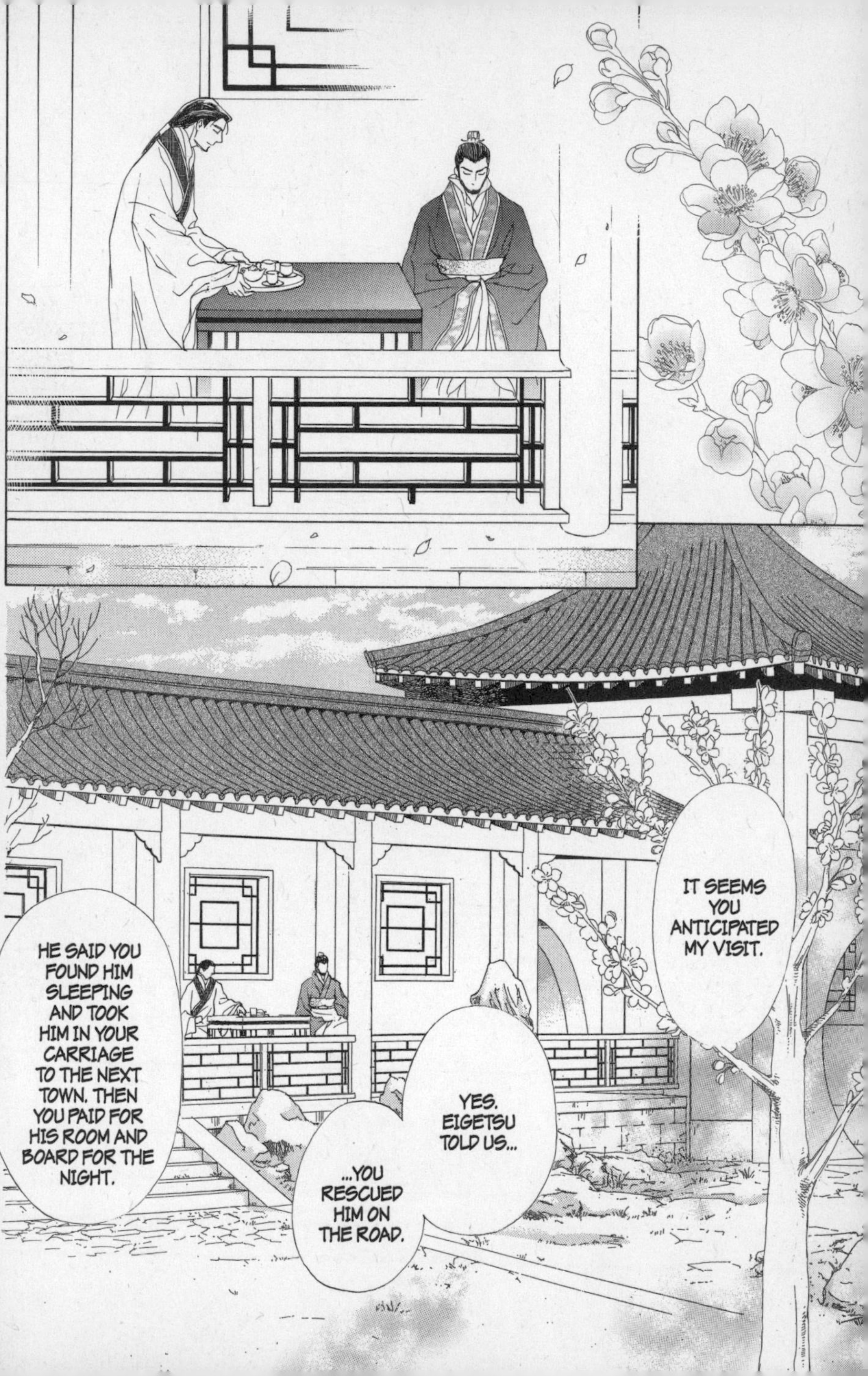
IT SEEMS YOU ANTICIPATED MY VISIT.
YES. EIGETSU TOLD US...
...YOU RESCUED HIM ON THE ROAD.
HE SAID YOU FOUND HIM SLEEPING AND TOOK HIM IN YOUR CARRIAGE TO THE NEXT TOWN. THEN YOU PAID FOR HIS ROOM AND BOARD FOR THE NIGHT.

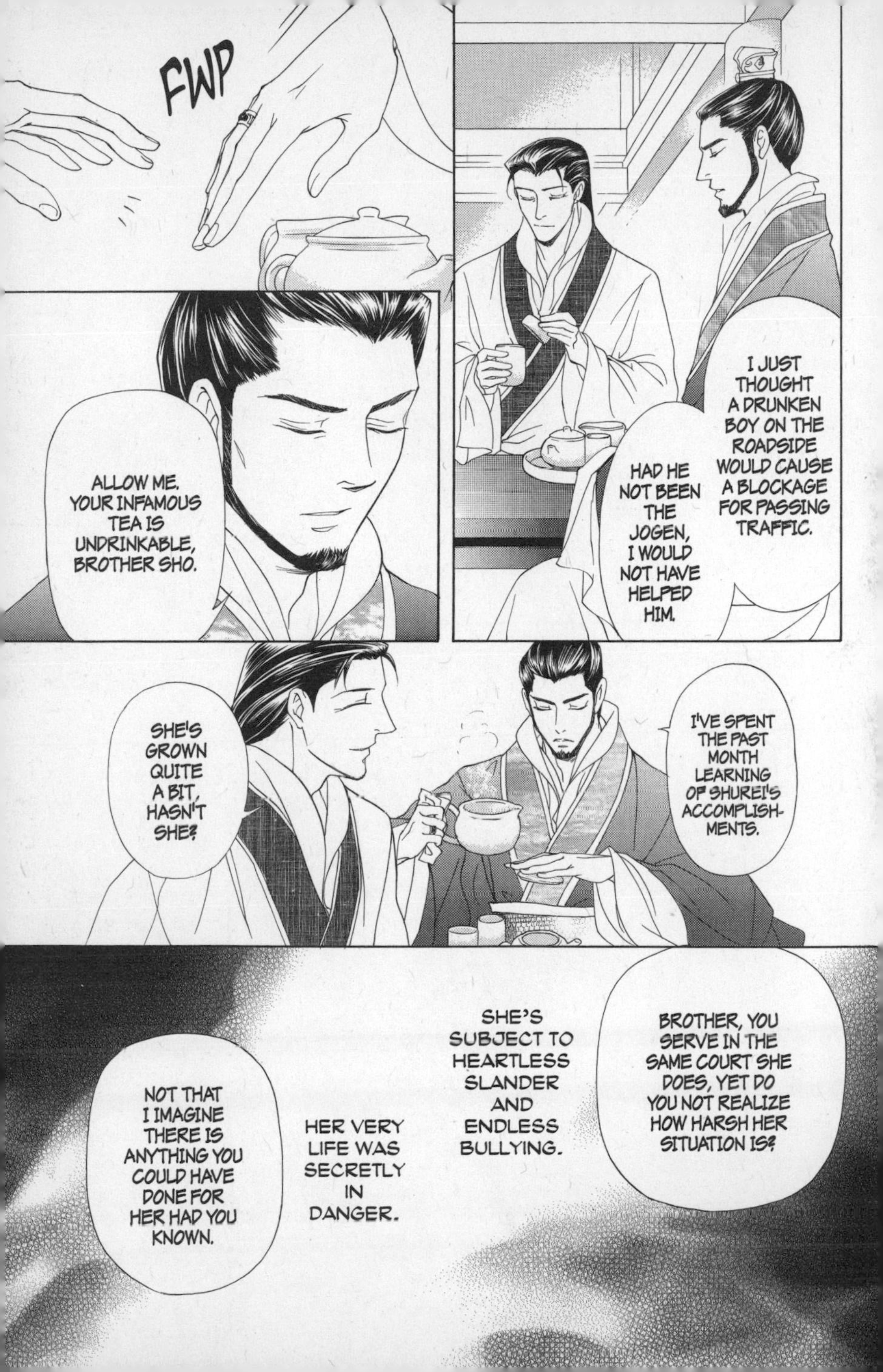
I JUST THOUGHT A DRUNKEN BOY ON THE ROADSIDE WOULD CAUSE A BLOCKAGE FOR PASSING TRAFFIC.
HAD HE NOT BEEN THE JOGEN, I WOULD NOT HAVE HELPED HIM.
FWP
ALLOW ME. YOUR INFAMOUS TEA IS UNDRINKABLE, BROTHER SHO.
I'VE SPENT THE PAST MONTH LEARNING OF SHUREI'S ACCOMPLISHMENTS.
SHE'S GROWN QUITE A BIT, HASN'T SHE?
BROTHER, YOU SERVE IN THE SAME COURT SHE DOES, YET DO YOU NOT REALIZE HOW HARSH HER SITUATION IS?
SHE'S SUBJECT TO HEARTLESS SLANDER AND ENDLESS BULLYING.
HER VERY LIFE WAS SECRETLY IN DANGER.
NOT THAT I IMAGINE THERE IS ANYTHING YOU COULD HAVE DONE FOR HER HAD YOU KNOWN.

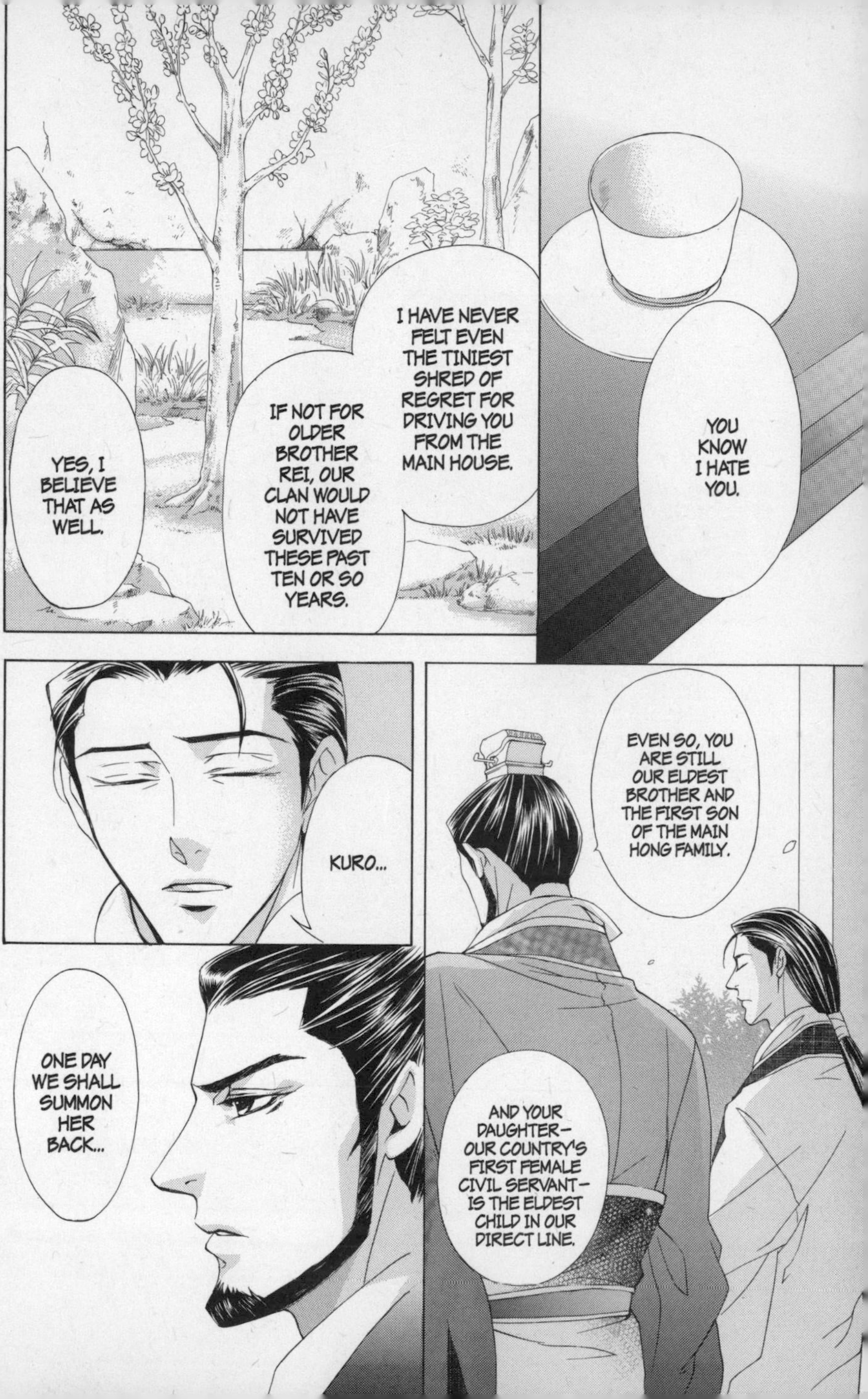
YOU KNOW I HATE YOU.
I HAVE NEVER FELT EVEN THE TINIEST SHRED OF REGRET FOR DRIVING YOU FROM THE MAIN HOUSE.
IF NOT FOR OLDER BROTHER REI, OUR CLAN WOULD NOT HAVE SURVIVED THESE PAST TEN OR SO YEARS.
YES, I BELIEVE THAT AS WELL.
EVEN SO, YOU ARE STILL OUR ELDEST BROTHER AND THE FIRST SON OF THE MAIN HONG FAMILY.
AND YOUR DAUGHTER—OUR COUNTRY'S FIRST FEMALE CIVIL SERVANT—IS THE ELDEST CHILD IN OUR DIRECT LINE.
KURO...
ONE DAY WE SHALL SUMMON HER BACK...

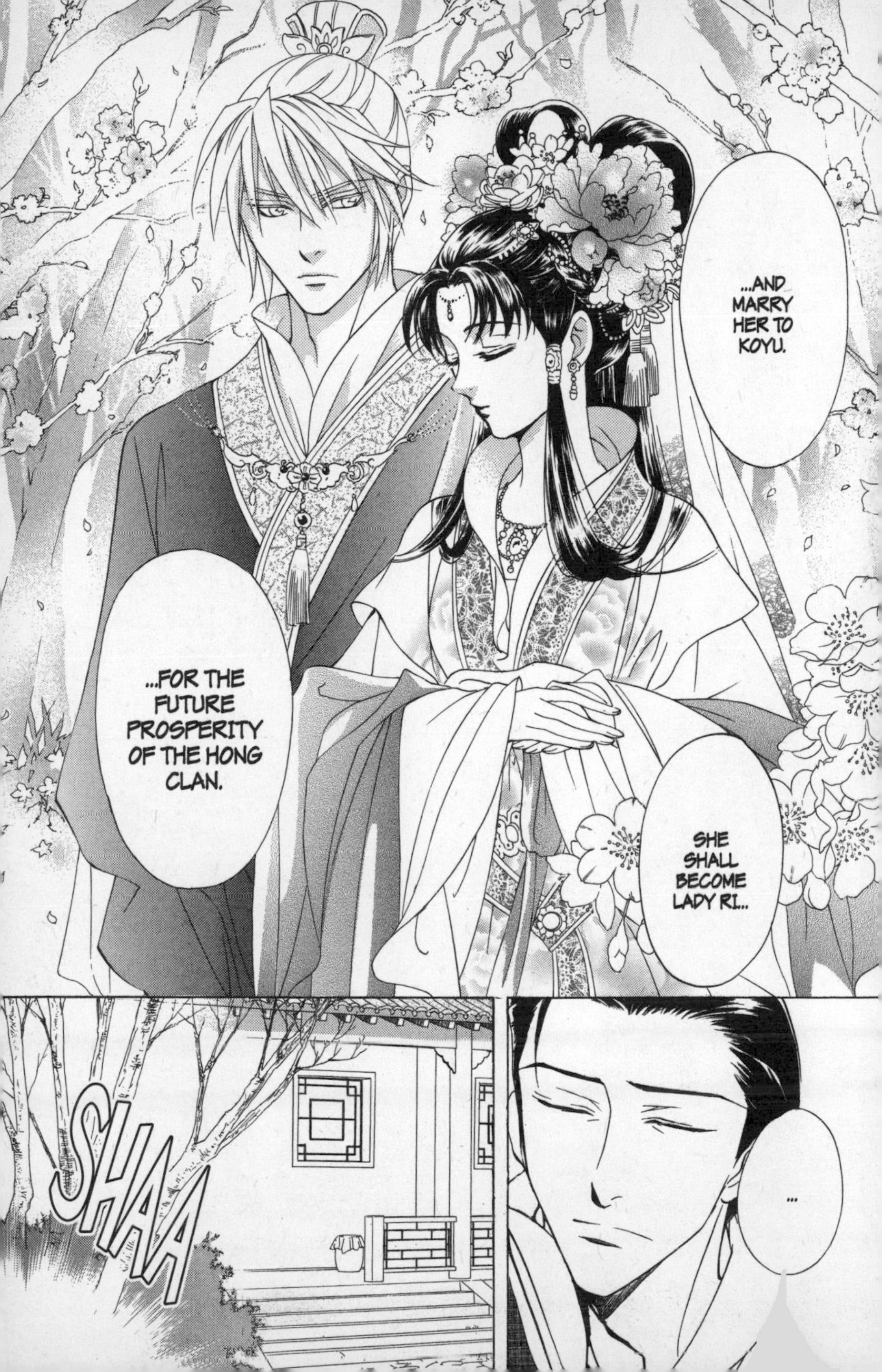
...AND MARRY HER TO KOYU.
SHE SHALL BECOME LADY RI...
...FOR THE FUTURE PROSPERITY OF THE HONG CLAN.
...
SHAA

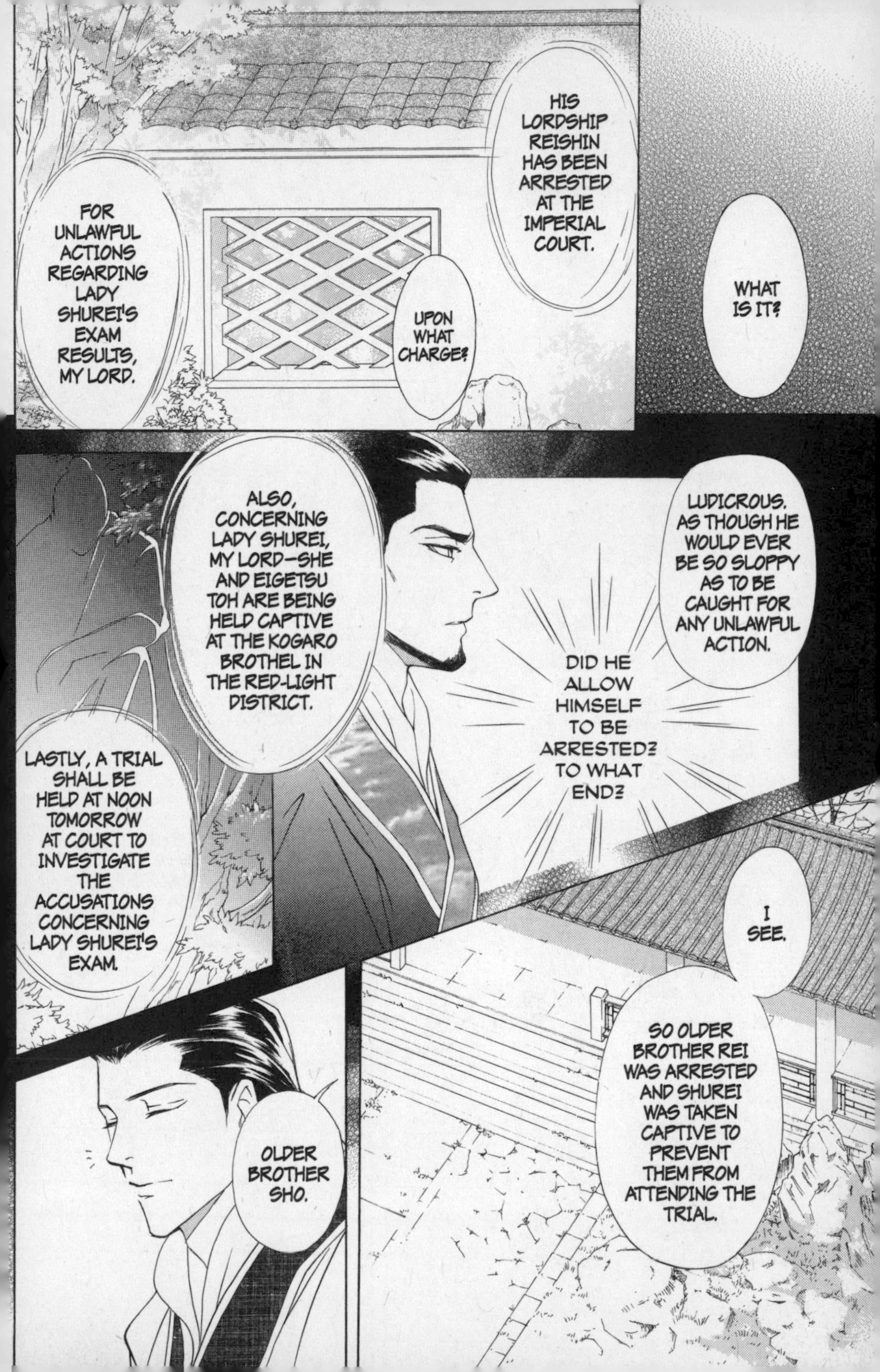
WHAT IS IT?
HIS LORDSHIP REISHIN HAS BEEN ARRESTED AT THE IMPERIAL COURT.
UPON WHAT CHARGE?
FOR UNLAWFUL ACTIONS REGARDING LADY SHUREI'S EXAM RESULTS, MY LORD.
LUDICROUS. AS THOUGH HE WOULD EVER BE SO SLOPPY AS TO BE CAUGHT FOR ANY UNLAWFUL ACTION.
ALSO, CONCERNING LADY SHUREI, MY LORD—SHE AND EIGETSU TOH ARE BEING HELD CAPTIVE AT THE KOGARO BROTHEL IN THE RED-LIGHT DISTRICT.
DID HE ALLOW HIMSELF TO BE ARRESTED? TO WHAT END?
LASTLY, A TRIAL SHALL BE HELD AT NOON TOMORROW AT COURT TO INVESTIGATE THE ACCUSATIONS CONCERNING LADY SHUREI'S EXAM.
I SEE.
SO OLDER BROTHER REI WAS ARRESTED AND SHUREI WAS TAKEN CAPTIVE TO PREVENT THEM FROM ATTENDING THE TRIAL.
OLDER BROTHER SHO.

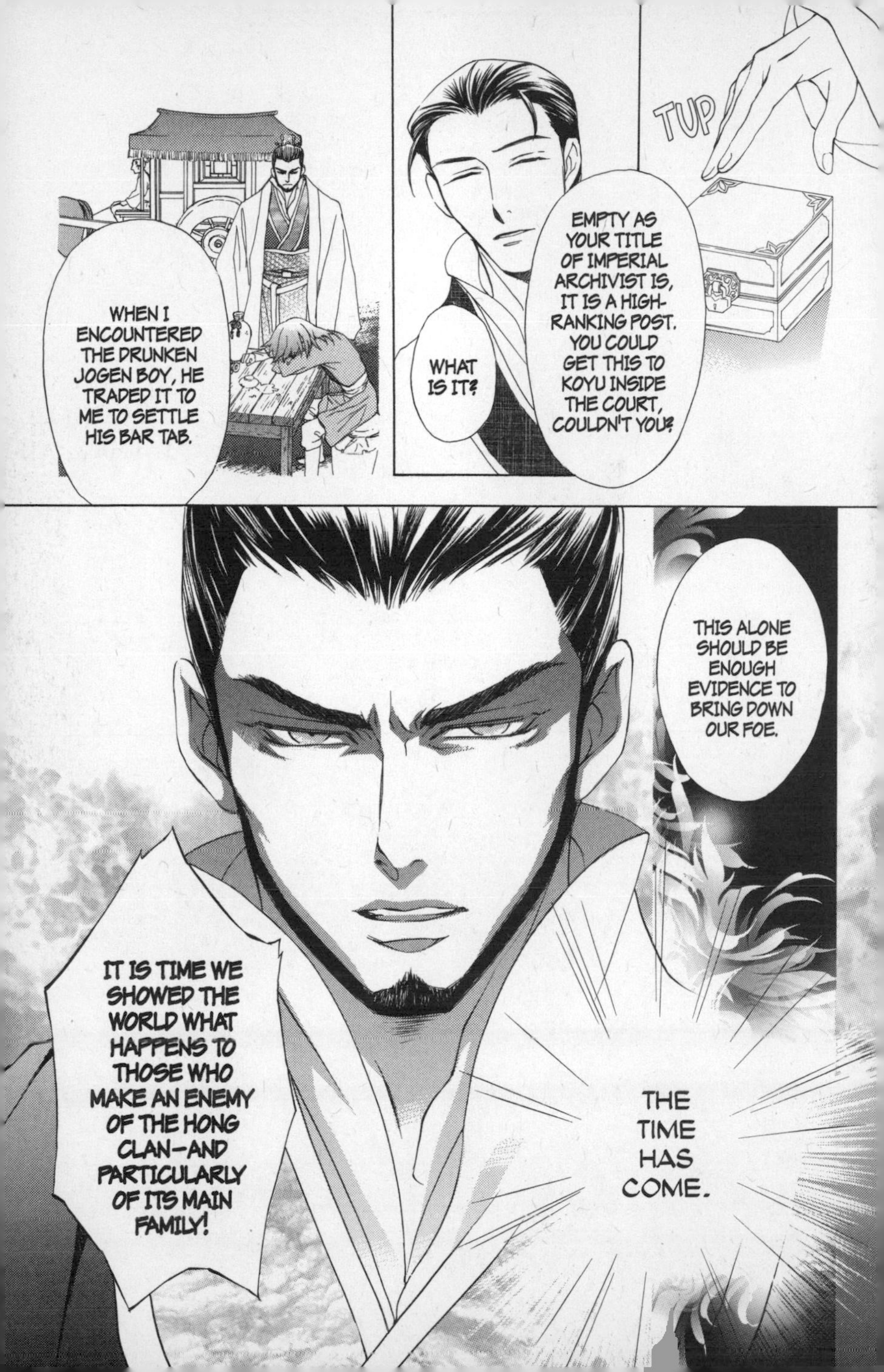
TUP
EMPTY AS YOUR TITLE OF IMPERIAL ARCHIVIST IS, IT IS A HIGH-RANKING POST. YOU COULD GET THIS TO KOYU INSIDE THE COURT, COULDN'T YOU?
WHAT IS IT?
WHEN I ENCOUNTERED THE DRUNKEN JOGEN BOY, HE TRADED IT TO ME TO SETTLE HIS BAR TAB.
THIS ALONE SHOULD BE ENOUGH EVIDENCE TO BRING DOWN OUR FOE.
IT IS TIME WE SHOWED THE WORLD WHAT HAPPENS TO THOSE WHO MAKE AN ENEMY OF THE HONG CLAN—AND PARTICULARLY OF ITS MAIN FAMILY!
THE TIME HAS COME.

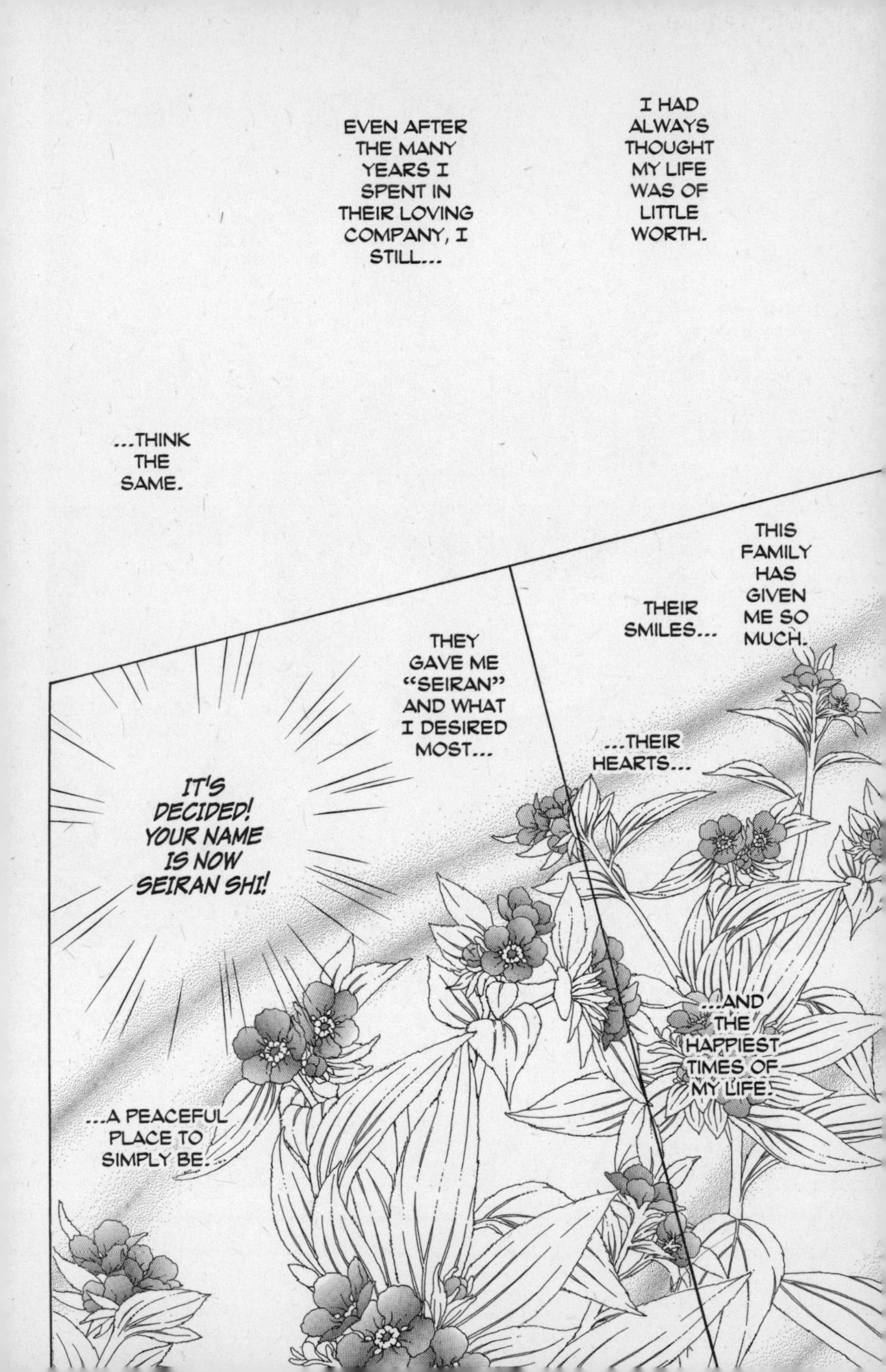
I HAD ALWAYS THOUGHT MY LIFE WAS OF LITTLE WORTH.
EVEN AFTER THE MANY YEARS I SPENT IN THEIR LOVING COMPANY, I STILL...
...THINK THE SAME.
THIS FAMILY HAS GIVEN ME SO MUCH.
THEIR SMILES...
...THEIR HEARTS...
...AND THE HAPPIEST TIMES OF MY LIFE.
THEY GAVE ME "SEIRAN" AND WHAT I DESIRED MOST...
IT'S DECIDED! YOUR NAME IS NOW SEIRAN SHI!
...A PEACEFUL PLACE TO SIMPLY BE...

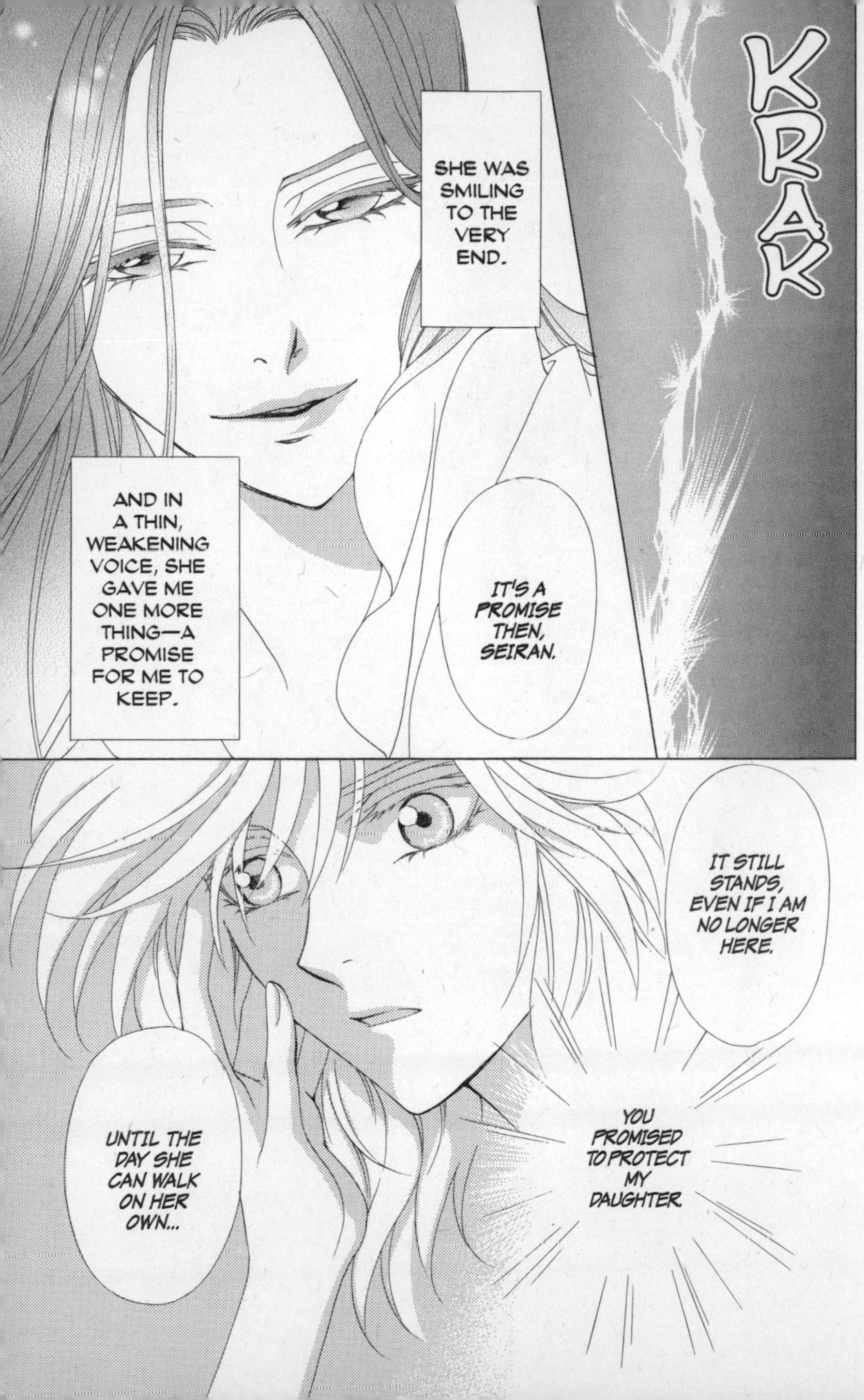
KRAK
SHE WAS SMILING TO THE VERY END.
AND IN A THIN, WEAKENING VOICE, SHE GAVE ME ONE MORE THING—A PROMISE FOR ME TO KEEP.
IT'S A PROMISE THEN, SEIRAN.
IT STILL STANDS, EVEN IF I AM NO LONGER HERE.
YOU PROMISED TO PROTECT MY DAUGHTER.
UNTIL THE DAY SHE CAN WALK ON HER OWN...

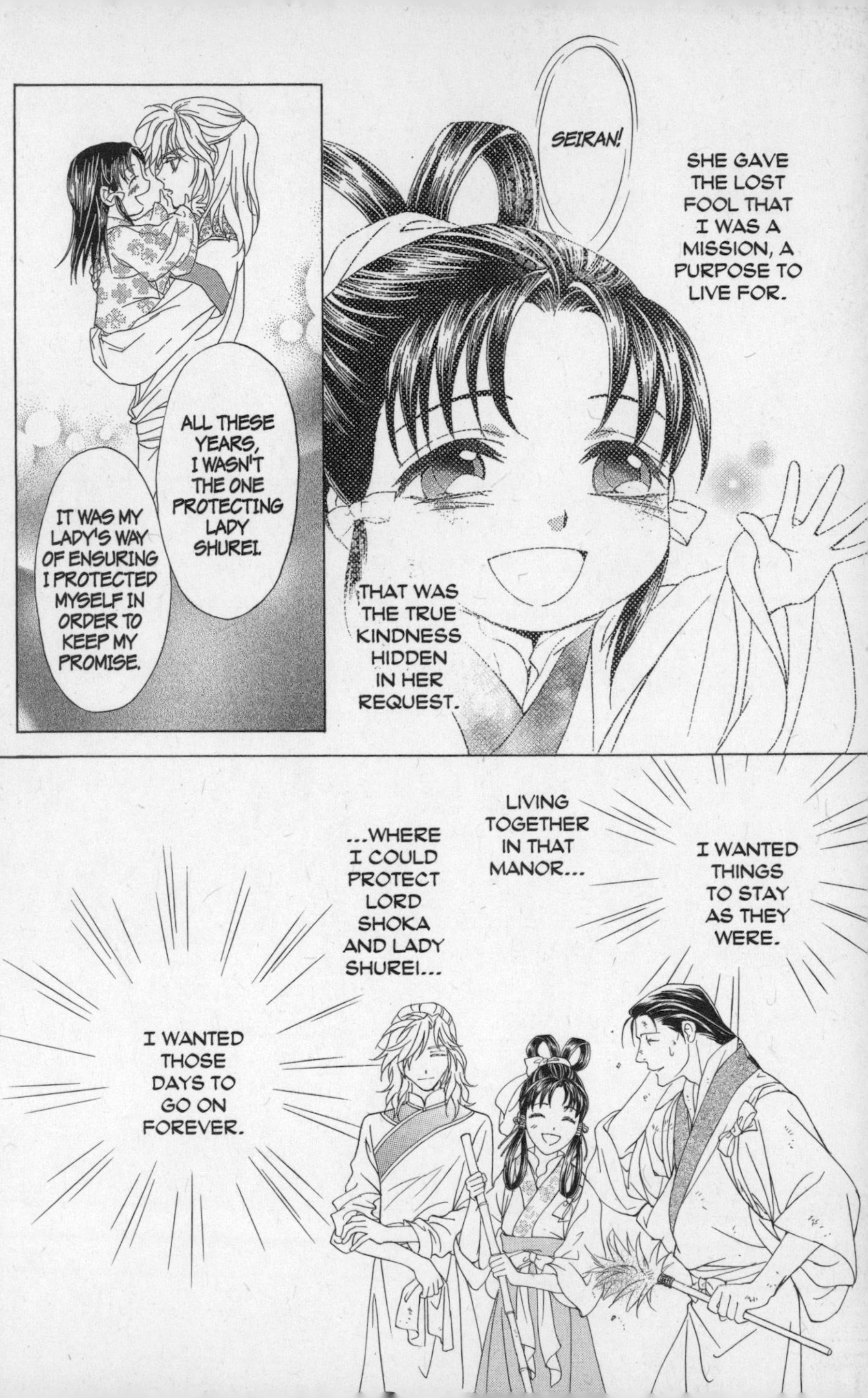
SEIRAN!
SHE GAVE THE LOST FOOL THAT I WAS A MISSION, A PURPOSE TO LIVE FOR.
THAT WAS THE TRUE KINDNESS HIDDEN IN HER REQUEST.
ALL THESE YEARS, I WASN'T THE ONE PROTECTING LADY SHUREI.
IT WAS MY LADY'S WAY OF ENSURING I PROTECTED MYSELF IN ORDER TO KEEP MY PROMISE.
I WANTED THINGS TO STAY AS THEY WERE.
LIVING TOGETHER IN THAT MANOR...
...WHERE I COULD PROTECT LORD SHOKA AND LADY SHUREI...
I WANTED THOSE DAYS TO GO ON FOREVER.

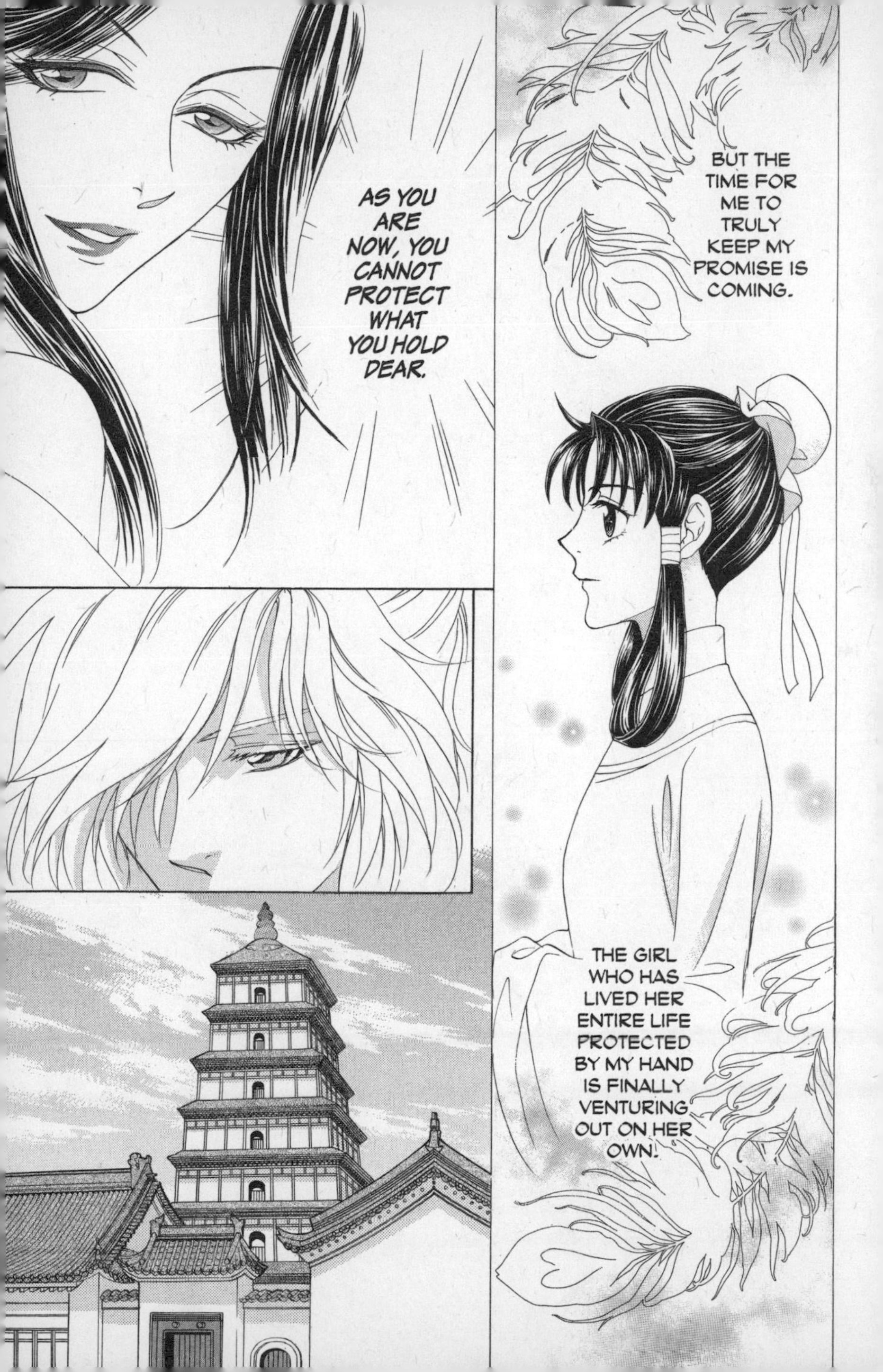
BUT THE TIME FOR ME TO TRULY KEEP MY PROMISE IS COMING.
THE GIRL WHO HAS LIVED HER ENTIRE LIFE PROTECTED BY MY HAND IS FINALLY VENTURING OUT ON HER OWN.
AS YOU ARE NOW, YOU CANNOT PROTECT WHAT YOU HOLD DEAR.

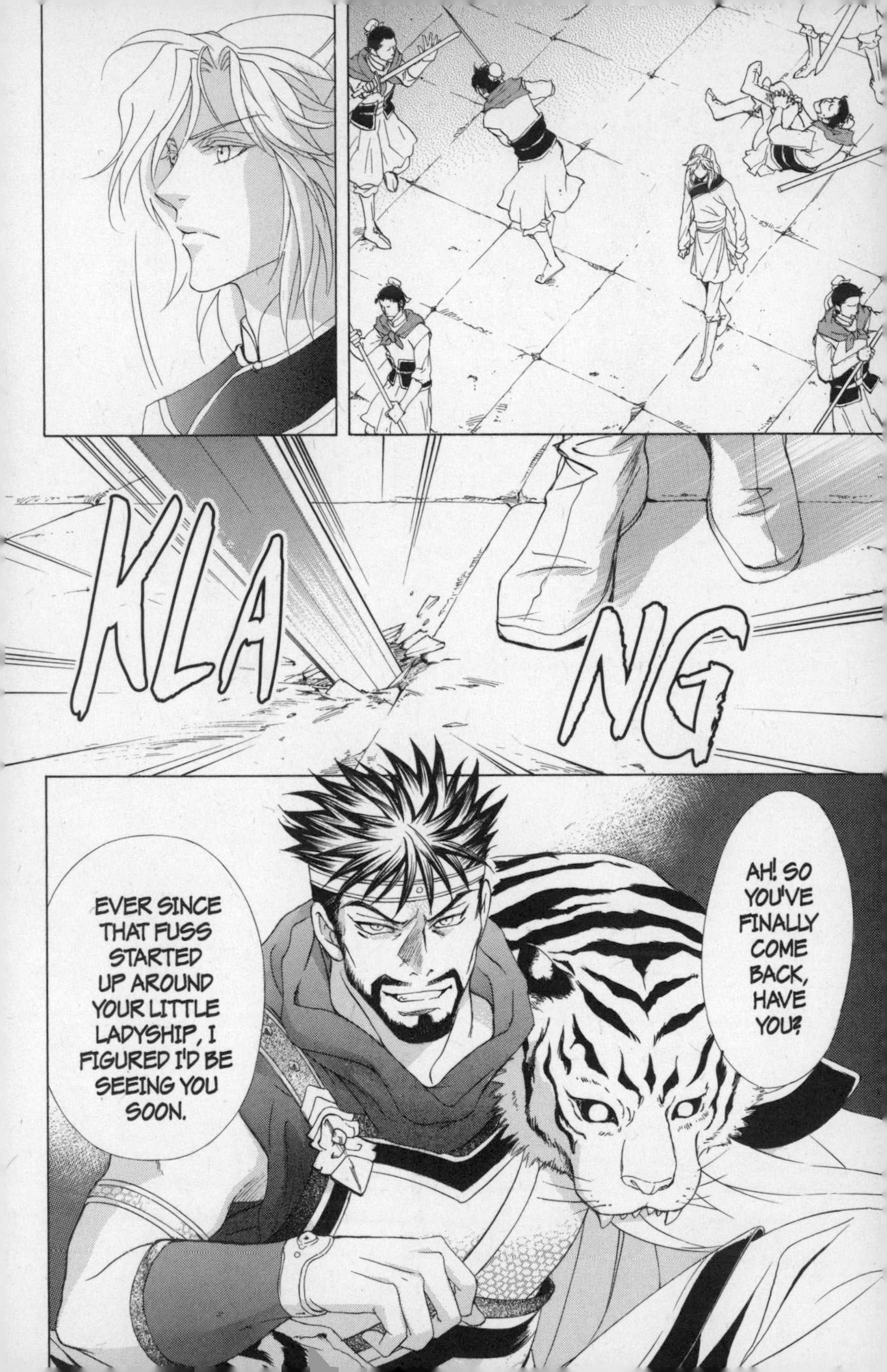
KLANG
AH! SO YOU'VE FINALLY COME BACK, HAVE YOU?
EVER SINCE THAT FUSS STARTED UP AROUND YOUR LITTLE LADYSHIP, I FIGURED I'D BE SEEING YOU SOON.

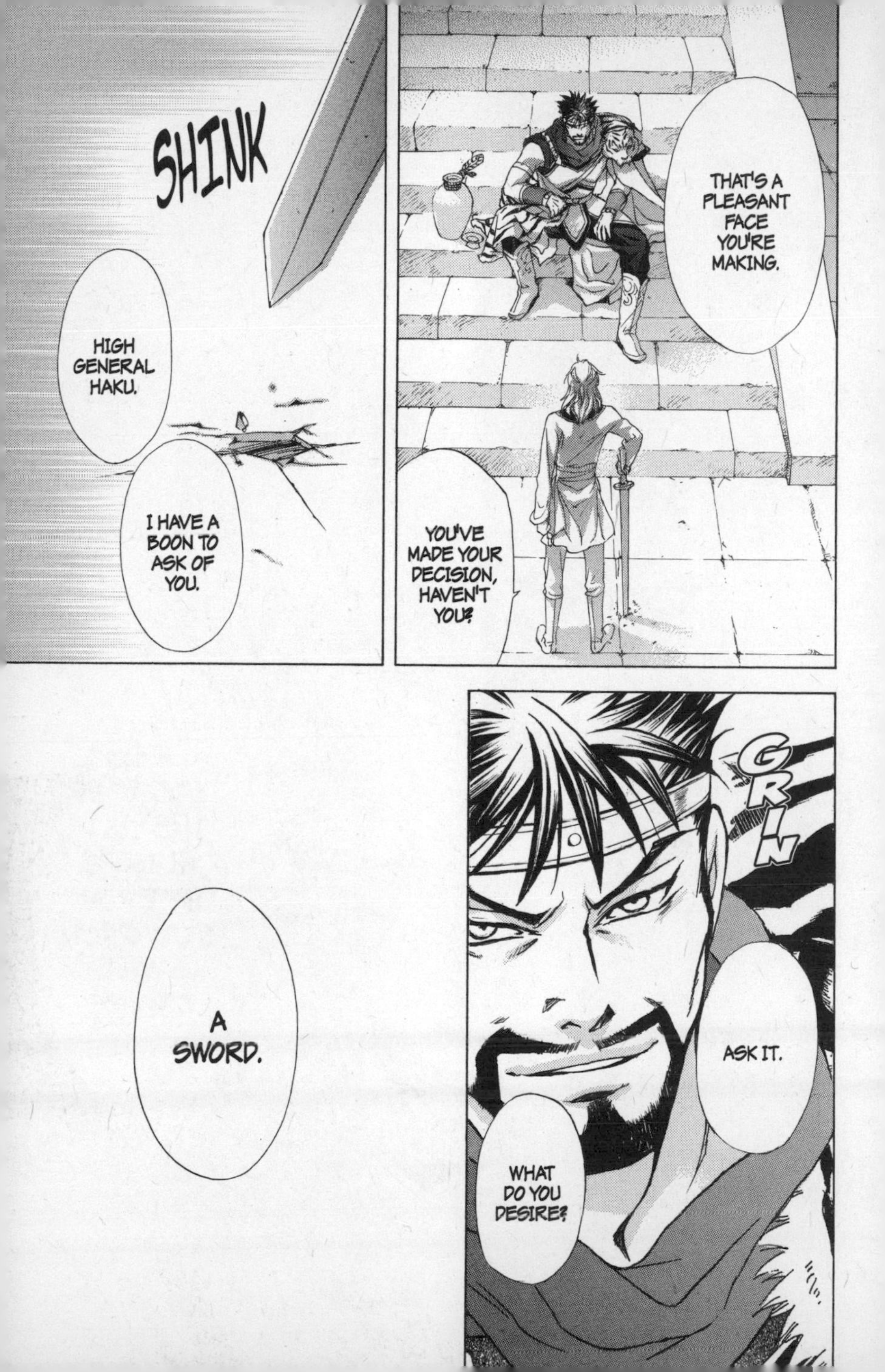
THAT'S A PLEASANT FACE YOU'RE MAKING.
YOU'VE MADE YOUR DECISION, HAVEN'T YOU?
SHINK
HIGH GENERAL HAKU.
I HAVE A BOON TO ASK OF YOU.
GRIN
ASK IT.
WHAT DO YOU DESIRE?
A SWORD.

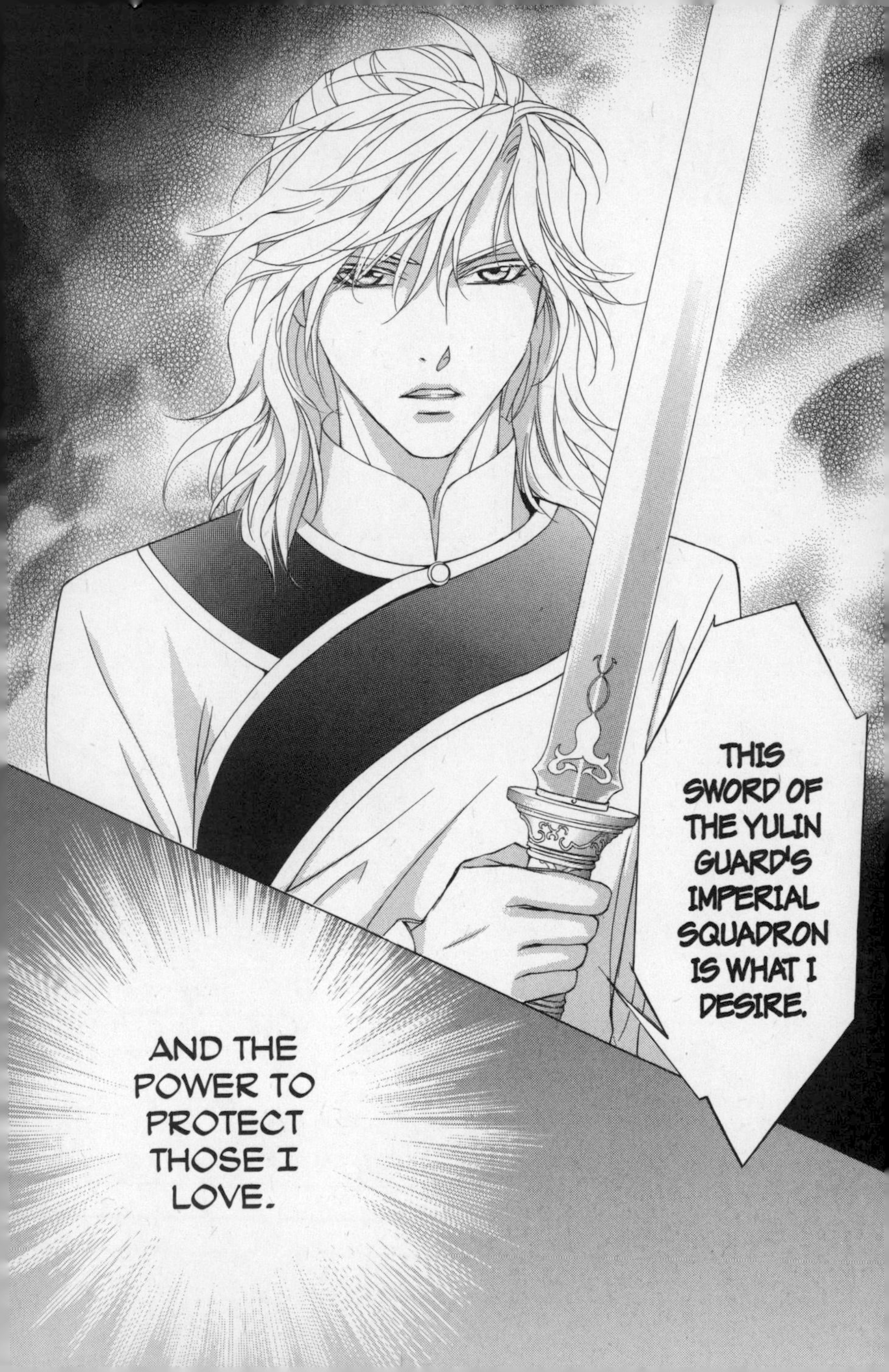
THIS SWORD OF THE YULIN GUARD'S IMPERIAL SQUADRON IS WHAT I DESIRE.
AND THE POWER TO PROTECT THOSE I LOVE.

The Story of
SAIUNKOKU

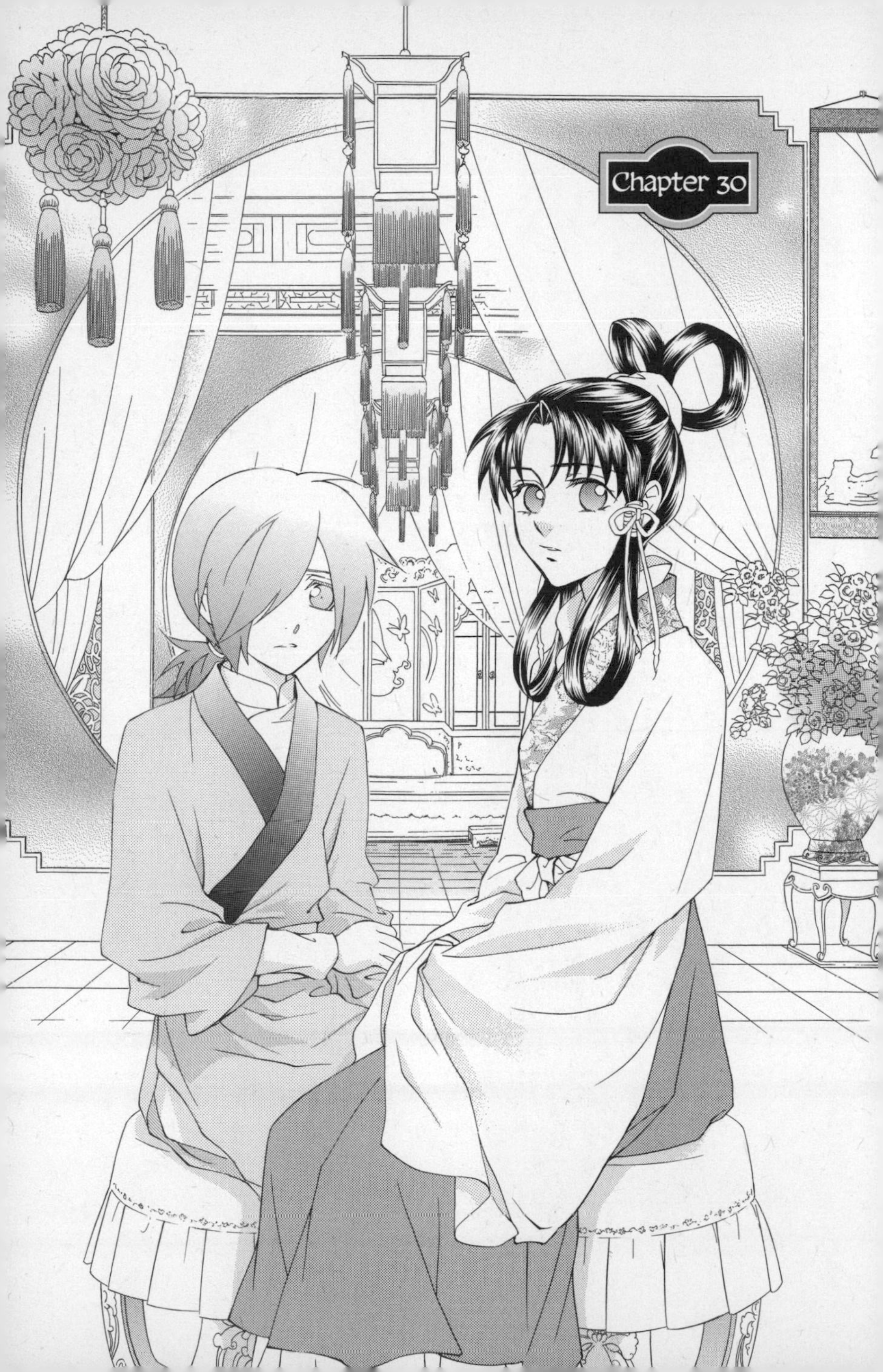
Chapter 30

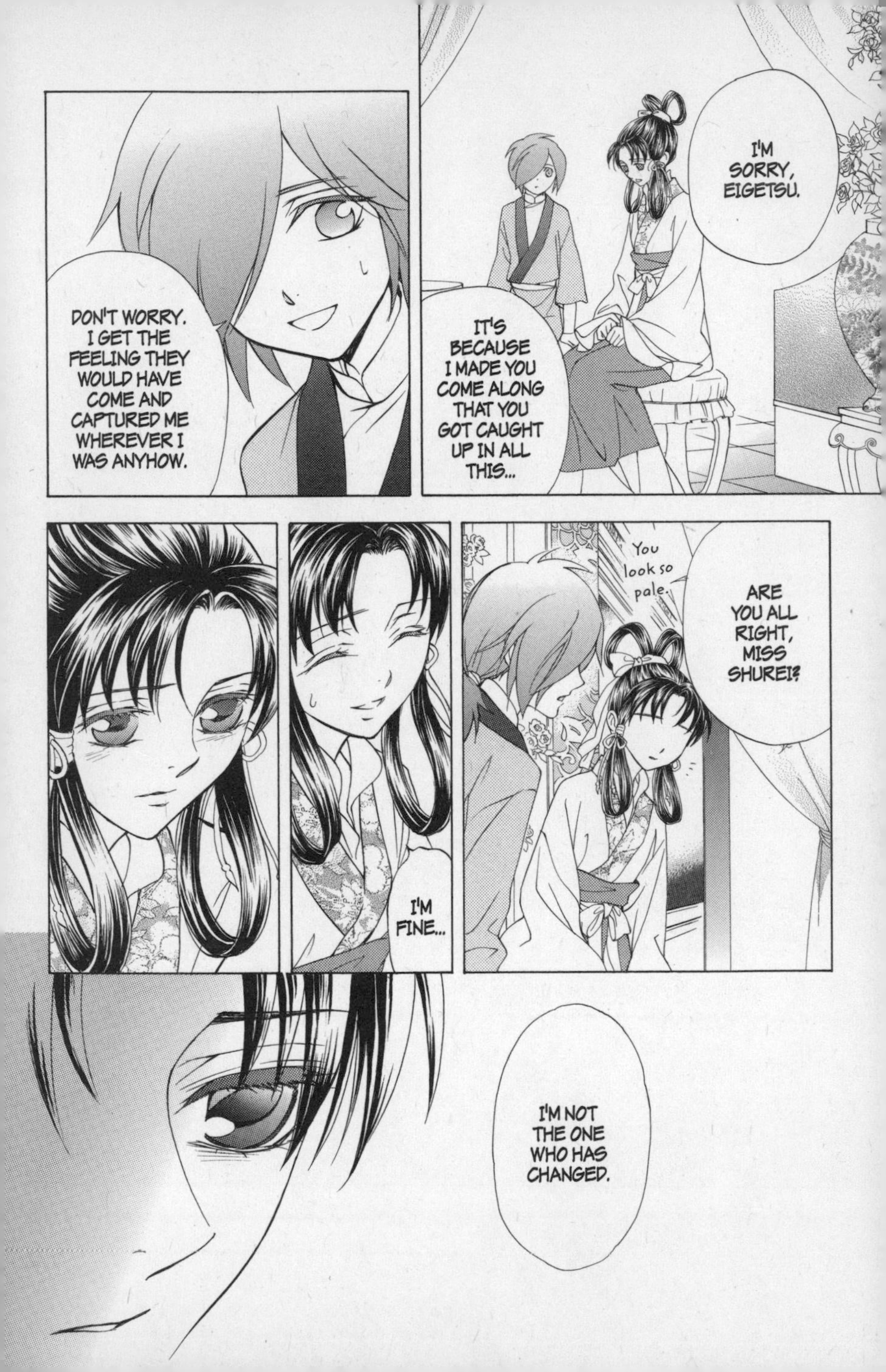
I'M SORRY, EIGETSU.
IT'S BECAUSE I MADE YOU COME ALONG THAT YOU GOT CAUGHT UP IN ALL THIS...
DON'T WORRY. I GET THE FEELING THEY WOULD HAVE COME AND CAPTURED ME WHEREVER I WAS ANYHOW.
ARE YOU ALL RIGHT, MISS SHUREI?
You look so pale.
I'M FINE...
I'M NOT THE ONE WHO HAS CHANGED.

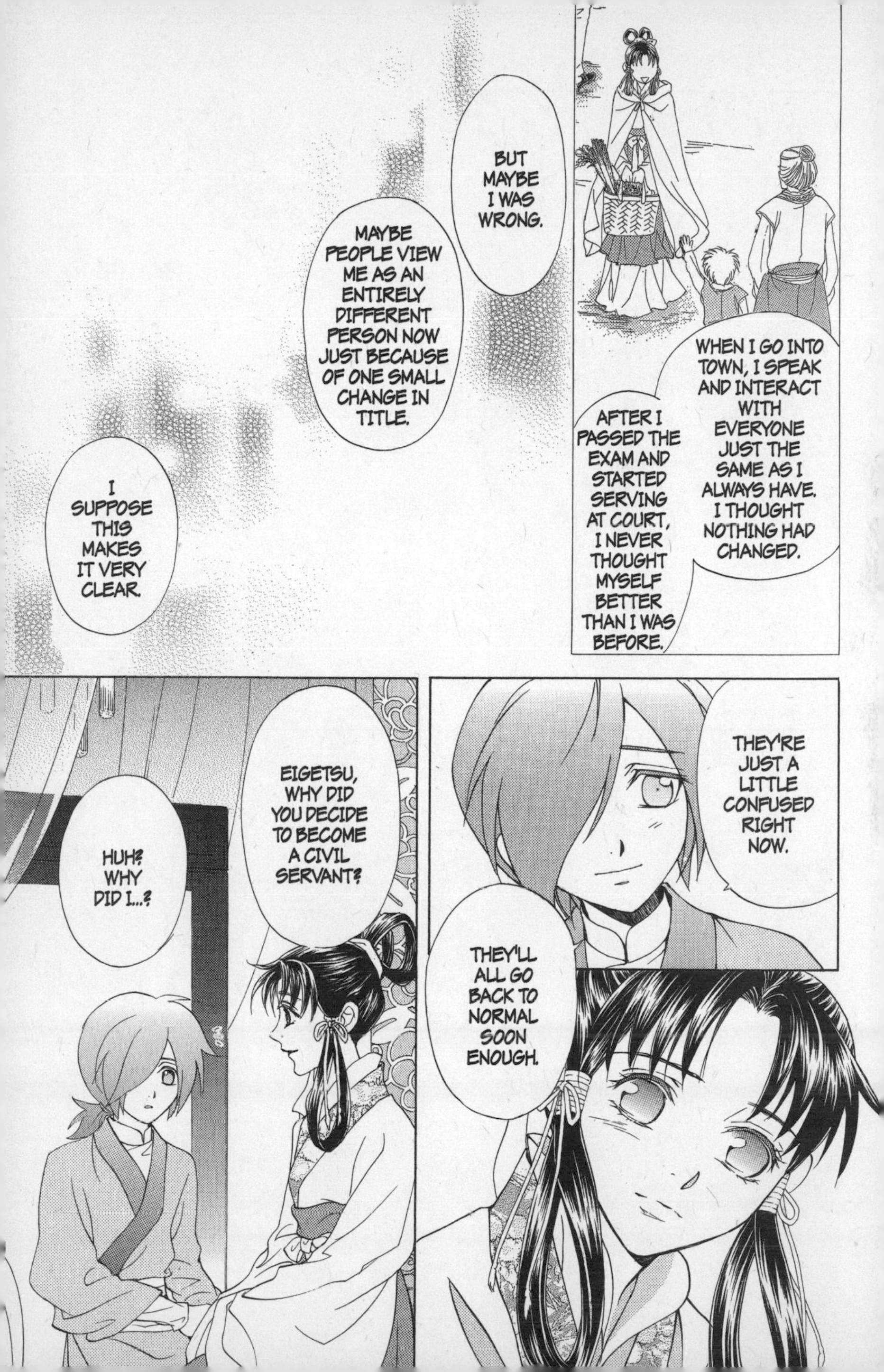
WHEN I GO INTO TOWN, I SPEAK AND INTERACT WITH EVERYONE JUST THE SAME AS I ALWAYS HAVE. I THOUGHT NOTHING HAD CHANGED.
AFTER I PASSED THE EXAM AND STARTED SERVING AT COURT, I NEVER THOUGHT MYSELF BETTER THAN I WAS BEFORE.
BUT MAYBE I WAS WRONG.
MAYBE PEOPLE VIEW ME AS AN ENTIRELY DIFFERENT PERSON NOW JUST BECAUSE OF ONE SMALL CHANGE IN TITLE.
I SUPPOSE THIS MAKES IT VERY CLEAR.
THEY'RE JUST A LITTLE CONFUSED RIGHT NOW.
THEY'LL ALL GO BACK TO NORMAL SOON ENOUGH.
EIGETSU, WHY DID YOU DECIDE TO BECOME A CIVIL SERVANT?
HUH? WHY DID I...?

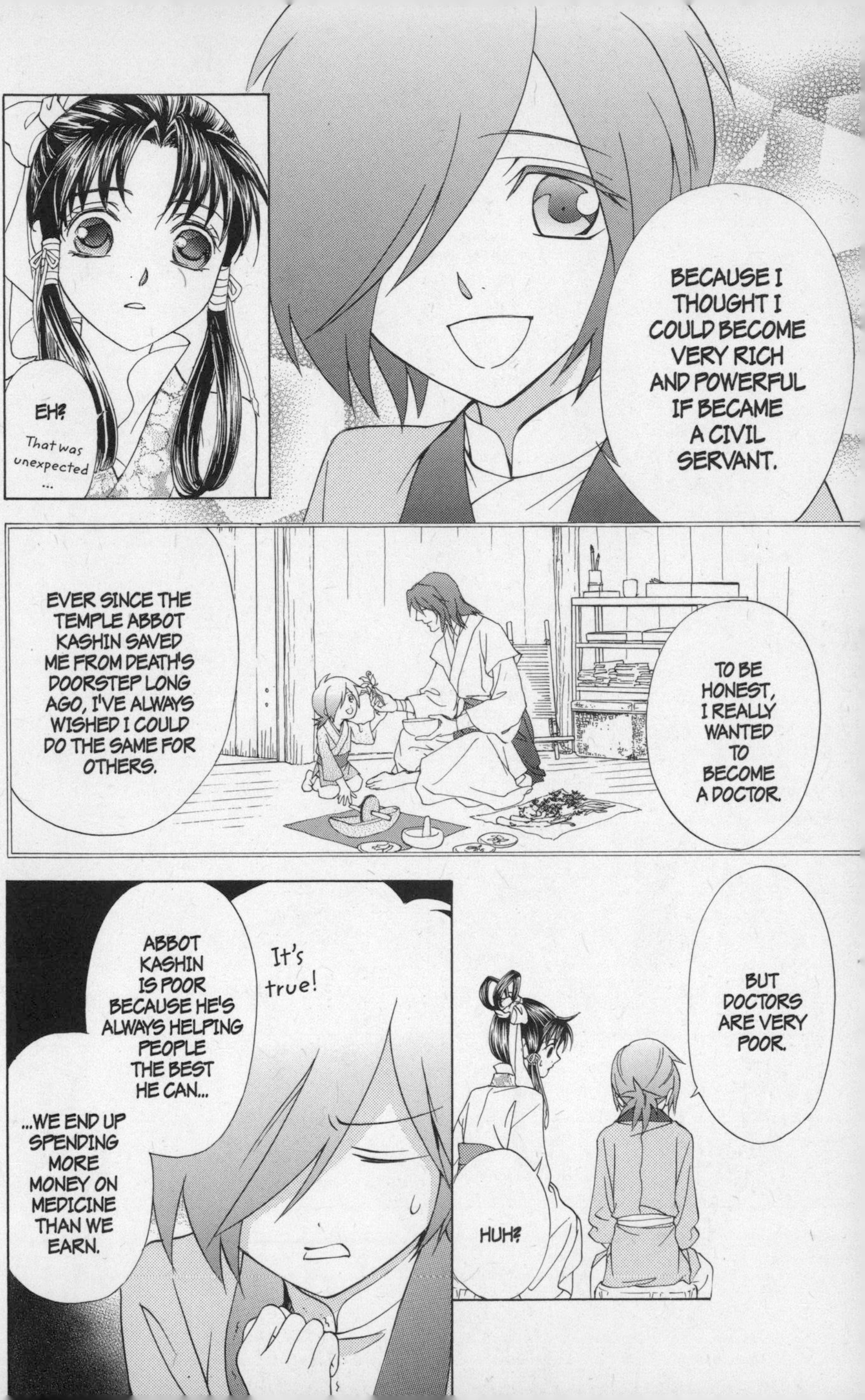
BECAUSE I THOUGHT I COULD BECOME VERY RICH AND POWERFUL IF BECAME A CIVIL SERVANT.
EH?
That was unexpected ...
TO BE HONEST, I REALLY WANTED TO BECOME A DOCTOR.
EVER SINCE THE TEMPLE ABBOT KASHIN SAVED ME FROM DEATH'S DOORSTEP LONG AGO, I'VE ALWAYS WISHED I COULD DO THE SAME FOR OTHERS.
BUT DOCTORS ARE VERY POOR.
HUH?
ABBOT KASHIN IS POOR BECAUSE HE'S ALWAYS HELPING PEOPLE THE BEST HE CAN...
It's true!
...WE END UP SPENDING MORE MONEY ON MEDICINE THAN WE EARN.

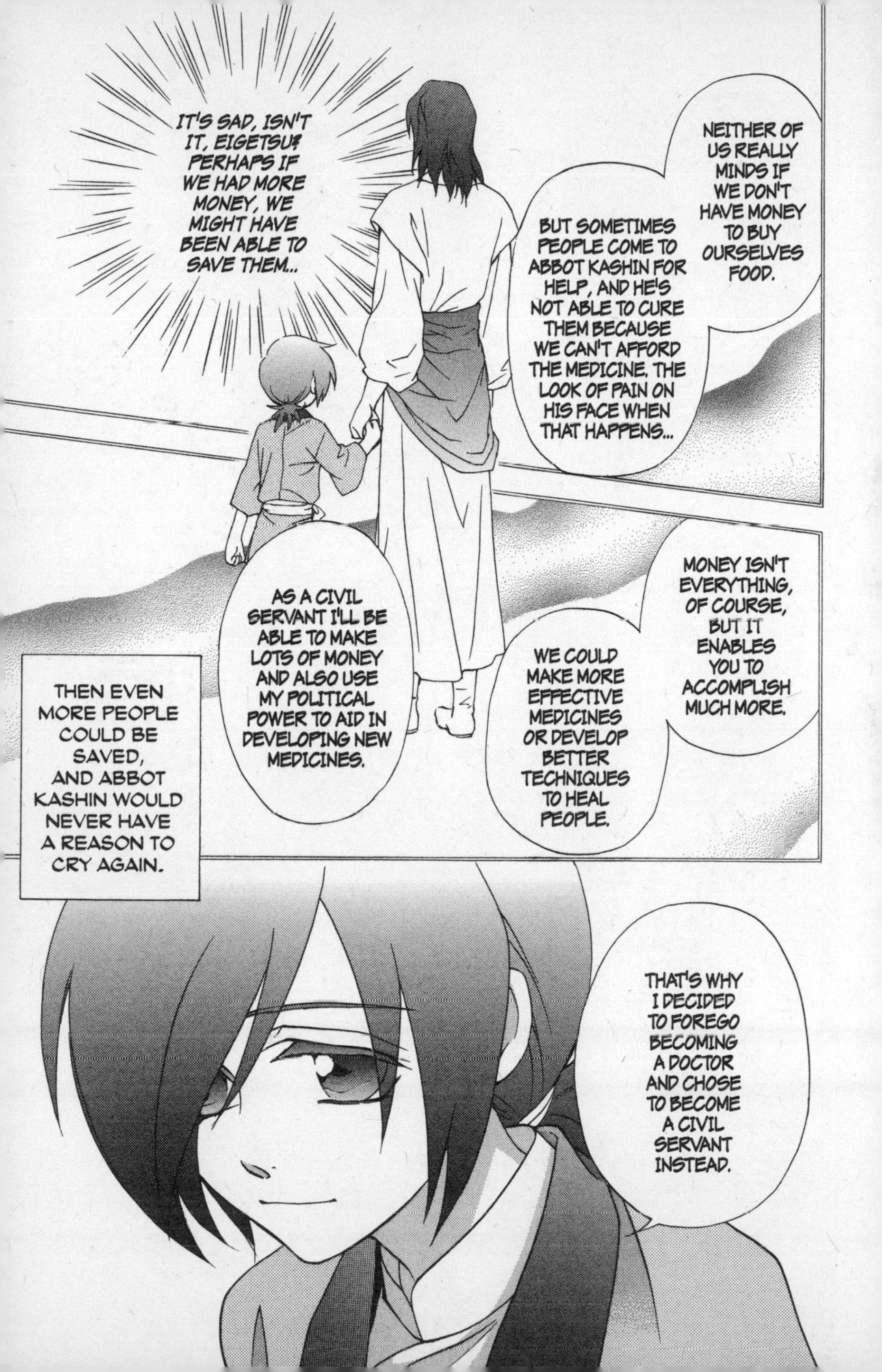
NEITHER OF US REALLY MINDS IF WE DON'T HAVE MONEY TO BUY OURSELVES FOOD.
BUT SOMETIMES PEOPLE COME TO ABBOT KASHIN FOR HELP, AND HE'S NOT ABLE TO CURE THEM BECAUSE WE CAN'T AFFORD THE MEDICINE. THE LOOK OF PAIN ON HIS FACE WHEN THAT HAPPENS...
IT'S SAD, ISN'T IT, EIGETSU? PERHAPS IF WE HAD MORE MONEY, WE MIGHT HAVE BEEN ABLE TO SAVE THEM...
MONEY ISN'T EVERYTHING, OF COURSE, BUT IT ENABLES YOU TO ACCOMPLISH MUCH MORE.
WE COULD MAKE MORE EFFECTIVE MEDICINES OR DEVELOP BETTER TECHNIQUES TO HEAL PEOPLE.
AS A CIVIL SERVANT I'LL BE ABLE TO MAKE LOTS OF MONEY AND ALSO USE MY POLITICAL POWER TO AID IN DEVELOPING NEW MEDICINES.
THEN EVEN MORE PEOPLE COULD BE SAVED, AND ABBOT KASHIN WOULD NEVER HAVE A REASON TO CRY AGAIN.
THAT'S WHY I DECIDED TO FOREGO BECOMING A DOCTOR AND CHOSE TO BECOME A CIVIL SERVANT INSTEAD.

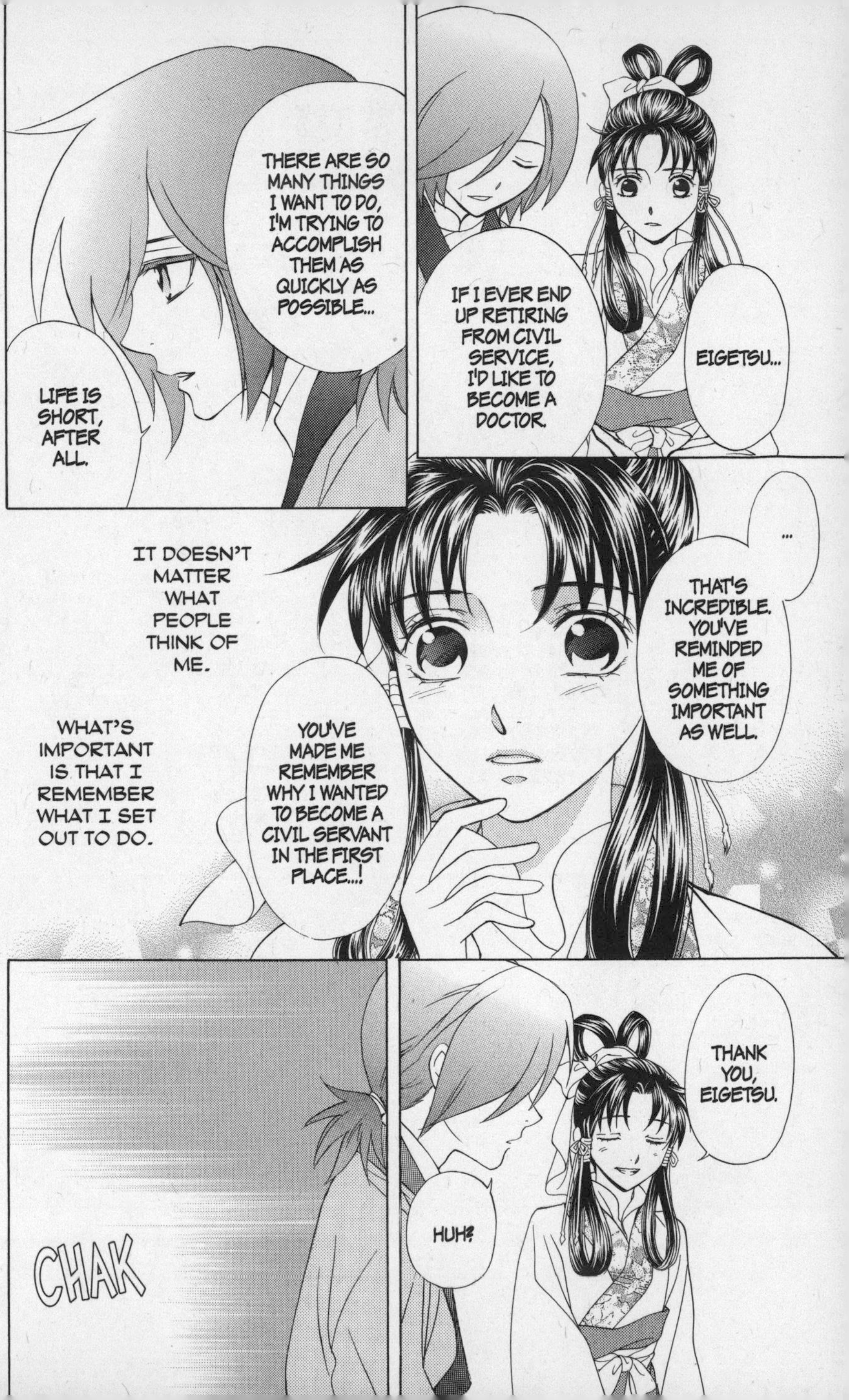
EIGETSU...
IF I EVER END UP RETIRING FROM CIVIL SERVICE, I'D LIKE TO BECOME A DOCTOR.
THERE ARE SO MANY THINGS I WANT TO DO, I'M TRYING TO ACCOMPLISH THEM AS QUICKLY AS POSSIBLE...
LIFE IS SHORT, AFTER ALL.
...
THAT'S INCREDIBLE. YOU'VE REMINDED ME OF SOMETHING IMPORTANT AS WELL.
YOU'VE MADE ME REMEMBER WHY I WANTED TO BECOME A CIVIL SERVANT IN THE FIRST PLACE...!
IT DOESN'T MATTER WHAT PEOPLE THINK OF ME.
WHAT'S IMPORTANT IS THAT I REMEMBER WHAT I SET OUT TO DO.
THANK YOU, EIGETSU.
HUH?
CHAK

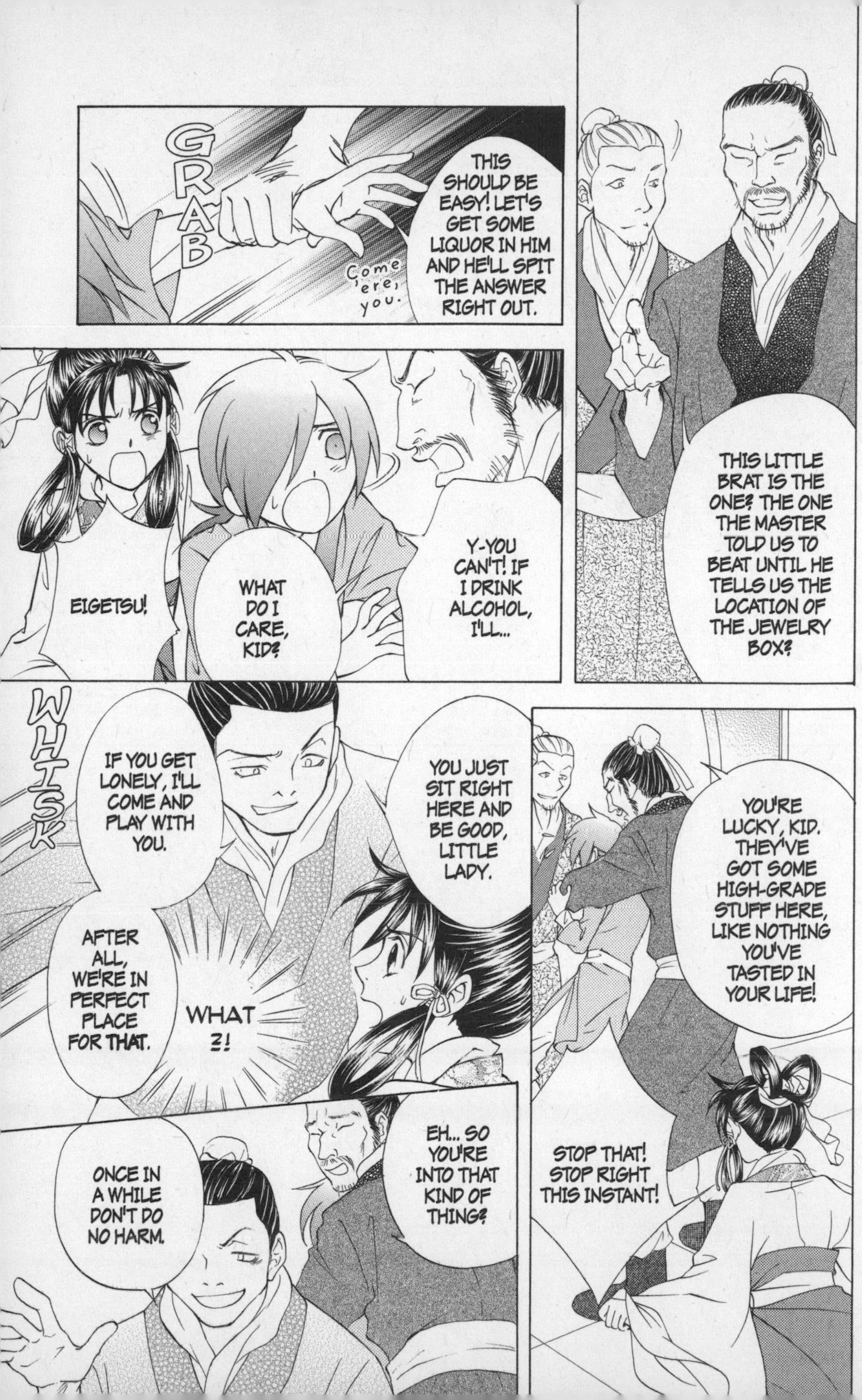
THIS LITTLE BRAT IS THE ONE? THE ONE THE MASTER TOLD US TO BEAT UNTIL HE TELLS US THE LOCATION OF THE JEWELRY BOX?
THIS SHOULD BE EASY! LET'S GET SOME LIQUOR IN HIM AND HE'LL SPIT THE ANSWER RIGHT OUT.
Come 'ere, you.
GRAB
Y-YOU CAN'T! IF I DRINK ALCOHOL, I'LL...
WHAT DO I CARE, KID?
EIGETSU!
YOU'RE LUCKY, KID. THEY'VE GOT SOME HIGH-GRADE STUFF HERE, LIKE NOTHING YOU'VE TASTED IN YOUR LIFE!
STOP THAT! STOP RIGHT THIS INSTANT!
YOU JUST SIT RIGHT HERE AND BE GOOD, LITTLE LADY.
IF YOU GET LONELY, I'LL COME AND PLAY WITH YOU.
WHISK
WHAT?!
AFTER ALL, WE'RE IN PERFECT PLACE FOR THAT.
EH... SO YOU'RE INTO THAT KIND OF THING?
ONCE IN A WHILE DON'T DO NO HARM.

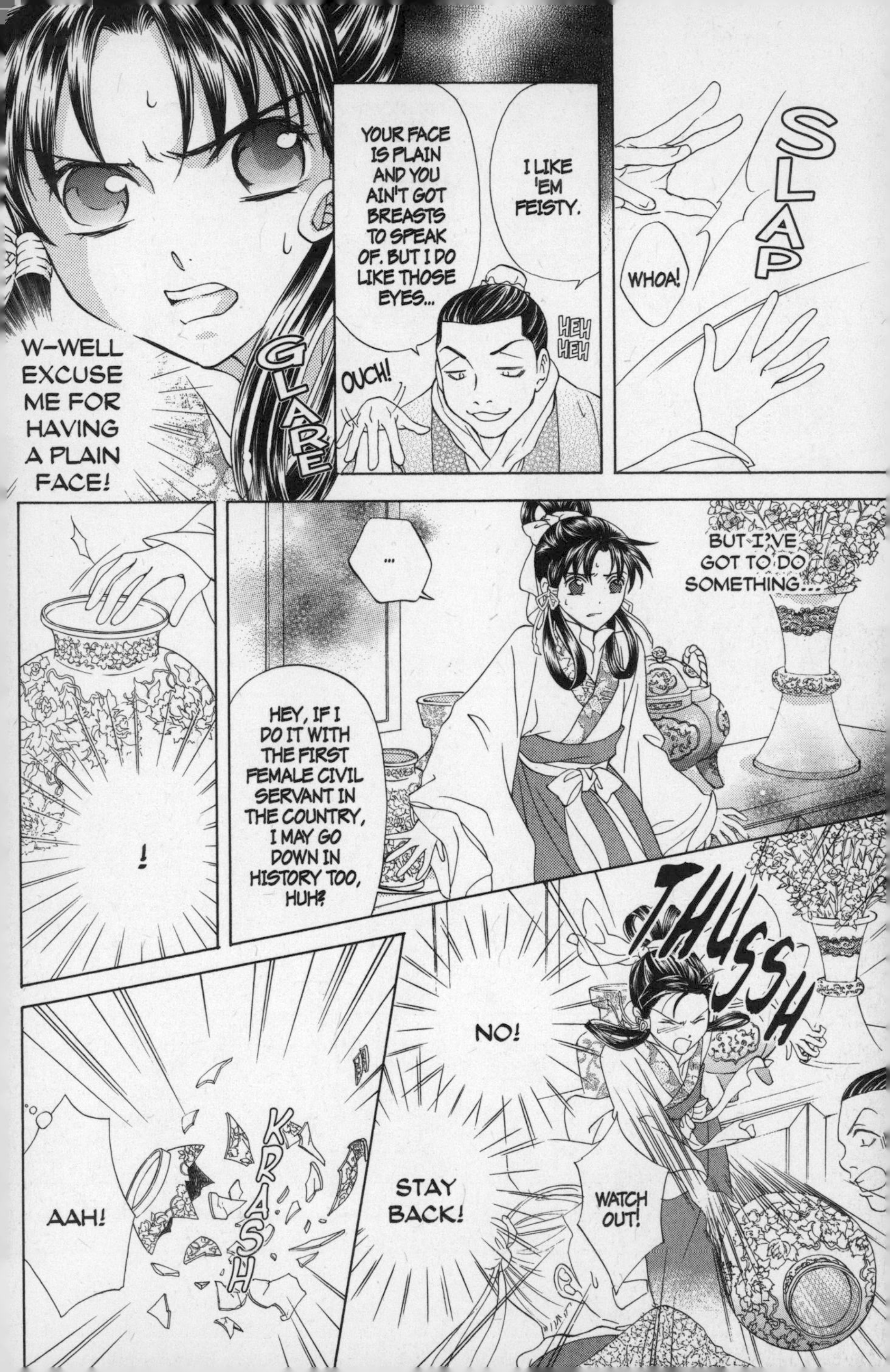
SLAP
WHOA!
I LIKE 'EM FEISTY.
YOUR FACE IS PLAIN AND YOU AIN'T GOT BREASTS TO SPEAK OF. BUT I DO LIKE THOSE EYES...
HEH HEH
OUCH!
GLARE
W-WELL EXCUSE ME FOR HAVING A PLAIN FACE!
BUT I'VE GOT TO DO SOMETHING...
...
HEY, IF I DO IT WITH THE FIRST FEMALE CIVIL SERVANT IN THE COUNTRY, I MAY GO DOWN IN HISTORY TOO, HUH?
!
THUSSH
NO!
WATCH OUT!
STAY BACK!
KRASH
AAH!

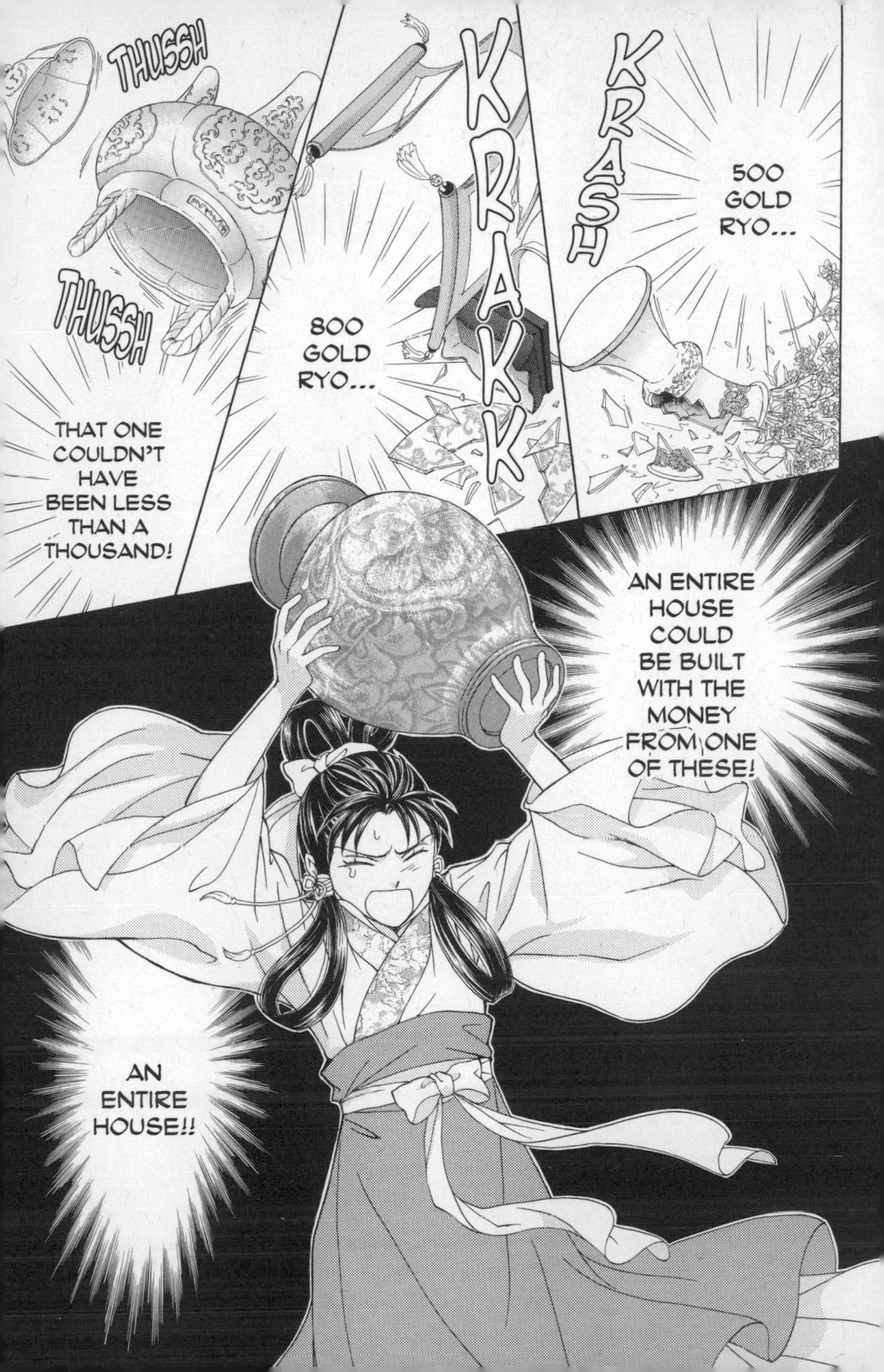
KRASH
500 GOLD RYO...
KRAKK
800 GOLD RYO...
THUSSH
THUSSH
THAT ONE COULDN'T HAVE BEEN LESS THAN A THOUSAND!
AN ENTIRE HOUSE COULD BE BUILT WITH THE MONEY FROM ONE OF THESE!
AN ENTIRE HOUSE!!

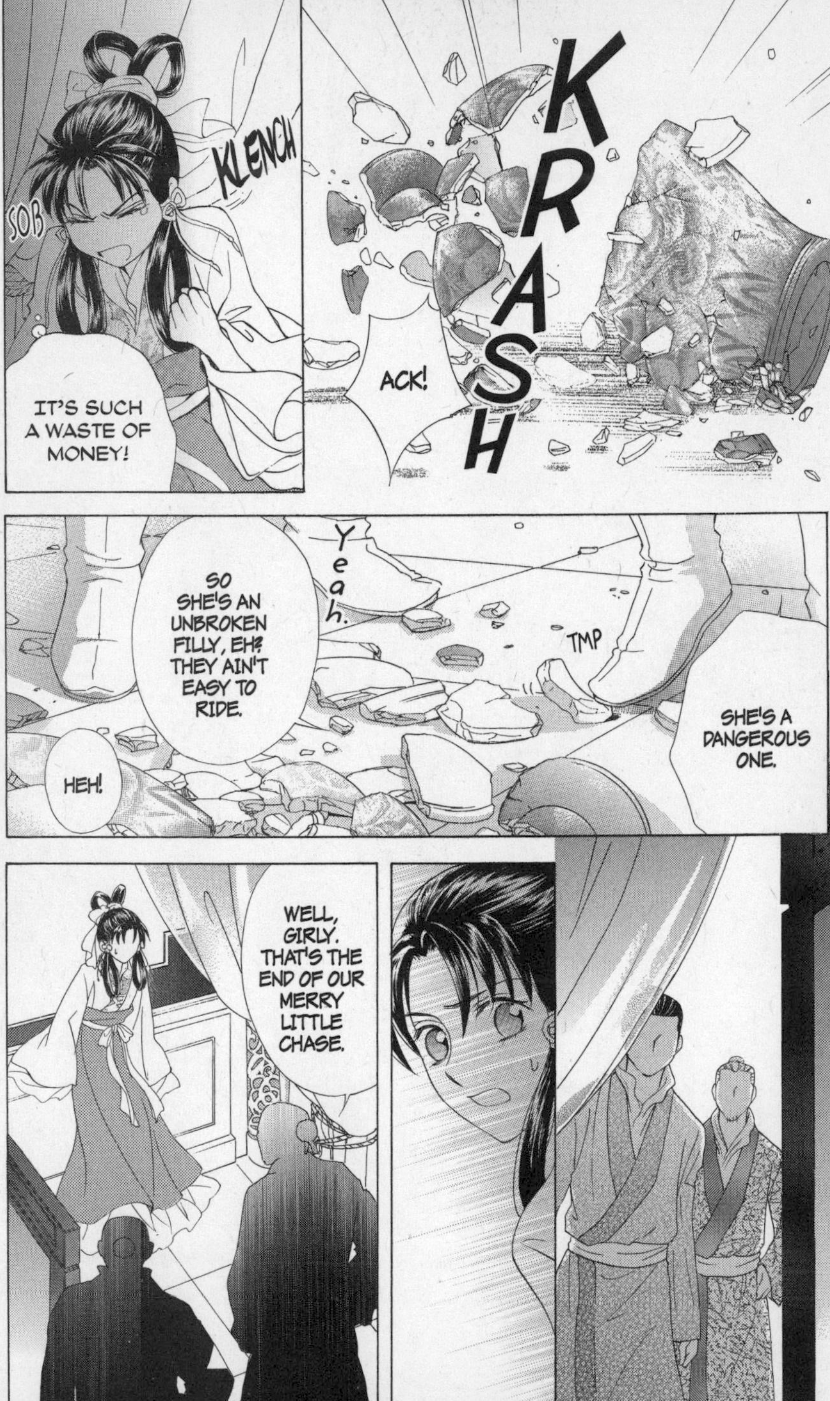
KRASH
ACK!
KLENCH
SOB
IT'S SUCH A WASTE OF MONEY!
SHE'S A DANGEROUS ONE.
TMP
Yeah.
SO SHE'S AN UNBROKEN FILLY, EH? THEY AIN'T EASY TO RIDE.
HEH!
WELL, GIRLY. THAT'S THE END OF OUR MERRY LITTLE CHASE.

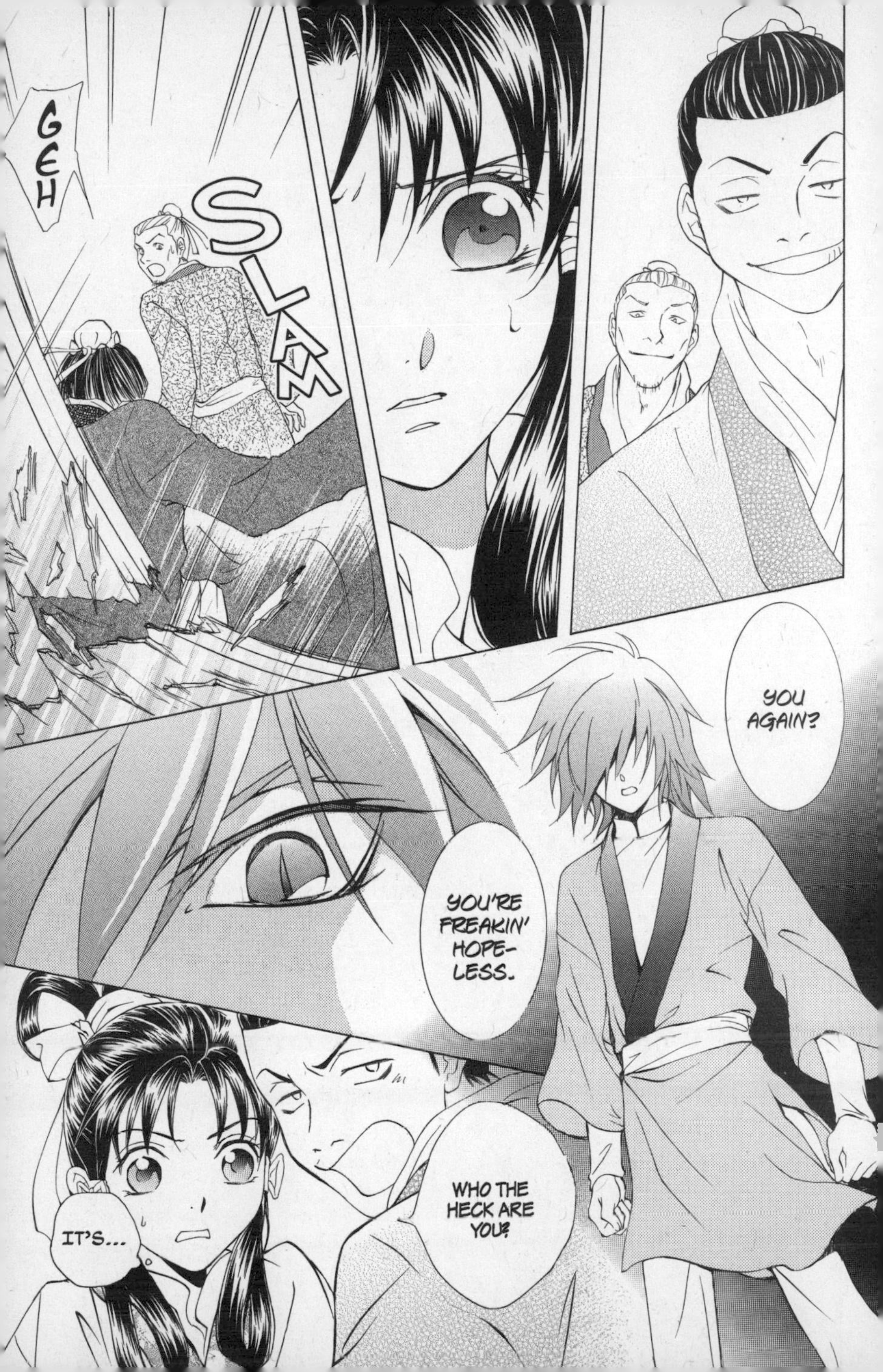
GEH
SLAM
YOU AGAIN?
YOU'RE FREAKIN' HOPE-LESS.
WHO THE HECK ARE YOU?
IT'S...

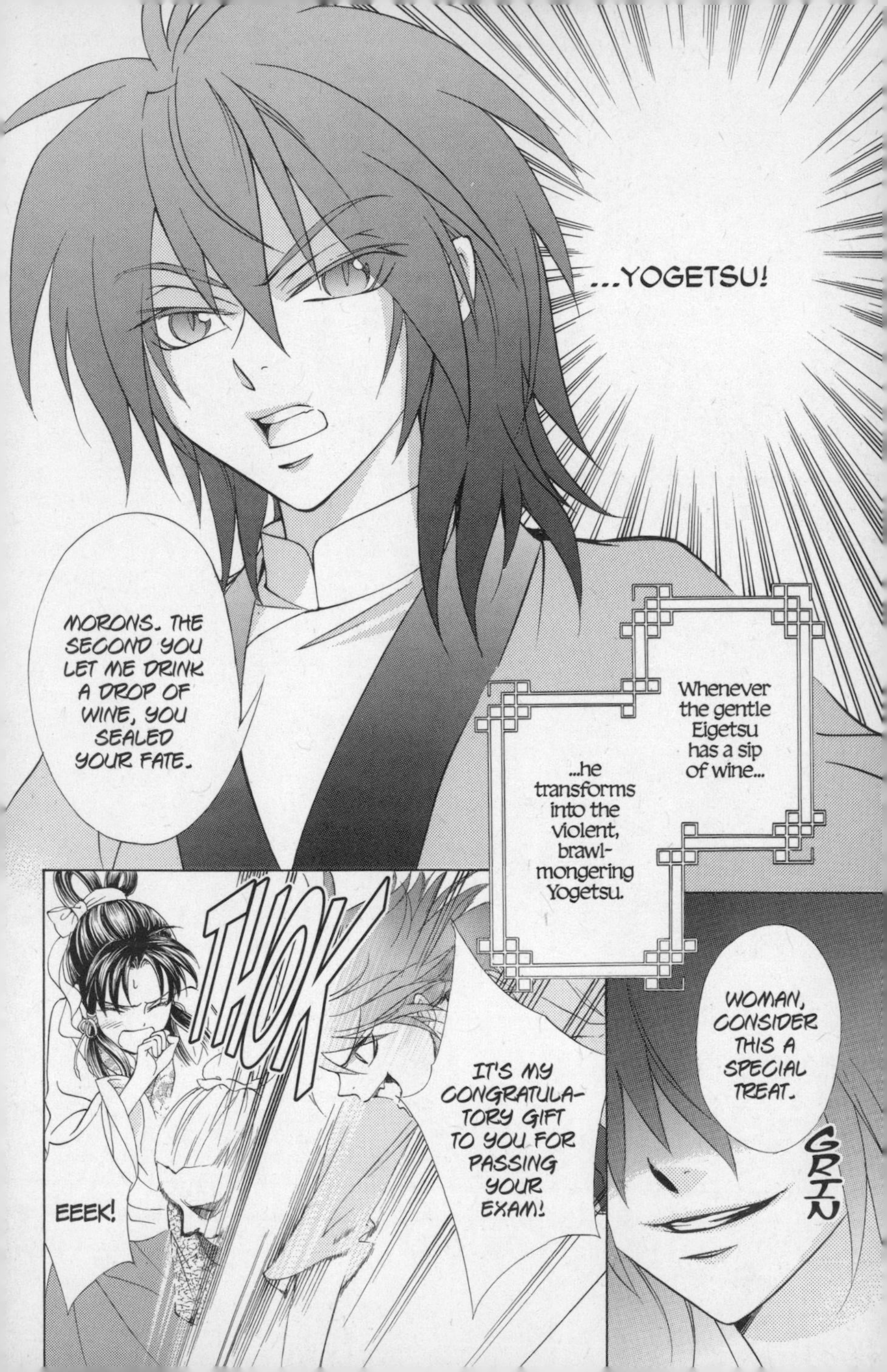
...YOGETSU!
MORONS. THE SECOND YOU LET ME DRINK A DROP OF WINE, YOU SEALED YOUR FATE.
Whenever the gentle Eigetsu has a sip of wine...
...he transforms into the violent, brawl-mongering Yogetsu.
WOMAN, CONSIDER THIS A SPECIAL TREAT.
GRIN
IT'S MY CONGRATULATORY GIFT TO YOU FOR PASSING YOUR EXAM!
THOK
EEEK!

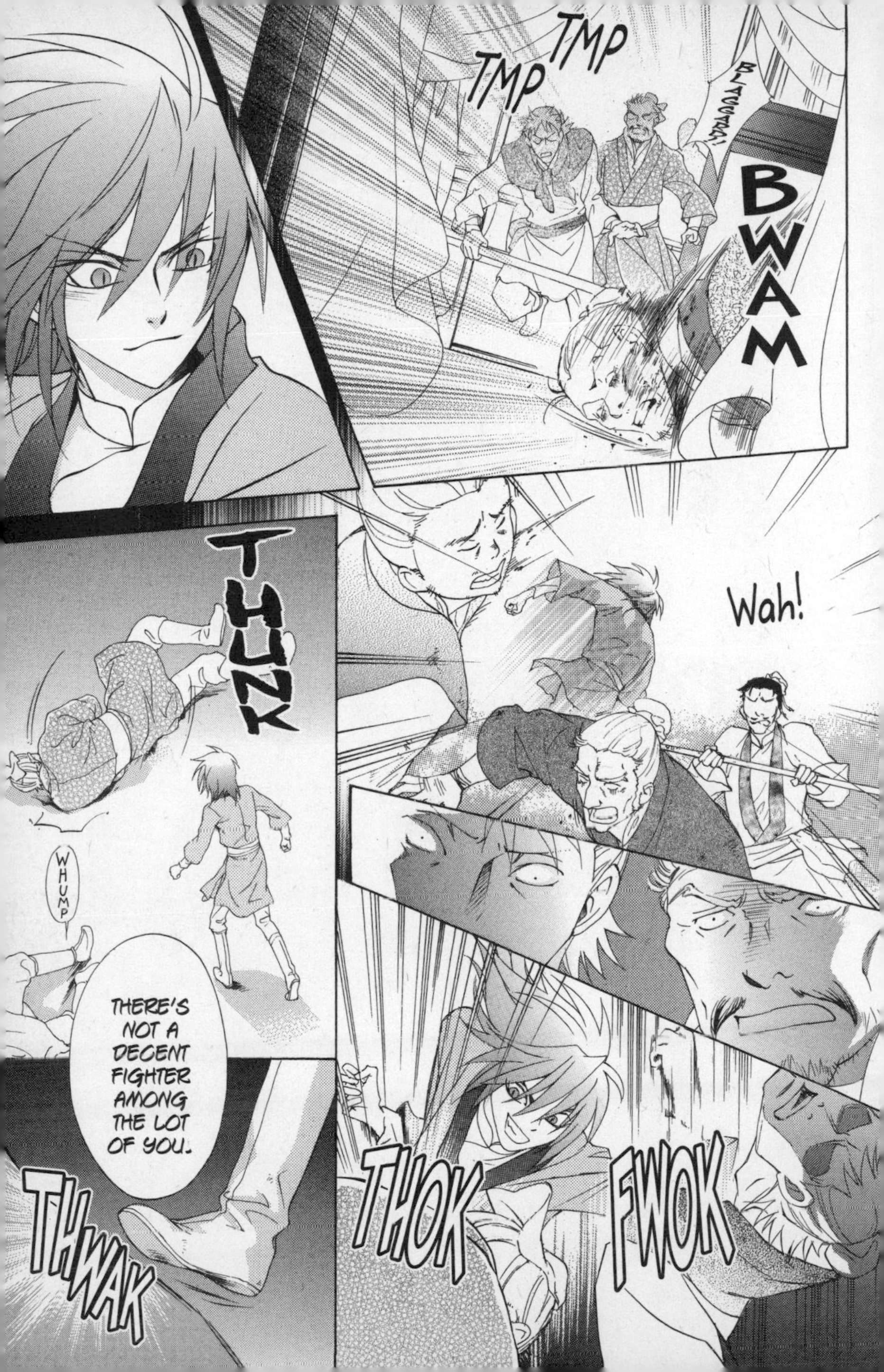
TMP TMP
BLAGGARDS!
BWAM
Wah!
THUNK
WHUMP
THERE'S NOT A DECENT FIGHTER AMONG THE LOT OF YOU.
FWOK
THOK
THWAK

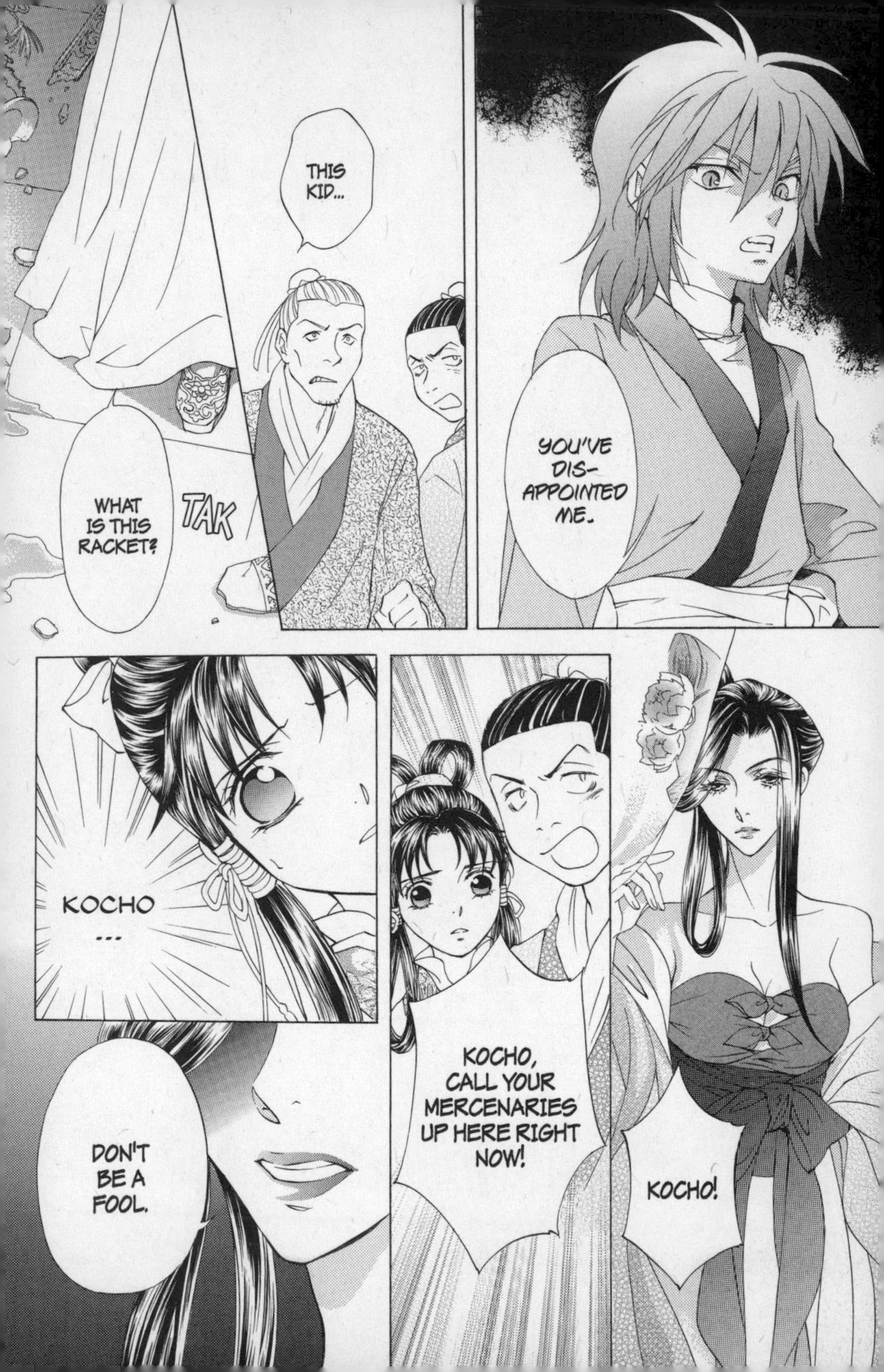
YOU'VE DIS-APPOINTED ME.
THIS KID...
TAK
WHAT IS THIS RACKET?
KOCHO!
KOCHO, CALL YOUR MERCENARIES UP HERE RIGHT NOW!
KOCHO ...
DON'T BE A FOOL.

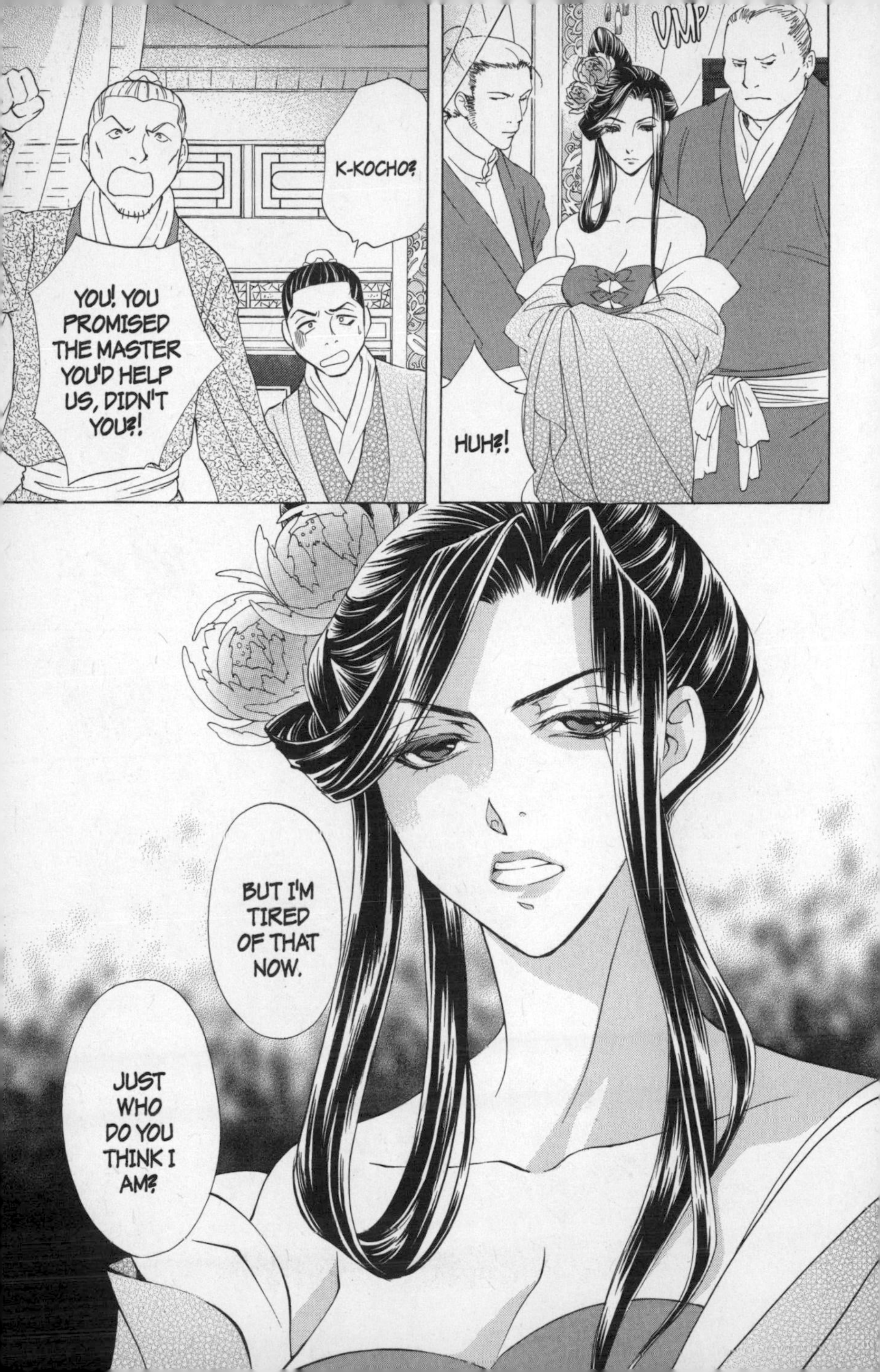
VMP
HUH?!
K-KOCHO?
YOU! YOU PROMISED THE MASTER YOU'D HELP US, DIDN'T YOU?!
BUT I'M TIRED OF THAT NOW.
JUST WHO DO YOU THINK I AM?

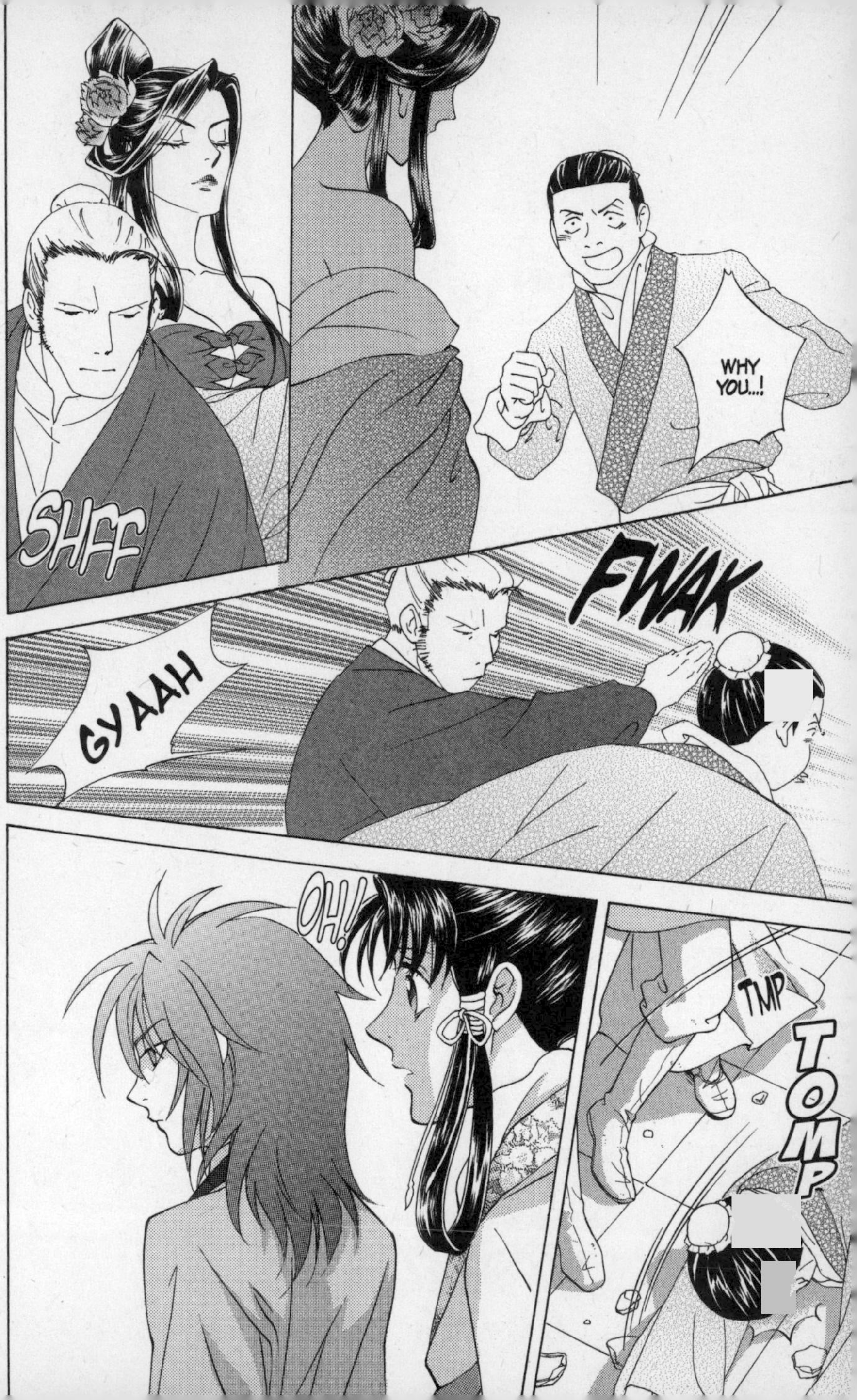
WHY YOU...!
SHFF
FWAK
GYAAH
TMP
TOMP
OH!

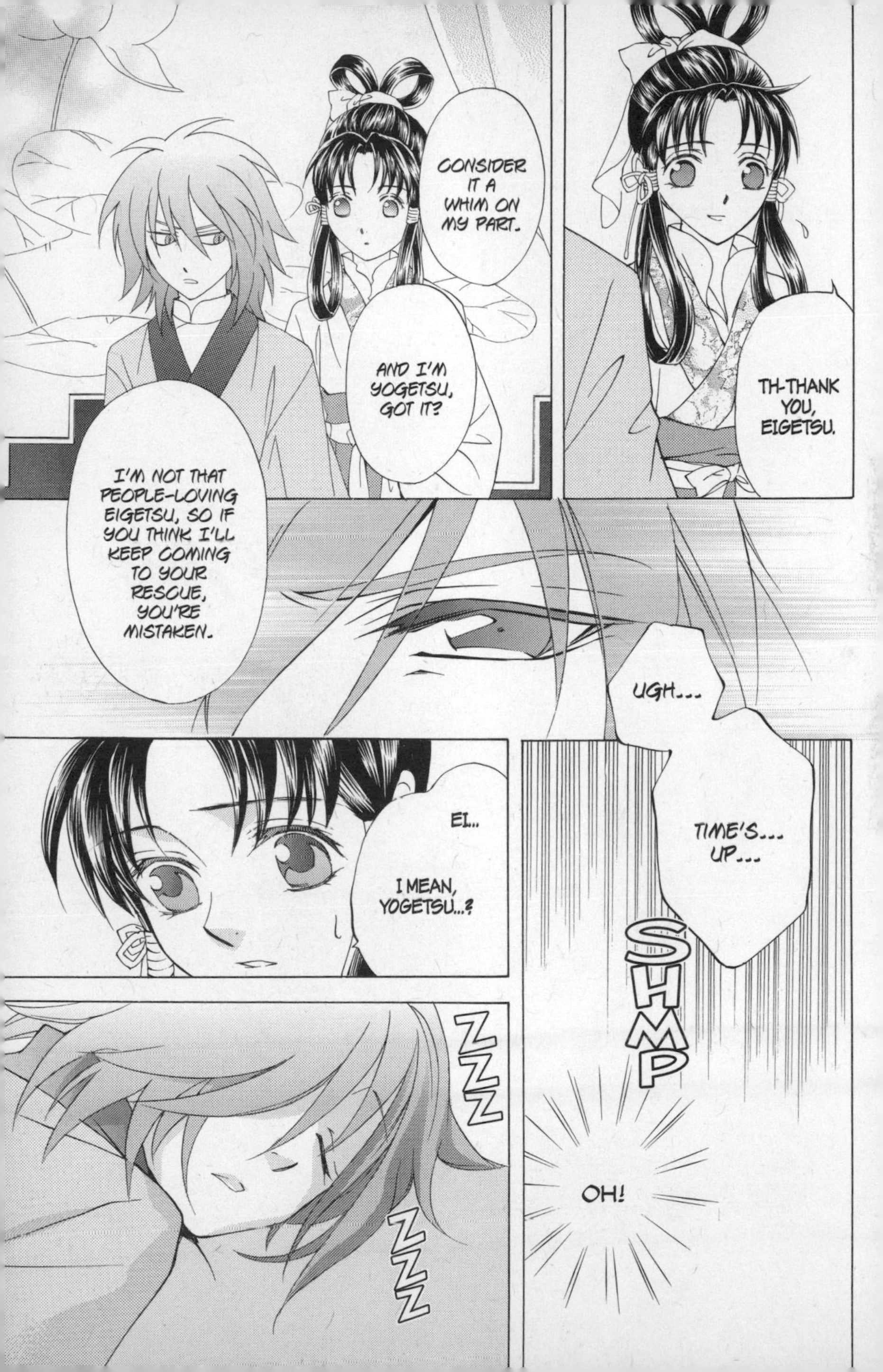
TH-THANK YOU, EIGETSU.
CONSIDER IT A WHIM ON MY PART.
AND I'M YOGETSU, GOT IT?
I'M NOT THAT PEOPLE-LOVING EIGETSU, SO IF YOU THINK I'LL KEEP COMING TO YOUR RESCUE, YOU'RE MISTAKEN.
UGH...
TIME'S... UP...
SHMP
OH!
EI...
I MEAN, YOGETSU...?
ZZZ
ZZZ

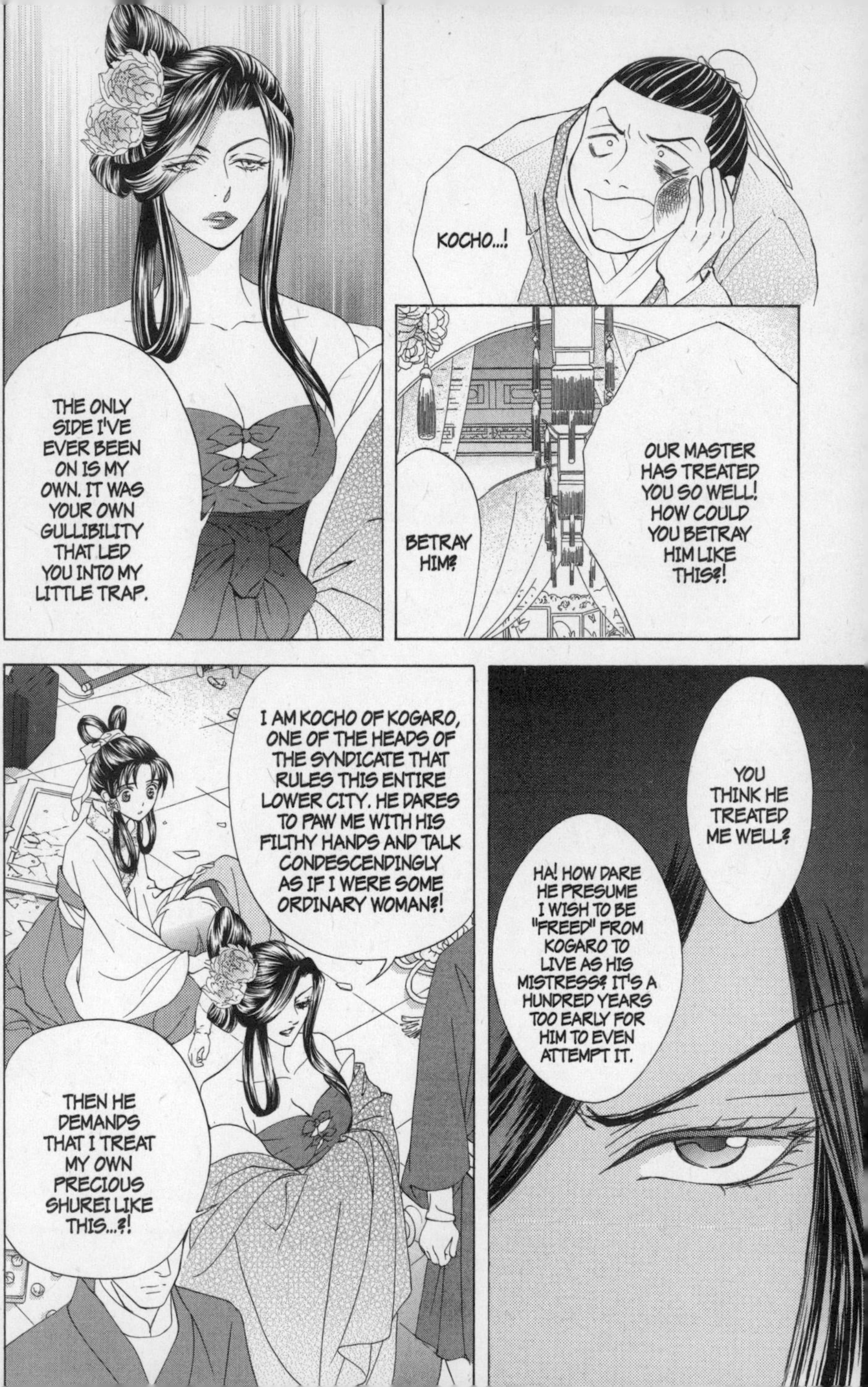
KOCHO...!
OUR MASTER HAS TREATED YOU SO WELL! HOW COULD YOU BETRAY HIM LIKE THIS?!
BETRAY HIM?
THE ONLY SIDE I'VE EVER BEEN ON IS MY OWN. IT WAS YOUR OWN GULLIBILITY THAT LED YOU INTO MY LITTLE TRAP.
YOU THINK HE TREATED ME WELL?
HA! HOW DARE HE PRESUME I WISH TO BE "FREED" FROM KOGARO TO LIVE AS HIS MISTRESS? IT'S A HUNDRED YEARS TOO EARLY FOR HIM TO EVEN ATTEMPT IT.
I AM KOCHO OF KOGARO, ONE OF THE HEADS OF THE SYNDICATE THAT RULES THIS ENTIRE LOWER CITY. HE DARES TO PAW ME WITH HIS FILTHY HANDS AND TALK CONDESCENDINGLY AS IF I WERE SOME ORDINARY WOMAN?!
THEN HE DEMANDS THAT I TREAT MY OWN PRECIOUS SHUREI LIKE THIS...?!

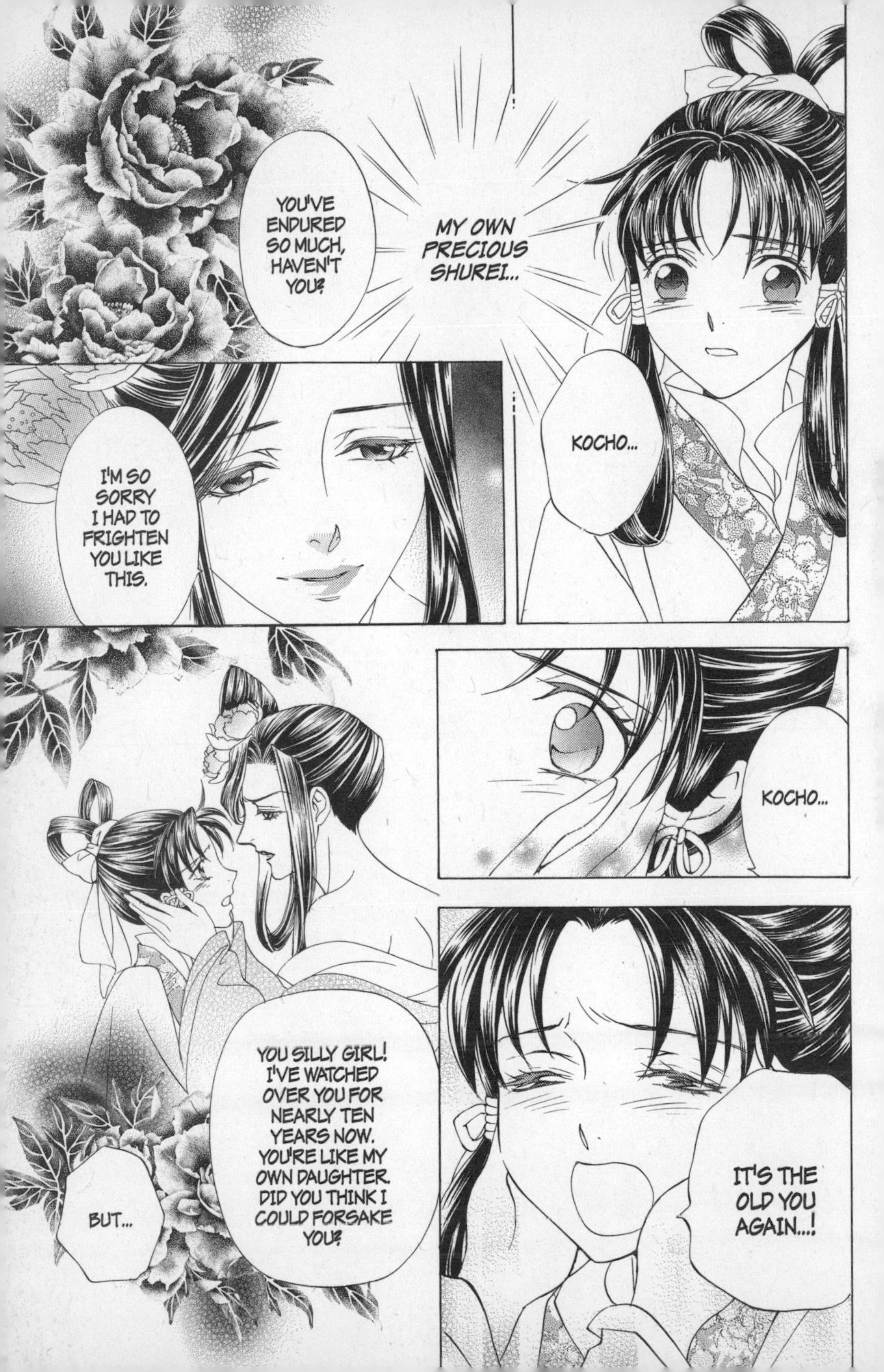
MY OWN PRECIOUS SHUREI...
KOCHO...
YOU'VE ENDURED SO MUCH, HAVEN'T YOU?
I'M SO SORRY I HAD TO FRIGHTEN YOU LIKE THIS.
KOCHO...
IT'S THE OLD YOU AGAIN...!
YOU SILLY GIRL! I'VE WATCHED OVER YOU FOR NEARLY TEN YEARS NOW. YOU'RE LIKE MY OWN DAUGHTER. DID YOU THINK I COULD FORSAKE YOU?
BUT...

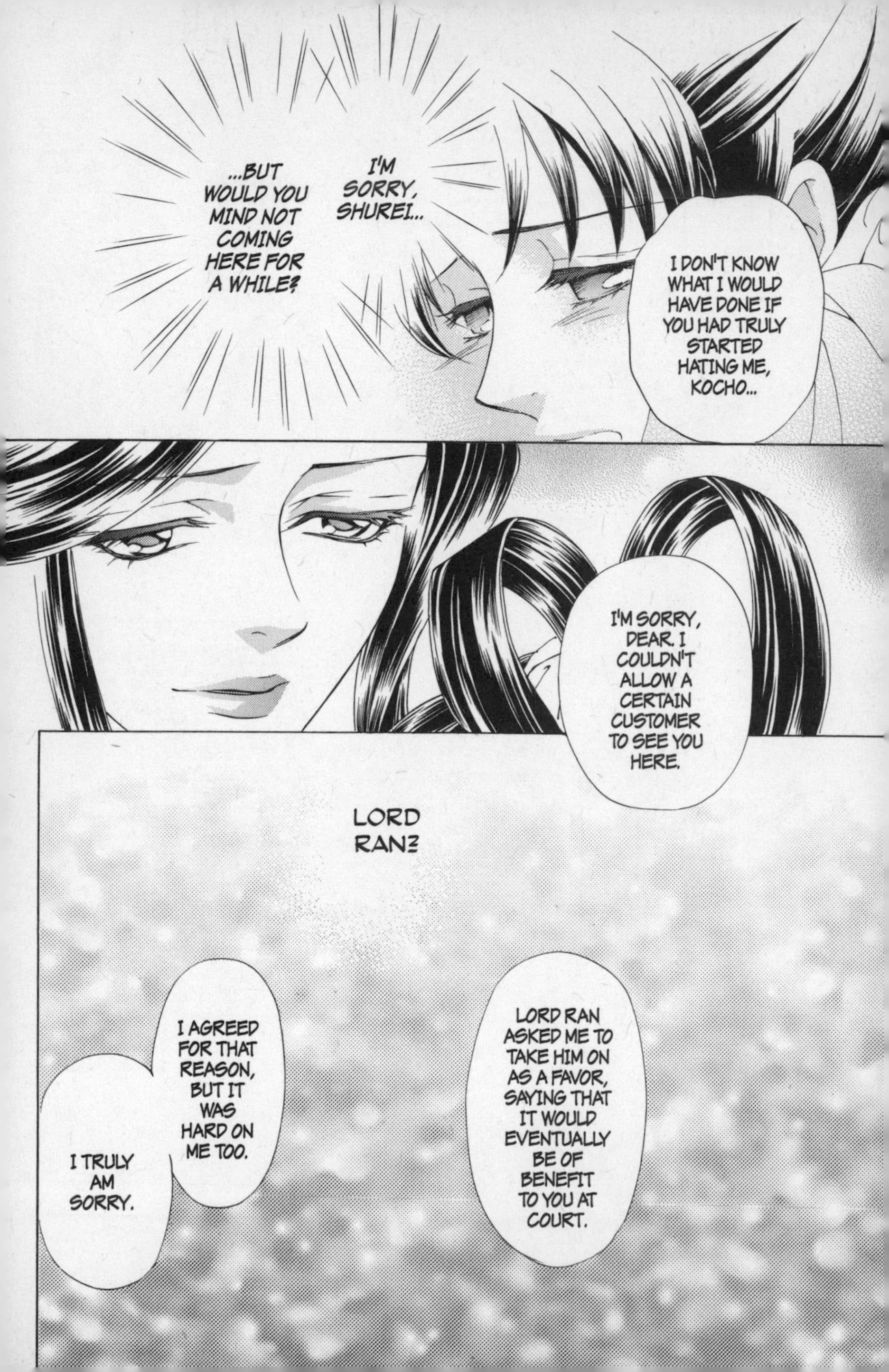
I DON'T KNOW WHAT I WOULD HAVE DONE IF YOU HAD TRULY STARTED HATING ME, KOCHO...
I'M SORRY, SHUREI...
...BUT WOULD YOU MIND NOT COMING HERE FOR A WHILE?
I'M SORRY, DEAR. I COULDN'T ALLOW A CERTAIN CUSTOMER TO SEE YOU HERE.
LORD RAN?
LORD RAN ASKED ME TO TAKE HIM ON AS A FAVOR, SAYING THAT IT WOULD EVENTUALLY BE OF BENEFIT TO YOU AT COURT.
I AGREED FOR THAT REASON, BUT IT WAS HARD ON ME TOO.
I TRULY AM SORRY.

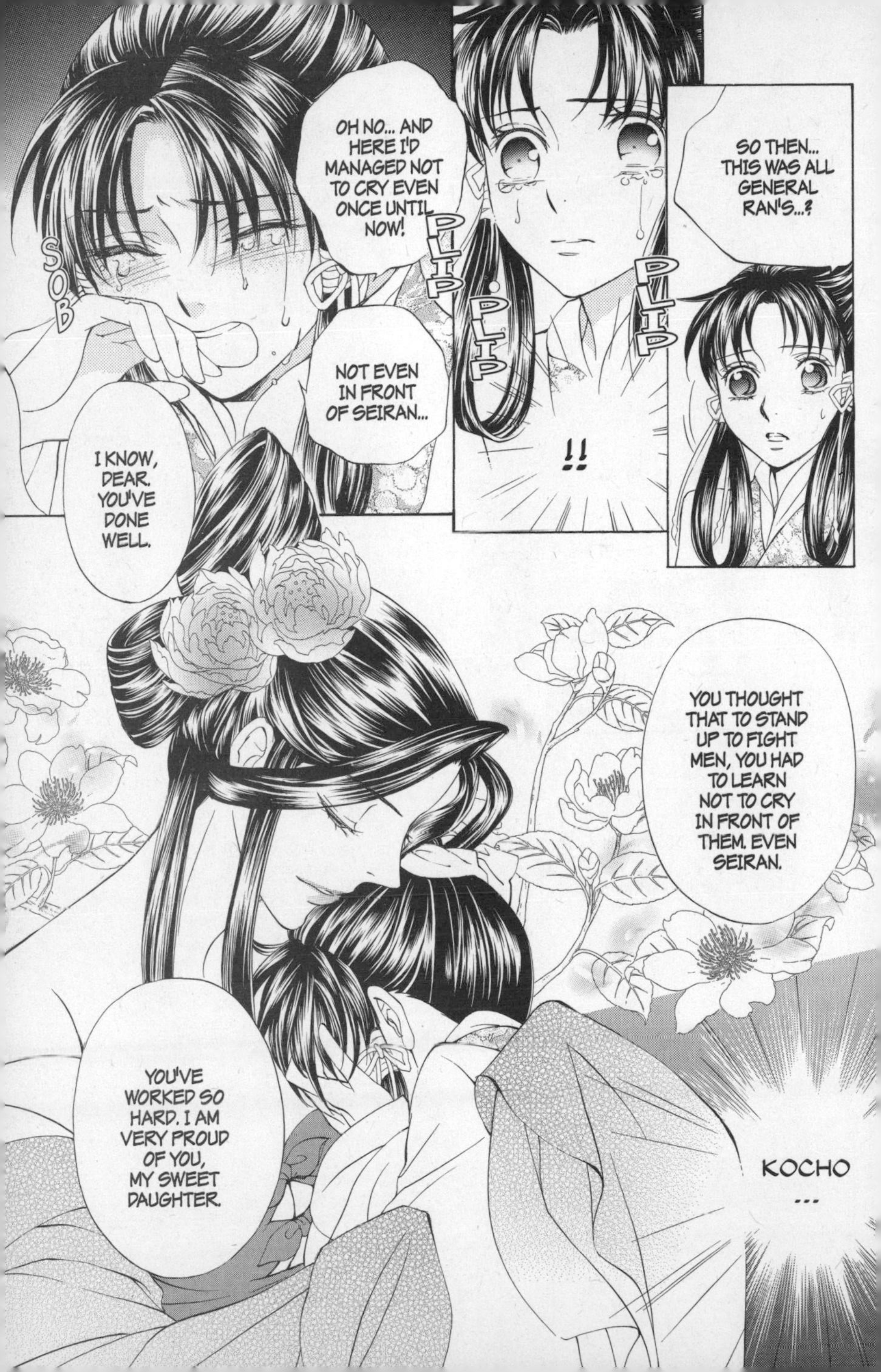
SO THEN... THIS WAS ALL GENERAL RAN'S...?
PLIP
PLIP
PLIP
!!
OH NO... AND HERE I'D MANAGED NOT TO CRY EVEN ONCE UNTIL NOW!
SOB
NOT EVEN IN FRONT OF SEIRAN...
I KNOW, DEAR. YOU'VE DONE WELL.
YOU THOUGHT THAT TO STAND UP TO FIGHT MEN, YOU HAD TO LEARN NOT TO CRY IN FRONT OF THEM. EVEN SEIRAN.
YOU'VE WORKED SO HARD. I AM VERY PROUD OF YOU, MY SWEET DAUGHTER.
KOCHO ...

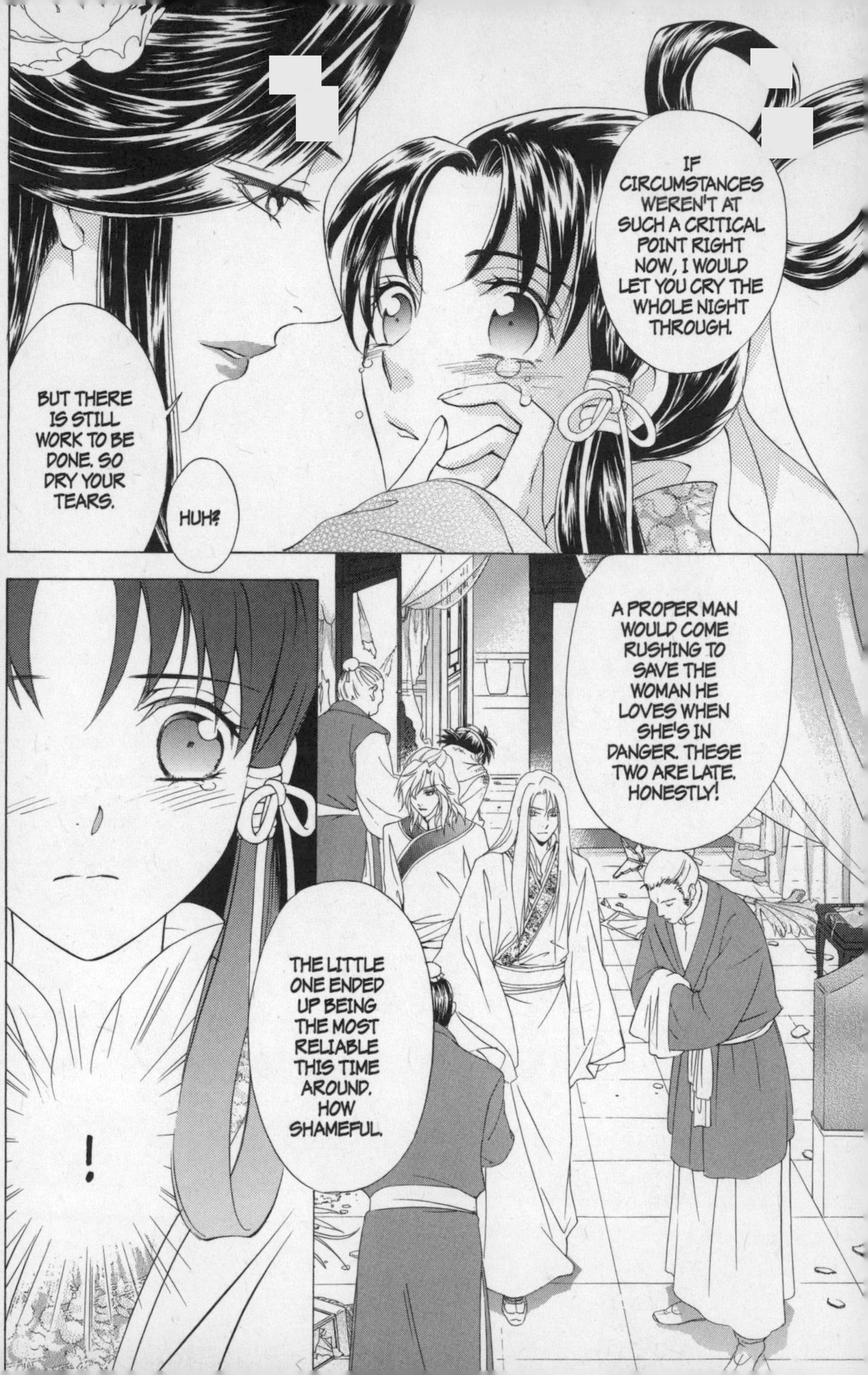
IF CIRCUMSTANCES WEREN'T AT SUCH A CRITICAL POINT RIGHT NOW, I WOULD LET YOU CRY THE WHOLE NIGHT THROUGH.
BUT THERE IS STILL WORK TO BE DONE. SO DRY YOUR TEARS.
HUH?
A PROPER MAN WOULD COME RUSHING TO SAVE THE WOMAN HE LOVES WHEN SHE'S IN DANGER. THESE TWO ARE LATE. HONESTLY!
THE LITTLE ONE ENDED UP BEING THE MOST RELIABLE THIS TIME AROUND. HOW SHAMEFUL.
!

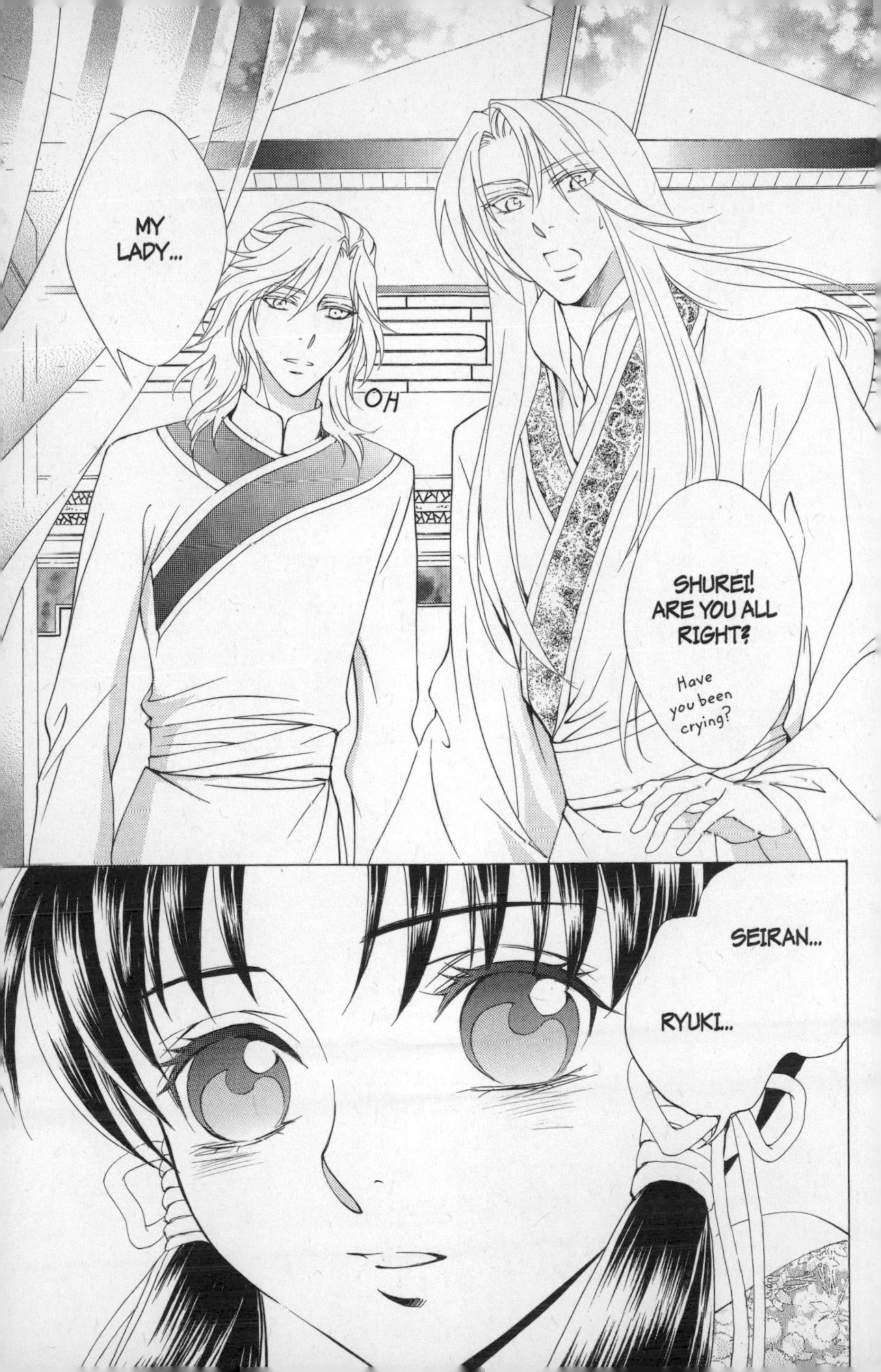
SHUREI! ARE YOU ALL RIGHT?
Have you been crying?
OH
MY LADY...
SEIRAN...
RYUKI...

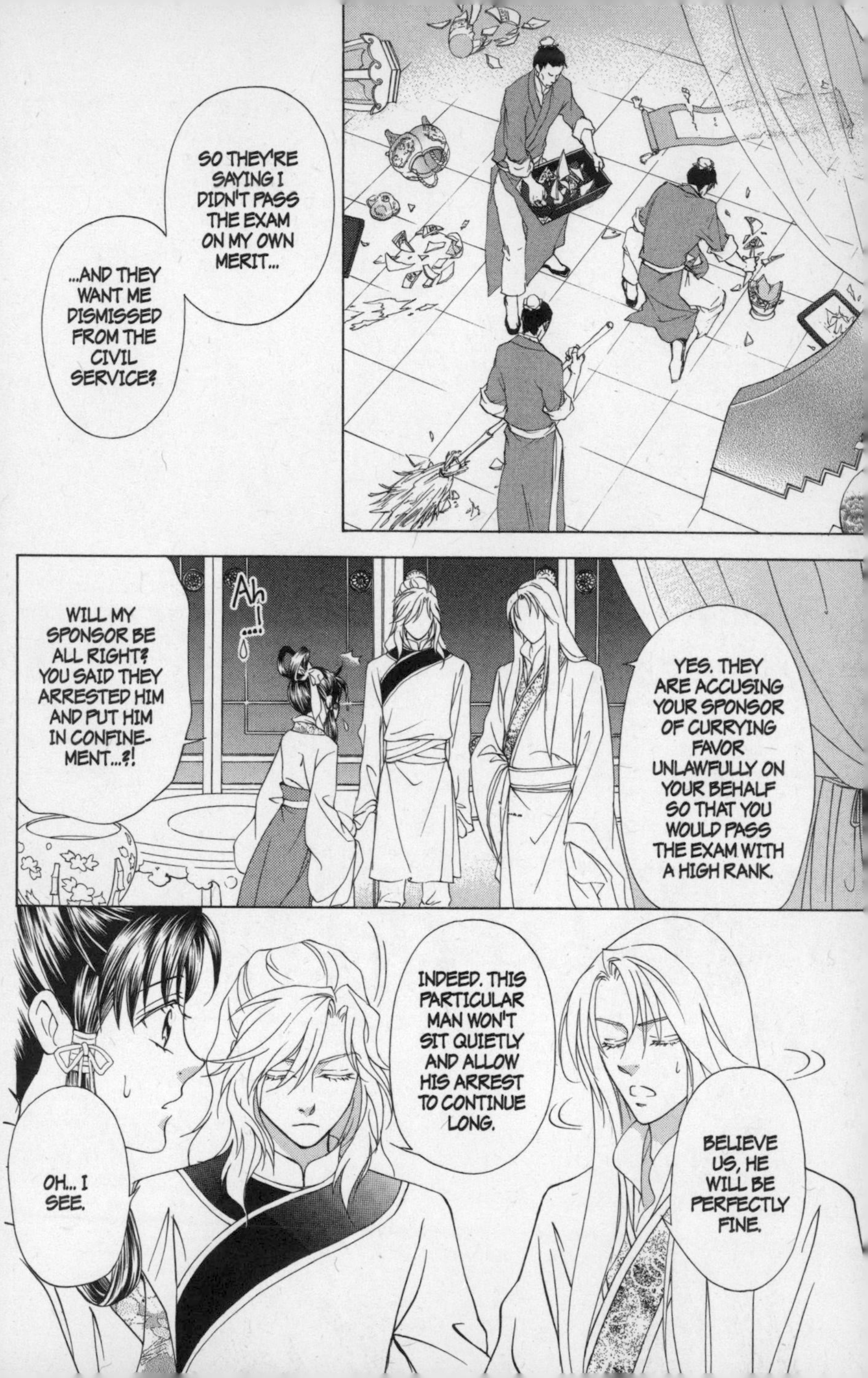
SO THEY'RE SAYING I DIDN'T PASS THE EXAM ON MY OWN MERIT...
...AND THEY WANT ME DISMISSED FROM THE CIVIL SERVICE?
WILL MY SPONSOR BE ALL RIGHT? YOU SAID THEY ARRESTED HIM AND PUT HIM IN CONFINE-MENT...?!
Ah...!
YES. THEY ARE ACCUSING YOUR SPONSOR OF CURRYING FAVOR UNLAWFULLY ON YOUR BEHALF SO THAT YOU WOULD PASS THE EXAM WITH A HIGH RANK.
INDEED. THIS PARTICULAR MAN WON'T SIT QUIETLY AND ALLOW HIS ARREST TO CONTINUE LONG.
BELIEVE US, HE WILL BE PERFECTLY FINE.
OH... I SEE.

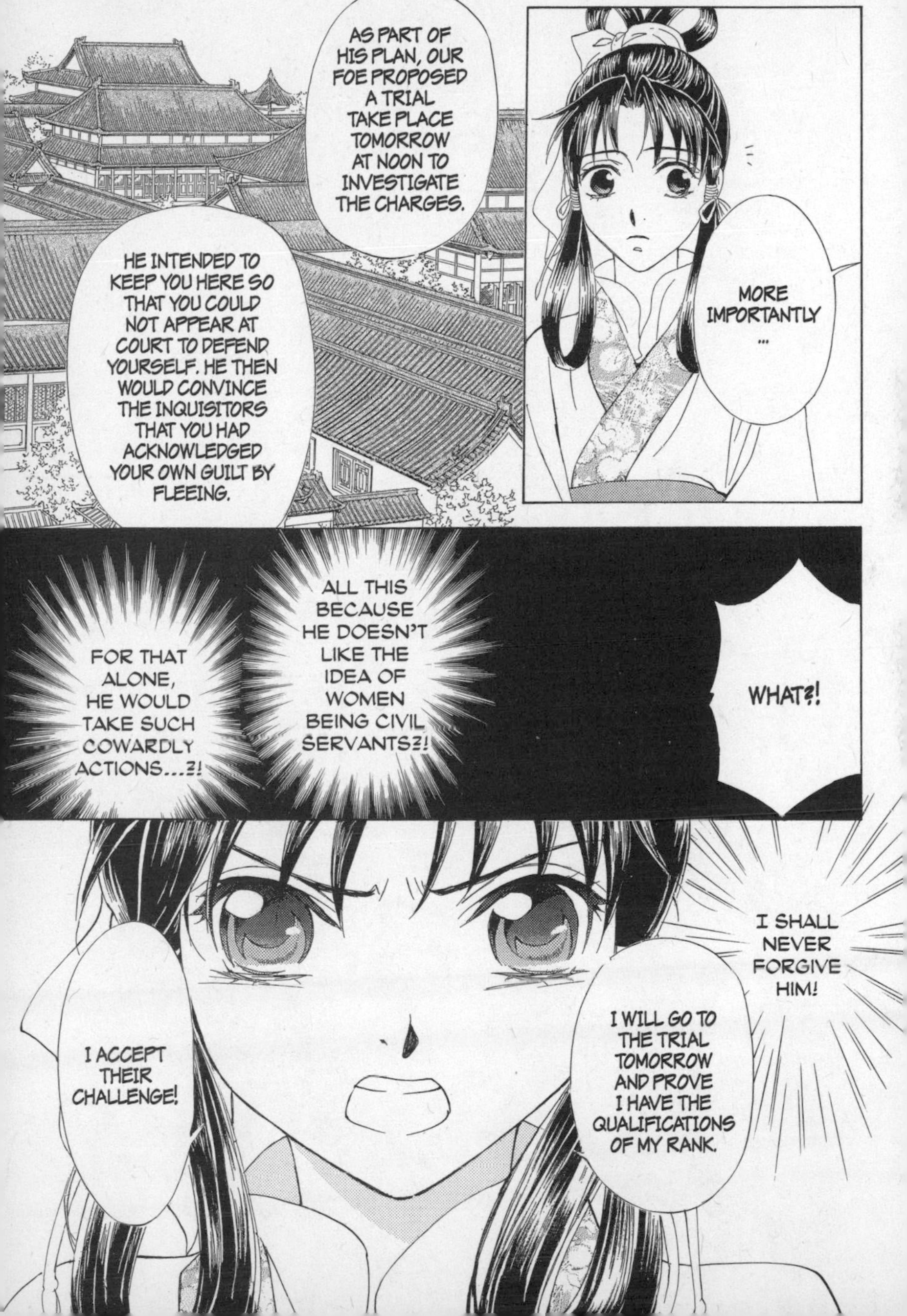
MORE IMPORTANTLY ...
AS PART OF HIS PLAN, OUR FOE PROPOSED A TRIAL TAKE PLACE TOMORROW AT NOON TO INVESTIGATE THE CHARGES.
HE INTENDED TO KEEP YOU HERE SO THAT YOU COULD NOT APPEAR AT COURT TO DEFEND YOURSELF. HE THEN WOULD CONVINCE THE INQUISITORS THAT YOU HAD ACKNOWLEDGED YOUR OWN GUILT BY FLEEING.
WHAT?!
ALL THIS BECAUSE HE DOESN'T LIKE THE IDEA OF WOMEN BEING CIVIL SERVANTS?!
FOR THAT ALONE, HE WOULD TAKE SUCH COWARDLY ACTIONS...?!
I SHALL NEVER FORGIVE HIM!
I WILL GO TO THE TRIAL TOMORROW AND PROVE I HAVE THE QUALIFICATIONS OF MY RANK.
I ACCEPT THEIR CHALLENGE!

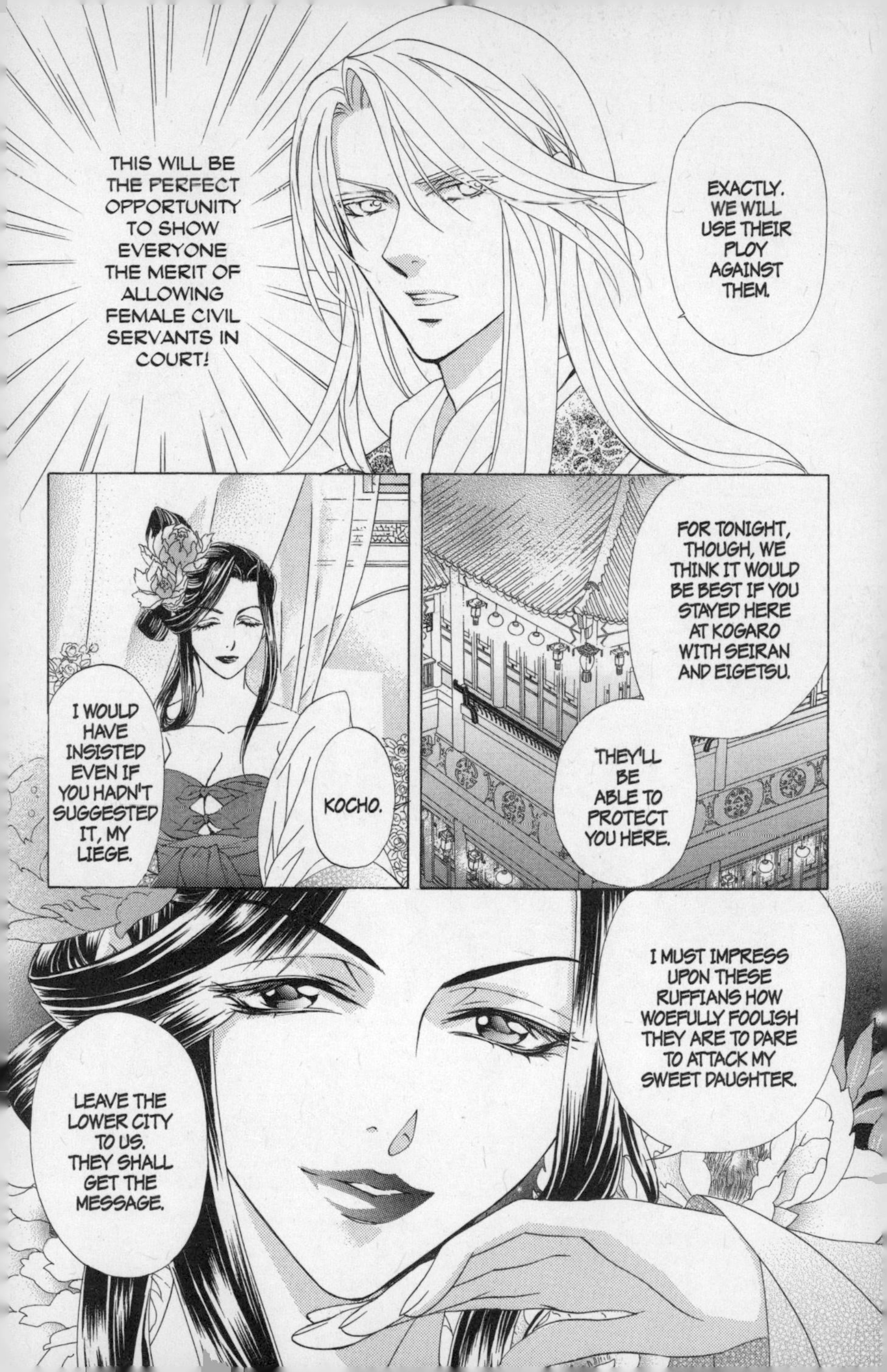
EXACTLY. WE WILL USE THEIR PLOY AGAINST THEM.
THIS WILL BE THE PERFECT OPPORTUNITY TO SHOW EVERYONE THE MERIT OF ALLOWING FEMALE CIVIL SERVANTS IN COURT!
FOR TONIGHT, THOUGH, WE THINK IT WOULD BE BEST IF YOU STAYED HERE AT KOGARO WITH SEIRAN AND EIGETSU.
THEY'LL BE ABLE TO PROTECT YOU HERE.
KOCHO.
I WOULD HAVE INSISTED EVEN IF YOU HADN'T SUGGESTED IT, MY LIEGE.
I MUST IMPRESS UPON THESE RUFFIANS HOW WOEFULLY FOOLISH THEY ARE TO DARE TO ATTACK MY SWEET DAUGHTER.
LEAVE THE LOWER CITY TO US. THEY SHALL GET THE MESSAGE.

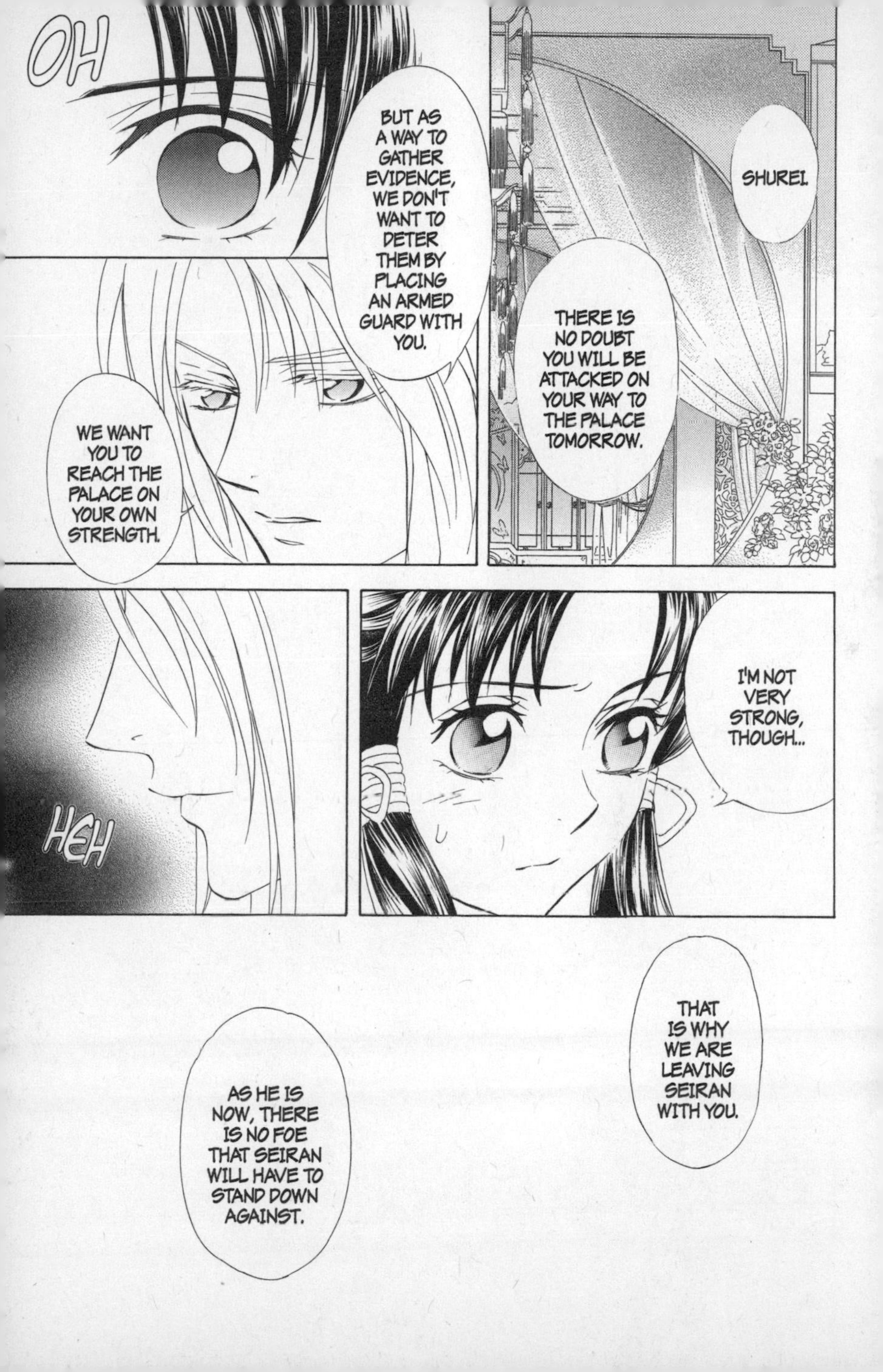
SHUREI.
THERE IS NO DOUBT YOU WILL BE ATTACKED ON YOUR WAY TO THE PALACE TOMORROW.
OH
BUT AS A WAY TO GATHER EVIDENCE, WE DON'T WANT TO DETER THEM BY PLACING AN ARMED GUARD WITH YOU.
WE WANT YOU TO REACH THE PALACE ON YOUR OWN STRENGTH.
I'M NOT VERY STRONG, THOUGH...
HEH
THAT IS WHY WE ARE LEAVING SEIRAN WITH YOU.
AS HE IS NOW, THERE IS NO FOE THAT SEIRAN WILL HAVE TO STAND DOWN AGAINST.

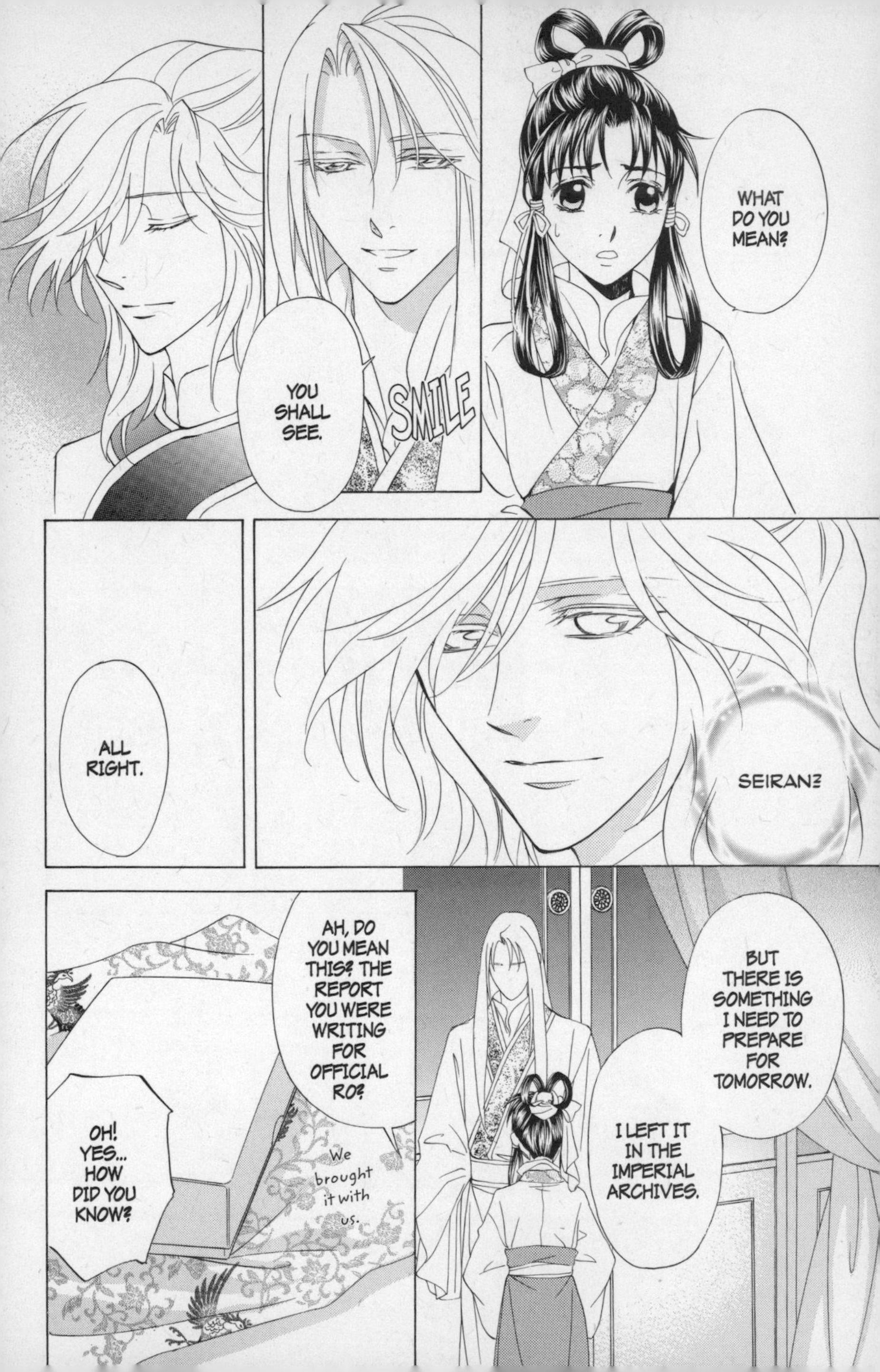
WHAT DO YOU MEAN?
YOU SHALL SEE.
SMILE
SEIRAN?
ALL RIGHT.
BUT THERE IS SOMETHING I NEED TO PREPARE FOR TOMORROW.
I LEFT IT IN THE IMPERIAL ARCHIVES.
AH, DO YOU MEAN THIS? THE REPORT YOU WERE WRITING FOR OFFICIAL RO?
We brought it with us.
OH! YES... HOW DID YOU KNOW?

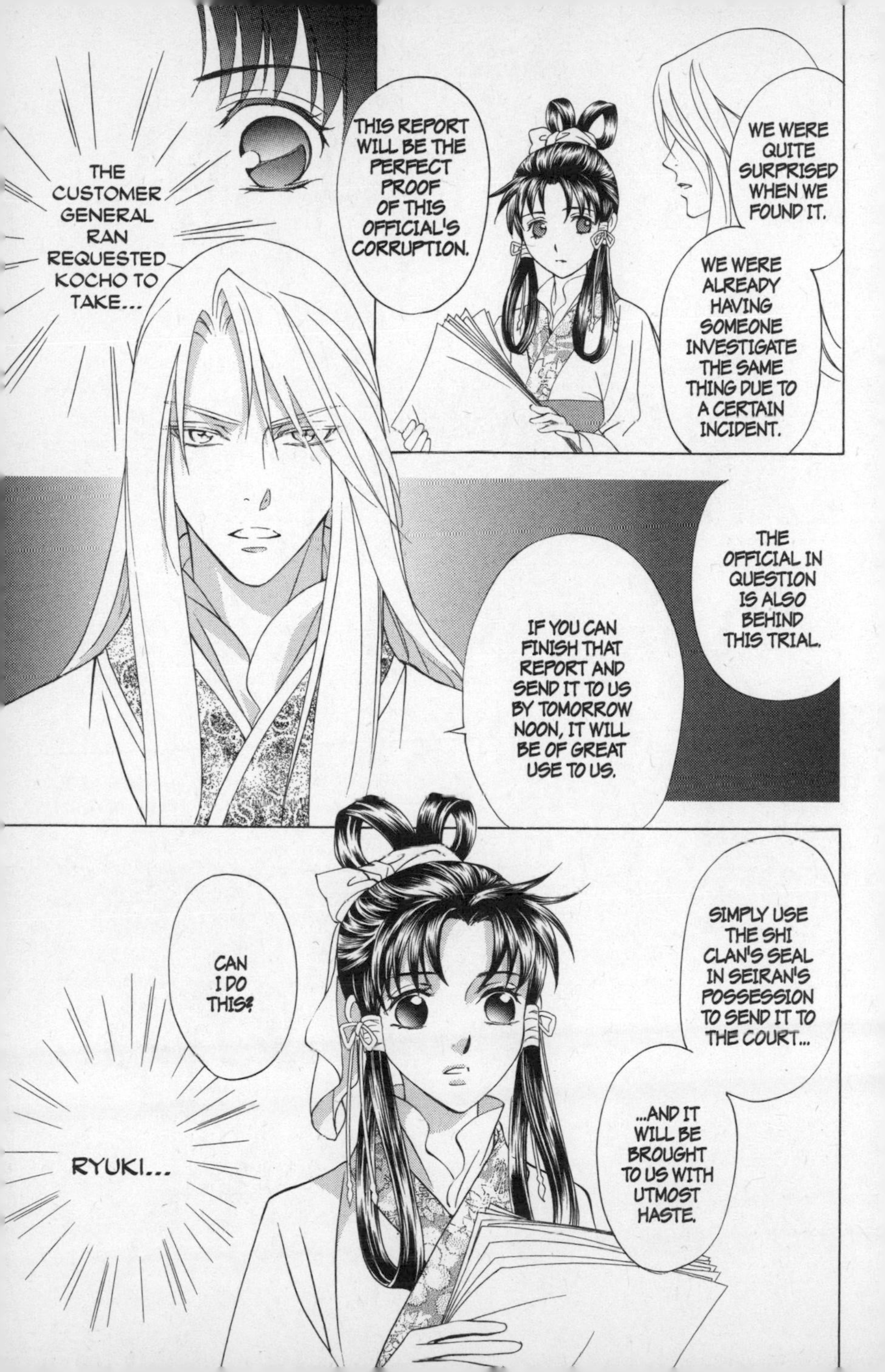
WE WERE QUITE SURPRISED WHEN WE FOUND IT.
WE WERE ALREADY HAVING SOMEONE INVESTIGATE THE SAME THING DUE TO A CERTAIN INCIDENT.
THIS REPORT WILL BE THE PERFECT PROOF OF THIS OFFICIAL'S CORRUPTION.
THE CUSTOMER GENERAL RAN REQUESTED KOCHO TO TAKE...
THE OFFICIAL IN QUESTION IS ALSO BEHIND THIS TRIAL.
IF YOU CAN FINISH THAT REPORT AND SEND IT TO US BY TOMORROW NOON, IT WILL BE OF GREAT USE TO US.
SIMPLY USE THE SHI CLAN'S SEAL IN SEIRAN'S POSSESSION TO SEND IT TO THE COURT...
...AND IT WILL BE BROUGHT TO US WITH UTMOST HASTE.
CAN I DO THIS?
RYUKI...

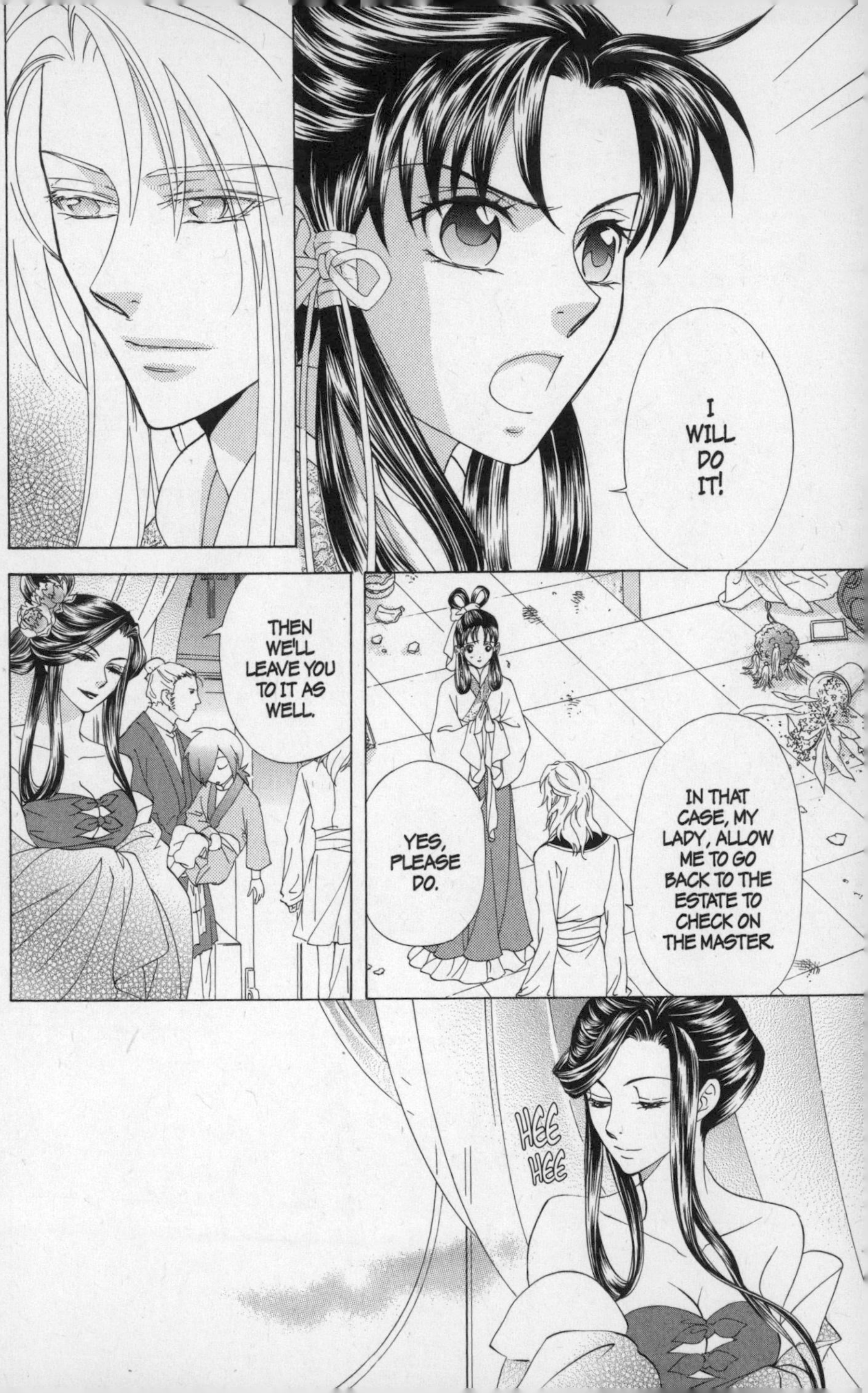
I WILL DO IT!
IN THAT CASE, MY LADY, ALLOW ME TO GO BACK TO THE ESTATE TO CHECK ON THE MASTER.
YES, PLEASE DO.
THEN WE'LL LEAVE YOU TO IT AS WELL.
HEE HEE

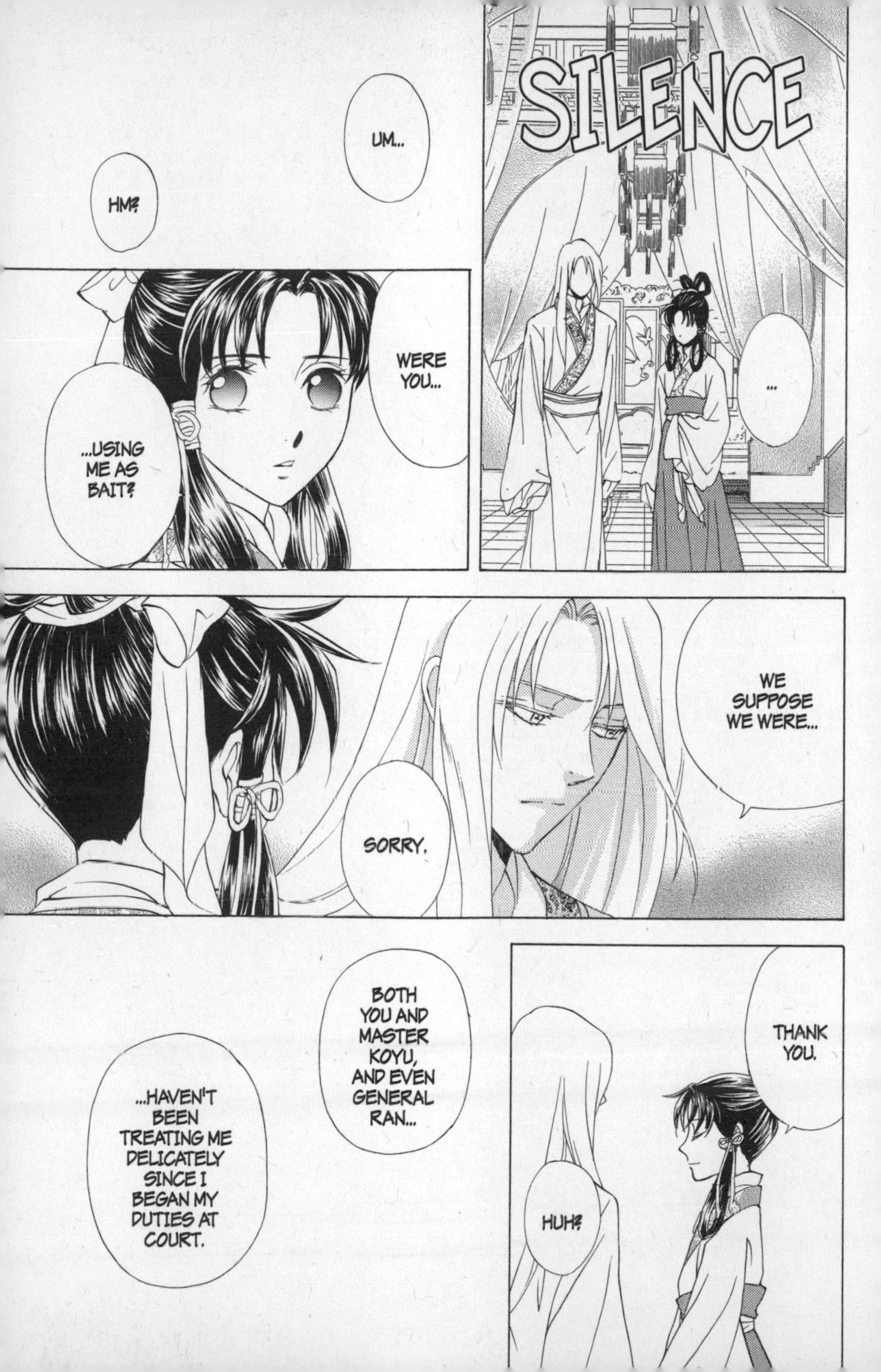
SILENCE
...
UM...
HM?
WERE YOU...
...USING ME AS BAIT?
WE SUPPOSE WE WERE...
SORRY.
THANK YOU.
HUH?
BOTH YOU AND MASTER KOYU, AND EVEN GENERAL RAN...
...HAVEN'T BEEN TREATING ME DELICATELY SINCE I BEGAN MY DUTIES AT COURT.

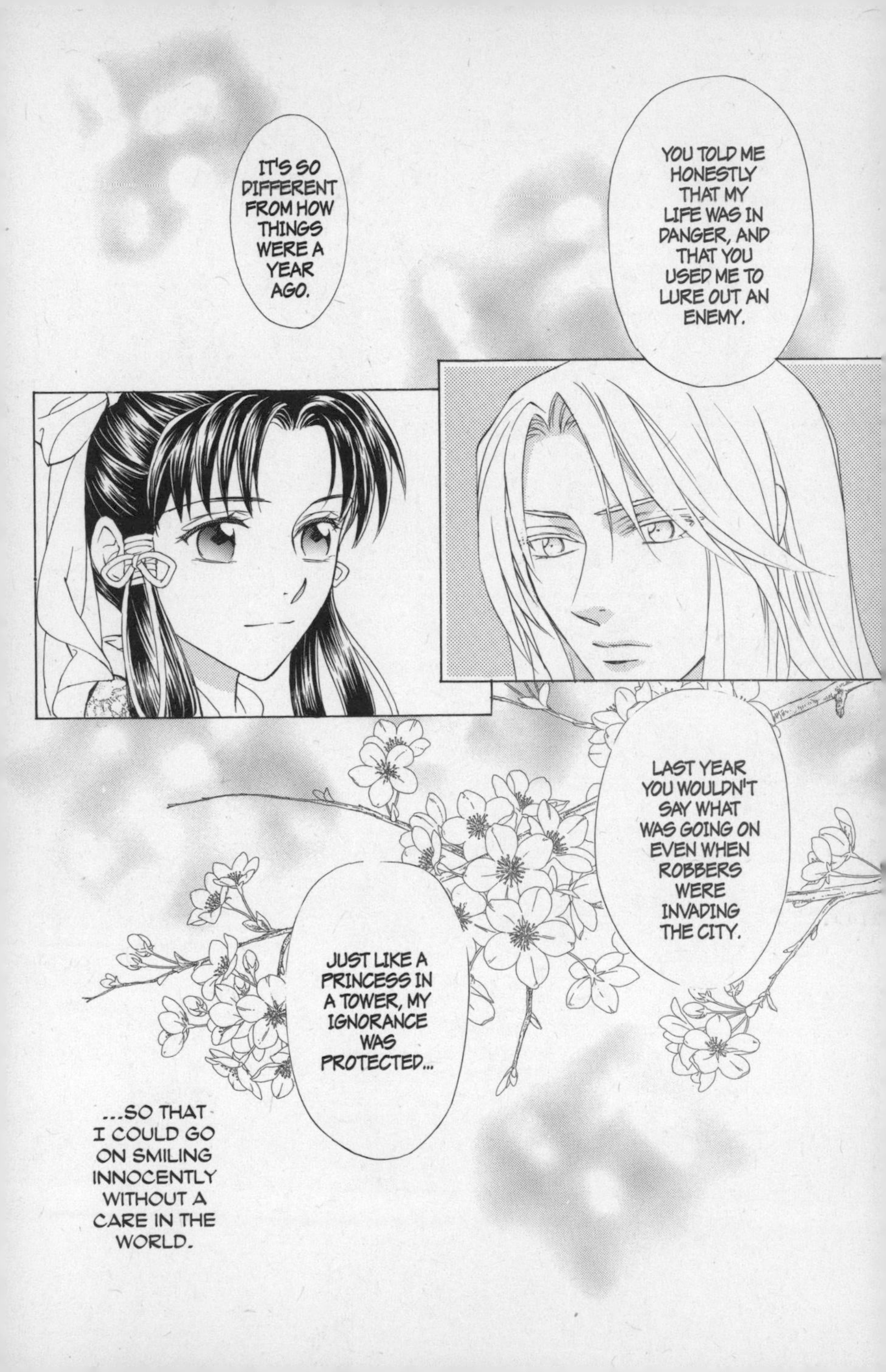
YOU TOLD ME HONESTLY THAT MY LIFE WAS IN DANGER, AND THAT YOU USED ME TO LURE OUT AN ENEMY.
IT'S SO DIFFERENT FROM HOW THINGS WERE A YEAR AGO.
LAST YEAR YOU WOULDN'T SAY WHAT WAS GOING ON EVEN WHEN ROBBERS WERE INVADING THE CITY.
JUST LIKE A PRINCESS IN A TOWER, MY IGNORANCE WAS PROTECTED...
...SO THAT I COULD GO ON SMILING INNOCENTLY WITHOUT A CARE IN THE WORLD.

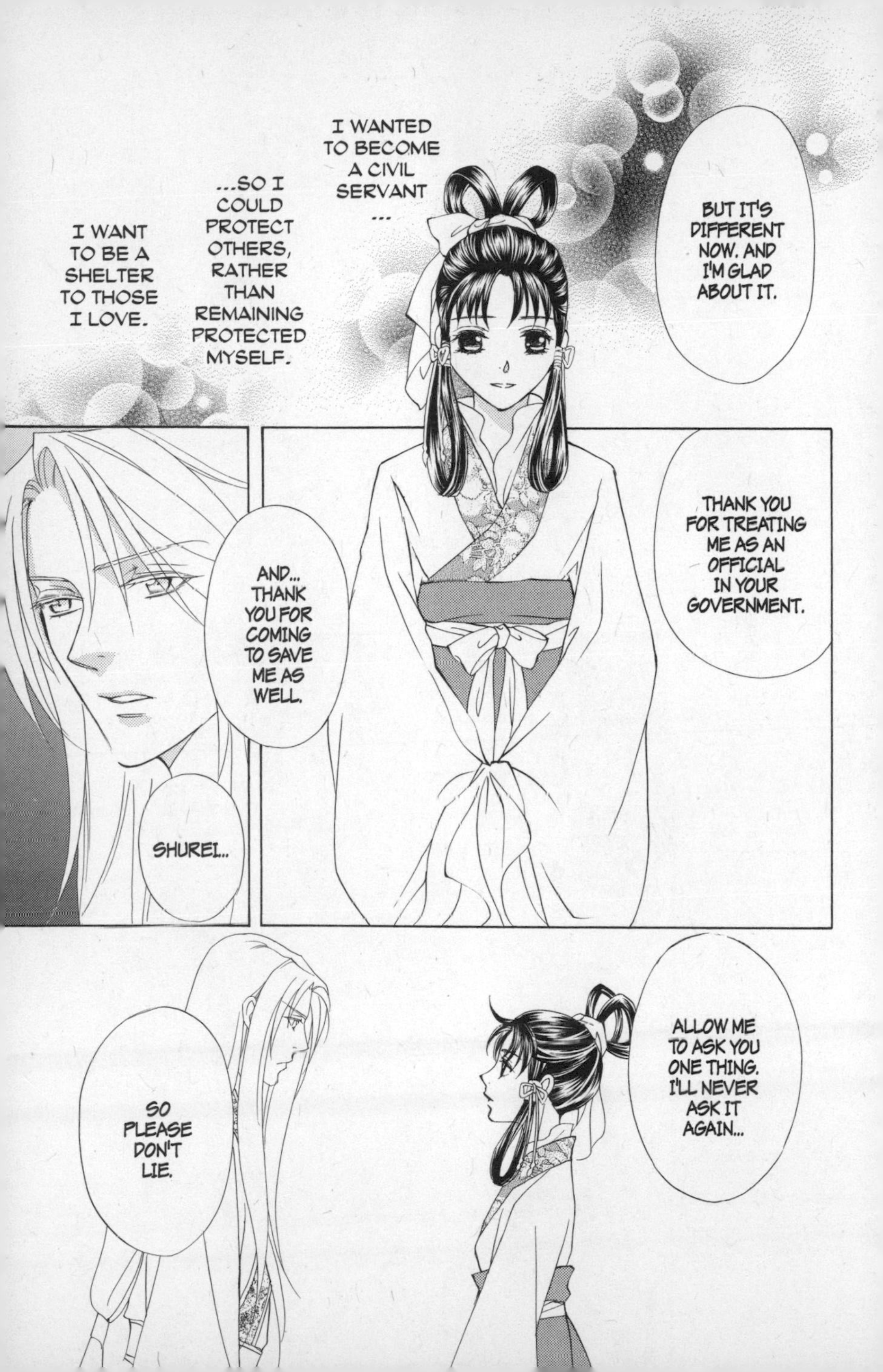
BUT IT'S DIFFERENT NOW. AND I'M GLAD ABOUT IT.
I WANTED TO BECOME A CIVIL SERVANT ...
...SO I COULD PROTECT OTHERS, RATHER THAN REMAINING PROTECTED MYSELF.
I WANT TO BE A SHELTER TO THOSE I LOVE.
THANK YOU FOR TREATING ME AS AN OFFICIAL IN YOUR GOVERNMENT.
AND... THANK YOU FOR COMING TO SAVE ME AS WELL.
SHUREI...
ALLOW ME TO ASK YOU ONE THING. I'LL NEVER ASK IT AGAIN...
SO PLEASE DON'T LIE.

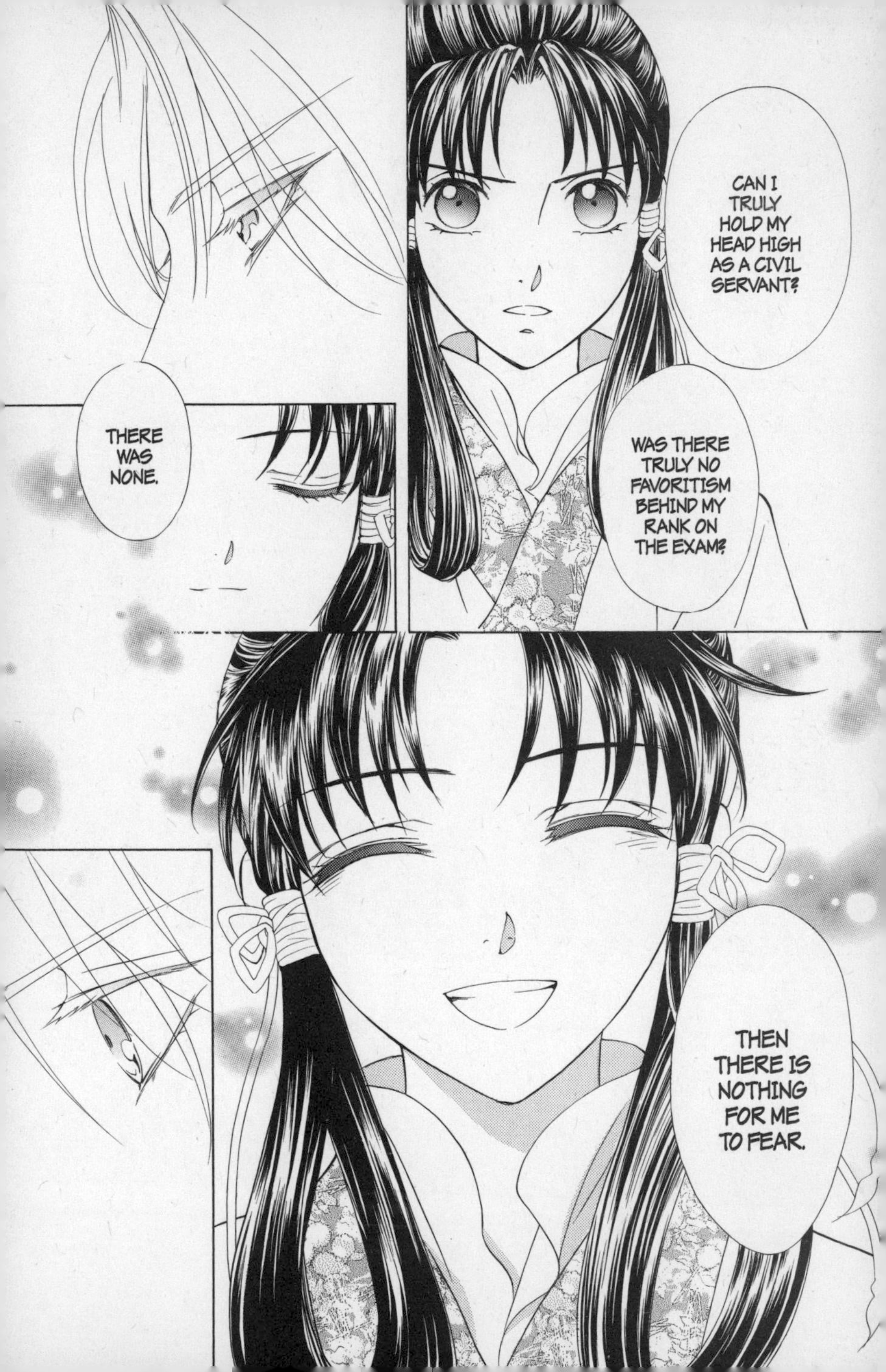
CAN I TRULY HOLD MY HEAD HIGH AS A CIVIL SERVANT?
WAS THERE TRULY NO FAVORITISM BEHIND MY RANK ON THE EXAM?
THERE WAS NONE.
THEN THERE IS NOTHING FOR ME TO FEAR.

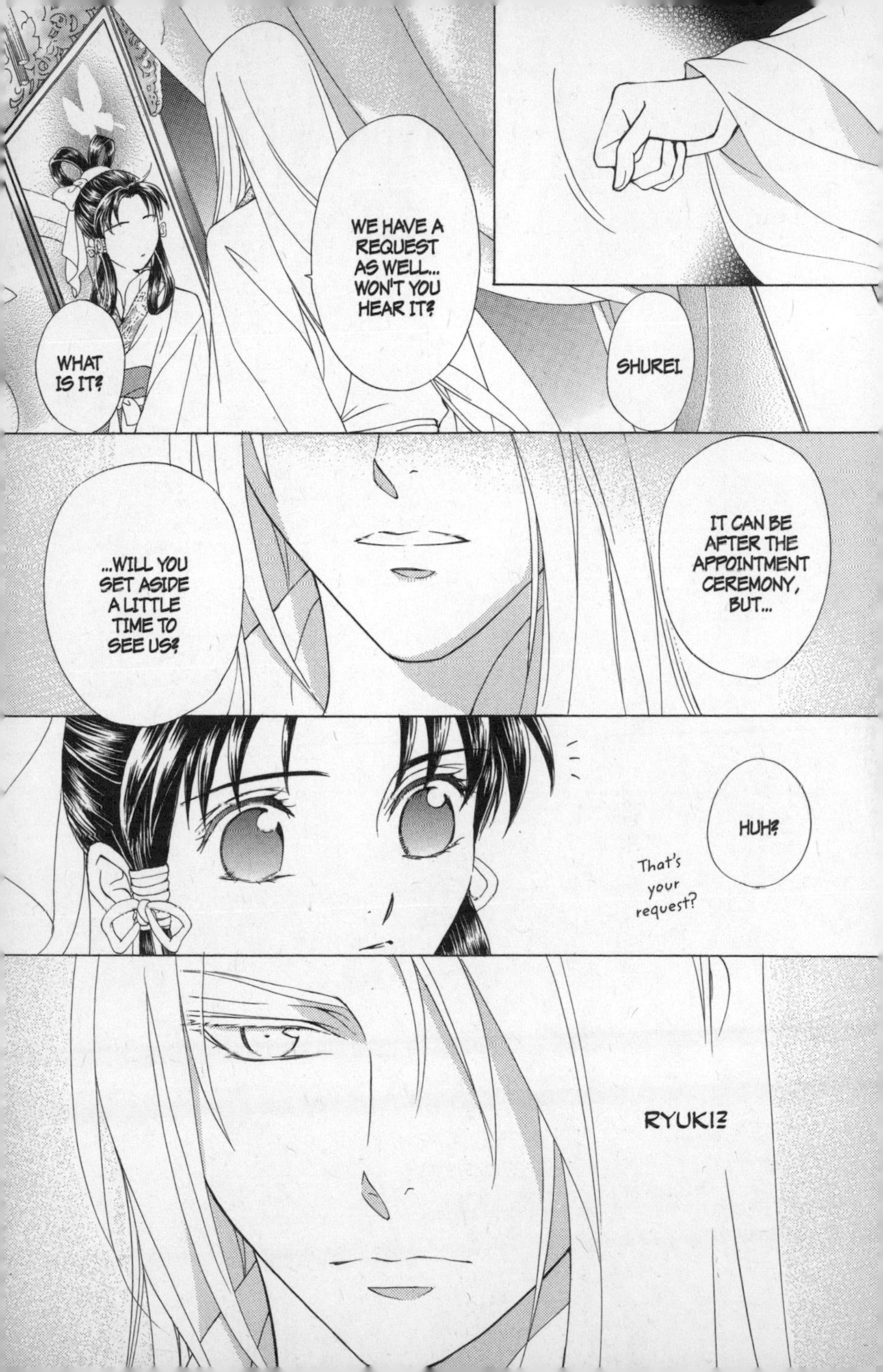
SHUREI.
WE HAVE A REQUEST AS WELL... WON'T YOU HEAR IT?
WHAT IS IT?
IT CAN BE AFTER THE APPOINTMENT CEREMONY, BUT...
...WILL YOU SET ASIDE A LITTLE TIME TO SEE US?
HUH?
That's your request?
RYUKI?

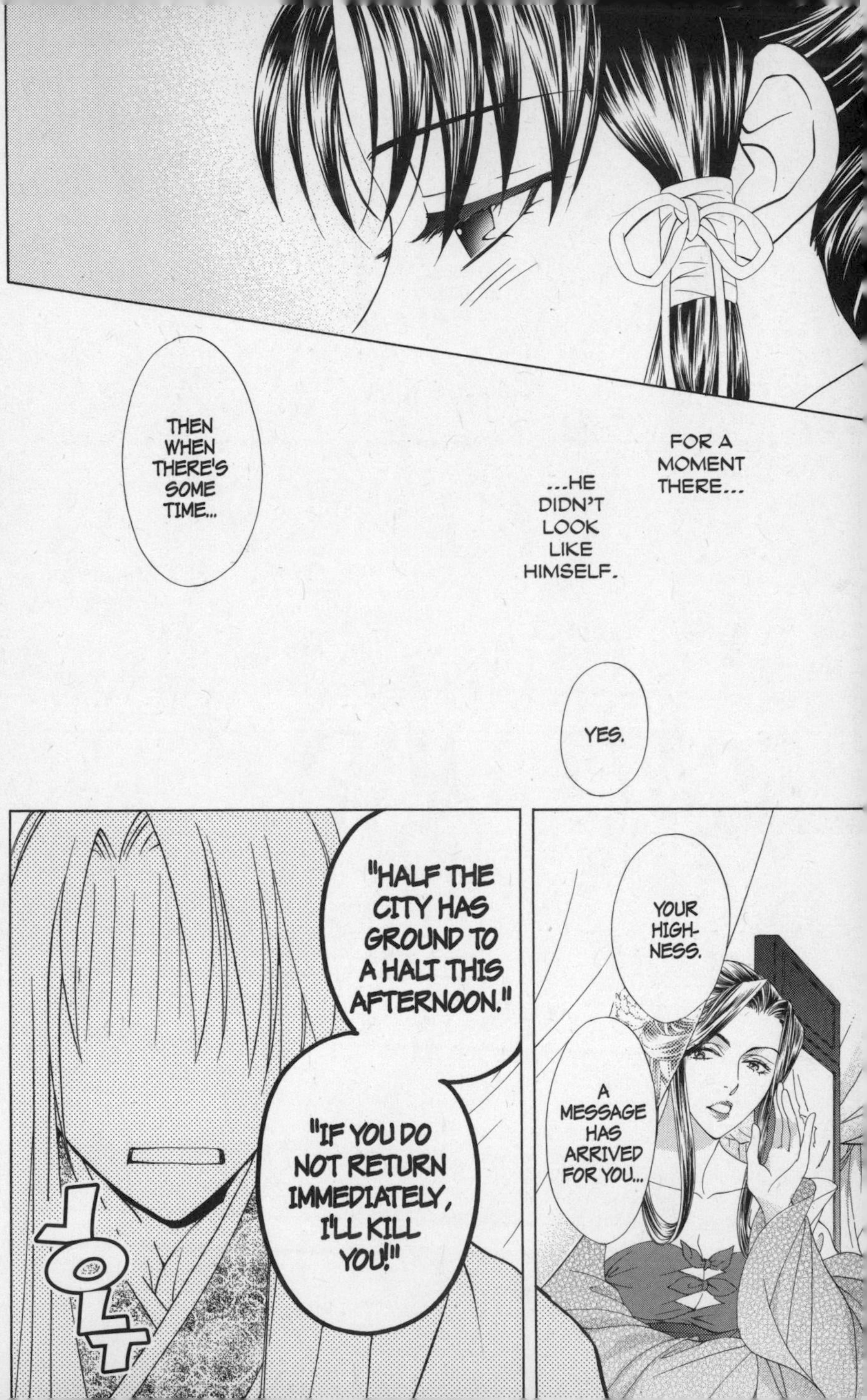
FOR A MOMENT THERE...
...HE DIDN'T LOOK LIKE HIMSELF.
THEN WHEN THERE'S SOME TIME...
YES.
YOUR HIGH-NESS.
A MESSAGE HAS ARRIVED FOR YOU...
"HALF THE CITY HAS GROUND TO A HALT THIS AFTERNOON."
"IF YOU DO NOT RETURN IMMEDIATELY, I'LL KILL YOU!"
JOLT

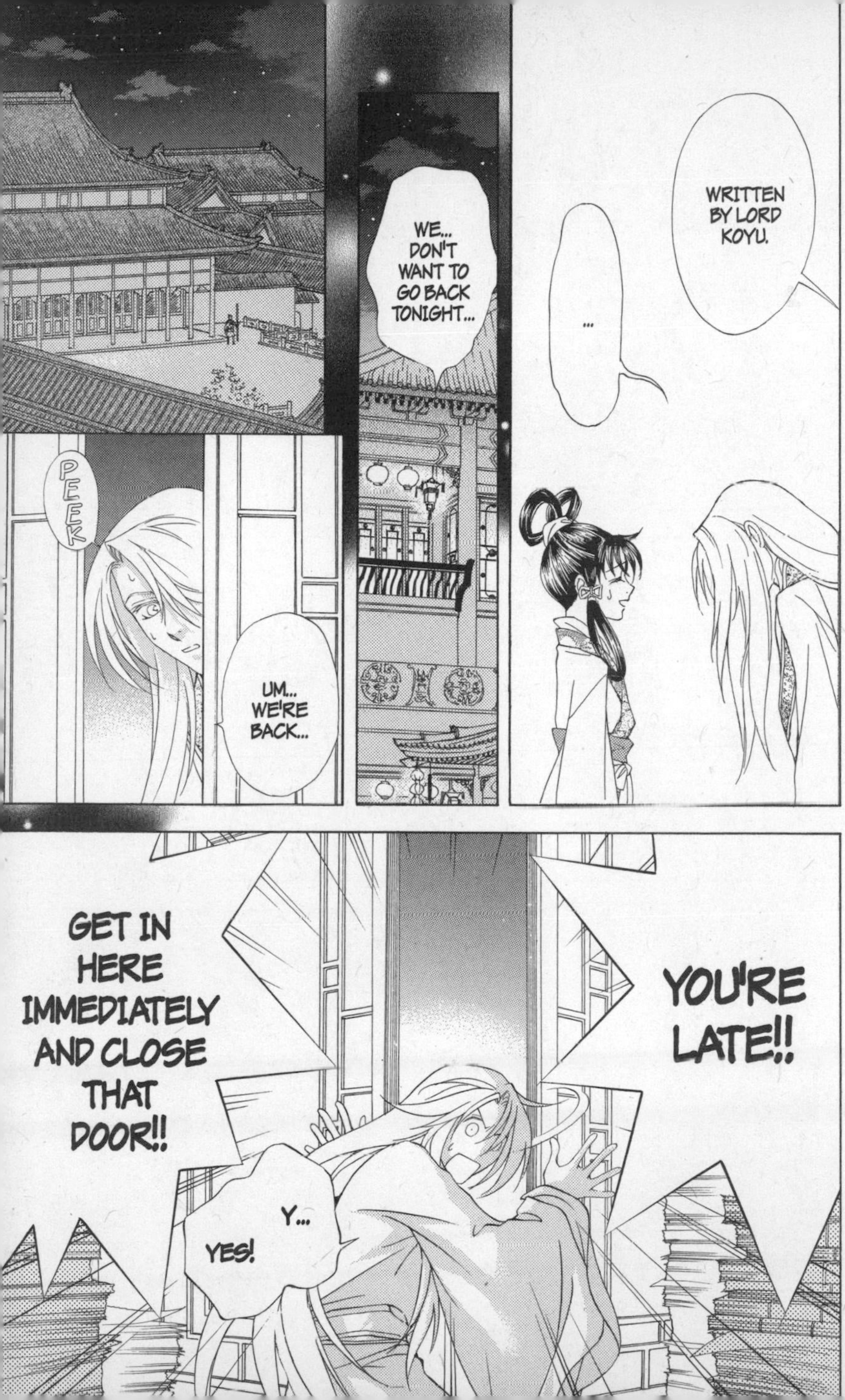
WRITTEN BY LORD KOYU.
...
WE... DON'T WANT TO GO BACK TONIGHT...
PEEK
UM... WE'RE BACK...
YOU'RE LATE!!
GET IN HERE IMMEDIATELY AND CLOSE THAT DOOR!!
Y...
YES!

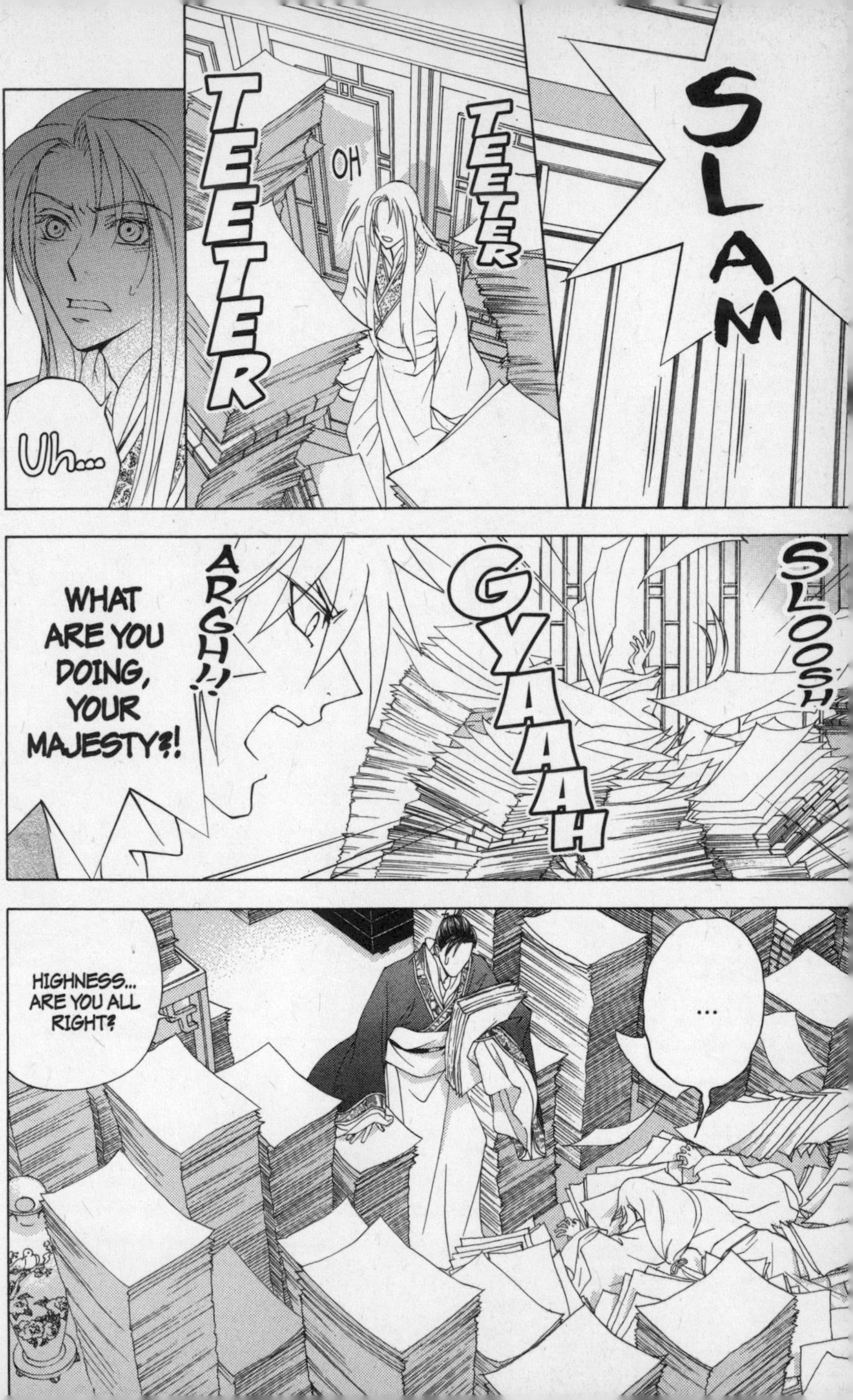
SLAM
TEETER
OH
TEETER
Uh...
SLOOSH
GYAAAH
ARGH!!
WHAT ARE YOU DOING, YOUR MAJESTY?!
...
HIGHNESS... ARE YOU ALL RIGHT?

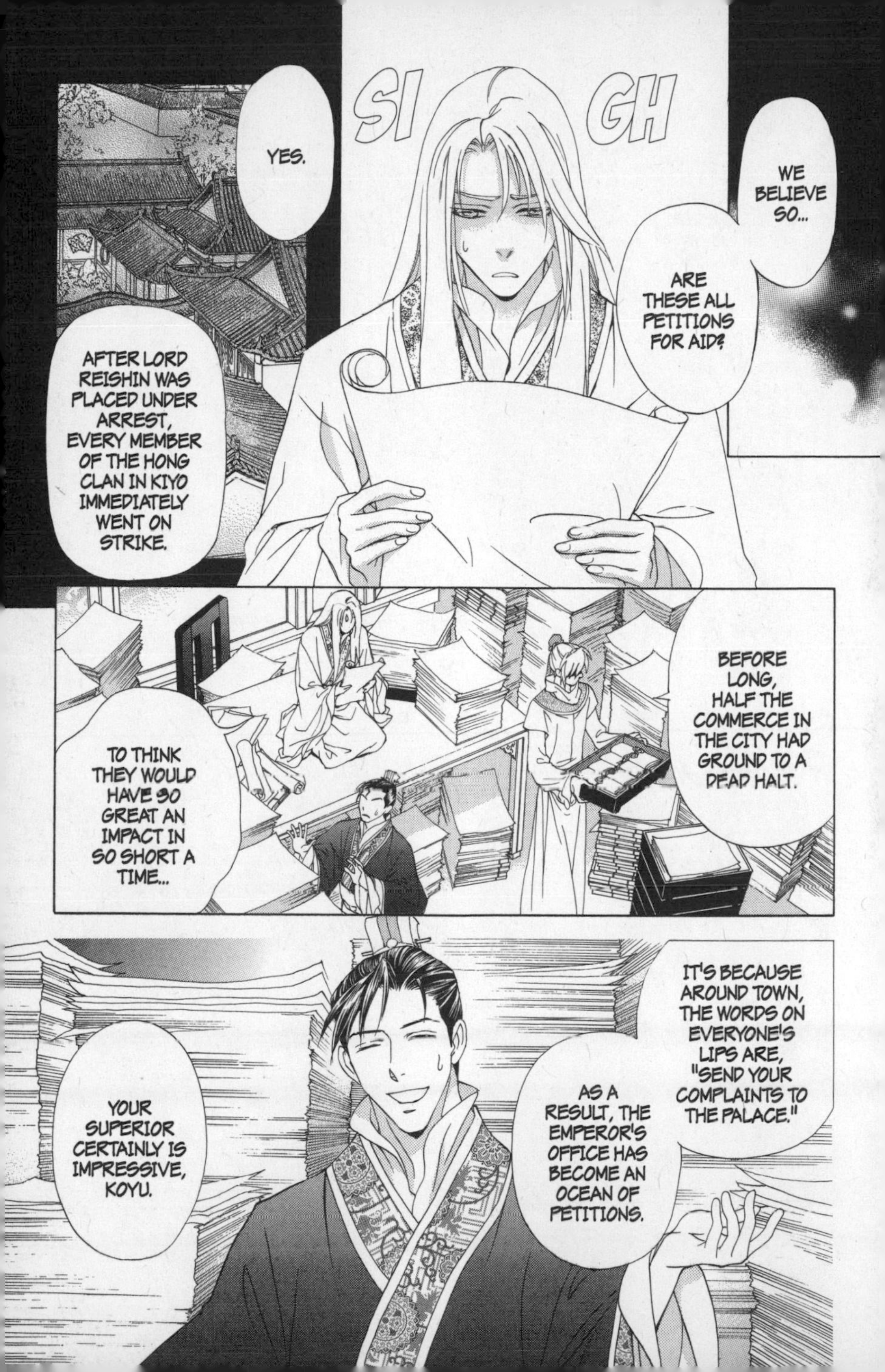
SIGH
ARE THESE ALL PETITIONS FOR AID?
WE BELIEVE SO...
YES.
AFTER LORD REISHIN WAS PLACED UNDER ARREST, EVERY MEMBER OF THE HONG CLAN IN KIYO IMMEDIATELY WENT ON STRIKE.
BEFORE LONG, HALF THE COMMERCE IN THE CITY HAD GROUND TO A DEAD HALT.
TO THINK THEY WOULD HAVE SO GREAT AN IMPACT IN SO SHORT A TIME...
IT'S BECAUSE AROUND TOWN, THE WORDS ON EVERYONE'S LIPS ARE, "SEND YOUR COMPLAINTS TO THE PALACE."
AS A RESULT, THE EMPEROR'S OFFICE HAS BECOME AN OCEAN OF PETITIONS.
YOUR SUPERIOR CERTAINLY IS IMPRESSIVE, KOYU.

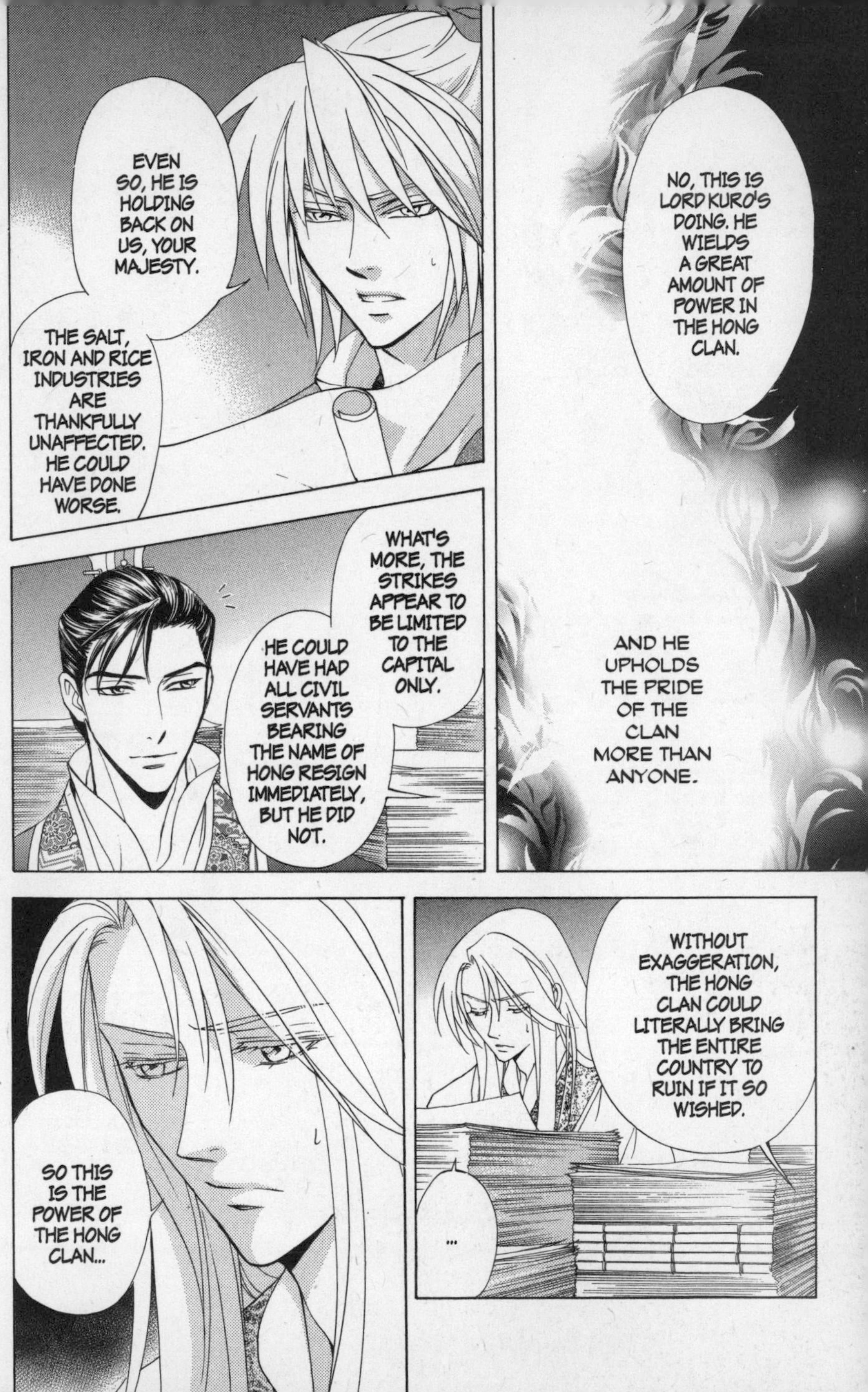
NO, THIS IS LORD KURO'S DOING. HE WIELDS A GREAT AMOUNT OF POWER IN THE HONG CLAN.
AND HE UPHOLDS THE PRIDE OF THE CLAN MORE THAN ANYONE.
EVEN SO, HE IS HOLDING BACK ON US, YOUR MAJESTY.
THE SALT, IRON AND RICE INDUSTRIES ARE THANKFULLY UNAFFECTED. HE COULD HAVE DONE WORSE.
WHAT'S MORE, THE STRIKES APPEAR TO BE LIMITED TO THE CAPITAL ONLY.
HE COULD HAVE HAD ALL CIVIL SERVANTS BEARING THE NAME OF HONG RESIGN IMMEDIATELY, BUT HE DID NOT.
WITHOUT EXAGGERATION, THE HONG CLAN COULD LITERALLY BRING THE ENTIRE COUNTRY TO RUIN IF IT SO WISHED.
...
SO THIS IS THE POWER OF THE HONG CLAN...

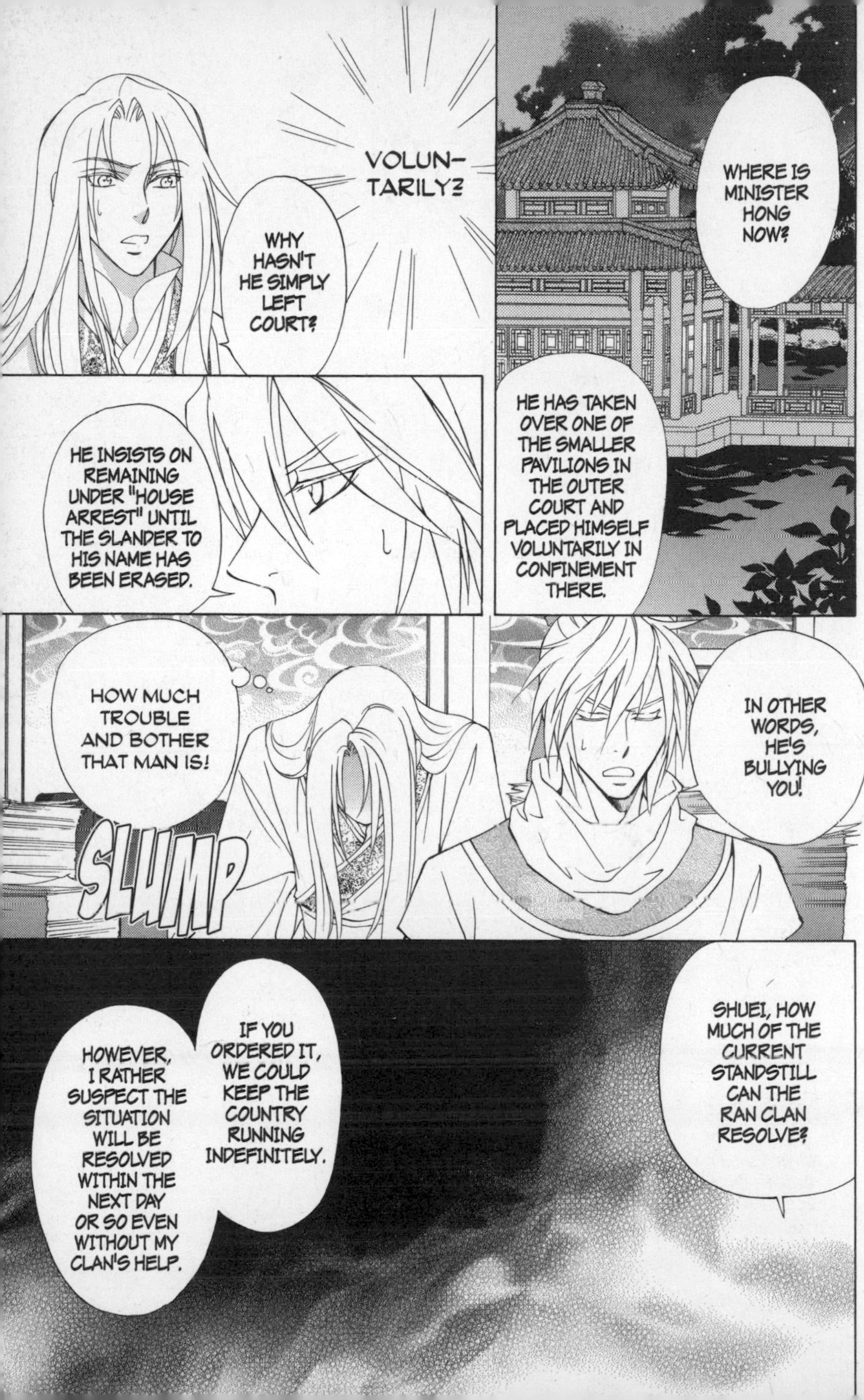
WHERE IS MINISTER HONG NOW?
HE HAS TAKEN OVER ONE OF THE SMALLER PAVILIONS IN THE OUTER COURT AND PLACED HIMSELF VOLUNTARILY IN CONFINEMENT THERE.
VOLUN-TARILY?
WHY HASN'T HE SIMPLY LEFT COURT?
HE INSISTS ON REMAINING UNDER "HOUSE ARREST" UNTIL THE SLANDER TO HIS NAME HAS BEEN ERASED.
IN OTHER WORDS, HE'S BULLYING YOU!
HOW MUCH TROUBLE AND BOTHER THAT MAN IS!
SLUMP
SHUEI, HOW MUCH OF THE CURRENT STANDSTILL CAN THE RAN CLAN RESOLVE?
IF YOU ORDERED IT, WE COULD KEEP THE COUNTRY RUNNING INDEFINITELY.
HOWEVER, I RATHER SUSPECT THE SITUATION WILL BE RESOLVED WITHIN THE NEXT DAY OR SO EVEN WITHOUT MY CLAN'S HELP.

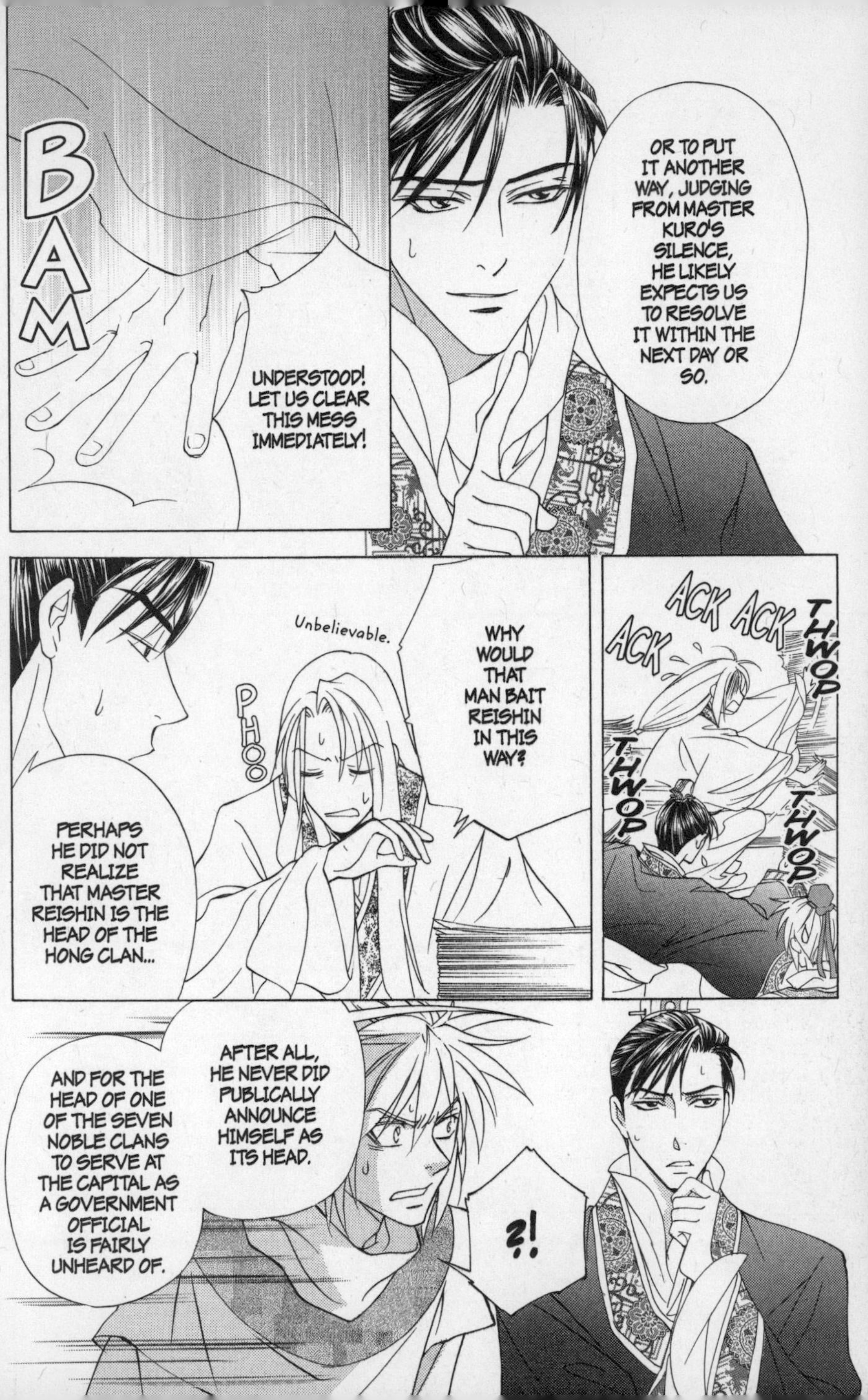
OR TO PUT IT ANOTHER WAY, JUDGING FROM MASTER KURO'S SILENCE, HE LIKELY EXPECTS US TO RESOLVE IT WITHIN THE NEXT DAY OR SO.
BAM
UNDERSTOOD! LET US CLEAR THIS MESS IMMEDIATELY!
ACK ACK
ACK
THWOP
THWOP
THWOP
THWOP
WHY WOULD THAT MAN BAIT REISHIN IN THIS WAY?
Unbelievable.
PHOO
PERHAPS HE DID NOT REALIZE THAT MASTER REISHIN IS THE HEAD OF THE HONG CLAN...
AFTER ALL, HE NEVER DID PUBLICALLY ANNOUNCE HIMSELF AS ITS HEAD.
AND FOR THE HEAD OF ONE OF THE SEVEN NOBLE CLANS TO SERVE AT THE CAPITAL AS A GOVERNMENT OFFICIAL IS FAIRLY UNHEARD OF.
?!

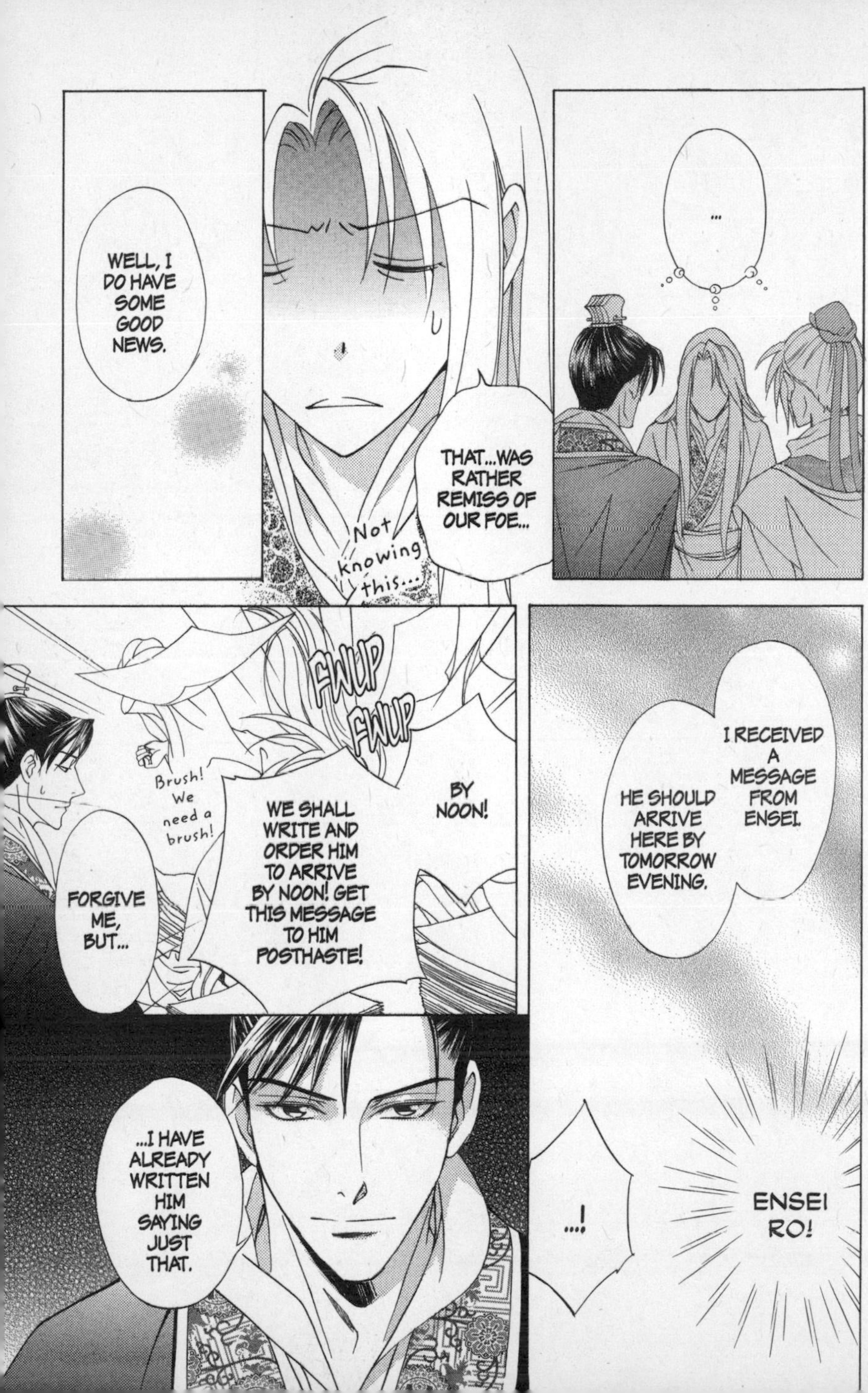
...
THAT...WAS RATHER REMISS OF OUR FOE...
Not knowing this...
WELL, I DO HAVE SOME GOOD NEWS.
I RECEIVED A MESSAGE FROM ENSEI.
HE SHOULD ARRIVE HERE BY TOMORROW EVENING.
ENSEI RO!
...!
FWUP
FWUP
BY NOON!
WE SHALL WRITE AND ORDER HIM TO ARRIVE BY NOON! GET THIS MESSAGE TO HIM POSTHASTE!
Brush! We need a brush!
FORGIVE ME, BUT...
...I HAVE ALREADY WRITTEN HIM SAYING JUST THAT.

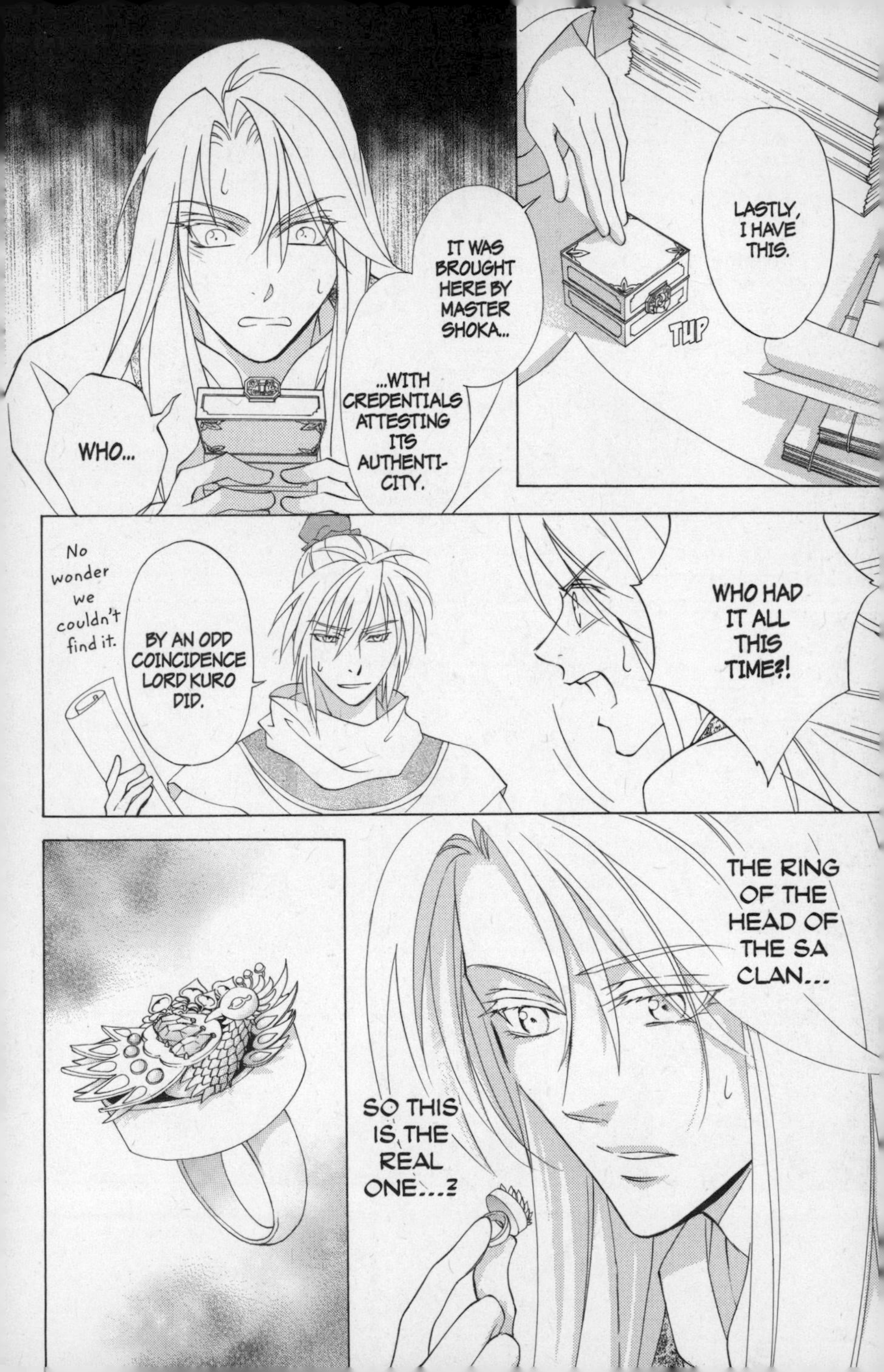
LASTLY, I HAVE THIS.
TUP
IT WAS BROUGHT HERE BY MASTER SHOKA...
...WITH CREDENTIALS ATTESTING ITS AUTHENTICITY.
WHO...
WHO HAD IT ALL THIS TIME?!
BY AN ODD COINCIDENCE LORD KURO DID.
No wonder we couldn't find it.
THE RING OF THE HEAD OF THE SA CLAN...
SO THIS IS THE REAL ONE...?

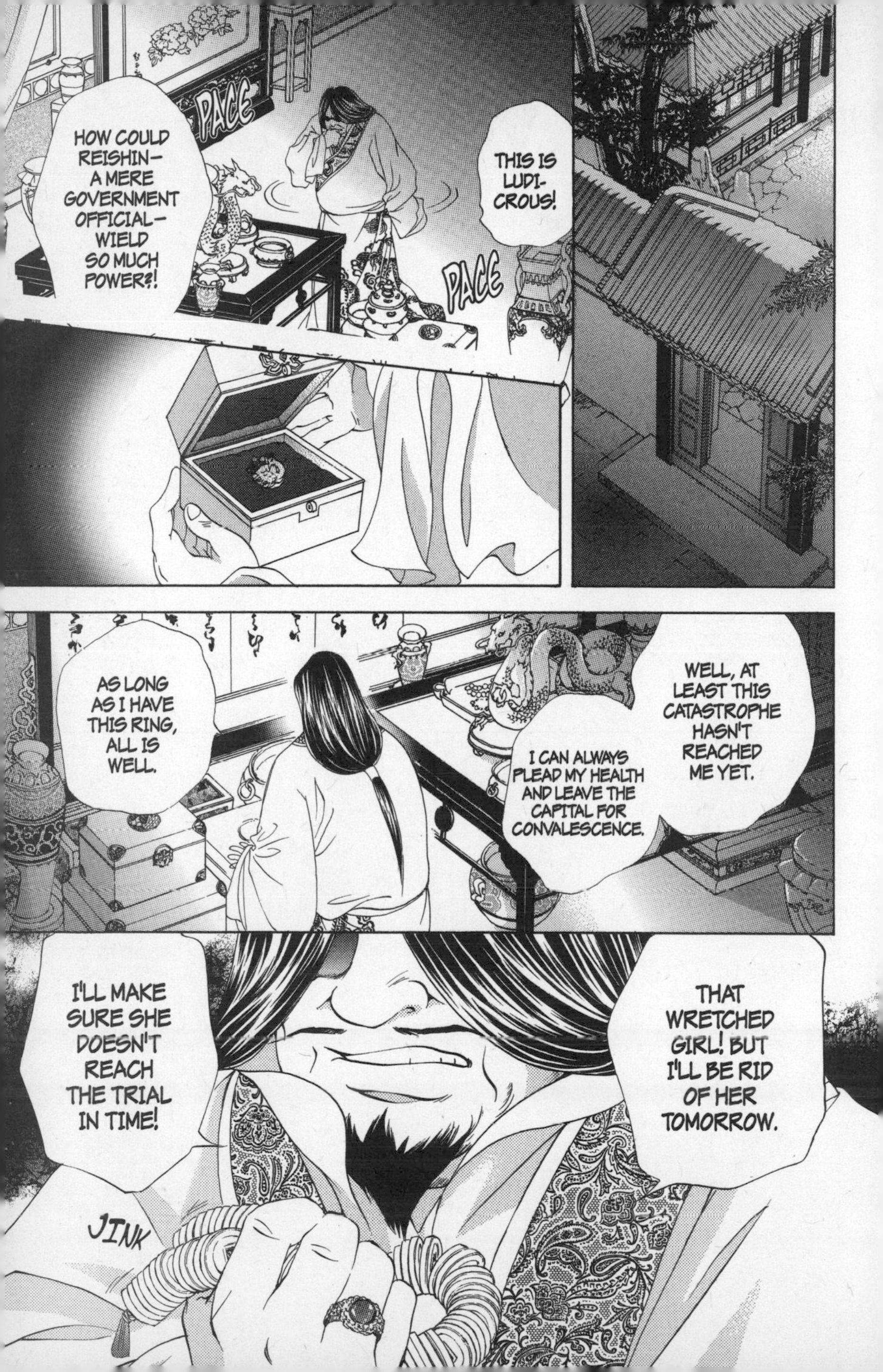
PACE
THIS IS LUDICROUS!
PACE
HOW COULD REISHIN—A MERE GOVERNMENT OFFICIAL—WIELD SO MUCH POWER?!
WELL, AT LEAST THIS CATASTROPHE HASN'T REACHED ME YET.
I CAN ALWAYS PLEAD MY HEALTH AND LEAVE THE CAPITAL FOR CONVALESCENCE.
AS LONG AS I HAVE THIS RING, ALL IS WELL.
THAT WRETCHED GIRL! BUT I'LL BE RID OF HER TOMORROW.
I'LL MAKE SURE SHE DOESN'T REACH THE TRIAL IN TIME!
JINK

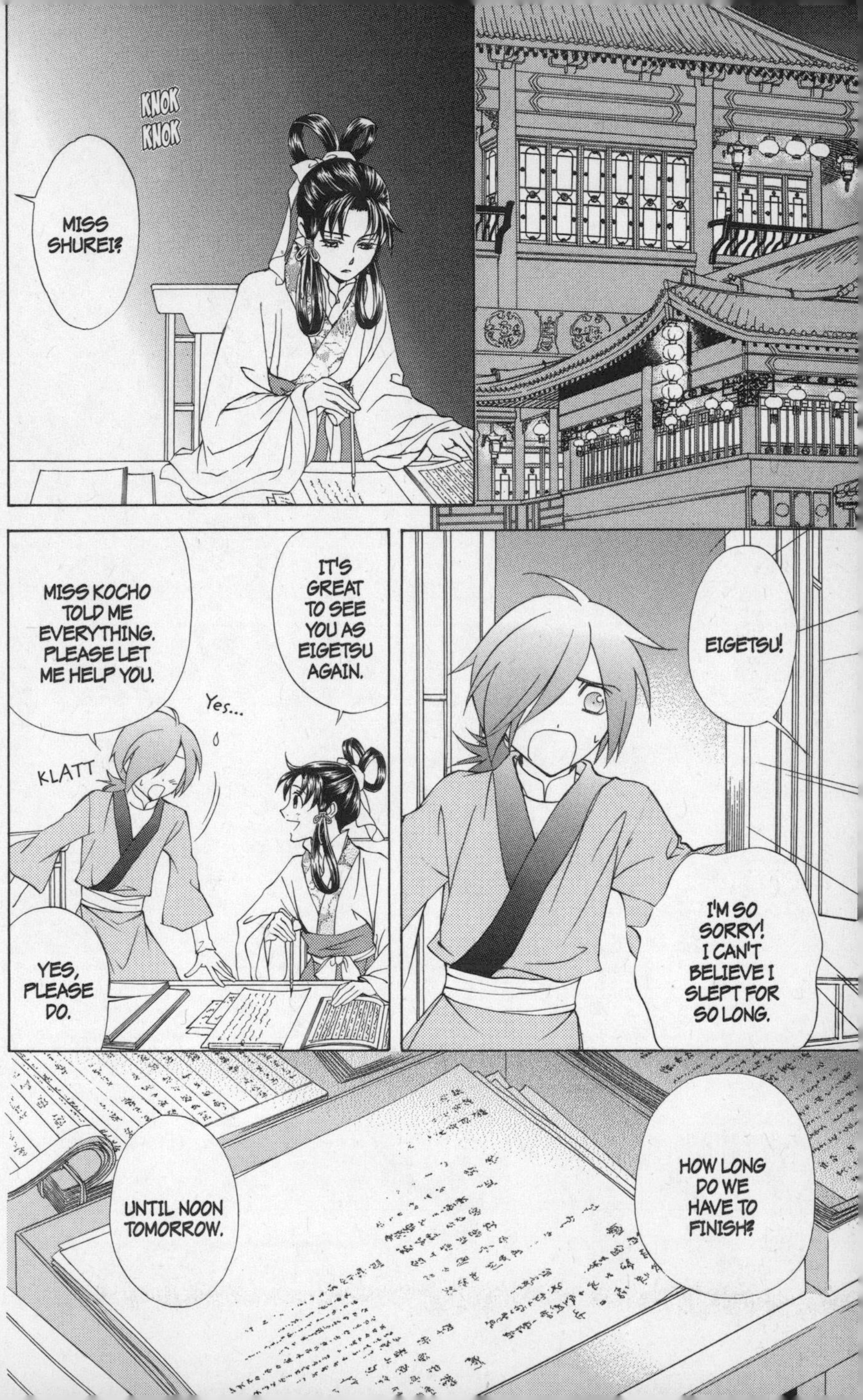
KNOK KNOK
MISS SHUREI?
EIGETSU!
I'M SO SORRY! I CAN'T BELIEVE I SLEPT FOR SO LONG.
IT'S GREAT TO SEE YOU AS EIGETSU AGAIN.
Yes...
MISS KOCHO TOLD ME EVERYTHING. PLEASE LET ME HELP YOU.
KLATT
YES, PLEASE DO.
HOW LONG DO WE HAVE TO FINISH?
UNTIL NOON TOMORROW.

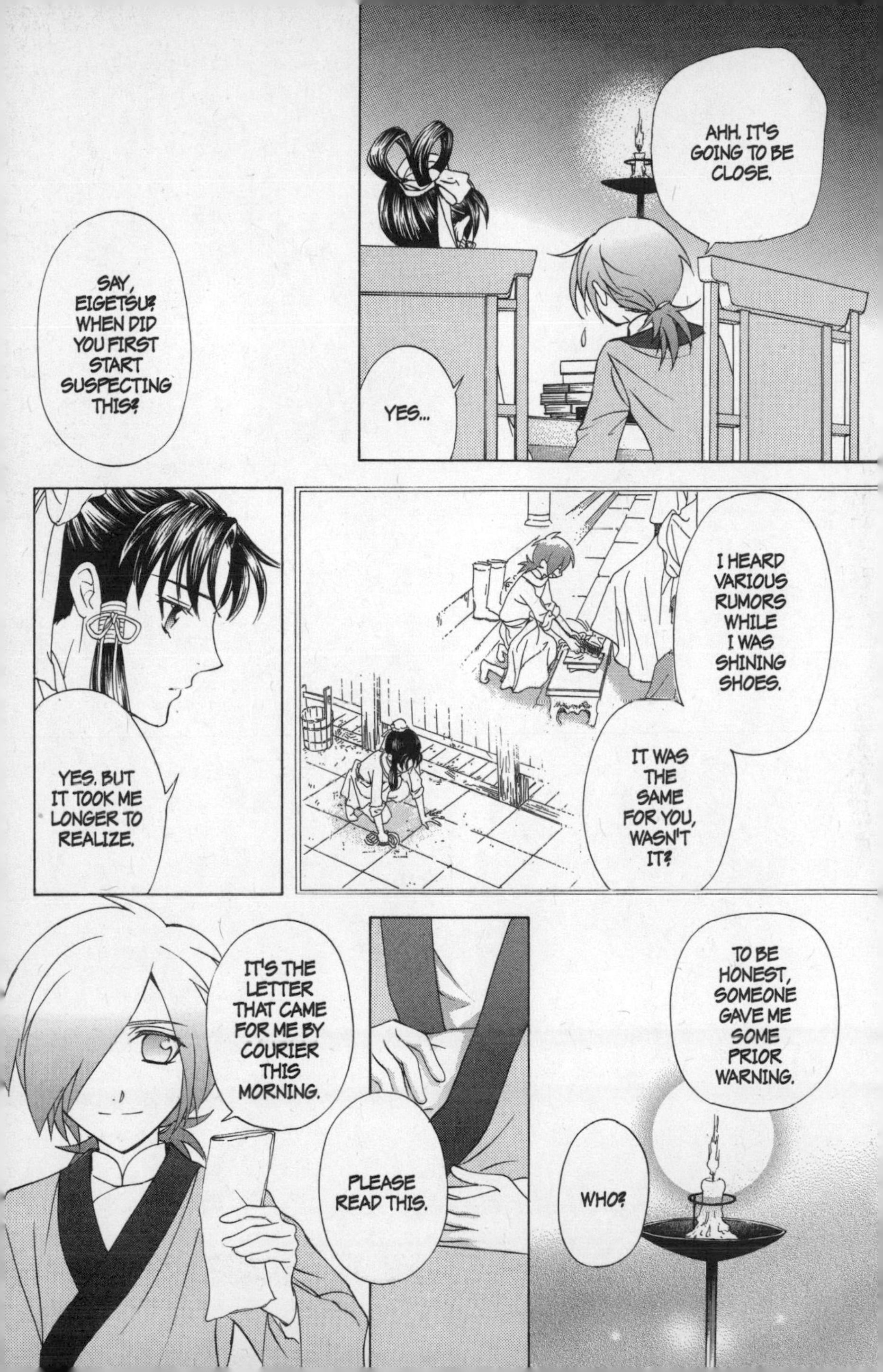
AHH. IT'S GOING TO BE CLOSE.
YES...
SAY, EIGETSU? WHEN DID YOU FIRST START SUSPECTING THIS?
I HEARD VARIOUS RUMORS WHILE I WAS SHINING SHOES.
IT WAS THE SAME FOR YOU, WASN'T IT?
YES. BUT IT TOOK ME LONGER TO REALIZE.
TO BE HONEST, SOMEONE GAVE ME SOME PRIOR WARNING.
WHO?
IT'S THE LETTER THAT CAME FOR ME BY COURIER THIS MORNING.
PLEASE READ THIS.

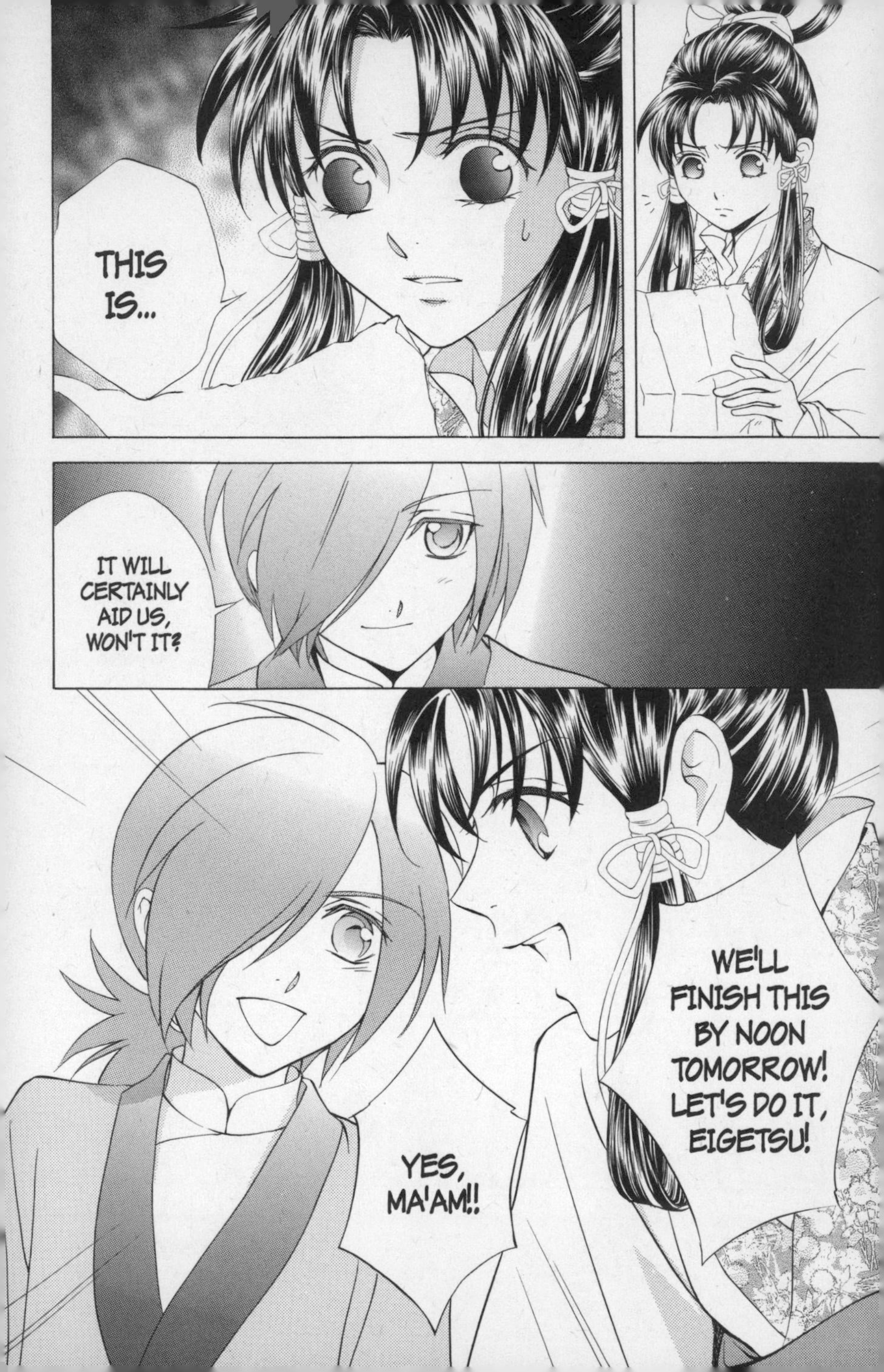
THIS IS...
IT WILL CERTAINLY AID US, WON'T IT?
WE'LL FINISH THIS BY NOON TOMORROW! LET'S DO IT, EIGETSU!
YES, MA'AM!!

TEP
TEP
TEP

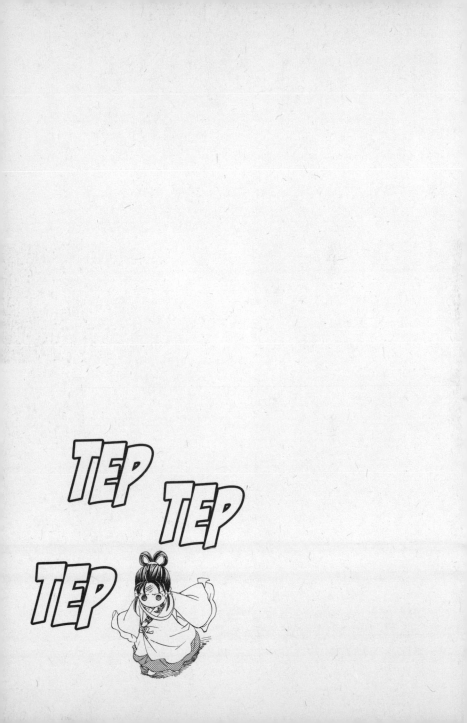

The Story of
SAIUNKOKU

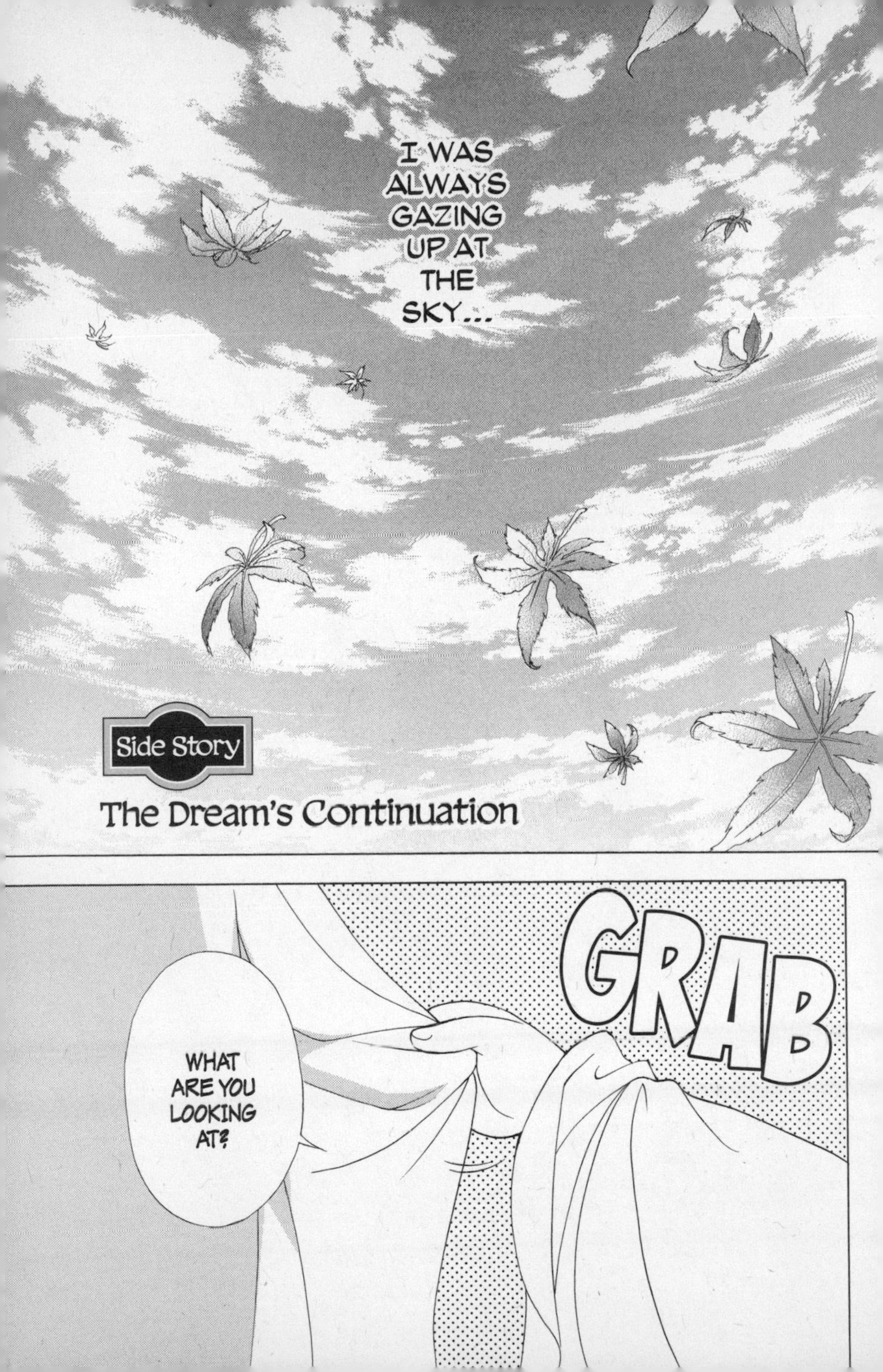
I WAS ALWAYS GAZING UP AT THE SKY...
Side Story
The Dream's Continuation
GRAB
WHAT ARE YOU LOOKING AT?

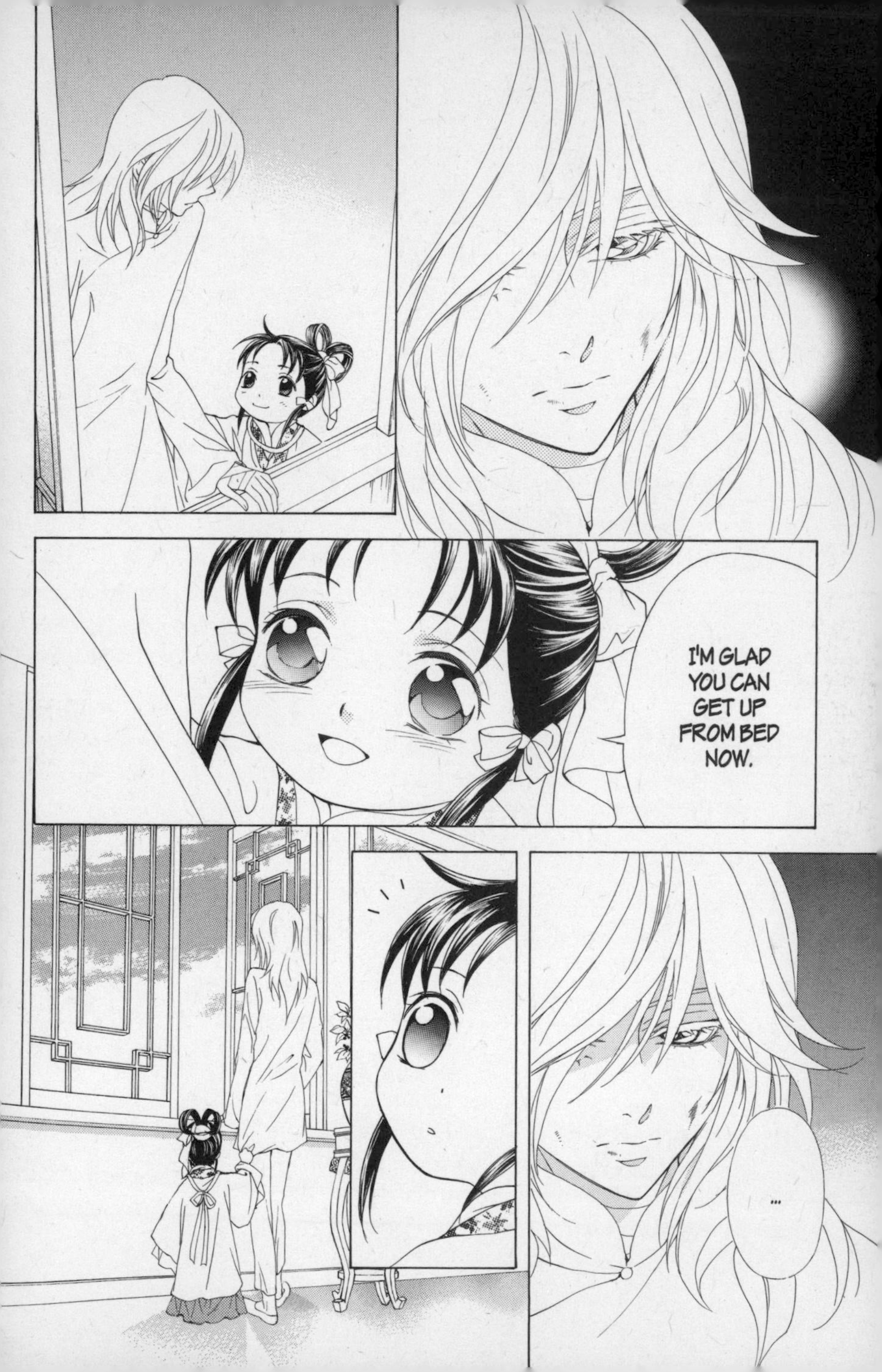
I'M GLAD YOU CAN GET UP FROM BED NOW.
...

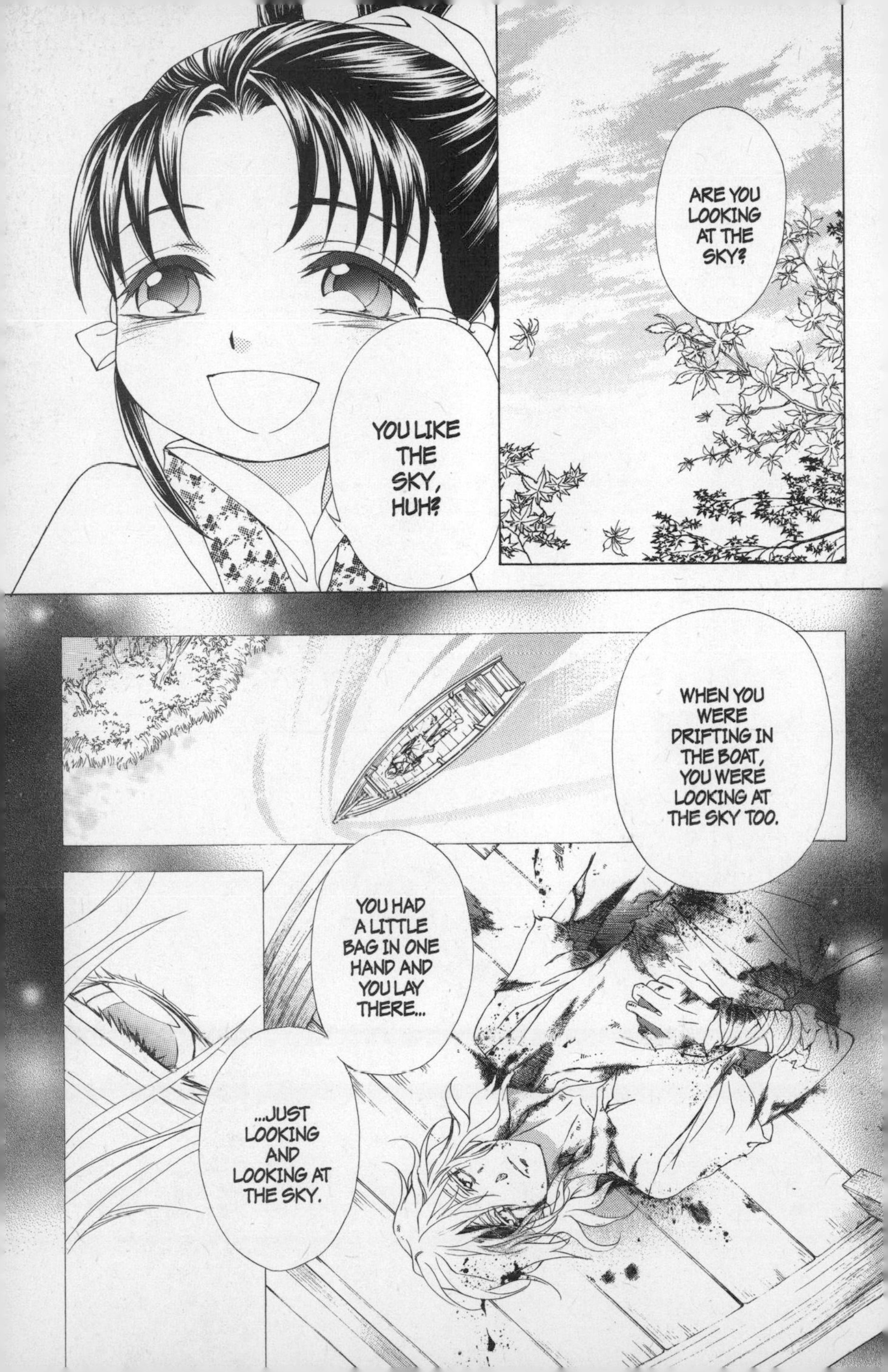
ARE YOU LOOKING AT THE SKY?
YOU LIKE THE SKY, HUH?
WHEN YOU WERE DRIFTING IN THE BOAT, YOU WERE LOOKING AT THE SKY TOO.
YOU HAD A LITTLE BAG IN ONE HAND AND YOU LAY THERE...
...JUST LOOKING AND LOOKING AT THE SKY.

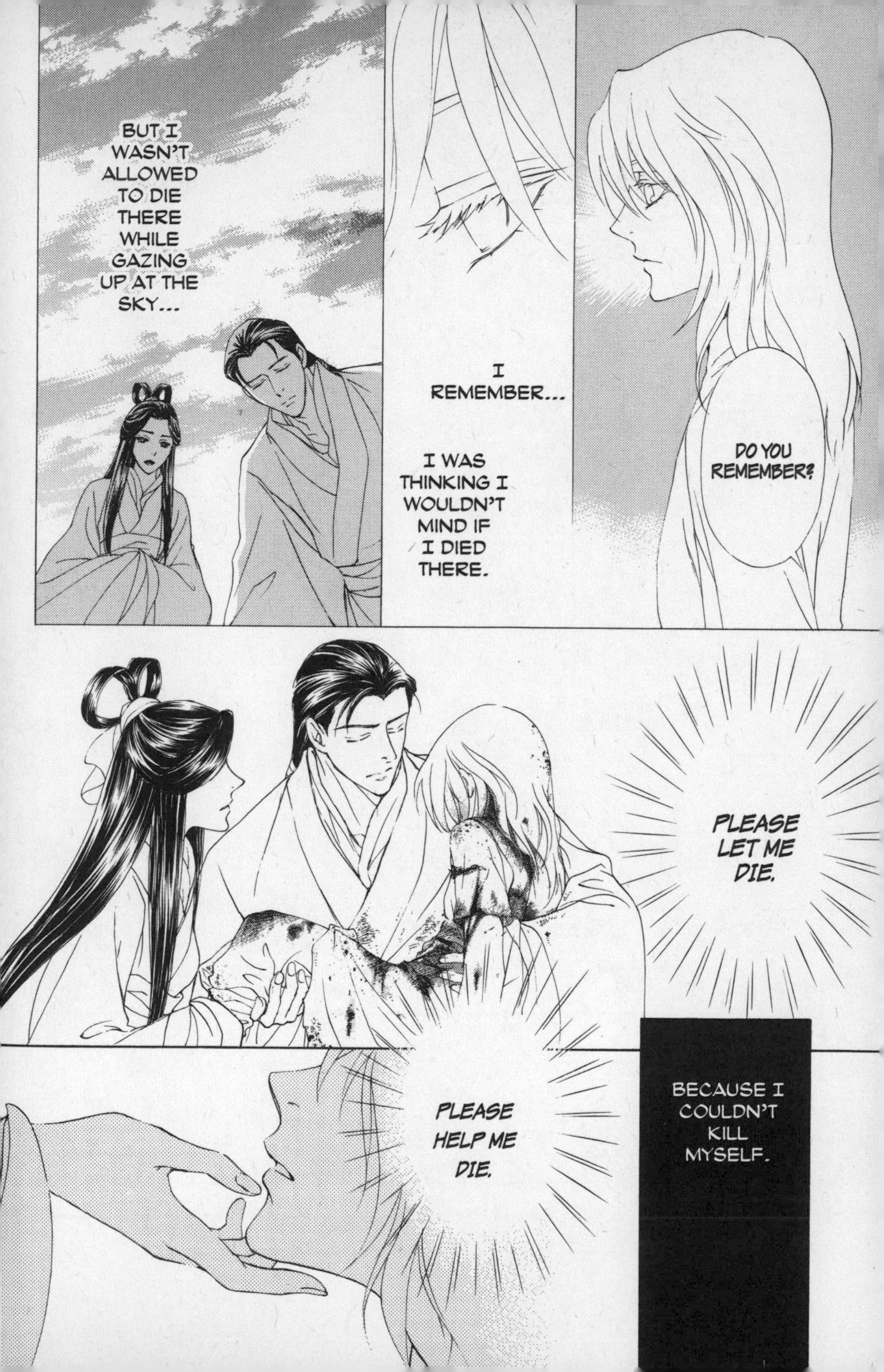
DO YOU REMEMBER?
I REMEMBER...
I WAS THINKING I WOULDN'T MIND IF I DIED THERE.
BUT I WASN'T ALLOWED TO DIE THERE WHILE GAZING UP AT THE SKY...
PLEASE LET ME DIE.
BECAUSE I COULDN'T KILL MYSELF.
PLEASE HELP ME DIE.

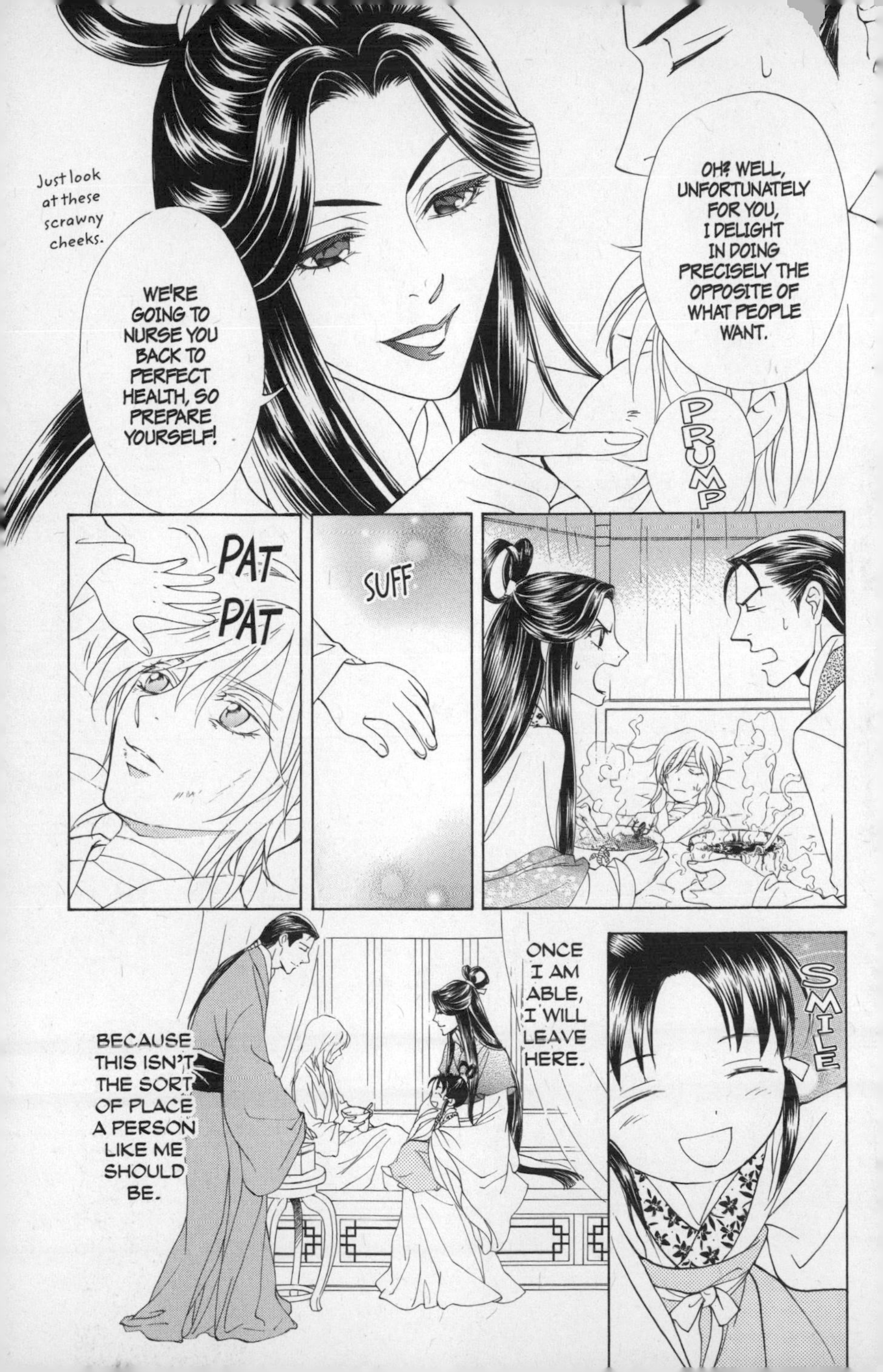
OH? WELL, UNFORTUNATELY FOR YOU, I DELIGHT IN DOING PRECISELY THE OPPOSITE OF WHAT PEOPLE WANT.
PRUMP
Just look at these scrawny cheeks.
WE'RE GOING TO NURSE YOU BACK TO PERFECT HEALTH, SO PREPARE YOURSELF!
SUFF
PAT PAT
SMILE
ONCE I AM ABLE, I WILL LEAVE HERE.
BECAUSE THIS ISN'T THE SORT OF PLACE A PERSON LIKE ME SHOULD BE.

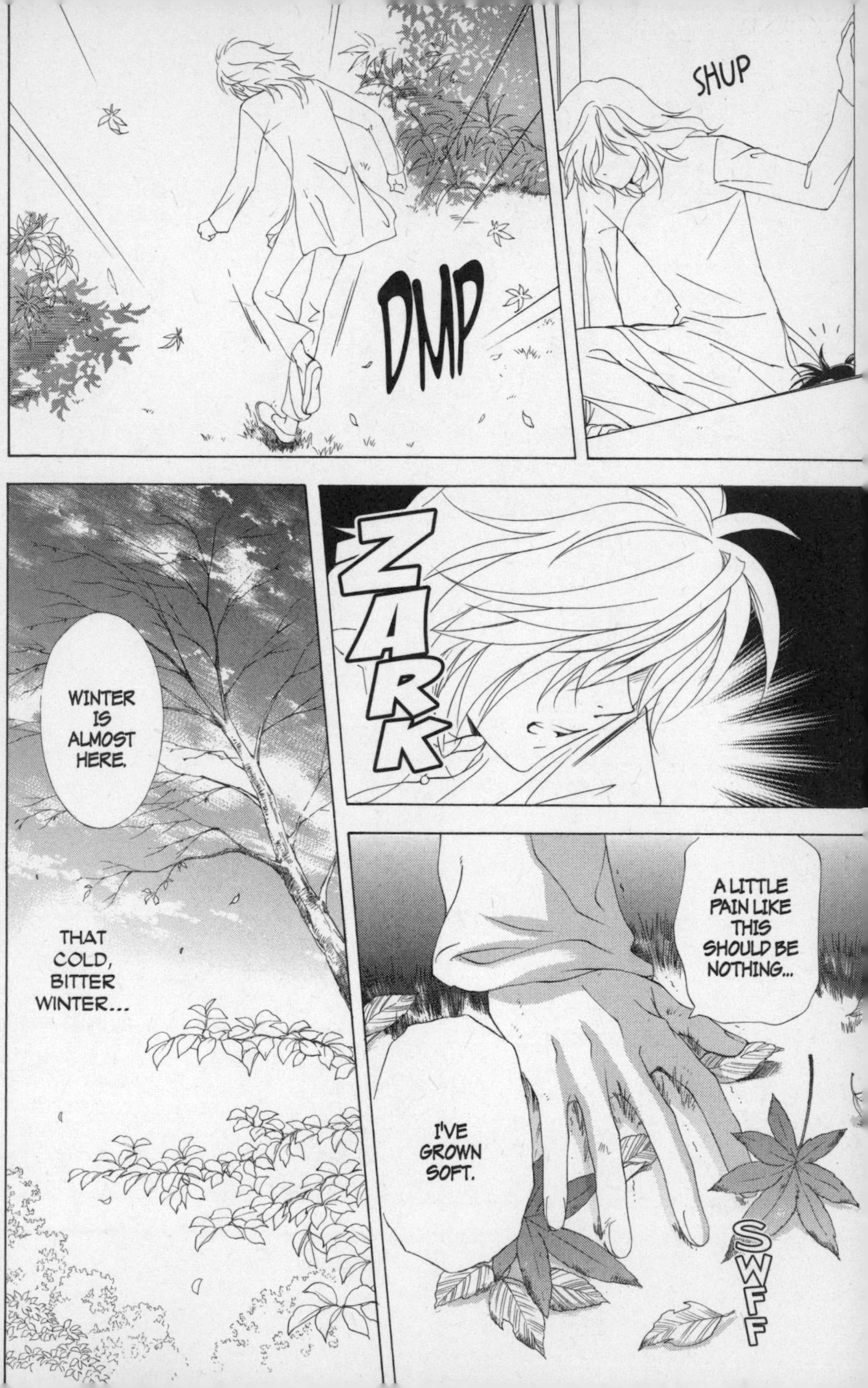
SHUP
DMP
ZARK
A LITTLE PAIN LIKE THIS SHOULD BE NOTHING...
I'VE GROWN SOFT.
SWFF
WINTER IS ALMOST HERE.
THAT COLD, BITTER WINTER...

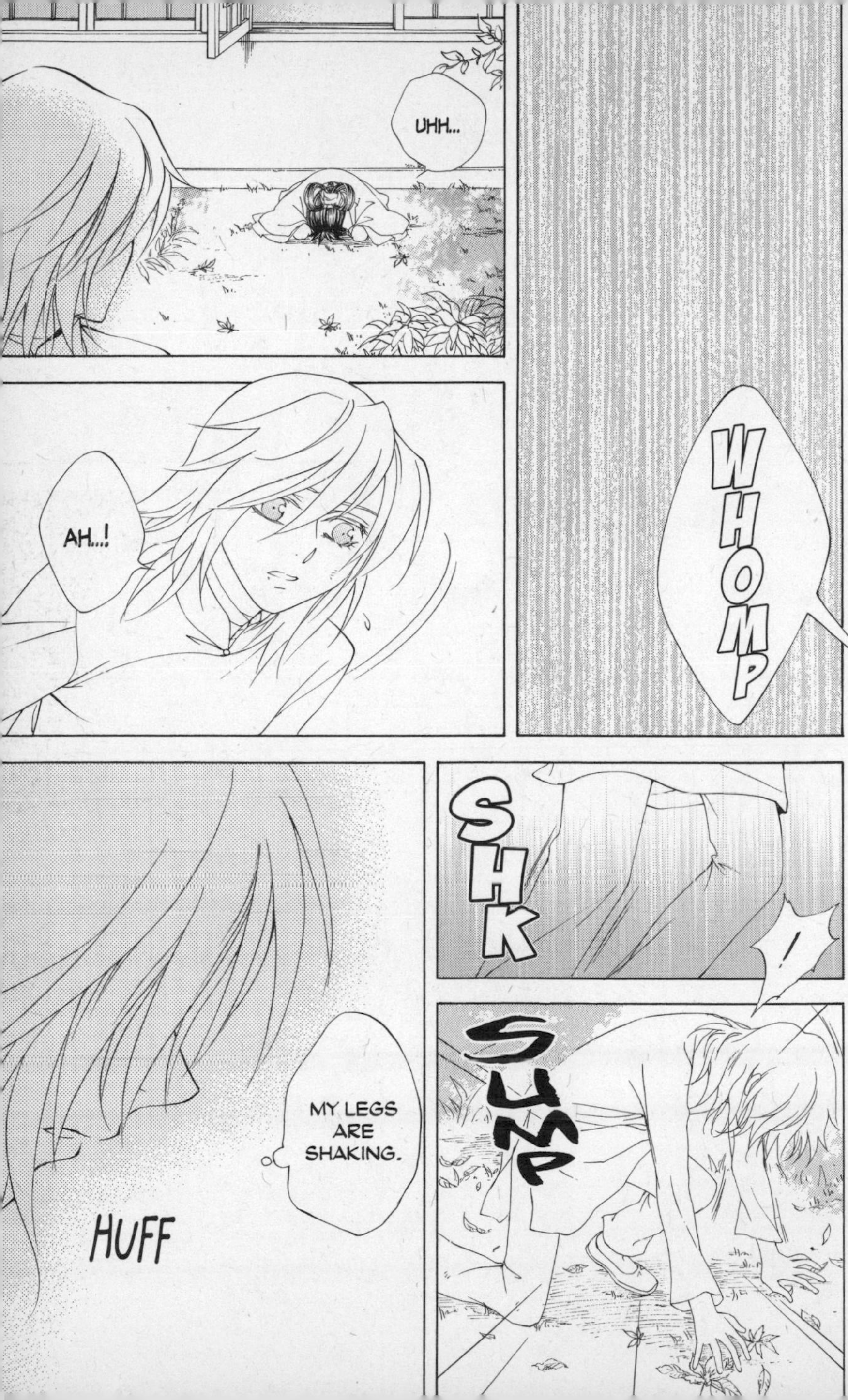
WHOMP
UHH...
AH...!
SHK
!
SUMP
MY LEGS ARE SHAKING.
HUFF

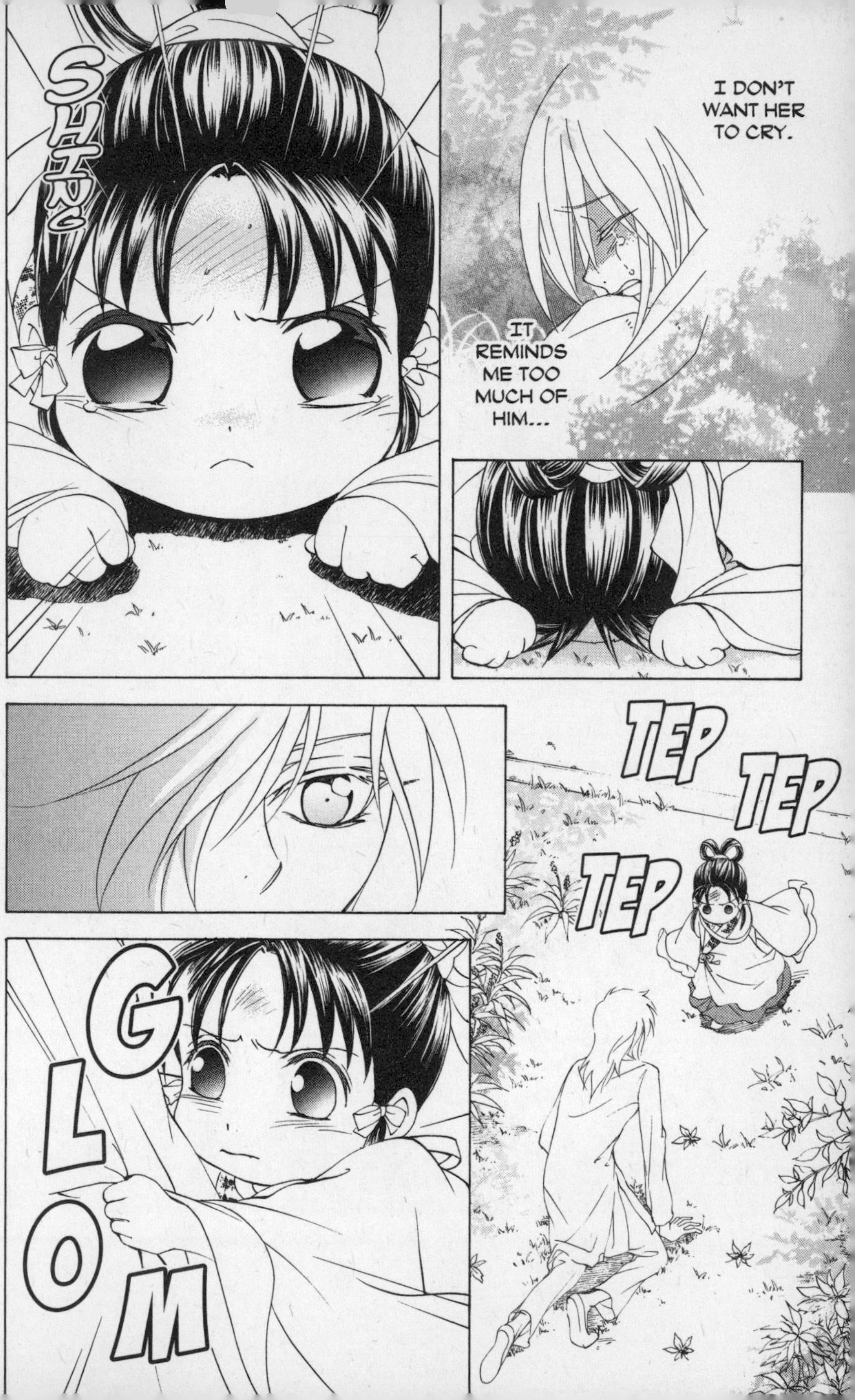

I DON'T WANT HER TO CRY.
IT REMINDS ME TOO MUCH OF HIM...
SHING
TEP TEP TEP
GLOMP

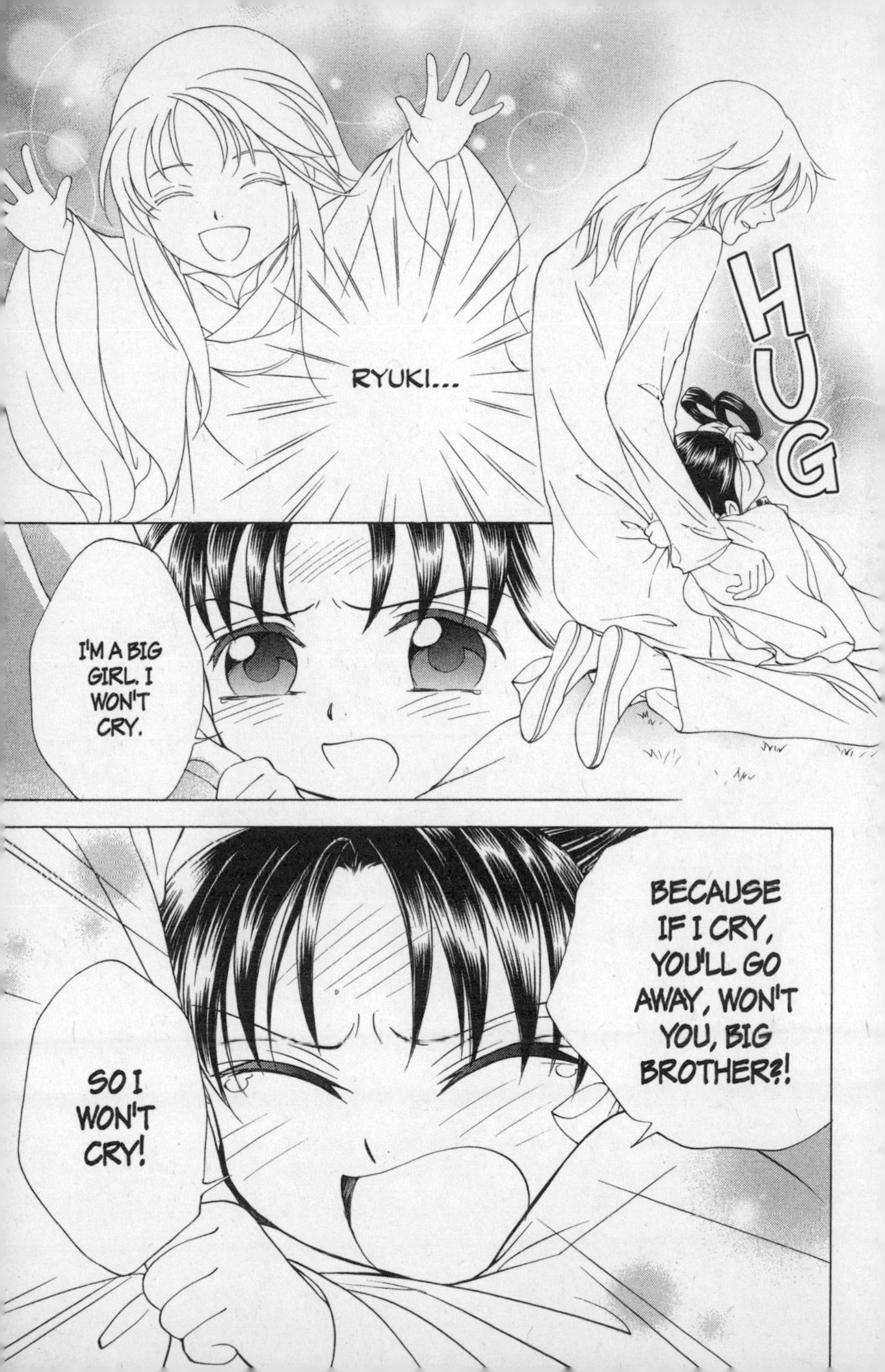
HUG
RYUKI...
I'M A BIG GIRL. I WON'T CRY.
BECAUSE IF I CRY, YOU'LL GO AWAY, WON'T YOU, BIG BROTHER?!
SO I WON'T CRY!

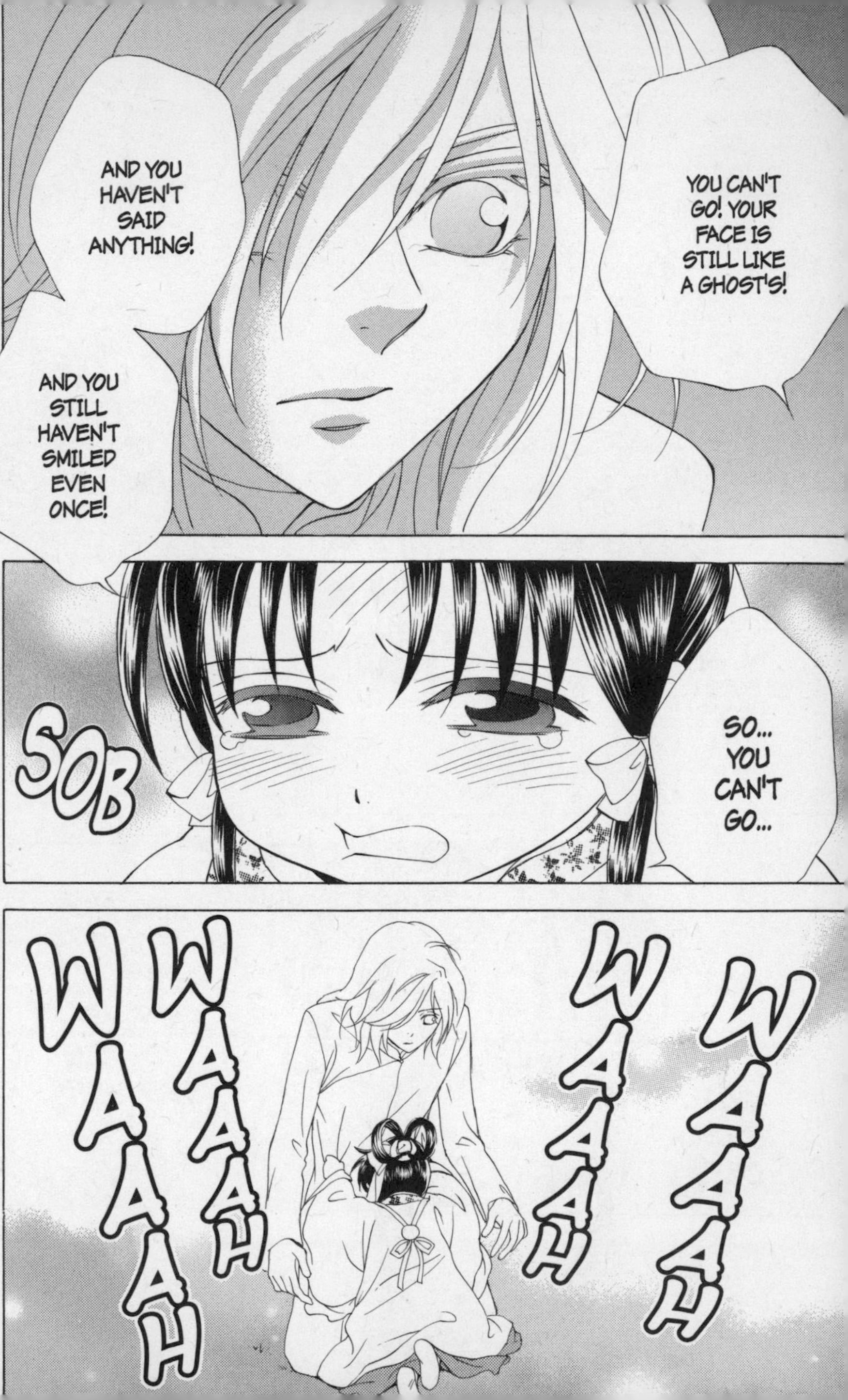
YOU CAN'T GO! YOUR FACE IS STILL LIKE A GHOST'S!
AND YOU HAVEN'T SAID ANYTHING!
AND YOU STILL HAVEN'T SMILED EVEN ONCE!
SO... YOU CAN'T GO...
SOB
WAAAAH
WAAAAH
WAAAH
WAAAAAH

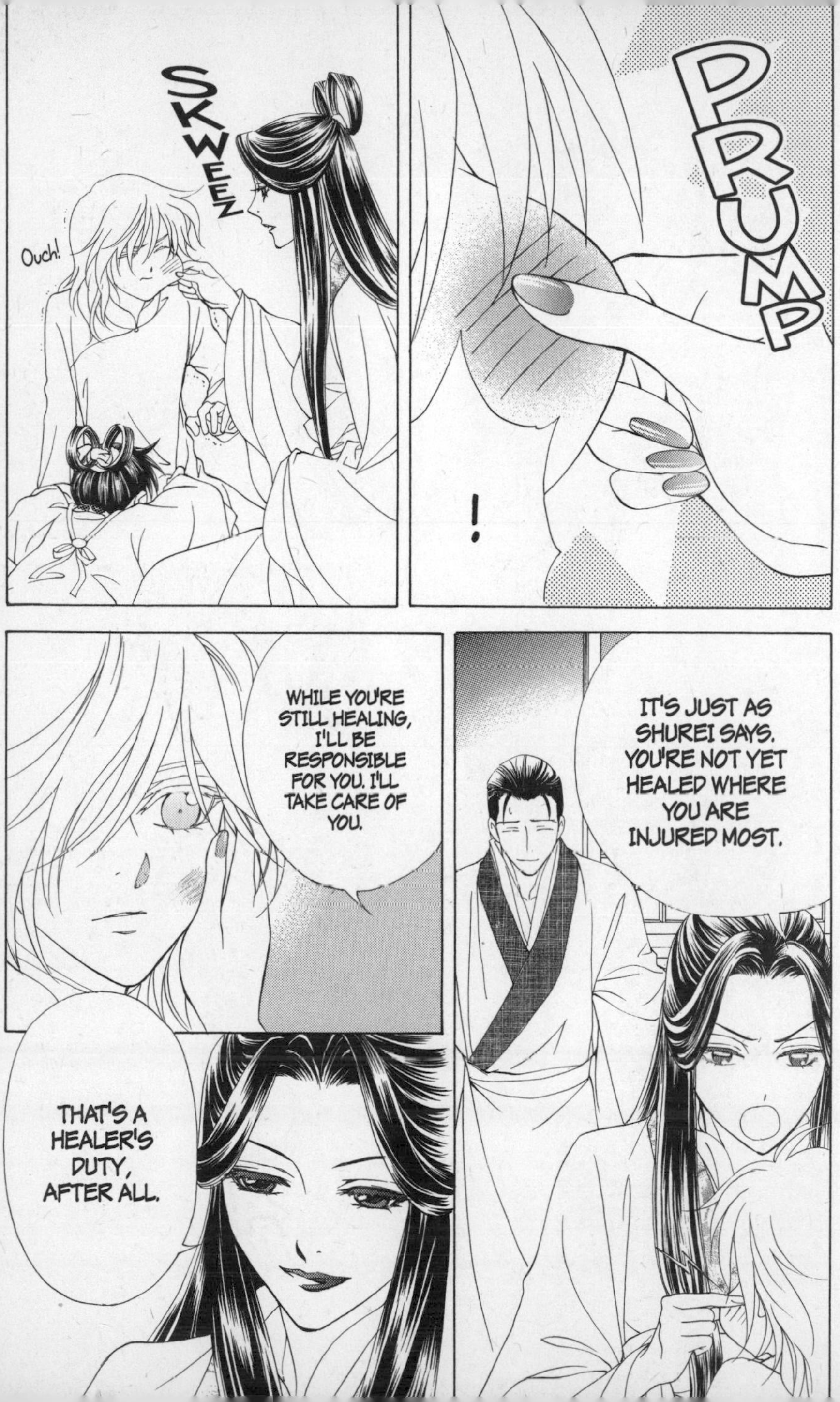
PRUMP
!
SKWEEZ
Ouch!
IT'S JUST AS SHUREI SAYS. YOU'RE NOT YET HEALED WHERE YOU ARE INJURED MOST.
WHILE YOU'RE STILL HEALING, I'LL BE RESPONSIBLE FOR YOU. I'LL TAKE CARE OF YOU.
THAT'S A HEALER'S DUTY, AFTER ALL.

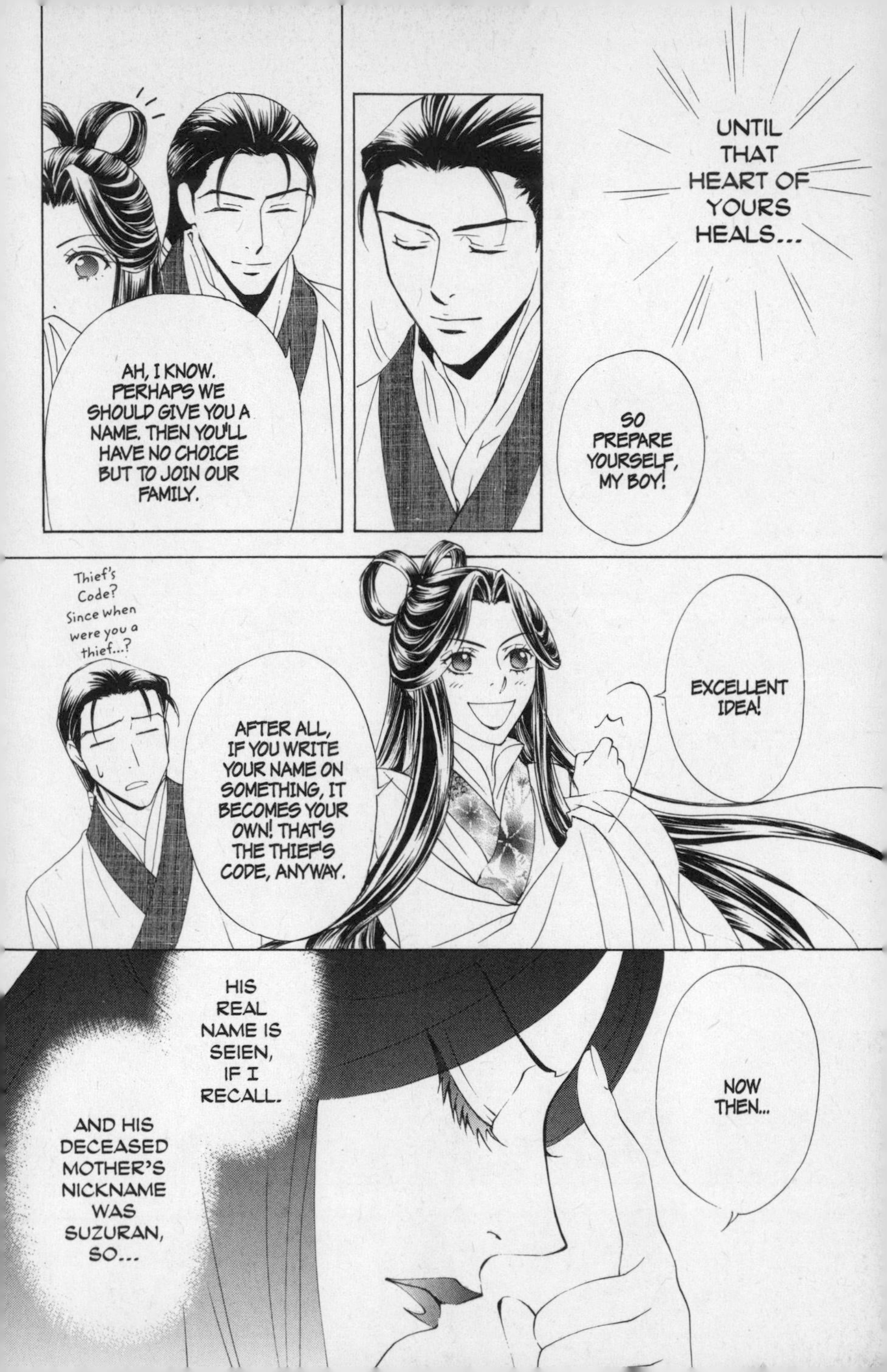
UNTIL THAT HEART OF YOURS HEALS...
SO PREPARE YOURSELF, MY BOY!
AH, I KNOW. PERHAPS WE SHOULD GIVE YOU A NAME. THEN YOU'LL HAVE NO CHOICE BUT TO JOIN OUR FAMILY.
EXCELLENT IDEA!
AFTER ALL, IF YOU WRITE YOUR NAME ON SOMETHING, IT BECOMES YOUR OWN! THAT'S THE THIEF'S CODE, ANYWAY.
Thief's Code? Since when were you a thief...?
NOW THEN...
HIS REAL NAME IS SEIEN, IF I RECALL.
AND HIS DECEASED MOTHER'S NICKNAME WAS SUZURAN, SO...

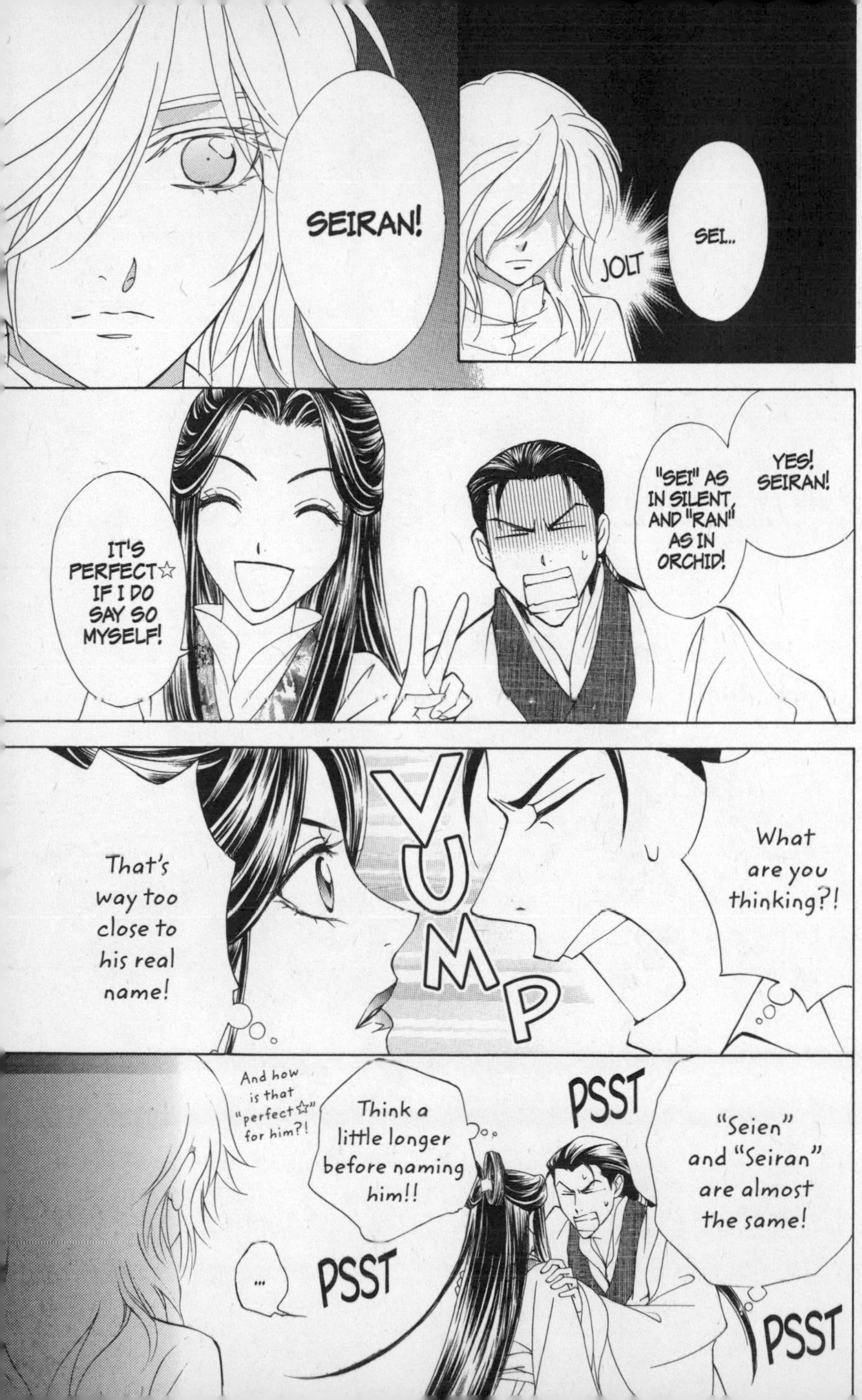
SEI...
JOLT
SEIRAN!
YES! SEIRAN!
"SEI" AS IN SILENT, AND "RAN" AS IN ORCHID!
IT'S PERFECT☆ IF I DO SAY SO MYSELF!
What are you thinking?!
VUMP
That's way too close to his real name!
"Seien" and "Seiran" are almost the same!
PSST
Think a little longer before naming him!!
And how is that "perfect☆" for him?!
PSST
...
PSST

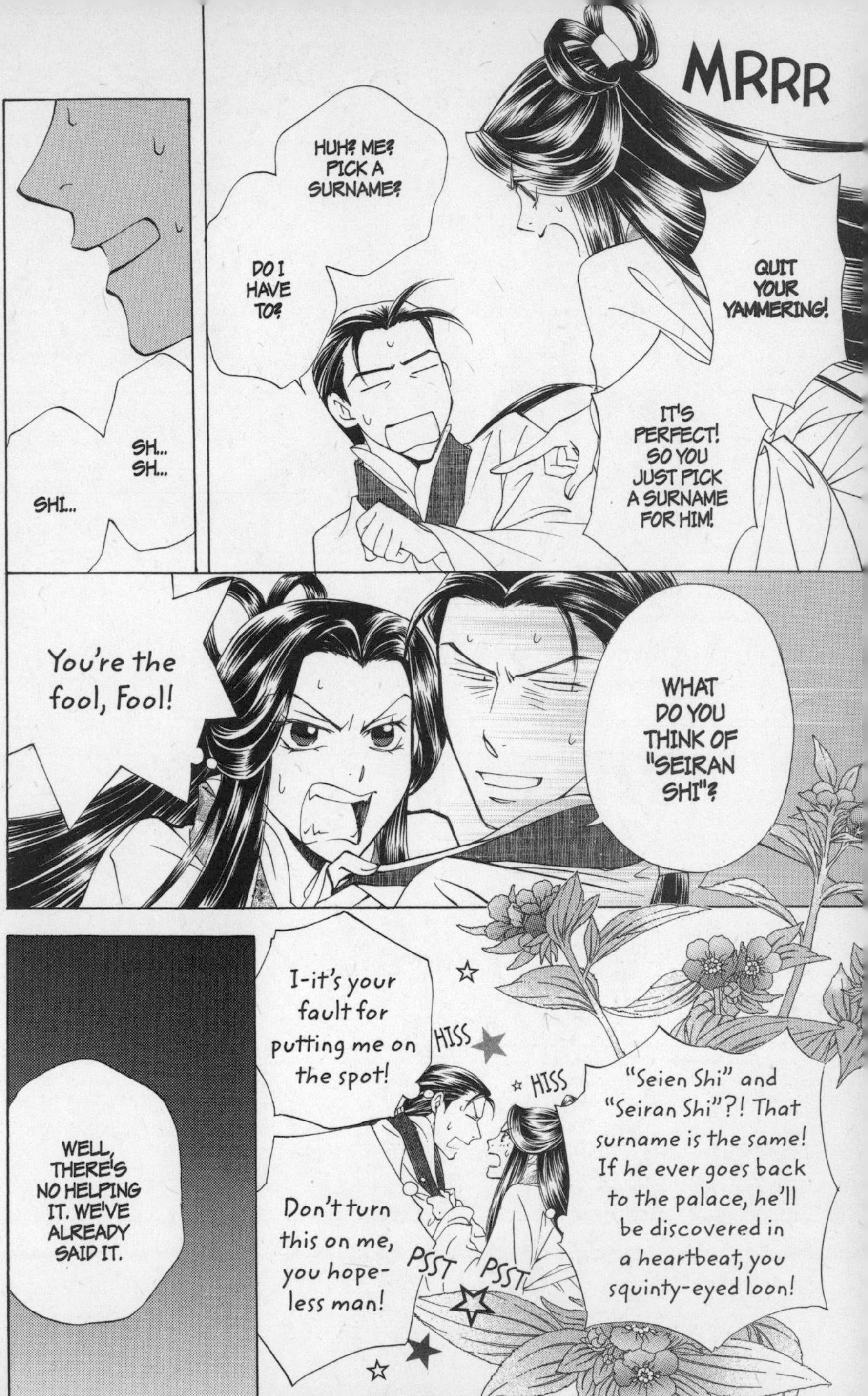
MRRR
QUIT YOUR YAMMERING!
IT'S PERFECT! SO YOU JUST PICK A SURNAME FOR HIM!
HUH? ME? PICK A SURNAME?
DO I HAVE TO?
SH... SH...
SHI...
WHAT DO YOU THINK OF "SEIRAN SHI"?
You're the fool, Fool!
"Seien Shi" and "Seiran Shi"?! That surname is the same! If he ever goes back to the palace, he'll be discovered in a heartbeat, you squinty-eyed loon!
HISS
HISS
I-it's your fault for putting me on the spot!
Don't turn this on me, you hopeless man!
PSST
PSST
WELL, THERE'S NO HELPING IT. WE'VE ALREADY SAID IT.

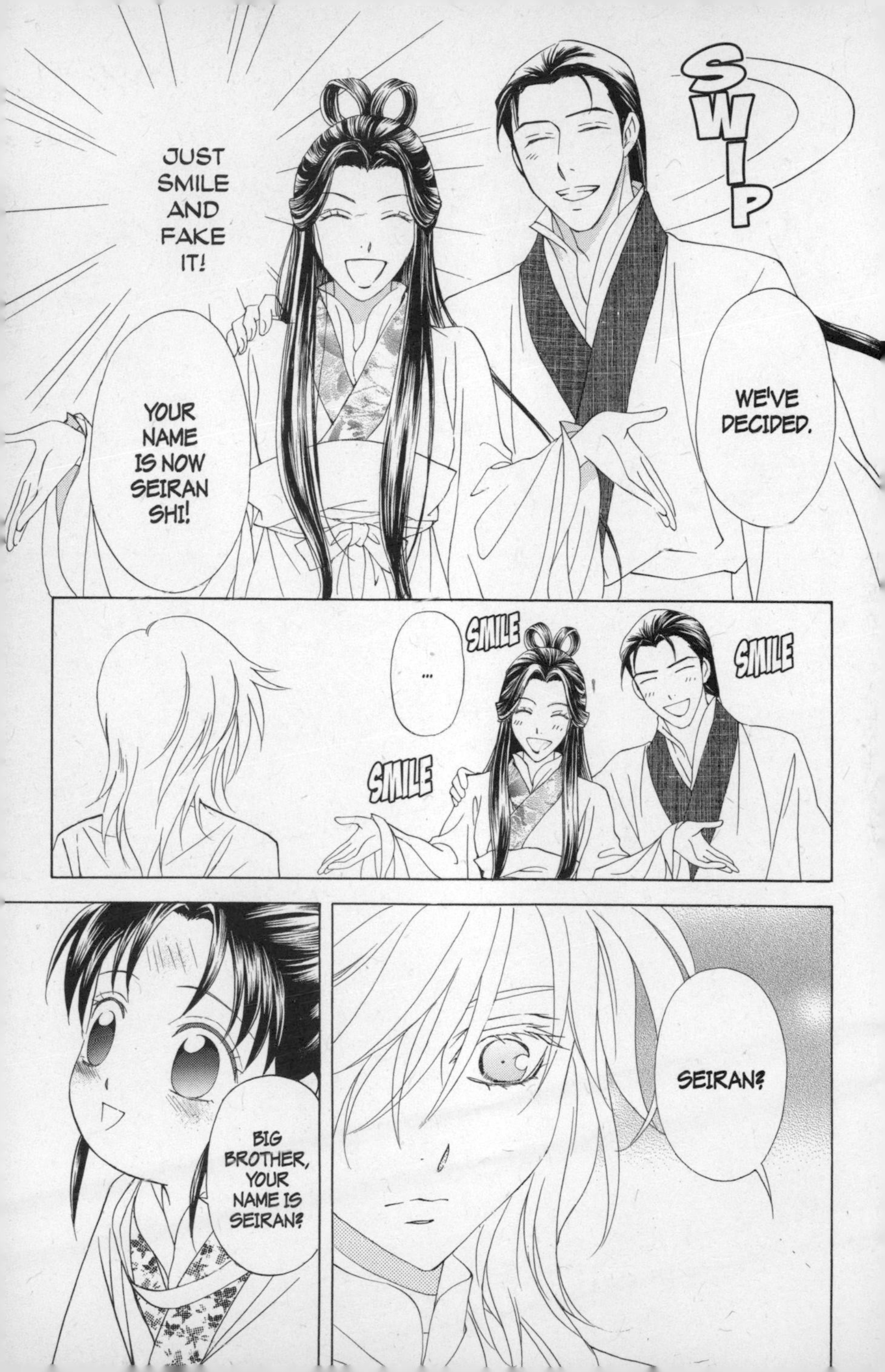
SWIP
WE'VE DECIDED.
JUST SMILE AND FAKE IT!
YOUR NAME IS NOW SEIRAN SHI!
SMILE
SMILE
...
SMILE
SEIRAN?
BIG BROTHER, YOUR NAME IS SEIRAN?

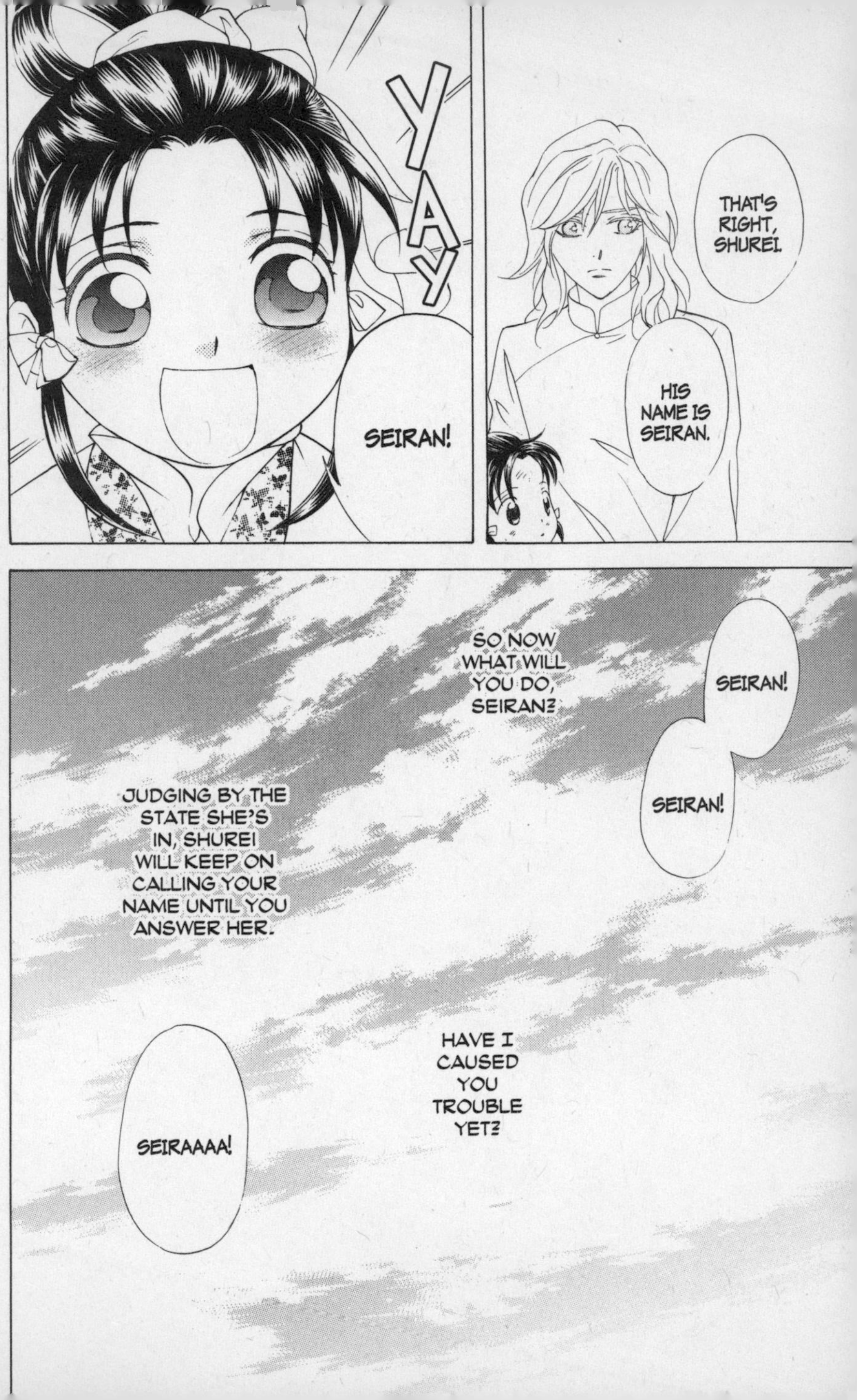
THAT'S RIGHT, SHUREI.
HIS NAME IS SEIRAN.
YAY
SEIRAN!
SEIRAN!
SEIRAN!
SO NOW WHAT WILL YOU DO, SEIRAN?
JUDGING BY THE STATE SHE'S IN, SHUREI WILL KEEP ON CALLING YOUR NAME UNTIL YOU ANSWER HER.
HAVE I CAUSED YOU TROUBLE YET?
SEIRAAAA!

The Story of
SAIUNKOKU

The Story of SAIUNKOKU Four-Panel Comics

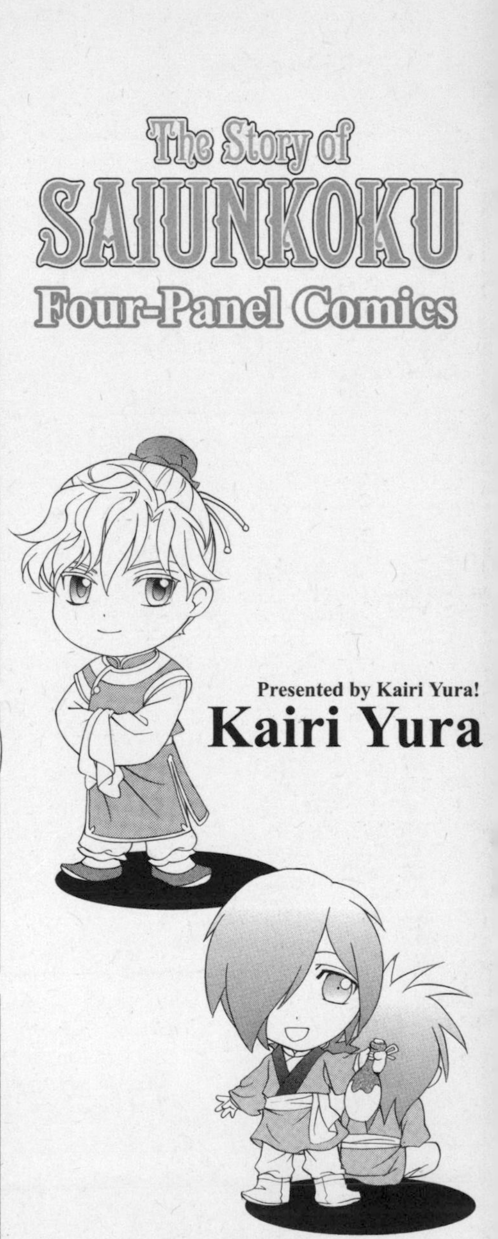

Presented by Kairi Yura!

Kairi Yura

Bargain Hunter Girl

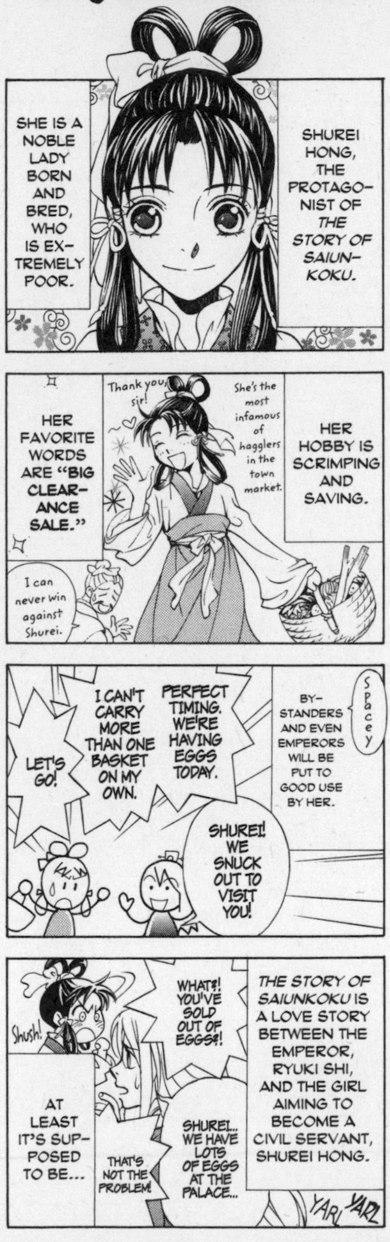
SHUREI HONG, THE PROTAGONIST OF THE STORY OF SAIUNKOKU.
SHE IS A NOBLE LADY BORN AND BRED, WHO IS EXTREMELY POOR.
HER HOBBY IS SCRIMPING AND SAVING.
She's the most infamous of hagglers in the town market.
Thank you, sir!
HER FAVORITE WORDS ARE "BIG CLEARANCE SALE."
I can never win against Shurei.
Spacey
BYSTANDERS AND EVEN EMPERORS WILL BE PUT TO GOOD USE BY HER.
PERFECT TIMING. WE'RE HAVING EGGS TODAY.
I CAN'T CARRY MORE THAN ONE BASKET ON MY OWN.
LET'S GO!
SHUREI! WE SNUCK OUT TO VISIT YOU!
THE STORY OF SAIUNKOKU IS A LOVE STORY BETWEEN THE EMPEROR, RYUKI SHI, AND THE GIRL AIMING TO BECOME A CIVIL SERVANT, SHUREI HONG.
WHAT?! YOU'VE SOLD OUT OF EGGS?!
Shush!
SHUREI... WE HAVE LOTS OF EGGS AT THE PALACE...
THAT'S NOT THE PROBLEM!
AT LEAST IT'S SUPPOSED TO BE...
YARI YARI

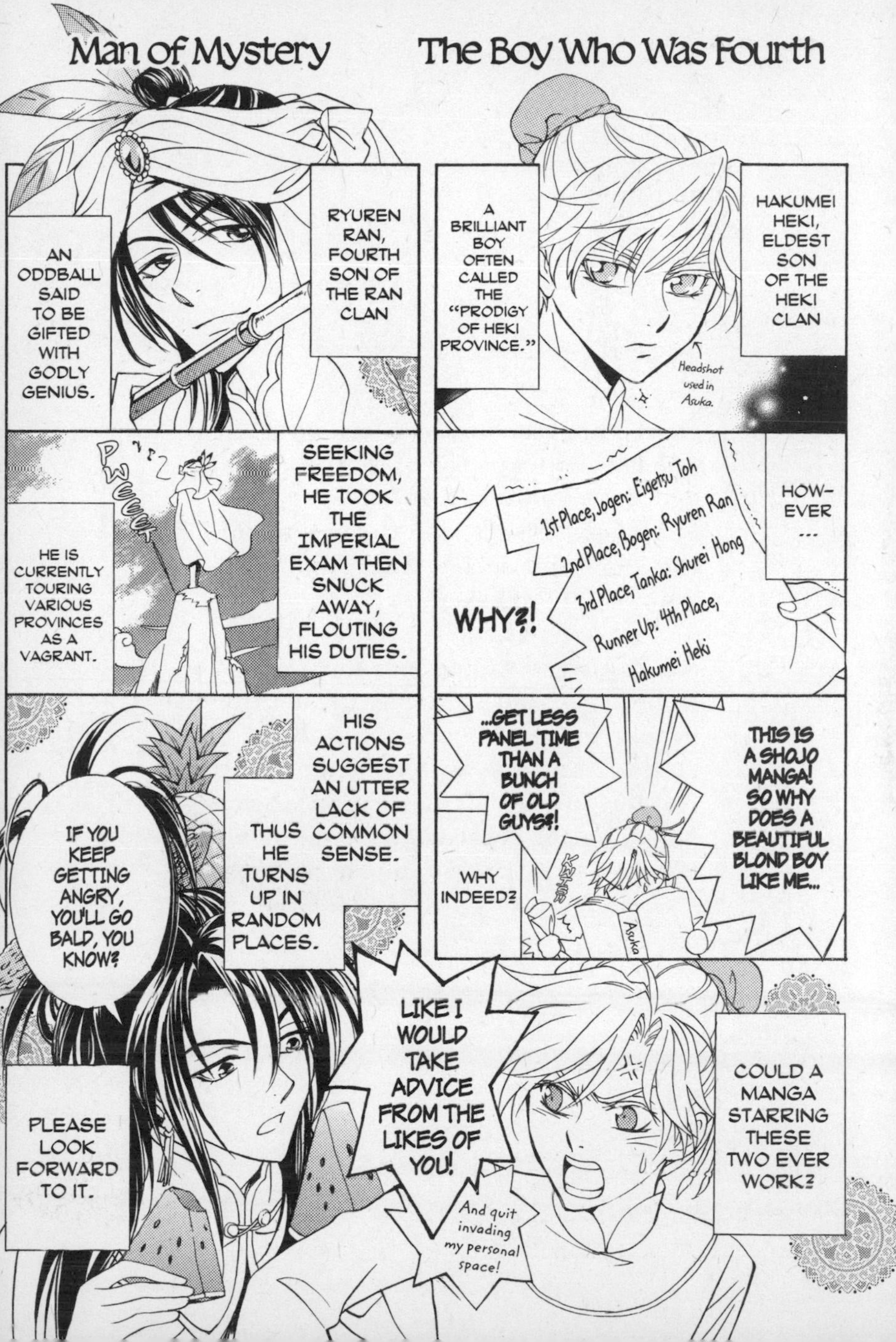
The Boy Who Was Fourth
HAKUMEI HEKI, ELDEST SON OF THE HEKI CLAN
A BRILLIANT BOY OFTEN CALLED THE "PRODIGY OF HEKI PROVINCE."
Headshot used in Asuka.
HOW-EVER ...
1st Place, Jogen: Eigetsu Toh
2nd Place, Bogen: Ryuren Ran
3rd Place, Tanka: Shurei Hong
Runner Up: 4th Place, Hakumei Heki
WHY?!
THIS IS A SHOJO MANGA! SO WHY DOES A BEAUTIFUL BLOND BOY LIKE ME...
...GET LESS PANEL TIME THAN A BUNCH OF OLD GUYS?!
WHY INDEED?
Asuka
COULD A MANGA STARRING THESE TWO EVER WORK?
LIKE I WOULD TAKE ADVICE FROM THE LIKES OF YOU!
And quit invading my personal space!
Man of Mystery
RYUREN RAN, FOURTH SON OF THE RAN CLAN
AN ODDBALL SAID TO BE GIFTED WITH GODLY GENIUS.
SEEKING FREEDOM, HE TOOK THE IMPERIAL EXAM THEN SNUCK AWAY, FLOUTING HIS DUTIES.
HE IS CURRENTLY TOURING VARIOUS PROVINCES AS A VAGRANT.
HIS ACTIONS SUGGEST AN UTTER LACK OF COMMON SENSE.
THUS HE TURNS UP IN RANDOM PLACES.
IF YOU KEEP GETTING ANGRY, YOU'LL GO BALD, YOU KNOW?
PLEASE LOOK FORWARD TO IT.

Kairi Yura was born on January 16. She is the illustrator of both the manga and the YA novels for *The Story of Saiunkoku*. She is also the creator of the *Angelique* series. Yura's hobby is going to the theater.

Sai Yukino was born on January 26. She is author of both the manga and the YA novels for *The Story of Saiunkoku*. She received an honorable mention and the Readers' Award for Kadokawa's Beans Novel Taisho Awards. When she's not busy writing, Yukino enjoys massages.

Shojo Beat

THE STORY OF SAIUNKOKU
Volume 7

Shojo Beat Edition

ART
KAIRI YURA
STORY
SAI YUKINO

Translation & English Adaptation/Su Mon Han
Touch-up Art & Lettering/Freeman Wong
Design/Yukiko Whitley
Editor/Nancy Thistlethwaite

Printed in the U.S.A.

Published by VIZ Media, LLC
P.O. Box 77010
San Francisco, CA 94107

10 9 8 7 6 5 4 3 2 1
First printing, May 2012

RATED T FOR TEEN

PARENTAL ADVISORY
THE STORY OF SAIUNKOKU is rated T for Teen and is recommended for ages 13 and up. This volume contains suggestive themes.

ratings.viz.com

VIZ media
www.viz.com

www.shojobeat.com

Stepping on Roses

Story & Art by **Rinko Ueda**
the creator of *Tail of the Moon*

Can't Buy Love

Sumi Kitamura's financial situation is dire.
Wealthy Soichiro Ashida has money to
spare. He'll help her out if she agrees to
be his bride. Will Sumi end up richer...
or poorer?

$9.99 USA / $12.99 CAN / £6.99 UK ★ | ISBN: 978-1-4215-3182-3

On sale at **store.viz.com**
Also available at your local bookstore or comic store

HADASHI DE BARA WO FUME © 2007 by Rinko Ueda/SHUEISHA Inc.
★ Prices subject to change

The VIZ Manga App has some new friends...

The world's best manga is now on the iPad,™ iPhone™ and iPod touch™

To learn more, visit viz.com/25years

From legendary manga like *Death Note* to *Absolute Boyfriend*, the best manga in the world is now available on multiple devices through the official VIZ Manga app.

- **Hundreds of volumes available**
- **Free App**
- **New content weekly**
- **Free chapter 1 previews**

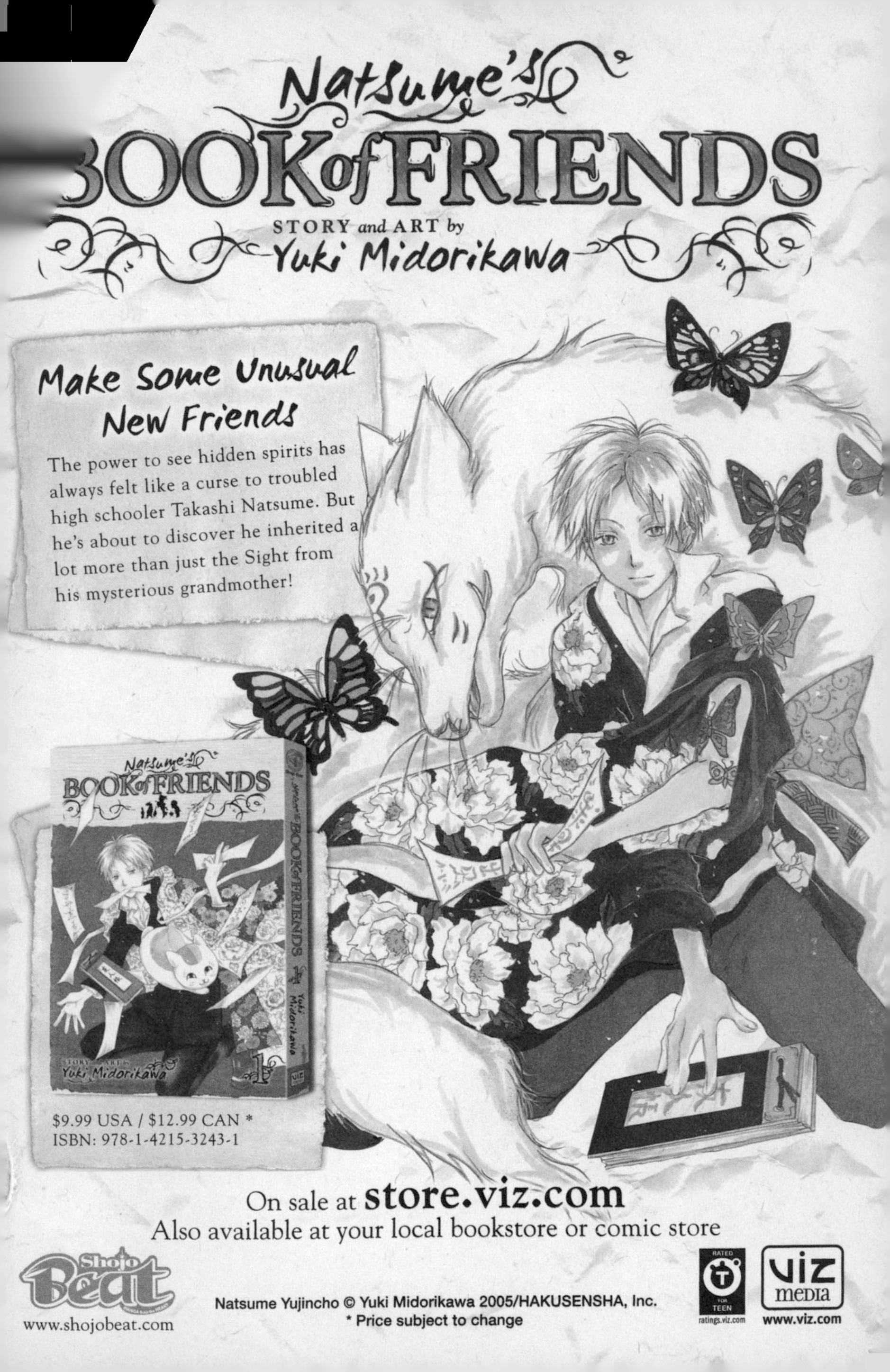
Natsume's
BOOK of FRIENDS
STORY and ART by
Yuki Midorikawa
Make Some Unusual New Friends
The power to see hidden spirits has always felt like a curse to troubled high schooler Takashi Natsume. But he's about to discover he inherited a lot more than just the Sight from his mysterious grandmother!
Natsume's BOOK of FRIENDS
STORY and ART by Yuki Midorikawa
$9.99 USA / $12.99 CAN *
ISBN: 978-1-4215-3243-1
On sale at store.viz.com
Also available at your local bookstore or comic store
Shojo Beat
www.shojobeat.com
Natsume Yujincho © Yuki Midorikawa 2005/HAKUSENSHA, Inc.
* Price subject to change
RATED T FOR TEEN
ratings.viz.com
VIZ media
www.viz.com

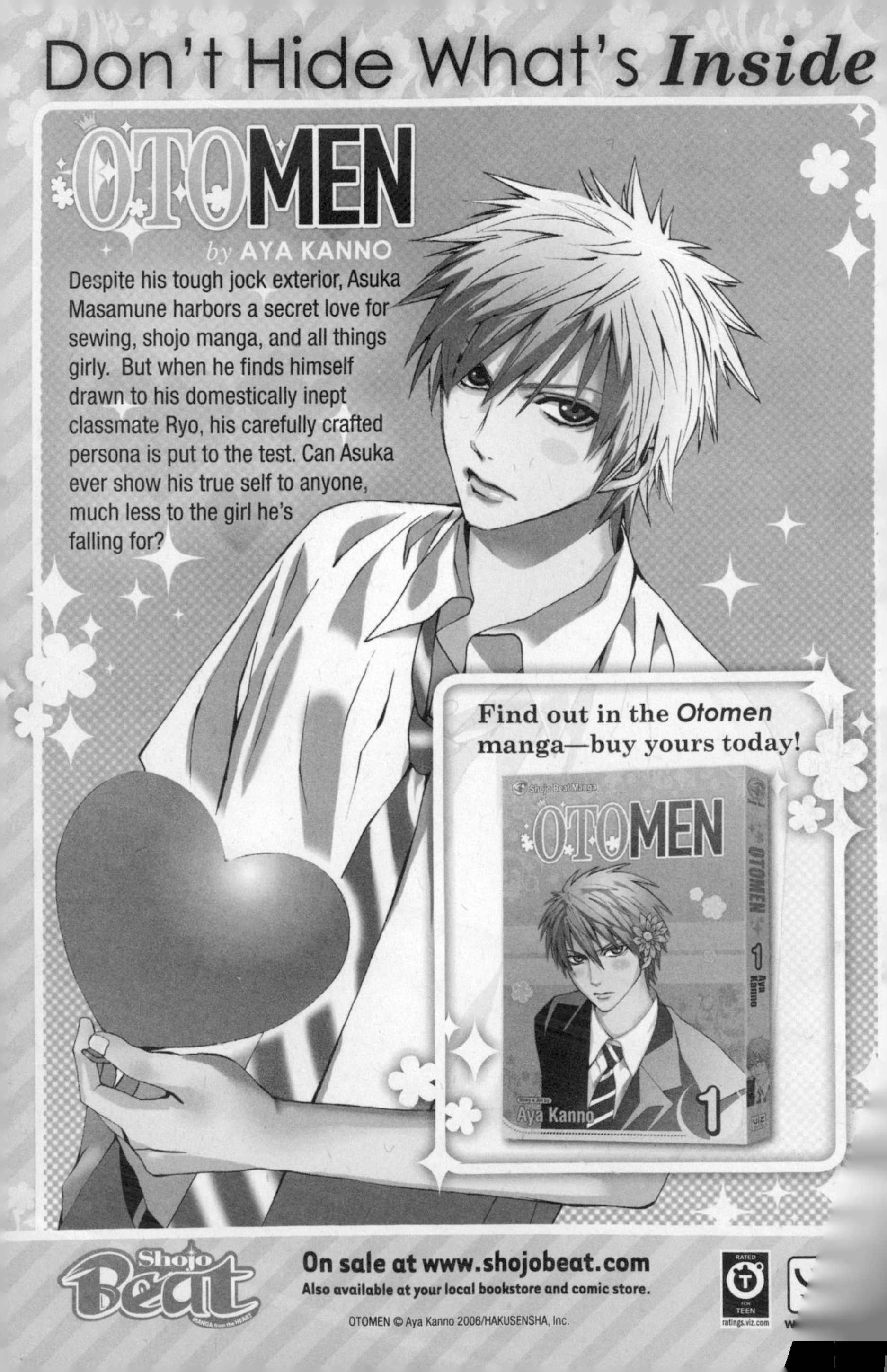
Don't Hide What's Inside
OTOMEN
by AYA KANNO
Despite his tough jock exterior, Asuka Masamune harbors a secret love for sewing, shojo manga, and all things girly. But when he finds himself drawn to his domestically inept classmate Ryo, his carefully crafted persona is put to the test. Can Asuka ever show his true self to anyone, much less to the girl he's falling for?
Find out in the Otomen manga—buy yours today!
Shojo Beat Manga
OTOMEN
1
Aya Kanno
Shojo Beat
MANGA from the HEART
On sale at www.shojobeat.com
Also available at your local bookstore and comic store.
OTOMEN © Aya Kanno 2006/HAKUSENSHA, Inc.
RATED
T
FOR TEEN
ratings.viz.com

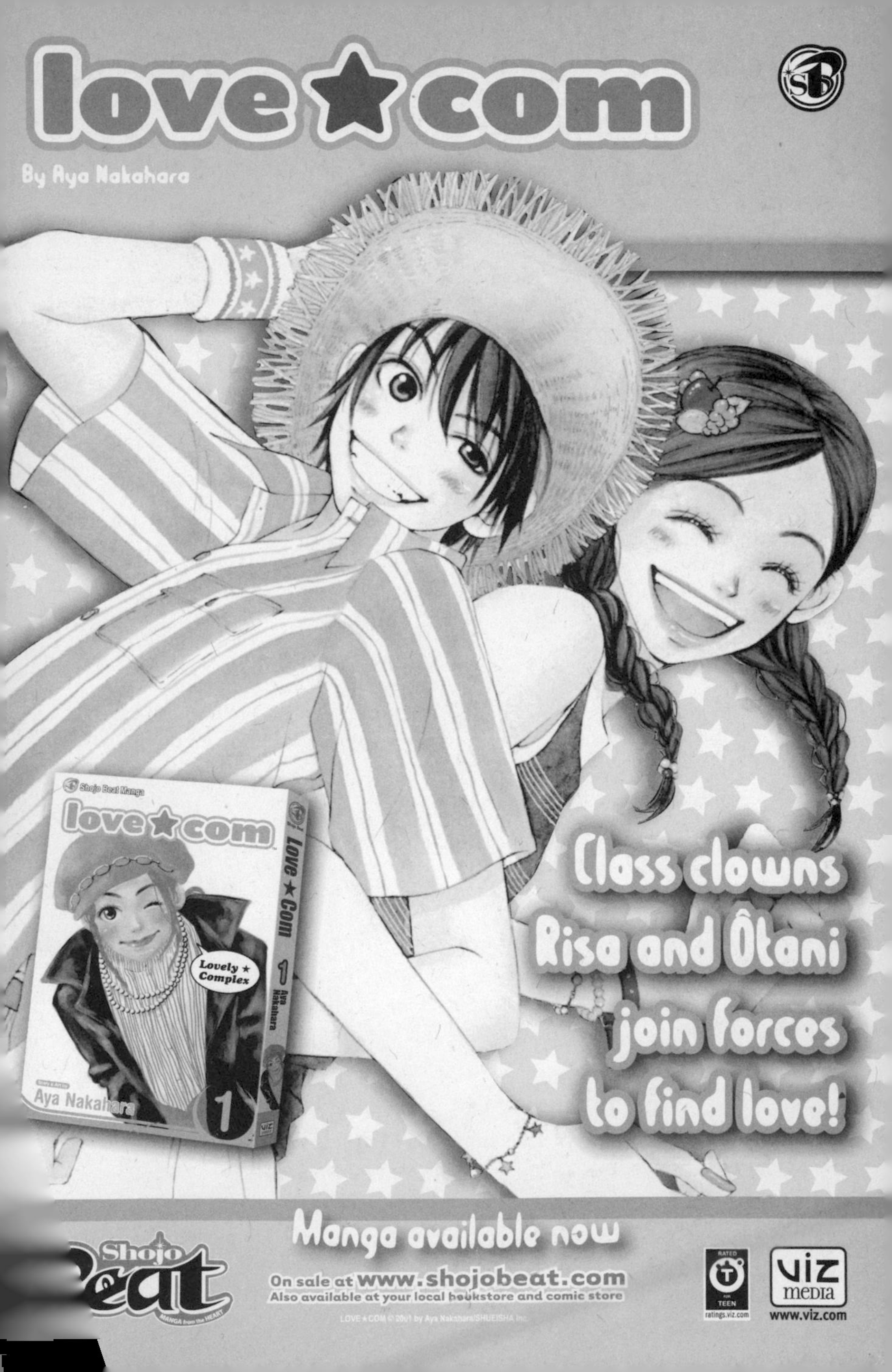
love★com
By Aya Nakahara
Shojo Beat Manga
love★com
Love★Com
1
Aya Nakahara
Lovely ★ Complex
Aya Nakahara
1
Class clowns
Risa and Ôtani
join forces
to find love!
Manga available now
Shojo Beat
MANGA from the HEART
On sale at www.shojobeat.com
Also available at your local bookstore and comic store
LOVE★COM © 2001 by Aya Nakahara/SHUEISHA Inc.
RATED T TEEN
ratings.viz.com
VIZ MEDIA
www.viz.com

High School DEBUT

By Kazune Kawahara

When Haruna Nagashima was in junior high, softball and comics were her life. Now that she's in high school, she's ready to find a boyfriend. But will hard work (and the right coach) be enough?

Find out in the *High School Debut* manga series—available now!

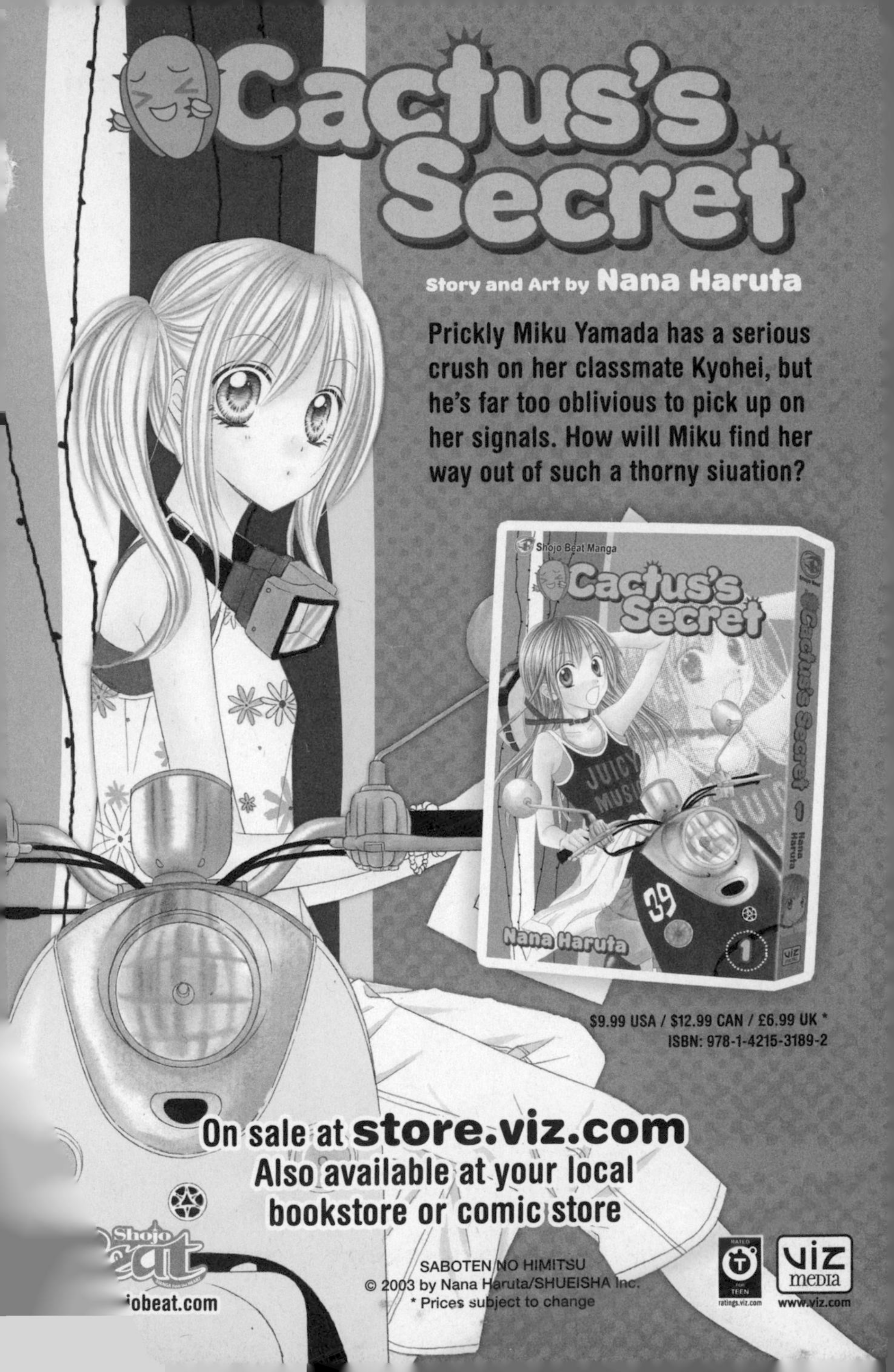
Cactus's Secret
Story and Art by Nana Haruta
Prickly Miku Yamada has a serious crush on her classmate Kyohei, but he's far too oblivious to pick up on her signals. How will Miku find her way out of such a thorny siuation?
Shojo Beat Manga
Cactus's Secret
Nana Haruta
1
$9.99 USA / $12.99 CAN / £6.99 UK *
ISBN: 978-1-4215-3189-2
On sale at store.viz.com
Also available at your local bookstore or comic store
SABOTEN NO HIMITSU
© 2003 by Nana Haruta/SHUEISHA Inc.
* Prices subject to change
RATED T FOR TEEN
ratings.viz.com
VIZ media
www.viz.com

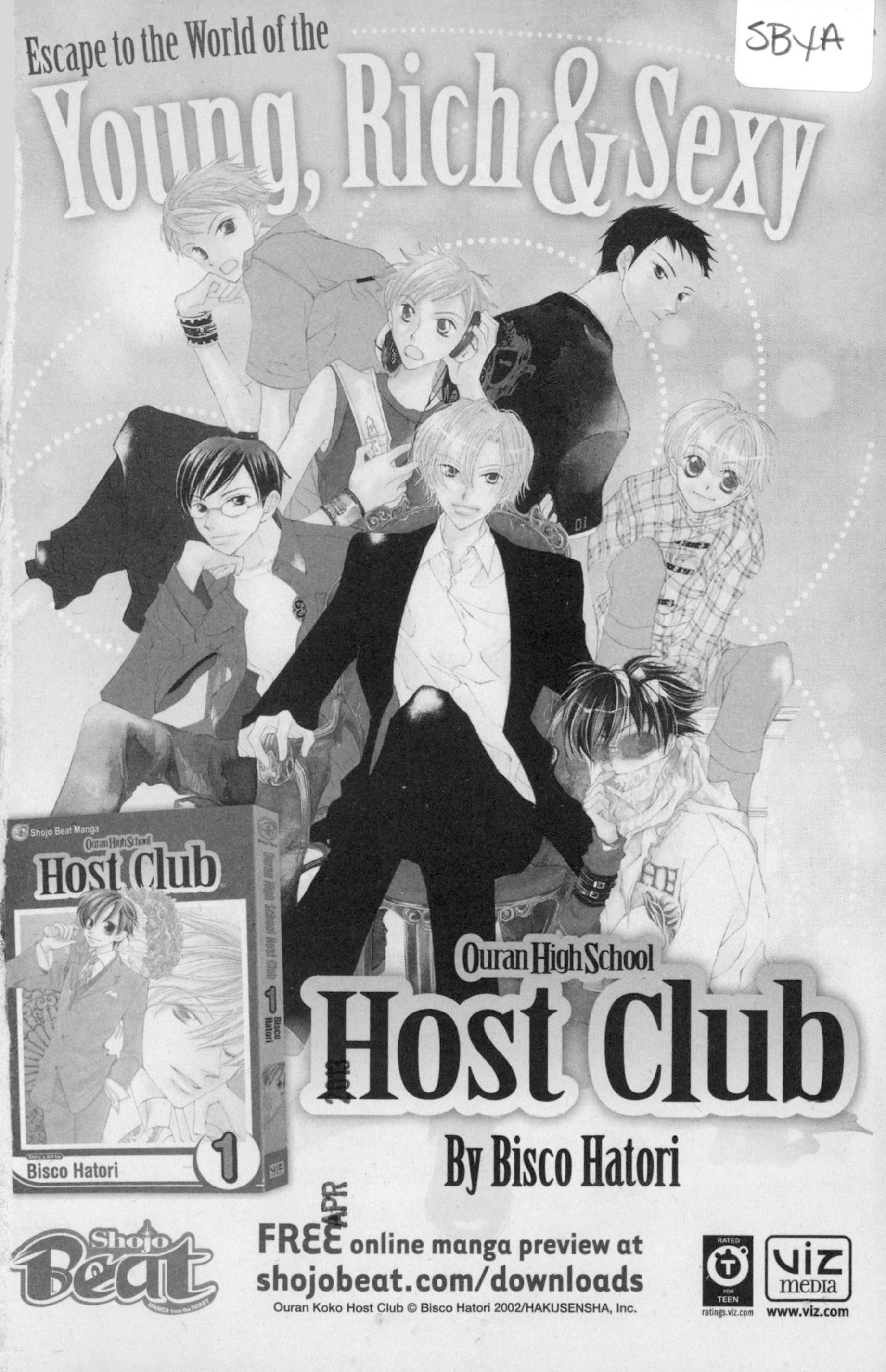
SBYA
Escape to the World of the
Young, Rich & Sexy
Shojo Beat Manga
Ouran High School
Host Club
Ouran High School Host Club
1
Bisco Hatori
Story & Art by
Bisco Hatori
1
Ouran High School
Host Club
By Bisco Hatori
APR
2013
FREE online manga preview at
shojobeat.com/downloads
Ouran Koko Host Club © Bisco Hatori 2002/HAKUSENSHA, Inc.
Shojo Beat
MANGA from the HEART
RATED
T
FOR TEEN
ratings.viz.com
viz media
www.viz.com